The City of Babylon

The 2,000-year story of Babylon sees it moving from a city state to the centre of a great empire of the ancient world. It remained a centre of kingship under the empires of Assyria, Nebuchadnezzar, Darius, Alexander the Great, the Seleucids and the Parthians. Its city walls were declared to be a Wonder of the World while its ziggurat won fame as the Tower of Babel. Visitors to Berlin can admire its Ishtar Gate. The supposed location of its elusive Hanging Garden is explained. Worship of its patron god Marduk spread widely while its well-trained scholars communicated legal, administrative and literary works throughout the ancient world, some of which provide a backdrop to Old Testament and Hittite texts. Its science also laid the foundations for Greek and Arab astronomy through a millennium of continuous astronomical observations. This accessible and up-to-date account is by one of the world's leading authorities.

STEPHANIE DALLEY is a member of the Oriental Institute, University of Oxford and an Honorary Senior Research Fellow of Somerville College. She has excavated in the Middle East and published cunei-form texts found in Iraq, Syria, and Jordan, and in museums in Baghdad, Oxford, London, and Edinburgh. She is the author of *The Mystery of the Hanging Garden of Babylon* (2013), which formed the basis for a successful TV documentary. Her other books include *Myths from Mesopotamia* (1986), *The Legacy of Mesopotamia* (1998), *Mari and Karana: Two Old Babylonian Cities* (1984), and *Esther's Revenge at Susa* (2007), some of which have been translated into other languages. She has lectured worldwide including at universities, schools, and societies, and taught for three decades at the Oriental Institute. She is a Fellow of the Society of Antiquaries of London.

The City of Babylon

A History, c. 2000 BC–AD 116

STEPHANIE DALLEY

University of Oxford

CAMBRIDGE
UNIVERSITY PRESS

CAMBRIDGE
UNIVERSITY PRESS

University Printing House, Cambridge CB2 8BS, United Kingdom

One Liberty Plaza, 20th Floor, New York, NY 10006, USA

477 Williamstown Road, Port Melbourne, VIC 3207, Australia

314–321, 3rd Floor, Plot 3, Splendor Forum, Jasola District Centre,
New Delhi – 110025, India

103 Penang Road, #05–06/07, Visioncrest Commercial, Singapore 238467

Cambridge University Press is part of the University of Cambridge.

It furthers the University's mission by disseminating knowledge in the pursuit of
education, learning, and research at the highest international levels of excellence.

www.cambridge.org
Information on this title: www.cambridge.org/9781107136274
DOI: 10.1017/9781316479728

First published 2021

Printed in the United Kingdom by TJ Books Limited, Padstow Cornwall

A catalogue record for this publication is available from the British Library.

Library of Congress Cataloging-in-Publication Data
Names: Dalley, Stephanie, author.
Title: The city of Babylon : a history, c. 2000 BC – AD 116 / Stephanie Dalley,
University of Oxford.
Description: Cambridge, United Kingdom ; New York, NY : Cambridge University Press,
2021. | Includes bibliographical references and index.
Identifiers: LCCN 2021002364 (print) | LCCN 2021002365 (ebook) | ISBN 9781107136274
(hardback) | ISBN 9781316501771 (paperback) | ISBN 9781316479728 (ebook)
Subjects: LCSH: Babylon (Extinct city) – History.
Classification: LCC DS70.5.B3 D33 2021 (print) | LCC DS70.5.B3 (ebook) |
DDC 935/.5–dc23
LC record available at https://lccn.loc.gov/2021002364
LC ebook record available at https://lccn.loc.gov/2021002365

ISBN 978-1-107-13627-4 Hardback
ISBN 978-1-316-50177-1 Paperback

Contents

Illustrations and Maps

Preface

Babylon developed from an insignificant city to a city state, to a kingdom, to the head of an empire, and then to an icon of scholarship, religion, and trade under the rule of foreigners. Here its history is drawn from the extraordinary wealth of Babylonian cuneiform texts, spanning the period from 2000 BC to AD 116, with inevitable gaps where a lack of sources precludes a smooth narrative. Archaeological work has also contributed to this account. I have tried to avoid an academic style while engaging with recent research and outlining matters that are unresolved or disputed. Research in Assyriology has made great strides during recent decades, and until now much of the material I describe has been available only in specialist publications.

For the reader who would like more illustrations, I recommend the three great catalogues of exhibitions on Babylon held in 2008–9: the French exhibition at the Louvre in Paris, the German at the Pergamum Museum in Berlin, and the English at the British Museum in London. Each contains interesting accounts of various topics based mainly on the objects in those exhibitions.[1]

The quantity of relevant publications is now so vast that a full bibliography would have overwhelmed the book. I have tried to give up-to-date references with which earlier work can be found. This has the unfortunate consequence that the pioneering work of earlier scholars seems to be ignored. I hope colleagues will not feel affronted if I have omitted to mention the source of a particular piece of evidence or interpretation, intending to produce a clear narrative derived from many details without including them all. The wise words of the Sumerologist Edmond Sollberger come to mind: 'Don't empty your drawers into your writing'.

I thank Michael Sharp of CUP for much detailed help and interest in the book and the Delegates of CUP for giving me a contract; Alwyn Harrison for careful editing; Judith Wilson for encouragement to begin such a big work; Alison Wilkins for preparing maps and plans and the Lorne Thyssen

---

[1] On the three exhibition catalogues, see Finkel and Seymour 2008; Marzahn 2008; André-Salvini 2008; see also, e.g., Seymour 2014; Thelle 2018.

Fund at Wolfson College Oxford for supporting the work; Michael Macdonald for keeping me up-to-date on finds from Arabia; Günter Vittmann on the dating of Papyrus Amherst 35; Robertus van der Spek, Wouter Henkelman, Christopher Metcalf, and Adam Howe for help with the bibliography; Michael Roaf and Elize Zomer for supplying me with material before it was published; Willemijn de Waal for checking that the inscribed palm sticks in Leiden University Library are indeed incised; Carole Hillenbrand for help with Arabic sources; Ian Cartwright at the Oxford Institute of Archaeology for expert help preparing illustrations; Janice Kwiatkowski for critical reading of an early draft; my sister Corinna Redman for improving the formatting of the bibliography; Elize Zomer for timely generosity in sharing her work on the *Epic of Gulkišar*; Tim Clayden for support in various ways; and above all my encouraging but ever-critical husband Christopher Dalley for improving my style. Mistakes that remain are entirely my responsibility. I would like to thank especially warmly all those scholars who have sent me monographs, offprints, and pdfs during the past half century, contributing hugely to keeping my morale afloat.

Babylon stood at the centre of an intellectual and religious society that developed long before the great monotheisms of Judaism, Christianity, and Islam. This is its story, extracted from brilliant discoveries by archaeologists and the scholars who elucidate cuneiform texts.

For a detailed guide to the architecture of temples, palaces and walls of Babylon, the 2021 book by Olof Pedersen, *Babylon The Great City* (Münster: Zaphon) is highly recommended.

Conventions

The letter *š* is pronounced like English *sh*, but is not used in this book in the names of deities, such as Shamash and Urash, with the exception of the god Aššur (to avoid the awkward spelling Ashshur), nor in place names such as Eshnunna. The city name Ashur is a conventional spelling used here to distinguish it from the eponymous god's name. Š is kept in royal names with the exception of the conventional spelling Ashurbanipal. Biblical names such as Nebuchadnezzar follow common usage. The letter *h* represents three different Semitic consonants, apart from its use with English *s* to represent *š*; *ṭ* and *ṣ* are 'emphatic' versions of *t* and *s*.

The pre-Christian era is indicated by BC (before Christ), the Christian era AD (*anno domini*). The second millennium BC is the period from 2000 to 1000 BC. The eighteenth century BC is the period 1800 to 1700 BC. The second century AD is the period from AD 100 to 200.

Long vowels in personal and place names are not marked, with the exception of Bēl, which is the Babylonian word 'Lord' equivalent to, but distinct from, West Semitic Baʿal, as Greek transcriptions show. Biblical Hebrew versions of names from English translations are occasionally used when they are considered conventional in modern English speech and literature. Ambiguities are explained in the indices where appropriate.

In king lists, // indicates a foreign king whose reign in part coincides with that of a king of Babylon.

Timeline

Kings Who Ruled in Babylon

This book follows the traditional 'middle chronology' for the second millennium.

Many of the dates are prone to slight adjustments.

The names of kings whose deeds are unknown or insignificant are omitted. For a complete list see, for example, Walker's appendix in Collon's *Ancient Near Eastern Art* (1995: 234–8) with the exception of late Seleucid and Parthian Arsacid rulers, for which Wiesehöfer 2001: 316–18 is followed.

All dates are BC unless specified as AD.

Ch. 3	1894–c. 1732	**First Dynasty**, first part, up to the Great Rebellion
		Sumu-la-El, Sumu-abum, Apil-Sin, Sin-muballiṭ, Hammurabi, Samsu-iluna
		Amorite kings
		Middle Bronze Age
Ch. 5	c. 1732–1592	First Dynasty, second part, from the Great Rebellion to the end of the dynasty
		Samsu-iluna, Abi-ešuh, Ammi-ṣaduqa, Ammi-ditana, Samsu-ditana
		Amorite kings
		Middle Bronze Age
Ch. 6	c. 1595–1223	Early **Kassite** kings and First **Sealand** Dynasty (14 of c. 36)
		Agum II kakrime
		Pešgaldarame, Ayadaragalama (placing uncertain)
		Burna-Buriaš I, Kara-indaš, Kurigalzu I, Kadašman-Enlil I, Burna-Buriaš II,
		Kurigalzu II, Nazi-maruttaš, Kadašman-Turgu, Kadašman-Enlil II, Kudur-Enlil, Šagarakti-šuriaš, Kaštiliaš IV
		Middle to Late Bronze Age
	1222–1155	Later **Kassite** kings
		Adad-šuma-iddina
		Adad-šuma-uṣur
		Meli-šipak

(*cont.*)

		Marduk-apla-iddina I
		Enlil-nadin-ahi
		Late Bronze Age
	1157–1026	Second dynasty 'of Isin' (3 of 11 kings)
		Itti-Marduk-balaṭu
		Nebuchadnezzar I
		Adad-apla-iddina
	1025–1005	Second dynasty of Sealand (1 of 3)
		Simbar-šipak
	1004–985	Bazi dynasty (3 kings, none listed)
	984–979	'Elamite' dynasty (1 of 1)
		Mar-biti-apla-uṣur
		Early Iron Age
Ch. 7	978–783	**Babylonian** kings (5 of 12)
		Nabu-mukin-apli
		Mar-biti-ahhe-iddina
		Šamaš-mudammiq
		Nabu-apla-iddina
		Marduk-zakir-šumi
		Late Iron Age I into Iron Age II
	769–703	**Chaldean and Sealand** kings + Assyrian overlords
		(18 of 23)
		Eriba-Marduk
		Nabu-šuma-iškun
		Nabu-naṣir
		Nabu-mukin-zeri
		Tiglath-pileser III
		Marduk-apla-iddina (Merodach-Baladan)
		Sargon II
		Sennacherib
	703–625	Merodach-Baladan II (again)
		Sennacherib (again)
		Bēl-ibni
		Aššur-nadin-šumi
		Mušezib-Marduk
		Esarhaddon
		Aššurbanipal
		Šamaš-šum-ukin
		Kandalanu
		Nabopolassar
		Late Iron Age II into Iron Age III
		Neo-Assyrian/Neo-Babylonian period
Ch. 8	625–562	**Neo-Babylonian kings**

(*cont.*)

		Nabopolassar
		Nebuchadnezzar II
Ch. 9	561–521	Amel-Marduk (Evil-Merodach)
		Neriglissar
		La-abaši-Marduk
		Nabonidus
		Cyrus II (the Great)
		Cambyses
		Bardiya aka Nebuchadnezzar III
		Neo-Babylonian to Achaemenid period
Ch. 10	521–331	**Achaemenid kings** (7 of 9) + two usurpers (indented)
		Darius I
		Xerxes
		Bel-šimanni
		Šamaš-eriba
		Artaxerxes I
		Darius II
		Arses = Artaxerxes II
		Artaxerxes III Ochus
		Darius III
		Late Babylonian/Achaemenid period
	331–305	**Macedonian** Greek kings
		Alexander III the Great
		Alexander IV (+ Antigonus)
	305–c. 164	**Seleucid** Greek kings (6 of many, to first Parthian conquest)
		Seleucus I
		Antiochus I
		Antiochus II
		Seleucus II
		Seleucus III
		Antiochus IV
		Late Babylonian/Hellenistic/Seleucid period
Ch. 11	145–125	**Late Seleucid kings** (2 of many)
		Demetrius II (first time)
		Antiochus VII
		Demetrius II (second time)
	247 BC–AD 127	**Parthian (Arsacid) kings** (8 of many)
		Arsaces I
		Mithradates I
		Phraates II
		Hyspaosines of Elymais/Maysan
		Artabanus II

(*cont.*)

	Mithradates II
	Gotarzes I
	Osroes
	Roman emperor
AD 116	Trajan

Note: The word 'dynasty' implies that all kings were related by blood. Babylonian king-lists may sometimes imply that the kings listed were selected by divination, not always related.

Written Languages and Their Scripts

c. 3200 BC–early AD

Sumerian The language of southern Mesopotamia, written in a cuneiform (literally 'wedge-shaped') script. It gave way around 2000 BC to Akkadian as a spoken language, but was still a prestigious written language until the disappearance of cuneiform script. Unrelated to any other known language. Its extensive narrative literature is different from that of Babylonian and Assyrian.

c. 2100 BC–c. 1500 BC

Amorite A West Semitic language spoken but perhaps not written throughout much of the Near East, probably comprehensible to Babylonians, its people being scarcely distinguishable by the time of Babylon's First Dynasty.

c. 2350 BC–early AD

Akkadian A general term for all dialects of Babylonian and Assyrian; an East Semitic language, written in cuneiform, with vowels shown.

Babylonian The dialects of central Mesopotamia, used for all kinds of texts, with a literary dialect for religious and other elite texts.

Assyrian A general term for all dialects of Assyria with distinctive features of grammar and phonetics, written in cuneiform script, mainly known from business, correspondence, and legal texts, no longer written after c. 600 BC.

c. 1500 BC onwards

Aramaic A West Semitic language used throughout the ancient Near East, written in alphabetic script mainly without vowels. Used for administrative, legal, and short royal inscriptions, with some semi-historical narrative literature.

1800–330 BC

Elamite Language of south-east Iran, notably in Khuzistan, possibly a branch of the Dravidian group related to Tamil. Written in a modified cuneiform script. Used for administration and royal inscriptions. No known narrative literature.

1500–1200 BC

Hittite Indo-European language of central Anatolia, related to Persian and Greek, written in a modified cuneiform script. Used for administration, divination, rituals, land grants, treaties, royal inscriptions including annals, literature partly derived from Akkadian.

For details of these languages as well as Greek, Ugaritic, Hurrian, Luvian, Old Persian, and Urartian, see R. D. Woodard's *Cambridge Encyclopedia of the World's Ancient Languages* (2004).

Note: The terms East and West Semitic are based on particular linguistic features as well as script. East Semitic Babylonian, written in cuneiform script, shows vowels; West Semitic mainly does not.

View from the Summer Palace built by Nebuchadnezzar II, where Alexander the Great died, looking west over the Euphrates. Credit: author 1967.

1 | Land and Peoples

An Introduction

There's not one atom on yon earth
But once was living man;
Not the minutest drop of rain
That hangeth in its thinnest cloud
But flowed in human veins …
Thou canst not find one spot
Whereon no city stood.

(Percy Bysshe Shelley, *Queen Mab*)

Babylon, the most famous city of central Mesopotamia, gave its name to the surrounding region, Babylonia, and to the ancient kingdom, culture, and language now known as Babylonian. It was one of many great cities clustering in that fertile land, where it rose to dominate the others and held its dominance for nearly 2,000 years. Long before Babylon rose to supreme power, other great cities had powerful kings, fine buildings, extensive literacy, and mighty gods, so it is surprising that Babylon was able to achieve and hold on to its exceptional status for such a long time.

Mesopotamian civilization in general is extraordinary for its unbroken traditions of cities and literacy, but it did not begin in Babylon. For more than a thousand years the land had nurtured great Sumerian cities such as Ur, Uruk, and Lagash, whose rulers were pioneers of architecture, art, and literature with a rich and complex cultural history. Monumental buildings stood proud in the centre of all the cities, elaborately built in mud brick. The region teemed with a fecund, well-fed population in huge old cities and was criss-crossed by a network of canals connecting them for irrigation and for transport. Irrigation protected the supply of food from episodes of drought that elsewhere could decimate populations and empty settlements. Babylonia the region inherited much of the early literature and architecture, for Babylon the city was a minor settlement in the ancient land of Sumer before it rose to prominence in the eighteenth century BC. When it did, many of the old Sumerian cities of the south, with literacy centred on the Sumerian language, continued to flourish.

1

Close to Babylon on its northern side were huge ancient cities, in particular Kish and Sippar, where the Babylonian language, also known as Akkadian, superseding Sumerian, had become the main language written in cuneiform before alphabets came into use. Most of the great centres of Sumerian (non-Semitic) language were in the southern cities. In the northern cities and in Babylon itself, Sumerian was studied and revered for its antiquity. In their literature, all the kings of Sumerian and Babylonian cities satisfied the need for indigenous heroes and great deeds from a legendary past, developing written literature from epic tales, hymns, and narratives of royal deeds. Their languages were also used for legal contracts, letters, and administrative records. Some sorts of inscription were bilingual in Sumerian and Babylonian. Linear alphabetic writing developed during the second millennium, but traces of it are rare because it was almost always used on organic materials that are not preserved.

The Sumerians and Babylonians were integrated into urban Mesopotamia. The relationship between their languages bears some similarities with that between ancient Greek and Latin, including the skilful reworking and transforming of old themes and forms. Bilgames the Sumerian adventurer-king became Gilgamesh the Babylonian hero-king, claimed by two different cities, Ur and Uruk, and publicly emulated by the kings of Babylon. In order to keep old traditions alive, the Babylonians became adept at producing bilingual inscriptions and at translating old Sumerian texts. They extended their expertise beyond Babylonia, teaching illiterate neighbours to develop their own literature, always written in a cuneiform script.[1]

Babylon city lies in an alluvial plain on a branch of the river Euphrates, positioned 33 N by 44 E, about 85 km south of modern Baghdad in the middle of modern Iraq. Today the head of the Gulf lies roughly 450 km to the south of Babylon; how much the shoreline at the edge of the delta may have changed from time to time in antiquity is one of the most contested topics in research.[2] A change of climate around 2000 BC in the area stretching from Lake Van in eastern Anatolia to the Arabian Gulf caused rainfall to decrease by 20–30 per cent, and conditions of drought may have lasted for around 200 years, causing settlements to be abandoned in marginal zones.[3] Towards the end of that period, the first dynasty of Babylon arose. Its position on a branch of the Euphrates surely kept it

---

[1] For the significance of this, see Feeney 2016: 1–44 and 199–235.
[2] Many studies are described by Potts 1997: 30–9.
[3] An overview with detailed bibliography is given by Ristvet and Weiss, introduction to Eidem and Ristvet 2011: xxxix–xli.

safe from starvation as long as irrigation canals were dug and maintained, and floodwater controlled, but the same was true of other great cities nearby. Water management was a crucial duty of Babylonian kings.

The sources of the two great rivers Euphrates and Tigris are close together, then diverge to flow through very different terrains before joining again in the marshes of southern Iraq; there their beds often shifted, whether from natural causes or being diverted by human action, so the landscape constantly changed. Owing to the delta-like terrain of Lower Mesopotamia, it is not certain how the rivers and canals flowed at any particular period of history. Areas of marshland formed in different areas at different times, turning good agricultural land into reed beds with expanses of standing water.[4] The whole area is very low-lying, and the rivers bring down silt which clogs canals, so that they must be cleared frequently; the canals and their banks thus rise ever higher above the level of the plain. Abandoned canals have left many long stretches of levees in the landscape. The two rivers flood at slightly different times, far too late to facilitate sowing and early growth of crops; their waters are hard to control, with unpredictable floods damaging crops and cities.[5] A high water table and the difficulties of draining excess water from fields, combined with a high rate of evaporation in summer months, led to intermittent and localized salination, which could cause crops to fail. The southern terrain was difficult to manage when Babylon began to impose central government; the location of Babylon city did not give it particular advantages over rival cities such as Uruk and Larsa. According to the *Epic of Atrahasis*, the gods found the work of maintenance so hard that they created mankind to toil on their behalf:

> The gods' load was too great, the work too hard, the labour too much. The gods had to dig out canals, had to clear channels, the lifelines of the land. For 3,600 years they bore the excess, hard work, night and day. They groaned and blamed each other, grumbled over the heaps of excavated soil.[6]

The nearby cities Kish, Borsippa, and Sippar were closely involved with the activities of the great capital at Babylon. Each had an illustrious past from earliest times, and had a patron deity of top prestige: the war-god Zababa, famous for oracles, at Kish; the creator god Tutu, later succeeded by Nabu, at Borsippa; and the Sun-god Shamash, lord of law and justice, at Sippar. They were all connected, with Babylon as the hub, by waterways,

---

[4] See Cole 1994.   [5] Ionides 1937.
[6] Translations given in this volume are my own except where attributed.

processional streets, linked festivals and ceremonies in which the gods visited each other. Not far beyond lay many other cities of varying fame and continuity.

Further beyond Babylon, the Fertile Crescent arches from the foothills of western Iran, across the south-east of modern Turkey, down through the river valleys and mountains of the Amanus and Lebanon. In this great arc of land grew the wild plants domesticated during the Neolithic Age, which became a major source of prosperity in Mesopotamia: wheat and barley, lentils and chickpeas, bitter vetch, sesame and flax.[7] Sheep, goats, and cattle were domesticated, not only allowing a steady supply of food, wool, and leather, but also enabling the textile industry for which Babylon became famous.[8] Nowadays the region is best known for its petroleum oil, a plentiful resource still obtainable even from surface seepages. Exploited in ancient times in the form of bitumen, it was invaluable for waterproofing: for boats, for mortar, and for containers.

Upstream the Euphrates gave access by boat and donkey[9] to north-west Syria, from where land routes led to the Levant and to the semi-desert of central Syria, through Palmyra to Damascus. The Tigris, on the other hand, was fed by many tributaries flowing fast from the Zagros Mountains, joining or intersecting land routes that extended into the eastern and northern mountains. So the twin rivers, beginning and ending so close together, gave completely separate access to different regions for resources, for trade, and for immigration, along the middle part of their courses. Those differences also meant that the Babylonians encountered a very wide variety of peoples, languages, and products. Sometimes unable to repel incursions, they had to absorb foreign immigrants into a diverse but assimilated population. The contrast with Egypt on the Nile, a single river with waterless desert on both sides, is striking: there the environment did not provide a comparable variety of immigrants.

To the east of both rivers in Babylonia, in the surrounding hills and the Zagros Mountains, lay rival foreign cities. Most persistent was the federation of rulers over an ill-defined land called Elam, one of whose capital cities was Susa in south-west Iran, at the edge of the Mesopotamian river lands.[10] The Elamites were neither Semites nor Iranians – their language may be related to the group known as Dravidian, which includes Tamil.[11]

---

[7] Zohary 1996.   [8] Breniquet and Michel 2014.
[9] A hybrid wild ass crossed with the onager, now extinct: Mitchell 2018: 87–95.
[10] See Potts 2016 and Alvarez-Mon, Basello, and Wicks 2018 for extensive information about Elamites.
[11] See briefly Stolper 2004: 61.

Late in the third millennium they adopted the Babylonian language and script for writing and education, and were conversant with its literature, before evolving their own tradition to record their language in an adapted form of cuneiform script. When the first dynasty of Babylon began, Elamite settlements were scattered, their people opportunists as raiders, or as foreign militias specializing in archery who would serve any master according to need. A few centuries earlier, when their royal capital Susa had been ruled by a governor appointed by the kings of Ur, the Elamites had rebelled and sacked the city of Ur, and would remain a looming presence on the eastern border of Mesopotamia throughout its history, as traders, invaders, and foreign soldiers, according to the balance of power at any particular time. Later they coalesced into a centralized kingdom rivalling Babylonia and managed briefly to take over the rule of Babylon on more than one occasion, as is known mainly from Babylonian records. From Susa they had two main routes into Mesopotamia: either directly westward across the rivers and marshy lands to the Lower Tigris, or by the uplands along the foothills of the mountains to the city of Der, gateway to the Diyala river valley, down to fertile land and the city of Eshnunna, the 'princely sanctuary'. Both routes gave easy access to the heartland of Babylonia; but the Elamites never established a long-lived dynasty in Babylon, perhaps preferring to raid and occasionally to control from a distance, until the conquest of Babylon by Cyrus in 538.

Various other ethnic or language groups contributed to the diversity of Babylonia, and founded successful dynasties there. Invading hordes of (West Semitic) Amorites – hardy soldiers from the western deserts – were held at bay for centuries until they established the First Dynasty of Babylon, and played a formative role in the history of the city. Perhaps from the Zagros Mountains between Iraq and Iran came the (non-Semitic) Kassites. They had served in militias during the First Dynasty of Babylon, and eventually took up the reins of power in Babylon itself, successfully integrating into Babylonian traditions, bringing very little evidence of their own origins. None of those groups – Elamites, Amorites, and Kassites – showed any aversion to royal marriages outside their own ethnic or language group.

When Cyrus the Great conquered Babylon, he behaved as a king chosen by the Babylonian gods, inserting himself into Mesopotamian tradition. As an Elamite with Persian links, he was hardly different from earlier foreign usurpers such as the Kassites, who founded a new dynasty in Babylon. The Persian Darius I, however, began an era of relative neglect for the city in 521, giving local priests an opportunity to take over duties previously expected of the king. Then Alexander the Great, before his untimely death there, clearly intended to foster the city's existing glory rather than forcing Macedonian culture upon its people. When his successors managed to restore firm rule, their Seleucid dynasty treated the city with respect, and business continued, though use of cuneiform writing was declining in favour of alphabetic Aramaic. Neither the Achaemenid Persians nor the heirs of Alexander absorbed Babylonian culture in the way that previous foreign kings, notably the Kassites, had done. Significantly, however, neither the Persian language nor Greek managed to displace Babylonian literature, which continued even when the Parthian (Arsacid) kings took over. Even under Parthian domination, which began in 141 BC, Babylon's influence was slow to wane, still to be traced early in the Christian era. Knowledge of the cuneiform culture emanating from Babylon became the preserve of priests and temples, still innovative in mathematics and astronomy, for several centuries before it came to an end. Little of its finest literature written in cuneiform script was translated into non-Semitic languages written in alphabetic scripts.

To the north up the Tigris was Assyria, with its traditional capital city Ashur. When Babylon's first dynasty arose, the people of Ashur had formed colonies of merchants based in Anatolian towns, and they profited from trade chiefly in tin and textiles, carried overland in caravans of donkeys. Their main language was a dialect of Babylonian. Eventually they established other royal cities such as Nineveh, further up the Tigris, from which they could set out on campaigns to forge an empire, leaving Ashur as a mainly ceremonial centre. They were great admirers of Babylonian culture, and treated it with reverence, even when they ruled the city of Babylon.

Further to the north were the Indo-Aryan Hittites, rough people from the harsh environment of the Anatolian highlands, who formed a centralized kingdom there during the latter half of the First Dynasty of Babylon, apparently content to raid cities in the fertile lowlands of Mesopotamia without governing there, but accepting instruction in Babylonian script and language from visiting scholars. Through the scribal curriculum they learnt some of the great works of cuneiform literature and creatively adapted them to their own civilization.

To the south of Babylon the great cities of deeper antiquity included Ur 'of the Chaldees', city of the Moon-god, and Uruk, home of the legendary hero Gilgamesh and the great goddess Inanna. They lay close to the sea with access to harbours and the Gulf; they were surrounded by marshland full of fish, birds, and reeds, so the region was generally known as the Sealand. Above all, the date palm flourished, providing so many resources, from food to rope, that its origin at the behest of the god Enki was celebrated in the Sumerian myth of *Inanna and Her Gardener Shukaletuda*, in which a raven watered the first date palm with a *shaduf*,[12] and climbed up it using a harness:

> Its brittle leaves enclose its palm heart. Its dried palm fronds serve for weaving. Its shoots are like a surveyor's shining line; they are fit for the king's fields. Its branches are used in the king's palace for cleaning. Its dates, which are heaped up alongside pure barley grains, are fit for the temples of the great gods.[13]

Its versatility is emphasized in the Babylonian *Dispute between the Date Palm and the Tamarisk*:

> In those days, on those nights, in years long ago,
> When the gods made the land firm and created cities for long-ago people,
> When they poured out mountains and dug out rivers, life of the land …
> They loved the black-headed people and gave them a king …
> The king planted a date palm in his palace;
> All around he planted a tamarisk …
> The trees were enemies, tamarisk and date palm became rivals …
> 'You, tamarisk, are a useless tree. Why, tamarisk, do your branches
> Bear no fruit? Our fruits are fit for the king's table,
> The king eats and the public says they are my gift.
> Thanks to me, the orchard gardener makes a profit and provides for the
>   queen.
> As a mother, she raises her baby, it eats the gift of my fertility,
>   And grows up.
> My fruit is always there for royalty'.[14]

The fecund goddess herself was sometimes envisaged as a female date palm. Date palms grow happily around Babylon, too, but lose their ability to produce ripe fruit at more northerly latitudes.[15] In the marshes of the south, many settlements were built from the reeds which grew abundantly in reed beds within the marshes, and cannot now be located by surface survey or excavation, for they were organic and disintegrated easily, leaving no trace. On alluvial land the efficient use of canals, tree plantations, and fish ponds presumably had a beneficial effect on the

---

[12] A *shaduf* consists of a pole moving on a pivot on top of a vertical beam. One end of the pole has a bucket suspended from it, the other has a weight acting as a counterpoise.

[13] See 'Inana and Shu-kale-tuda', ETCSL, also Volk 1995.

[14] My own translation after Cohen 2013: 177–98.

[15] Depending on precise climatic conditions, see Giovino 2007: 91–102.

local microclimate, providing shade and local water in the great heat of summer.

To the west, on the Middle Euphrates lay Mari, capital of early kings 'of Mari and Hana'.[16] Although Mari declined swiftly when Babylon sacked the city about 1760 BC, its power shifted to nearby cities, and the region became known simply as Hana, a kingdom that lasted for a further half-millennium. Among its major cities were Harran and Guzana (the biblical Gozan). Hana benefitted not only from the east–west trade on the great river, but also from the desert road to Palmyra, and to the fertile lands bordering the river Habur, which flowed into the Euphrates from the long mountain range in the north known as the Tur Abdin. Hana maintained a very conservative tradition of writing records, keeping to the scribal habits of the early eighteenth century for several hundred years.[17]

All of those groups admired and emulated the literate culture of Babylon and adapted some of its written works to their own needs. With deep roots in the written literature of ancient Sumer, the Babylonians were already developing a varied range of compositions that were not simply aping those of earlier times: they were innovative, producing works of science and narrative that were admired throughout the known world.

Many of the itinerant tribes on the fringes of Babylonia included not only the hunter-gatherers of prehistory, but also pastoralists, whether semi-nomadic tent dwellers (in Mesopotamia) or cave dwellers (in mountainous and rocky areas), who were available for seasonal labour such as digging and clearing canals, making mud bricks, sowing and harvesting crops in exchange for cereal, beer, oil, and dates, the staples of daily diet. The ability to make tents would have been an innovation that changed and extended the patterns of semi-nomadic lifestyle in a region lacking caves and rock shelters. For much or all of the region's history, Mesopotamian cities would have had tented encampments outside the city walls. The pastoral tent dwellers relied on a symbiotic relationship with the city: they could pasture their flocks on fields at certain times of year, and were available for labour, especially for sowing and harvesting. The *Law of Hammurabi* §58 refers to how an aspect of this interaction was regulated to mutual benefit:

> If, after the flocks have come up from the irrigated land when the rope has been wound around the city gate, the shepherd has left flocks on the field and allowed the flocks to graze the field, the shepherd shall guard the field

---

[16] The kingdom of Hana was later known as Hanigalbat or Habigal; see Podany 2002, Fales 2014, and Da Riva 2017b.

[17] Podany 2016.

on which he allowed them to feed, and at harvest he shall measure out 60 *kor* (perhaps 18,000 litres) of barley per *iku* (acre) of land to the owner of the field.

When flocks are allowed to graze on young barley shoots, only a small loss of the crop results, especially if the sowing has been deliberately crowded to allow for grazing when the plants are immature.[18] The lifestyle of desert Bedouin known in recent times, dependent on camels, could not develop until the camel was domesticated for transport, around 1000 BC; that was one of many striking changes that would have transformed some of the city's facilities.[19]

Babylon's competitors were many, yet, as we shall see, it succeeded in rising above them by various different strategies, architectural, religious, literary, educational, and legal. Although the city suffered some terrible episodes of defeat and subsequent impoverishment, yet it managed each time to regenerate, building on the strength of its deep-rooted culture, invoking a history of past success and prosperity while helping its conquerors to adapt to their new circumstances. Many were the changes of dynasty, some of them founded by immigrants or invaders from other ethnic groups: Amorites, then Kassites from western Iran, later Persians from south-western Iran, and then Macedonians. Throughout those influxes Babylon continued to maintain and adapt its traditional cuneiform script and literature: culturally, the city did not yield to its conquerors, but won them over.

So who were the real Babylonians? Were they the kings who sat on the throne of Babylon, regardless of their ethnic origins? In fact, it was the city itself, its temples, scholars, and written culture, that kept the line of tradition going for two thousand years, instilling in its rulers a strong sense of duty, but able to thrive without royal patronage. Foreigners who settled became Babylonians.

Monarchy was the only form of government in Babylonia. Ostensibly kingship was hereditary; as an institution the gods had sent it from heaven at the dawn of history, and imposed heavy responsibilities which the king shared with his advisers. If a king proved irresponsible, the gods would withdraw kingship from him: in the Babylonian *Epic of Gilgamesh*, when the young king of Uruk behaved atrociously, his people prayed to the gods rather than deposing him. A good king took counsel from a group of men who could act for him in his absence. By means of public ceremonies, prayer, royal art, and religious rituals, kings kept in

---

[18] Oates and Oates 1976, quoting Adams 1965: 169.   [19] Magee 2014: 204–13.

close contact with the gods. Their main duties were to feed the gods and their people, to create wealth through trade, and to protect the land from flooding and invasion. In early times, legitimate succession (not necessarily by the first-born son) was so important officially, and ancestry so crucial, that a usurper would manipulate his genealogy to prove that he was not 'son of a nobody'. The word 'son' had a wide meaning implying not only direct descent but also the relationship of any male to his ruler, including adoption.

Every ruler had a duty to revere his royal ancestors as well as the gods, for his success depended on the support from the grave of predecessors. This duty exerted a strong control on the king's exercise of power. In royal inscriptions the influence of deceased predecessors is manifest in the claim by the king to understand old inscriptions which were kept on display, or were found when great buildings were repaired. The link of direct descent weakened over time, so eventually a king could admit to being 'son of a nobody', but an emphasis on local heritage and the importance of past history is evident at all periods from the use of archaic script on a new statue of a god, or a foundation inscription. On old statue bases, inscriptions were copied and studied, to perpetuate the fame of successes long past. Cuneiform writing as well as statuary played an important role in confirming continuity, stability, and royal control.

To extend and maintain domination over a widespread group of cities rather than just raiding them, a ruler needed clear communication with a common language and good connections by road, canal, and river. Perhaps the greatest achievement of ancient Mesopotamia was to spread its Babylonian language through the written word, backed up by a systematic education, far beyond home territory, among peoples whose many languages and dialects were entirely different: Elamites, Hittites, Kassites, and others. This unity allowed business contracts, treaties, and letters to facilitate a broad economy to the benefit of the central power. Babylon was neither the first nor the only city to have and use written language: nearby Kish and Sippar, for instance, were no different in that respect. By contrast, peoples of the mountains and deserts surrounding Mesopotamia, isolated from each other by harsh terrain, presumably lacked a common native tongue. Even city dwellers of adjacent lands such as the Elamites did not develop an independent literature. Babylonia is extraordinary for developing by far the richest and most varied literature in the pre-Greek world. This feat is all the more remarkable because, as Feeney remarks, 'Although nothing seems more natural than that a nation should have a literature, there is nothing inevitable or predictable about it'.[20]

In modern times, different languages are popularly linked to supposed ethnic and biological groups, but that link is demonstrably false in ancient Babylonia.[21] For instance, the Amorites, speaking a language related to Babylonian, settled in the cities of central Mesopotamia around 2000 BC without, as far as we know, bringing past traditions recorded in writing. The Sumerian tale *The Marriage of Martu* recounts how the Amorite god, despite his unattractive appearance, disgusting personal habits, and execrable lifestyle, managed to attract the love of a city girl, and was absorbed into city life to enjoy the pleasures of plentiful food, splendid festivals, and taverns with beer. Thus the Amorites inserted themselves into the deep heritage of literacy developed by the Sumerians and Babylonians, and often took Babylonian names for themselves and their children. Later intruders in Mesopotamia – Kassites, Elamites, Chaldeans – show a similar adoption and reverence for the ancient literacy already entrenched there, even though none of them came from a group that spoke a Semitic language. Above all in Babylonia the cuneiform writings of more ancient times could be read, cited, and revised, reassuring people in times of change and insecurity that stability was linked to the successes of strong kings from past times.

Civilization and central control by major cities had begun with the division of land into fields irrigated by a network of canals, and with the effective storage of food. Uncivilized people in the vicinity were denigrated as people who did not know fields, and the skills of pastoralists as shepherds and stockmen were recognized as less sophisticated but useful: 'The highland Martu-people (Amorite westerners), ignorant of agriculture', brought spirited cattle, kids, and fat-tailed sheep as offerings to the city temple, but were compared unfavourably with those who had dwellings in a city adorned with beautiful temples, where people ate delicious food, drank splendid drinks, took baths for festivals, wore fine clothes, and celebrated by dining with friends.[22] Urban and non-urban groups in society were not necessarily distinct, for sedentary farmers living mainly in villages and farmsteads benefitted from a symbiotic relationship with pastoralists, who were often contracted by both farmers and city dwellers. Uncivilized people from the mountains, who were much fitter than the city dwellers, were useful for guarding and fighting, and often formed militias who occupied forts serving the great cities. The king had to control the different

---

[20] Feeney 2016: 37 and 235.   [21] Barth 1969.   [22] Black et al. 2004: 118.

groups within the population, exploiting their potential and controlling their activities through laws.

Before Babylon began to record the existence of its earliest kings in the nineteenth century BC, it was a place of so little importance that it played no part in the great myths and epics of earlier times. The name of Gilgamesh, and the many stories about him, are not linked to the city, nor is any version of the Flood story, nor the myths of Etana, Anzu, Ishtar's Descent to the Underworld, Nergal, or Ereshkigal. Even when the *Epic of Atrahasis*, with the Creation of mankind and the Flood as its central themes, was written around the nineteenth century BC, the city of Babylon did not feature. Babylon inserted itself into the mythological past through subsequent compositions, most notably the *Enūma Eliš* (*Epic of Creation*). This shows how strong the tradition of those earlier myths was, and how the kings of Babylon accepted and revered the antiquity of the archaic cities, eventually adjusting the *Sumerian King-List* so that Babylon replaced other versions to insert itself as the first city in human history to have a king. Previously, several different cities had claimed to be the earliest, each inserting its own name. Kish was perhaps earliest, Eridu took its turn, Babylon was the last to claim the honour.[23]

A more or less centralized system of education helped to stabilize the Babylonian language, and made it an instrument of royal control, but that did not stop it changing over the centuries to such an extent that at the end of its history, grammar and vocabulary bore little resemblance to their earliest forms. Lexical 'dictionary' texts were updated to keep up with the changes in vocabulary. So the term 'Babylonian' for the whole time span, though useful, is rather misleading. Its complex pre-alphabetic script used wedge-shaped signs that have various different values as syllables (such as *mu* and *kal*), logograms (signs that represent a whole word), and determinatives (which indicate a category such as 'objects made of pottery').[24] The writing system was used by many of Babylon's neighbours and rivals. Its adoption was voluntary, linked to prestige, not conquest, and the system was usually adapted and simplified.

The written records of Babylonia can be divided into three major groups. First to attract attention in the early days of western scholarship were monumental and royal inscriptions, some of them inscribed on stone as well as clay. Their texts, written to show the greatness of the king, his public image, prestige, and authority, have what we might now call an ideological bias, and are not always reliable in relating the success or failure of royal

[23] Steinkeller 2003; Marchesi 2010.   [24] Labat and Malbran-Labat 1995.

deeds; occasionally clear evidence for blatant contradictions comes to light, sometimes showing that different versions were acceptable, and did not require harmonizing. Individual cities had their own king-lists, all of them following a traditional pattern of one king directly succeeded by the next, each with the number of years of his rule; the gods were responsible for bringing a dynasty to an end and transferring power to the next city. This is the tradition of the *Sumerian King-List* which extended back into legendary times, when some of the earliest kings had the names of constellations. During the First Dynasty of Babylon, the tradition was centralized so that versions of later Babylonian king-lists are found with kings almost all of whom are known from inscriptions of their own times. They do not contain legendary material, and they may ignore co-regencies and overlaps. Around the beginning of the second millennium, a tradition of chronicles began, in which the major events of each king's reign were briefly given in chronological order. The information may be more impartial than royal inscriptions in documenting events, and shows a keen interest in making a permanent record of events involving kings.

Second are texts of literary content, written on unbaked clay.[25] They are usually found in the form of short extracts from the school curriculum for young scribes, or texts from the libraries of their instructors, including hymns, epics, manuals, dictionaries, and ritual texts, some with incantations. Entire compositions have to be reconstructed from these extracts, from fragments of different dates and versions, by modern scholars stumbling through the variations and errors of apprentice scribes. A tradition of written commentaries on these compositions is found dating from the eighth to the second century BC.[26]

Third are archival texts, which include legal contracts, official letters, and business and administrative texts such as deliveries of goods.[27] Legal documents concerning real estate are hard to interpret, but receive much attention because land ownership is crucial to describing the economy. How much land, if any, was truly freehold in private ownership?[28] Letters of the king's family and his officials concern the minutiae of local as well as international events, but some are now understood to be partly fictitious texts composed within the school tradition, inventive in the colourful character that they attribute to the king. Administrative texts, often

[25] They are sometimes labelled 'canonical', a hotly disputed term. See, e.g., Lim 2017.
[26] Frahm 2011.
[27] Some scholars prefer the term 'dossier' for a group in a single category. All such groups are likely to be remnants of a larger group.
[28] Goddeeris 2002: 328 and 336.

found in palaces rather than temples, show that the ruler was ultimately responsible for recording goods and deliveries, which were documented in daily, monthly, and annual records, usually dated. Enormous quantities of luxury goods – mainly of metals, gemstones, and textiles – are recorded, with a value based not only on the material itself but also on the distance from the material's source and the expense of labour. How much trade was financed and conducted on behalf of the king or the temple, and how much was private, at any particular period, is hard to determine. So-called 'rations' were the salaries of specialist workers. Much production was not intended for daily use but provided luxuries conspicuously consumed at festivals and banquets. The people and the king both donated currency metal to temples at festivals, thus using temples as treasuries.[29] Each group of texts has its own terminology, inconsistent through time and place.

There are several reasons why many texts on clay tablets cannot be dated: many have no date, or the date is broken away; many are copies, which may either use a current script or imitate an older one; and some deliberately use old sign forms and select archaic values of signs.

The ancient Babylonians were aware that stone and clay had survived even from the legendary past 'before the Flood':

> Make, then, tablets of stone and others of clay, and write on them … If by water the Lord judge our race, the tablets of clay will be dissolved and the tablets of stone will remain; if by fire, the tablets of stone will be shattered and the tablets of clay will be baked.[30]

There were times when waxed wooden or ivory writing-boards, hinged to turn like the pages of a book, as well as papyrus, parchment, copper, lead, and wooden sticks or the midribs of date palm leaves, were in common use. Beautiful complete copies of the great works of literature, perhaps also of official correspondence, were written on writing-boards which have not survived because they were made of organic materials, so we must reconstruct whole compositions piecemeal from clay tablets. Clay tablets are found in great quantities, but only on particular sites and for particular periods. There are long intervals between prolific finds of clay tablets, when one may not infer that writing ceased, since organic materials were sometimes preferred. When, eventually, Aramaic became the main language for writing, perhaps as early as the seventh century, both cuneiform script and, to a large extent, clay were abandoned for an alphabet on

---

[29] Sallaberger 2013.

[30] Quotation from *The Books of Adam and Eve*, Charles 1913: 152. I thank Stephanie West for this reference.

organic materials: letters were written in ink on parchment or potsherds or incised on clay or palm frond midribs.[31] The fact that clay tablets and cuneiform writing tell us only a part of the story is emphasized in the following chapters. But certain wise old scholars in the venerable institutions of Babylonia continued to keep records on clay alongside those on parchment. Papyrus was seldom used in Babylonia, and parchment (made from animal skins) was probably not used until late in its history.[32] According to the value of the material, and the time and expense required for preparation, writing-boards were the most prestigious medium, parchment and clay less so.

What kind of a city was Babylon? A question that applies to all the great cities of the ancient Near East is: did they develop into towns from primitive villages and then expand and change into cities? Were they market towns with good links by canal or river? Were they encircled by forts? Or did they begin as ceremonial centres of worship for an itinerant population, sacred places of intermittent assembly around which an elite first settled in order to service the needs of its deities, and to honour ancestors? If the latter, those religious centres are likely also to have been burial grounds where famous leaders were either interred or represented by statues, figurines, or standing stones in which the spirits of the dead were immanent.[33] A king of the First Dynasty of Babylon called upon his remote and legendary ancestors to partake in a funerary feast, presumably carrying on a long-standing tradition.[34] The grave of an ancestor could be an identifiable repository of weapons, available for living descendants: a letter shows it was acceptable for a king to open the tomb of a royal ancestor and take out bronze weapons.[35]

In lands other than Mesopotamia, some early sites that were special places of assembly apparently did not develop into cities with royal palaces, but persisted purely as centres of worship. Some of them are different from those of Lower Mesopotamia because they are based around natural features that radiate a numinous presence, such as mountaintops, unusual rock formations, springs at the sources of rivers. In Babylonia, artificial places had to be designed and built to create an impressive environment for spiritual engagement, requiring imagination

---

[31] For palm frond midribs, see Breton 1999: 112–13; Drewes and Ryckmans 2016. Also Hamidović 2014; Colonna d'Istria 2012: no. 48. See also Chapter 6, below, and Figure 6.3.

[32] Paper was invented in China around the second century AD. See Munro 2014: 61.

[33] See Mumford 1961: 7–10; Finlayson 2014; also Goring-Morris and Belfer-Cohen 2014: 152; Schmidt 2010: 239–54.

[34] See Chapter 5 p. 123 below.   [35] Text A 2177 from Mari, c. 1700 BC. See Jacquet 2012: 131–2.

and the transfer of concepts from the natural to the built environment. Most prominent was the ziggurat ('temple tower'), which represented a mountain peak close to heaven and had roots like a tree reaching down to the Underworld; Babylon's ziggurat was an outstanding example of such an artificial mountain, close to the temple of the city's patron god. Greek texts give some idea of its function: 'All agree that it was exceedingly high, and that in it the Chaldeans[36] made their observations of the stars, whose risings and settings could be observed accurately by reason of the structure's height'.[37] At the top was a room with a table and chair;[38] one imagines a rota of astronomers sitting there under the night sky with a clear view to the horizon, to record the results of their watch. Each temple was the home of a deity and his divine family, represented by statues. There they received their food and clothing as offerings, and heard the prayers of their worshippers. Temples and palaces were the two architectural expressions of power; city walls and gates kept the place secure, with a ring of forts beyond. Kings resided in a 'palace', which refers to a large administrative building with offices and workshops for activities such as textile manufacture, beer-brewing, and the distribution of bitumen. Wealth, partly controlled by the temples, was used less for personal extravagance than for adorning the gods, entertaining foreign diplomats, making offerings to ancestors, and sustaining militias with supplies of food and clothing. When ceremonial centres stored foodstuffs and other goods with a view to sacrifice as well as secular redistribution, a defensive wall with gates had to be added to the place, with areas within the walls available for housing the elite, as well as space for driving sheep and other domesticated animals in to safety at night.

One cannot exclude the possibility that Babylon developed simply from a small agricultural settlement with useful links by river and canal to other centres, and grew prosperous through the exertions of its farmers. The choice of the hoe to symbolize the city's god, and the special significance for Babylon of the constellation known as *ikû* ('the field'), now known to us as part of Pegasus,[39] helps to reinforce the fact that Babylon lay in central Mesopotamia, a region currently regarded as the birthplace of irrigation

---

[36] The name 'Chaldean' was used by Greek writers in Late Antiquity to mean astrologers and astronomers, rather than its earlier, indigenous application to a tribal group of Babylonians. It could also refer to the Aramaic language and script. See Chapter 7 below, pp. 172–3.

[37] Diod. Sic. II.9.4. The description, if true, cannot have referred to Babylon's ziggurat, which was a ruin before the arrival of Alexander the Great.

[38] Hdt I.181 f. This is an enticing image, but questionable.   [39] Ambos 2013: 164–5.

agriculture. A Sumerian song praises the hoe, which was present at the creation of the world, made the first bricks, and was instrumental in building the first cities and temples:

> Hoe makes everything prosper, hoe makes everything flourish.
> Hoe means good barley, hoe is overseer.
> Hoe means brick moulds, hoe lets people exist.
> It is hoe that is the strength of young manhood.
> Hoe and basket are the tools for building cities.
> It builds proper houses, it cultivates proper fields.
>   You, O hoe, extend good agricultural land!
> Hoe overcomes for its owner fields that resisted their owner,
> fields that did not submit to their owner.
> It chops the heads off vile esparto grasses, pulls them out by their
>   roots and tears at their stalks;
> Hoe subdues the *hirin* weeds.
> Hoe is the tool whose fate was fixed by father-god Enlil.
> Famous hoe![40]

Babylon's location, like that of other cities, on the bank of a watercourse, meant that it had at least one quay where boats for transport, trade and ceremonies congregated. Thus its situation was no different from other cities nearby, so one must look for reasons to explain why Babylon outstripped them. Each city had its own territory of agricultural land, but its borders did not necessarily join those of neighbouring cities. Beyond the reach of canals lay pasture land and steppe with grazing rights shared to more-or-less-agreed schedules by various pastoral tribes. Caravans of traders, diplomatic missions, and armies therefore passed inevitably through open country where they were susceptible to raids and ambushes, beyond the reach of a central authority.

Fertile soil and well-regulated irrigation made it easy to produce a surplus of food, and canals linking the cities made distribution simple. Forts protected the nodal points. These factors are key to a certain level of trade, both for home markets but also for export to less fertile lands. Growing cereals, oil plants, dates, and many other foods, and breeding and tending animals for meat, dairy products, and leather, was essential also for maintaining the cult in the great cities, keeping the goodwill of the gods. This was one of the driving forces behind social and cultural development. Temples were meeting places, festivals were markets. The bigger the temples and festivals, the bigger the markets, attracting both buyers and

---

[40] Translation adapted from Black et al. 2004: 314.

sellers. As many records show in detail, the god had regular, daily meals and 'ate' first; the food and drink offerings presented to the cult image were handed on to temple personnel and their dependents and to the palace, ensuring a vital connection between piety, loyalty, and food. Regular and irregular festivals throughout the year meant that crowds of people visited the various cities to partake of the gods' largesse, taking the opportunity also to exchange goods. This kept the central temples as the focus of local trading, with festivals described in texts as days of rejoicing accompanied by music and feasting.

Much as one would like to know population sizes for cities at any particular period, we cannot do so reliably, neither by taking a sample of brick-built houses within the walls as excavated by modern archaeologists nor by tracing from surface or aerial survey. In addition to other imponderables, tents made from leather or textiles seldom leave recoverable traces of their presence. But the recorded size of various armies and groups of levied soldiers gives at least an indication of relative manpower and how it increased over the centuries. The *Epic of Atrahasis* has as its main theme recurrent overpopulation, which could only be rectified by famine, disease, or flood. The comforts of urban life with plentiful food made it easy to raise large families, but unstoppable expansion led to problems that were recognized in early antiquity, and contraceptives were developed.[41]

Textual evidence for epidemics is sometimes linked to the movements of great armies introducing a disease into an unprotected population. Within the city, a supply of clean water is one of the best ways to avoid contagion. Even during the earliest dynasty of Babylon the great buildings and streets were supplied with clean water through systems of linked terracotta pipes. The discovery of milk teeth from piglets in several urban excavations reveals that domestic waste was largely disposed of by the indiscriminate appetites of piglets.[42] Contagion from vessels used by the sick and then shared by the healthy was understood, as we know from a letter. A king of Mari having heard that a woman was ill with a fever, wrote to his wife:

> She has stayed a lot at the palace, and has come into contact with many other women. Now, take strict measures: nobody must drink from the cup she drank from; nobody must sit on the seat she sat on, and nobody must lie on the bed she lay on. She must not have contact with the many other women. That fever is contagious.[43]

---

[41] Biggs 2000; Böck 2013.   [42] Grigson 2007: 106–7.   [43] Dossin 1978: no. 129.

This understanding did not preclude valid alternatives: demons and malicious magic could also be blamed for illnesses, and the great gods themselves could withdraw their protection from a pious person without cause. Incantations were effective and popular; they were poetic, individual compositions, not repetitive works for wide distribution, but literary works of extreme complexity.

Sheep and goats yielded abundant wool for textiles. Some of the work was done in palace workshops. A single administrative text from the time of Hammurabi in the eighteenth century BC gives the number of workers and the number of days required to produce special textiles for the king and for gods: several thousand days' labour of specialist workers.[44] Other texts show that dyestuffs, both mineral and botanical, were traded from far away. In special daily rituals the statues of the gods were arrayed in the finest garments. Social status was expressed through clothing and soft furnishings, which were among the most prestigious diplomatic gifts.

Technical progress in metalworking, in glass production, in cutting and carving hard gemstones, and in the construction of wheels, can be traced from texts in combination with material and pictorial evidence. Imported raw materials allowed indigenous innovation, craftsmanship, and ingenuity to flourish. Eventually Babylon served as a market for gemstones. Lapis lazuli, brought in from Afghanistan and sent on to the Levant and to Egypt, was especially valuable because it represented the night sky and the appearance of heaven. Agate could be cut and then given artificial banding to produce eye stones for the statues of gods and for highly prized dedications. Expert and highly technical glassware, developed in the second millennium, can be distinguished by its different ingredients from glass produced in other regions.[45] In Babylonia, a technique for producing colour-glazed bricks developed, adding lustre to its widespread reputation for fine brickwork, including vaulted roofs and arched doorways.

Babylon became a colourful city with fine architecture, using its eminence to trade in luxury goods for internal use or for prestigious exchanges. Its religious ceremonies became the most lavish in the world, its prestige attracted the best diplomatic gifts, its legal and financial expertise gave assurance to its merchants. Before the end of the Bronze Age, its citizens were exempt from corvée and taxation, and were forbidden to carry weapons within the city. Military troops were quartered in the nearby city of Kish, or in the forts that encircled Babylon. This exclusion of

---

[44] Lackenbacher 1982.   [45] See Chapter 6, pp. 139–40.

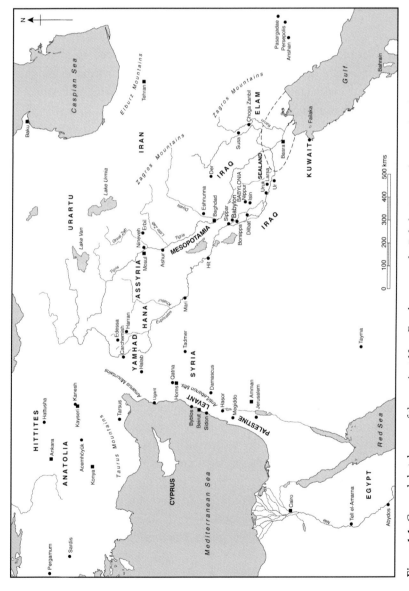

Figure 1.1 General sketch map of the ancient Near East known to the Babylonians in the second and early first millennium BC. Credit: Alison Wilkins and author. Modern cities are marked with squares.

weapons allowed its citizens and visitors to enjoy a relatively peaceful existence provided that the ruler maintained law and order.

That Babylonian architecture, literature, and astronomy survived down to the beginning of the Christian era can now be documented and dated from recent research on cuneiform texts. Evidence has been slow to emerge, because most scholars did not expect the civilization to have lasted into those late times. Early archaeologists did not look for or recognize the significance of late levels, not least on the site of Babylon, where erosion and looting had destroyed or muddled the evidence, and a framework for dating pottery and other finds had not yet been developed. Biblical and classical texts, as well as cuneiform records, were used naively to extract supposedly historical facts. Changes in environmental conditions, such as salination and the height of the water table, shifts in the shoreline at the head of the Gulf, major changes in canals and in the course of the Tigris, are now being investigated with modern techniques to give remarkable results.

2 | Discoveries and Excavations

> From the top of a mound one looks out over an apparently deserted world.
> Mounds rise everywhere – one can see perhaps sixty if one counts.
> Sixty ancient settlements . . . Here was the busy part of the world. Here
> were the beginnings of civilisation.
>
> (Agatha Christie, *Come, Tell Me How You Live*)

Modern scholars trying to trace the history of Babylon began from almost complete ignorance, burdened by preconceptions and prejudices. When excavations of the ancient city took place from 1899 to 1917, biblical and classical sources still dominated knowledge of Babylon. Several books of the Old Testament focused on Nebuchadnezzar II's capture of Jerusalem, his sacking of its temple, and taking its people to exile in Babylonia. Subsequent writers and redactors of biblical texts naturally emphasized that Babylon, the ultimate enemy of Jerusalem, was inherently evil, a view reinforced as the great monotheisms – Jewish, Christian, and Muslim – used the name and reputation of Babylon to denigrate pagan beliefs and actions. Egypt, on the other hand, was regarded as essentially benevolent. Early visitors travelling from Europe to the site of Babylon could only be uncertain about the size of the city as they surveyed the eroded and looted mounds of brick debris. Each tried to decide which mound concealed the remains of the Tower of Babel, and which the Palace of Nebuchadnezzar.

The biblical book of Daniel, written several centuries after the lifetime of Nebuchadnezzar II, gives an extreme view, representing its religion to be as fragile as one of its composite statues (2:32–5):

> a great statue of extreme brightness, stood before you, terrible to see. The head of this statue was of fine gold, its chest and arms were of silver, its belly and thighs of bronze, its legs of iron, its feet part iron, part earthenware. While you were gazing, a stone broke away, untouched by any hand, and struck the statue, struck its feet of iron and earthenware and shattered them. And then, iron and earthenware, bronze, silver, gold all broke into small pieces as fine as chaff on the threshing floor in summer. The wind blew them away, leaving not a trace behind.

Such imagery as this, interpreted literally, influenced the early appreciation of Babylonian culture. The great gap in time between the actual life of Nebuchadnezzar and the much later composition of the book of Daniel was ignored, due to an urge to find 'real' history rather than a court tale.

Greek and Roman historians had less contact with Babylon than the Hebrews did. Herodotus, whether or not he visited Babylon in person (scholarly arguments persist), relayed some, at least, of his stories from hearsay, and delighted his readers with anecdotes of epic heroes and warlike heroines, but failed to mention the fabled Hanging Garden.[1] He gave the circuit of the city walls as some 60 miles, rather than the modern estimate of 11, and a colourful description of the temple tower, the ziggurat that overshadowed the great temple of Marduk, who is 'Bēl the Lord'. His writings were set against a backdrop of great conquests, vast, successive empires, and the extraordinary campaigns in which the Assyrians and Babylonians – whom Greek writers sometimes confused – won their reputation for tyranny and famous exploits. From the writings of various ancient historians came opposing views: kings were either effete and dominated by their women, or warlike, cruel, and merciless. The works of these classical and biblical writers were very well known to the educated westerners who travelled in later times and looked for the places they mentioned.

At the site where Babylon once stood in all its glory, 85 km south of modern Baghdad, a vast and perplexing cluster of high mounds gave contours to the Inner City. Greek visitors were accustomed to stone buildings, and could not assess the shapeless heaps of mud brick. As a material of great flexibility which could be recycled completely, unbaked brickwork was easily knocked down or repaired with no need for fresh material. Thus whole layers of occupation may vanish, along with evidence for upper storeys and roofing. At least one of the mounds consisted of rubble from the collapsed ziggurat, removed by elephants during the Seleucid period. The unappealing rubble of ancient cities in southern Mesopotamia belies their intrinsic worth, and requires of the tourist great leaps of imagination.

Some of the quarters of the citadel were given the names of more ancient cities. Babylonians used them as a symbol of their domination, reflecting the city's role as the centre of religion: Eridu, which had been the first city to receive kingship from the gods; Nippur; and Kullab, where ancient Uruk's temple of the Sky-god was located. Babylon itself had several names: Ka-dingira, the 'Gate of God(s)', Shu-anna, the 'Hand of Heaven', Tintir, of uncertain meaning, and Babil, likewise. These names are now

---

[1] Dalley 2003: 171–89.

identified with individual areas in the citadel and elsewhere, some of them corresponding to the modern names of mounds.[2]

As a religious centre inclusive of the gods of other cities, Babylon's centrality was instituted by its patron god Marduk, who proclaimed to the gods in the *Epic of Creation*:

> I shall make a house to be a luxurious dwelling for myself . . .
> And I shall establish my private quarters, and confirm my kingship.
> Whenever you come up from the Apsu for an assembly
> Your night's resting place shall be in it, receiving you all.
> Whenever you come down from Heaven for an assembly,
> Your night's resting place shall be in it, receiving you all.
> I hereby name it Babylon, home of the great gods.
> We shall make it the centre of religion.

Parts of Babylon's huge site[3] eventually proved to contain not only two palaces attributed to Nebuchadnezzar, but also the great Ishtar Gate on the Processional Way, the temple of the great goddess Nin-mah, and the temple of the great god Bēl-Marduk. The mound now known as Amran[4] to the south of the biggest palace on the Kasr (Castle) mound takes its name from the mosque of ʿAmran Ibn ʿAli, where the holy imam of that name was buried; eventually the deep foundations of the great temple tower were found but no superstructure, disappointing expectations of finding the original Tower of Babel there. In the mounds called Homera and Merkes to the east of Kasr, private houses of important families were found. In the mound known as Babil[5] situated some way to the north, the remains of Nebuchadnezzar's Summer Palace were eventually excavated. In the village Jumjumiya to the south-west near a part of the citadel wall, the Cyrus Cylinder was discovered.[6] To add to the visitor's confusion, Herodotus described the Euphrates as running through the middle of the city, but the river has changed its course, both in antiquity and in more recent times.[7]

For reports of early travellers when the land was under Ottoman rule, we are dependent on the chance survival of written accounts.[8] Chief among them

---

[2] The dates of their introduction are uncertain.

[3] Kasr (Qasr), also called Mujellibeh, included the two areas called Südburg and Hauptburg by the German excavators. They comprise the citadel.

[4] Also spelt Omran.   [5] Also known as Mujellibeh, confusingly.

[6] The two fragments recently identified in the British Museum presumably come also from the area of the citadel wall.

[7] For problems of dating early changes in the riverbed, see Boiy 2004: 78–9.

[8] Detailed accounts of early visits and excavations are to be found in Lloyd 1947; Reade 2008a: 112–17 and Reade 2008b: 124–5; several authors ed. André-Salvini 2008: 505–25.

is the itinerary of Benjamin of Tudela, a Spanish rabbi whose main interest was in the large populations of Jews who revered the synagogue of Daniel, the shrines of Ezekiel and Jonah, and other famous Hebrews who had lived in Babylonia. He travelled during the twelfth century, in between the Second and Third Crusades, and reported on Babylon rather dismissively:

> To Babylon one day; this is the ancient Babel and now lies in ruins, but the streets still extend thirty miles. Of the palace of Nebuchadnetsar the ruins are still to be seen, but people are afraid to enter it on account of the serpents and scorpions, by which it is infested.[9]

He also visited the nearby site of Borsippa, a huge spread of rubble-strewn remains, and thought its still impressive, partly vitrified temple tower was the biblical Tower of Babel. Babylon's own temple tower had been dismantled long before his visit, giving him no option but to rely on the description given by Herodotus in the fifth century BC. Herodotus, in giving the length of Babylon's walls as 60 miles, may have thought that Borsippa was a part of Babylon just as Rabbi Benjamin did.

Rabbi Benjamin may not have been aware that Babylon had its own literate culture, so his impressions depended only on heaps of brick ruins. The term 'cuneiform', derived from a Latin word meaning 'wedge-shaped', is now used for the script in which Babylonian and several other contemporary languages were written.[10] But the word was not introduced until 1686, when Engelbert Kämpfer, visiting the handsome stone monuments at Persepolis, the impressive and well-preserved stone-built city of Darius I, far to the east of Babylon, copied inscriptions of Achaemenid Persian rulers which would remain undeciphered for more than a century. At that time, some people thought the signs represented some kind of ornament, or had magic power; some thought they were derived from Egyptian hieroglyphs. In 1667 Samuel Flower, an agent of the East India Company who had also been to Persepolis, made the first known copy of a cuneiform inscription, but no importance was attached to it in Europe, where it was dismissed as graffiti carved by soldiers in more recent times.[11]

Other travellers of various nationalities who visited Babylon before the nineteenth century included Gasparo Balbi, a Venetian jeweller who visited the site in 1579, and the English merchant John Eldred in 1583, who thought that the ruined remains of a ziggurat at Aqer Quf – the

[9] Asher 1907: 106.
[10] These include Hittite, Hurrian, Urartian, Elamite, and Old Persian, with some modifications made for each.
[11] Rogers 1915: I, 95–100.

Figure 2.1 Small black limestone boulder recording a grant of land, found in 1786 by André Michaux, gardener of Louis XIV, not far from Babylon. Eleventh century BC. Height 45 cm. Credit: Commons.Wikimedia.org/w/index.php?curid=640357. By Unknown, Public Domain. Bibliothèque Nationale, Paris.

rather well-preserved site of Dur-Kurigalzu near Babylon – included the Tower of Babel. In the seventeenth century an Italian priest, Pietro della Valle, brought back to Rome inscribed cylinder seals. In 1767, the Danish explorer Carsten Niebuhr brought back accurate copies of cuneiform inscriptions from Persepolis. Although he did not visit Babylon, his copies paved the way for the later work on the decipherment of Babylonian script and language. The French priest Joseph de Beauchamp, consul in Baghdad from 1780 to 1785, who excavated in Babylon, admired the impressive but uninscribed basalt 'Lion of

Figure 2.2 Symbols sculpted on the domed top of the *kudurru*-stone of Marduk-nadin-ahhe, king of Babylon, brother of Nebuchadnezzar I. Early eleventh century BC. Credit: Hinke 1907: fig. 12.

Babylon' uncovered by locals in 1776, and took inscribed bricks to Paris, to intrigue would-be decipherers. Various inscribed objects drawn or collected by those travellers came back to western Europe, where they stimulated curiosity about the lost culture of ancient Mesopotamia long before methodical excavation began. A fine black limestone boulder carved with sculpture in relief and a well-chiselled inscription had been found around 1786 in a 'garden of Semiramis', on the Tigris south of Ctesiphon, the legendary name of Semiramis giving it a supposed link with Babylon. Known as the Caillou Michaux after the French botanist André Michaux, gardener at Versailles, who had visited Babylon between 1783 and 1785, it was taken to France, and now belongs to the collection in the Bibliothèque Nationale de France, Cabinet des médailles. When that collection moved from Versailles to Paris in the eighteenth century, it began to attract a variety of other collections from aristocrats interested in antiquities, so Paris became a focus for scholarship in ancient Mesopotamian art and inscriptions. Those 'arrow-headed' signs connected with the name of Semiramis helped to shift interest to Babylon from the inscriptions more easily visible on Achaemenid Persian stone buildings at Persepolis.

Discoveries in Babylon by westerners from the seventeenth to the late nineteenth century were mainly haphazard. A great number of clay tablets and other artefacts reached London and other western cities, partly due to sporadic activities of East India Company officials who were posted to Mesopotamia from 1798 onwards. Tales of their acquisition show what enormous difficulties faced not only those explorers, but also the scholars who even now try to organize and make sense of the artefacts, especially the clay inscriptions. Just how chaotic and unregulated those early finds were can be seen from the following sketch of intermittent events and how the objects were understood at the time.

At that time, the East India Company employed British agents who were based in Baghdad or Basra, well-educated men who spent their spare time hunting, riding, and exploring the vicinity. If interesting antiquities came to light, they sent them to London through the efficient transport services of the Company, which actually ordered its employees to find and to send back inscribed bricks. Hugely significant was the East India House Inscription of Nebuchadnezzar II, probably found in Babylon, which played a key role in the decipherment of cuneiform Babylonian.[12] A light-coloured stone measuring 56.5 cm x 50.1 cm, it is beautifully inscribed in archaic cuneiform, imitating the style of Nebuchadnezzar's illustrious predecessors. In 1801 it went on display in the India Museum, founded in London to house the many curiosities collected by employees of the East India Company; two years later, the cuneiform inscription was published in London using the new technique of lithography, which was invented around 1796. That book heralds the beginning of scholars' ability to study inscriptions without having to travel to the Middle East and endure the various dangers of journeying beyond Europe.

It was the East India House Inscription that allowed a major breakthrough in decipherment by the brilliant scholar-clergyman Edward

---

[12] Registered as BM 129397. It gives the archaic forms of cuneiform signs that correspond to later forms used in duplicate texts written on clay.

Hincks, whose parish in Northern Ireland was far from the scholarly men of London. The archaic signs gave a near-duplicate of an inscription on a clay prism which used contemporary sign forms, the later script of Nebuchadnezzar's own time, with variant spellings. Hincks had contributed to the earlier decipherment of Egyptian hieroglyphs, giving him invaluable experience in a non-alphabetic script; and he made significant progress in the decipherment of Old Persian. By 1849 he had realized that the language of Babylonian and Assyrian texts was a Semitic one. In comparing variants on the East India House Inscription, he was able to show not only variation in sign forms, but also that two different signs could represent the same word or part of a word; moreover, most of the signs could be read in more than one way. These complexities dashed any hopes that would-be decipherers may have had that they would soon be able to read new texts swiftly and accurately. As for writing a competent history of Mesopotamia, that goal stretched far into the future as scholars wrestled with the difficulties of establishing a firm chronology. The existence of the India Museum in the heart of London during the early nineteenth century must have generated interest long before the British Museum began to form its collection from the ancient Near East; but Nebuchadnezzar's intriguing contribution would have been swamped by the eclectic and eccentric objects that crowded in from the Indian subcontinent. The collection was dissolved in 1879 after two unsatisfactory rehousings; many objects were distributed among London's great museums, but Nebuchadnezzar's stone inscription was not donated to the British Museum until 1938.

Most notable among the representatives of the East India Company in Mesopotamia was the precocious Claudius Rich, sociable and energetic, a brilliant linguist, already well-travelled when he was appointed British Resident in Baghdad in 1808 at the age of twenty-one, and already married, having 'commanded promotion by mere merit', in the words of his powerful father-in-law. The previous holder of that post had been given consular powers; Baghdad and Basra thus became a focus for increased diplomatic activity. Rich visited the site of Babylon in 1811, and set some workmen to dig on his behalf for several years; he purchased 'a large black stone, with figures and inscriptions on it' which was said to come from the mound Amran.[13] On the Kasr mound Rich's workmen uncovered the colossal basalt statue of a lion on a pedestal, with a defeated figure lying beneath the animal, static in design and unfinished in appearance, 'cut out of coarse

[13] It is now recognized as a *kudurru* ('boundary stone'), of the eleventh century BC.

grey granite', which was rediscovered and recorded in drawings several decades later by a brief French expedition; being inordinately heavy, it remains on the site to this day, its origin and significance still uncertain.[14]

Rich published the first accurate topographical plan of Babylon, as well as excellent copies of some cuneiform inscriptions made by his painstaking secretary. In his published account he made the fine observation that 'the height of these mounds greatly deceive one; from their immense extent and gradual descent into the level plain, appearing much lower than they really are'.[15] Dismayed by the appearance of the ruins and the landscape in general, Rich attributed the waste of good fertile land to overtaxation and the greed of short-term Ottoman administrators, themselves preceded by the Mongols who had rampaged through the country destroying canals and other vital installations.

Rich stayed in touch with Georg Grotefend (1775–1853), a school teacher in Göttingen who had puzzled over some cuneiform inscriptions (they were Old Persian, not Babylonian) found by Carsten Niebuhr at Persepolis – both men came from the same part of Hanseatic Germany – and Grotefend had bet some drinking companions that he could decipher cuneiform. He won his bet: the first announcement of a breakthrough on the names and titles of Persian kings in 1802 evidently became known to Rich through his secretary's correspondence with Grotefend, but that preliminary step was not followed by further progress. By then there was much interest in the script and its potential for full decipherment: in Germany, England, Ireland, Denmark, and France. But nobody was yet in a position to anticipate the difficulties of the whole task and the very long time it would take – a century would have been a conservative figure – to obtain reliable editions and translations.

Rich died young of cholera. Eventually, in 1825, his widow sold his 'extensive and valuable collection' of antiquities to the British Museum, presumably having decided that it was a more appropriate place than the museum of the East India Company. Rich had been pivotal to fieldwork on Babylon, publishing his map and finds, exertions that encouraged the earliest stages of decipherment. Appreciating the importance of his work, his widow published more of it from his notes after his death.

Interest in deciphering ancient languages became fashionable: Palmyrene, Old Persian, and, most spectacularly, Egyptian hieroglyphs.

[14] Rich 1839: 36 and 65. The statue is apparently basalt, not granite, see Moorey 1999: 30. See Chapter 7, pp. 201–2 below, for a new suggestion for its date and significance.
[15] Rich 1839: 10.

Almost every decipherment was beset by rivalries and 'honourable failures' as scholars struggled to outdo each other;[16] only quite recently has the main credit for deciphering Babylonian cuneiform, once claimed by the dashing Sir Henry Creswicke Rawlinson, been attributed to the reclusive elderly clergyman Edward Hincks.[17] A spirit of personal and nationalist competition among European and American scholars writing mainly in English, German, and French ensured a western-based scholarship which has made it difficult ever since for Middle Eastern scholars to engage in the study.

At that time Baghdad had no museum of its own. Even in Constantinople the Ottoman Imperial Museum, founded in 1872, did not open until 1880. Since there were still no museums elsewhere in the Middle East, and those in western Europe still concentrated on collections of Egyptian, Greek, and Roman antiquities as well as much later western art, it is hardly surprising that Babylonian finds were dispersed among many wealthy families and institutions such as schools and libraries, even though the Ottoman central administration passed a law to restrict the export of antiquities in 1874.[18] One group of tablets, now known as the Kasr Archive, was found at Babylon by various diggers and looters at different times, its provenance established when the team of the German archaeologist Robert Koldewey found some too. The archive is now known to consist of more than 200 tablets and has had to be reassembled from (so far) ten institutions on several different continents.[19]

In France, the Louvre had begun collecting such antiquities in 1826, when Champollion, famous as the decipherer of Egyptian hieroglyphs, became director. Then it began to collect Egyptian antiquities, stimulated especially by Napoleon's conquest of Egypt. Babylonian antiquities took longer to catch public interest. Although an Assyrian gallery was later opened for wonderful Assyrian palace sculptures found at Khorsabad, a royal Assyrian city of the eighth century BC, far to the north of Babylon, there was less interest in remains from Babylonian sites, on which large-scale stone sculptures and impressive objects for display were very rarely found. Although the British Museum had been established much earlier, in 1753, the emphasis at that time was on collecting classical and Egyptian antiquities, and Mesopotamian antiquities were relegated to the basement. But the reading public would soon be able to engage with cuneiform inscriptions because handmade copies would shortly be reproduced in

---

[16] Daniels 1995: 81–93.   [17] See Cathcart 1994: 1–29 and Daniels 1994: 30–57.
[18] Ismail 2011: 87.   [19] Stolper 1990: 195–205.

books by lithography. The new technique allowed thousands of copies to be printed from a single engraving made on stone or metal rather than wood. As a result, the extraordinary literacy of Babylonia began to attract interest.[20]

In 1851 two French archaeologists were sent to excavate at Babylon on behalf of the French government, but their finds, loaded onto a raft for transport to Basra with a view to reaching the Louvre, sank and were never recovered; no records survive. Conditions were extremely difficult, with treacherous agreements, robbers, and open extortion at every turn.

The big impetus for progress in research and decipherment came not from these rather desultory explorations, but from more glamorous discoveries on excavations in the Assyrian royal cities of the north, in Nineveh, Nimrud, and Khorsabad, sponsored in part by the British Museum and the Louvre, in the mid-nineteenth century.[21]

George Smith visited Babylon on behalf of the British Museum, having discovered in the latter a cuneiform text from Nineveh giving the story of the Flood. That link with the Bible, announced in 1876, aroused enormous interest in Britain. Apart from literature with biblical connections, Smith had a strong interest in dated legal contracts written in cuneiform on tablets of unbaked clay, in order to work out a precise chronology of rulers. When he arrived in Baghdad, he bought about 800 'objects' from a dealer on his first visit, and 2,600 on his second visit. Despite his death in Aleppo after a terrible journey, the tablets reached London, driving a scholar at the British Museum, William Boscawen, to despair, as he made endless promises to deliver while failing to turn up for work. He must have been overwhelmed by the task; he reported to the Keeper of Antiquities on one occasion that 2,500 tablets had just arrived.[22] There was enough work in that single delivery to keep a whole team of Assyriologists occupied for a couple of generations, quite apart from the need for a system of storage and conservation.

Many tablets urgently need to be treated to stop them crumbling but not until after the Second World War was a programme to conserve them begun. They were already in poor condition when they arrived in the British Museum, for several reasons:

> Generally speaking, an Arab digger contracts with two or three individuals to provide them with a certain quantity of antiquities, and when he cannot supply each individual with the same number or quality of objects, he breaks a most valuable inscription to divide amongst them.[23]

[20] Michaux 1800: 86–7.   [21] Larsen 1996.   [22] Evers 1993.   [23] Rassam 1897: 262.

Also, many of the tablets, being of unbaked clay, had soaked up brackish water, so when they were dug out and dried, salt crystals erupted on the surface, making the inscription illegible, so they were simply discarded: 'A large number of the records had crumbled to pieces as soon as they were removed, for they were found in damp soil impregnated with nitre (salt)'.[24] A further cause of damage was the transport by donkey or mule on rough roads to the river and on to the sea, followed by the unpacking and repacking insisted on by various officials as the consignments of the fragile texts made their way to London via India. When at last they arrived in the British Museum, the number and size of the deliveries 'placed an intolerable strain on the recording system of the Department'. Despite the best efforts of insufficient staff, registration of each acquisition was sometimes chaotic.[25] Tablets from Babylon arrived mixed with others from nearby sites such as Sippar and Kish.[26] Unofficial digging in Babylon in the 1870s yielded about 10,000 tablets, among them the library of Marduk's great temple Esagila, the 'House with High Top'. This collection dates from the Seleucid period, but was ignored by scholars, who supposed that a tide of Hellenization had drowned out the local culture.

Hormuzd Rassam, who worked at Babylon between 1878 and 1882 on behalf of the British Museum, and was mainly authorized to find inscriptions, was experienced in excavation from working at Nineveh with a British team. At that time, the gradual decipherment of the cuneiform script was eagerly followed by high society in Britain because of its potential for biblical links. But Rassam was not supported by any illustrator or cuneiform expert, and despite developments in photography at that time, he scarcely made use of the new invention for lack of expertise and equipment. He was unable to excavate Esagila for he found that it lay 21 m beneath the surface. He was disappointed in his hopes of finding splendid stone inscriptions to rival those in the Assyrian royal cities to the north, where winged bulls and lions of limestone protruding from the earth, palace sculptures and stelas, were so much more enticing: 'Nothing of any great magnitude has ever been discovered in the ruins of Babylon, in comparison to the bas-reliefs and colossal mystic figures found in Assyria'.[27] Rassam's excavations were desultory and poorly supervised,[28]

---

[24] Rassam 1897: 394.   [25] Reade 1986: xxvi.

[26] Many of the tablets are now known to come from Babylon and individual archives are still being identified.

[27] Rassam 1897: 267.

[28] Reade 1993; a more disinterested account is given by Ismail 2011: 99–106 and 227–9.

but one discovery clearly interested him greatly: at Babil, the site of Nebuchadnezzar II's Summer Palace, he uncovered 'four exquisitely-built wells of red granite in the southern centre of the mound; three of which were situated in a parallel line within a few feet of each other, and one was some distance from them in a southeasterly direction. Each well is built of circular pieces of granite',[29] each block of stone about 3 ft high. They were joined at the base to an 'aqueduct'. Rassam thought they were designed to irrigate the Hanging Garden of Babylon.[30]

Nothing visible on the surface at Babylon indicated the site of the temple tower, the great ziggurat of the god Bēl-Marduk. Unlike Rabbi Benjamin in the twelfth century, Rassam did not think that the vitrified temple tower at Borsippa (modern Birs Nimrud) 4 miles away, was the 'Tower of Babel'; and he made the alternative suggestion that Herodotus' length of 60 miles for the walls of Babylon might be based on the understanding that the mound of Uhaimir, part of the city of Kish, about 7 miles (11 km) from Babylon, was included.[31] The gods of both those cities, we now know, were included in ceremonial processions and rituals for the great New Year Festival of Babylon. Thus a concept of 'Greater Babylon' might have dictated Herodotus' estimate, based on the route taken by the god Bēl-Marduk for Babylon's prestigious eleven-day festival, visiting shrines in all three cities.

Disappointing the expectations of its excavators and the British Museum, Babylon produced far fewer inscriptions on stone, no royal stelas to show what the great Nebuchadnezzar looked like, and far fewer links with the history of Israel and Judah than were yielded by the great Assyrian cities in the north. Rassam had previously found at Babylon the famous Cyrus Cylinder, which was immediately publicized as a link to biblical narrative and misinterpreted as a unique record granting freedom to enslaved foreigners.[32] Less easily appreciated were the many clay tablets that had been displaced in antiquity: 'In those ruins we always found inscribed tablets mixed up with the rubbish'.[33] Nevertheless, Rassam sent back an enormous number to London; but many tablets from excavations were sold locally on the open market and found their way into various collections in the west. Some were bought from dealers by Wallis Budge, the Keeper of Antiquities, for the British Museum, when he visited

---

[29] Now described as 'red brecchia'. See n. 40, below.   [30] Rassam 1897: 394.
[31] Uhaimir is one of the mounds of the very ancient city of Kish, and is now known, like Borsippa, to have been linked to Babylon by a processional way.
[32] See Chapter 9, pp. 269–72, below.   [33] Rassam 1897: 348.

Iraq.[34] Austen Henry Layard, who excavated mainly at Nineveh and Nimrud, had procured an agreement with the Ottoman government, lasting for four years, that only duplicate antiquities need be handed over to the Imperial Museum in Constantinople, so almost all finds were legally exported.[35] The workmen on the site were allowed to take possession of all bricks, continuing a tradition of reusing these second-hand building materials.

In Berlin, the new Vorderasiatisches Museum took over a collection of antiquities in 1899, coinciding with the decision to promote German excavations in the Middle East. By the time Rassam had retired from the field, German politicians and engineers were working towards obtaining permission and finance to build a railway from Berlin to Baghdad and on to Basra. In 1899 the final agreement was concluded between the Ottoman government and the Germans under Kaiser Wilhelm II: mining rights within 20 km of the proposed railway track were granted, and digging included the excavation of antiquities, allowing all mined materials, including archaeological finds, to be exported to Germany. Since the route of the proposed track passed many visible ancient sites, German archaeologists chose the best sites for their excavations.[36] Those choices included Babylon. An astute journalist wrote in the *Daily Mail* of 13 June 1899 that Britain was losing ground in the international rivalry for productive archaeological sites, overtaken by Germany thanks to its alliance with Ottoman Turkey.

Even before that agreement was reached, a German archaeological excavator had been appointed for Babylon: Robert Koldewey. He was fully backed from Berlin by a learned society specifically set up, in the year before his excavations began at Babylon, to support archaeological research in the Middle East: the Deutsch Orient-Gesellschaft or German Oriental Society, which undertook to support not only the digging but also the publication of excavation results. The Society profited both financially and promotionally from the enthusiastic support of the Kaiser Wilhelm II, who was well aware that Britain and France had great national museums in which they could display discoveries from the Middle East. Neither Britain nor France, despite their museums, gave comparable support to their archaeologists. Expectations ran high because so many imposing monuments had already come to light.

---

[34] Ismail 2011: 99–106, 124–30, 167–9, 176–9, 268. In 1934, when the national museum was established in Baghdad, a fairer division of antiquities became law.

[35] For a brilliant account of Layard's work in context, see Larsen 1996.

[36] The sites in Iraq included Ashur, traditional capital of Assyria, and Uruk, legendary city of the hero Gilgamesh. There were others in Syria and Turkey.

Robert Koldewey was a superb choice. He had trained as an architect, a field which involved draftsmanship, painting, and art history; and he had already worked on major sites in the eastern Mediterranean and in Babylonia before directing his attention and an able team to Babylon. He was forty-three years old when he began to dig there, dashing around the huge site in the raised and upholstered sidecar of a motorcycle in a plume of dust, unfazed by extremes of heat as if in reaction against the lifestyle of his father, who had been an arctic explorer. He was an energetic and practical organizer, and got on well with local Arabs and western colleagues alike, though not so well with the diplomacy required for the Ottoman authorities in Constantinople. Much more than just a field archaeologist, he published promptly and extensively, with drawings, plans, and photographs. Above all, out of the drab ruins he was able to project his vision of the grandiose, monumental, and colourful city. He envisaged the great king Nebuchadnezzar II in the sixth century residing in his gigantic Southern Palace, parading along the magnificent Processional Way, through the Ishtar Gate now famous once again from its reconstruction in the Pergamum Museum in Berlin. He gave substance to the legends of the Old Testament and the Greek writers, and to the reality of Babylon's own great civilization. Properly equipped for photographic recording, and supported by, among others, Walter Andrae (who went on to become the excavator of the Assyrian capital city of Ashur), Koldewey's investigations were carried out all year round, from March 1899 for eighteen years. His work was unremitting, through the baking heat of summer and the cold rains of winter, as well as the early years of the First World War.

Koldewey's team uncovered the plan of the city on the eastern side of the river, as it had existed in the time of Nebuchadnezzar II, and plotted the contours of the whole area. On the published map of the ruins and in subsequent aerial photographs it was clear that the river Euphrates had been diverted at some point in antiquity, to the detriment of many important Babylonian buildings.

One of the first big discoveries was made in September of his first year. It was a damaged block of white limestone measuring 118 x 132 cm sculpted in relief and bearing the inscription of a man named 'Šamaš-reš-uṣur, governor of the land of Suhu and the land of Mari', who claimed to have introduced beekeeping into his kingdom on the Middle Euphrates.[37] Nothing was known of him from other sources. Ninety years later, some clay tablets turned up from the same site, showing at long last that the

---

[37] Frame 1995: 278–323. See Chapter 8, Figure 8.4.

enthusiastic honey gatherer was a petty ruler of the eighth century who traced his ancestry back to Hammurabi king of Babylon a thousand years earlier.

While Koldewey was fully occupied in excavating, in 1901–2 his work was given an unexpected impetus by French excavators' discovery of the great stela of Hammurabi in the Persian site of Susa, inscribed with the famous law code more than a thousand years before Nebuchadnezzar, and taken in triumph to the Louvre. It had been looted by the Elamites, arch-enemies of Babylon, and was never retrieved in antiquity. This made it all the more urgent for the German team to try to uncover buildings in the lower strata beneath the huge remains of Nebuchadnezzar's time. Because biblical interests were still so dominant in Mesopotamian archaeology, the discovery of the law code immediately evoked comparison of Hammurabi with Moses; a rash of books, many of which put Moses before Hammurabi in their titles, appeared between 1903 and 1907.[38] The wonderful column of polished black stone shows Hammurabi receiving the insignia of kingship from the Sun-god of justice, and has a near-perfect text with his laws inscribed below the image. So splendid and imposing was that monument, 2.25 m high, that the pre-biblical history of Babylon grew up around it, putting Hammurabi at the centre of the city's fame, although no records of Hammurabi had yet been found at Babylon. The stela is so tall that most photographs show only the scene carved at the top; one must visit the Louvre to appreciate the full impact of the whole monument.

Although the excavators at Babylon usually reached the water table before attaining the strata of Hammurabi's time – a limitation that put the earlier remains of mud-brick buildings beyond reach – they made good use of a rare period when the water table sank unusually low, allowing some early houses and their contents to be reached, and some contracts dated to the reign of Hammurabi were triumphantly brought to the surface. As if to compensate for the dearth of tablets dating to the time of Hammurabi, other sites with other excavators began to yield thousands of clay tablets, all including correspondence with the king of Babylon, whose reputation grew as the amount of information about him increased.

The colossal stone lion on his pedestal, recorded by the French expedition nearly fifty years earlier, was still at Babylon as if promising further riches for the German excavators. And of course hopes were high that the famous Hanging Garden would be found to give a physical presence to that

---

[38] E.g. Cook 1903; Jeremias 1903; Ensor 1904; Grimme and Pilter 1907.

Figure 2.3 Stela of black stone with complete text of Hammurabi's laws beneath a scene showing the king receiving the rod and ring of kingship from the Sun-god as lord of justice. The stone is probably a basalt resembling diorite. Eighteenth century BC. Height 2.25 m. Credit: Commons.Wikimedia, JoyofMuseums.com. Louvre Museum.

most elusive world wonder. But Koldewey did not find definite evidence for it, although he made a proposal out of a sense of desperation, calling it the garden of Semiramis rather than of Nebuchadnezzar; in no respect did the location within the palace match the accounts of the well-known classical writers, as he was well aware. Several other locations were proposed later. A convincing solution was not found until 2013.[39] Koldewey managed to dig deep to reach the walls of a tiny part of the great Esagila, temple of Marduk, but could not expose more because of the 21 m of overlay that Rassam had measured.

[39] Dalley 2013.

Figure 2.4 The lower part of Koldewey's deep trench above Esagila, temple of Marduk. Only a very small part of the building was excavated. Credit: Koldewey 1911: illustration 60.

Koldewey continued to work at Babylon through much of the First World War, while German engineers struggled in vain to complete the railway from Berlin to Baghdad. The excavations ended during the war, in 1917, when the Ottoman Turks withdrew from Baghdad and the British army marched in, with consequent disruption of all arrangements; the expedition house on the site was looted when the German team left. Some of its tablets were eventually sold by dealers, some were given false provenances. At that time there was still no museum in Baghdad, so archaeologists were responsible for the security and storage of all their finds. Not until 1922 did the situation change, when Gertrude Bell from England was appointed honorary Director of Antiquities in Iraq. She had visited Babylon in 1920, and she founded the National Museum of Antiquities in Baghdad two years later. For the first time Baghdad rather than Constantinople was legally entitled to a fair share of the antiquities found by foreign excavators.

Koldewey did thorough work of surveying, digging, recording, and eventually publishing in detail. The ground plans of many buildings and walls ostensibly from the reign of Nebuchadnezzar II were traced in their entirety. When the Processional Way was excavated in the centre of Babylon, it was found to be 250 m long, flanked by walls 7 m thick, with towers and bastions, set on a bedding that raised it up to 14 m above the original ground level, paved with white limestone slabs, and side-paving of red brecchia.[40] At its northern entrance once stood a sculpted and inscribed stela of Nabonidus, and a fragment from a stela of Darius I.

In later years, after the First World War and again after the Second, excavations at Babylon were intermittent; nevertheless, important discoveries continued to be made, and new understandings developed, especially where inscribed bricks of Nebuchadnezzar had been reused by later builders. This meant that public buildings had been occupied for many centuries after that king's death. Building on the work of Koldewey, Iraqi archaeologists in 1979 excavated in Babylon, notably finding the temple of the god Nabu-of-Vats, 'the temple that bestows a sceptre on the land', within the centre of the main citadel. It housed many school texts, about 2,000 clay tablets deposited as an offering to the god as patron of writing, many from the time of Nebuchadnezzar II.[41]

That temple was still in use at the height of the Roman Empire.[42] It has been astounding to find such clear evidence, both in archaeology and in texts, for the continuation of Babylonian religious buildings and rituals into the Roman Imperial period.

---

[40] Marzahn 1994. This red brecchia may be the 'red granite' identified by Rassam as the stone used to surround the great wells; if so, those wells may now be dated to Nebuchadnezzar II.

[41] See George 1992: 24 and 310–12.

[42] Hauser 1999: 220, dated from a reference to it in an astronomical diary for 78 BC.

Figure 2.5 The first national Iraq Museum of Antiquities in Baghdad, thanks to Gertrude Bell; opened in 1926. Credit: Noorah Al-Gailani.

Despite all the exertions and discoveries of the various explorers and archaeologists at Babylon, only about 3 per cent of the huge site within the inner walls has been excavated. From that percentage the limitations of this account can be judged.

When the earliest cuneiform signs were discovered, they were thought to be decorative patterns, not writing. When individual cuneiform signs were found to have several different values and could have very different shapes according to period and region, it took many painstaking revisions of manuals before a reliable edition could be produced. That process continues today.[43] New excavations and chance discoveries inevitably change our understanding of Babylon's history.

The decipherment of cuneiform texts, whether Sumerian or Babylonian, was a slow process involving major misunderstandings and premature theories. Was Sumerian a 'sacred language' invented by Semitic people in Babylonia? Could some of its linguistic structures be recognized as belonging to an Indo-European mould and related to Greek or Sanskrit? Difficulties in assigning a function to a multitude of Sumerian particles on verbs were only resolved in the 1970s when the structure of the verbal system, very different from that of Semitic or Indo-European (Aryan) languages, was recognized. Only gradually were translations improved and misunderstandings cleared up.[44]

Inscriptions on stone dominated the efforts of early Assyriologists because they recorded the deeds of kings recognizable from biblical and classical texts, and the stone was sometimes in good condition. Unbaked clay tablets, emerging from the soil by the basket-load, were usually damaged, often quite cursively written, and, at first sight, offered unexpected contents such as lists of words, or allusive incantations, monotonous accounts, and records of administration. The general public lost its enthusiasm during years when spectacular finds were not forthcoming. To read 'a laundry bill in Babylonic cuneiform' was derisively proclaimed in *The Pirates of Penzance* as the ultimate example of useless knowledge from antiquity, reflecting the tedium of ephemeral daily records, which outnumbered more glamorous royal inscriptions, literary texts, and legal documents.

During much of the twentieth century, archaeology was considered to be 'the handmaid of history', producing a field of knowledge to support the

---

[43] Labat and Malbran Labat 1995.   [44] See, e.g., Cooper 1991: 47–66.

information derived from written sources, especially biblical and classical. In Babylonia the situation proved to be unexpectedly complicated. For instance, on huge sites where excavators can uncover only a tiny fraction of a city, it was common, on finding an ashy level that implied the violent destruction of one or more buildings, to assume that a defeat and total sacking implied by texts was the cause. In a similar vein, if one area of a site was abandoned for a while, leaving a deposit recognizable as evidence for desertion, it was common to assume abandonment of the entire city, and to pick out textual 'evidence' to support the deduction. Particularly misleading, we now understand, were texts of lamentation which were not necessarily wailing over catastrophic destruction as a literal event but accompanied the repair of temples – even minor renovations – and the reinstallation of divine statues, whose temporary removal symbolically endangered the whole city; the plight of its citizens was exaggerated in order to persuade the gods to relent and return. A group of omens linked to supposed historical events seemed to give reliable information until it was realized that esoteric play on words and signs gave a misleading impression of connection with a historical event.

When levels of ash or abandonment seal earlier deposits of pottery, one might think that a careful typology showing changes of style would allow the dating of different levels, as with early Greek and Aegean pottery. Unfortunately, the ancient Mesopotamians put a relatively low value on pottery, so that it was rarely subject to changes of fashion, and remained the same for long stretches of time. Despite keen efforts to find hallmarks of change, only when there was a rare import from Greece or the Aegean, where fashions changed frequently, could a Babylonian level be dated with some precision. Cylinder seals, too, with or without inscriptions, could be unreliable for precise dating because they were cherished as heirlooms, or skilfully recut. So inscriptions and tablets were the main evidence for dating, but few were found. In other words, the early dating of levels at Babylon, as on other sites, is liable to improvement. Even royal building inscriptions are notorious for being taken out of a building and then put back into a new one by later royal builders to demonstrate pious respect for predecessors. As we shall see, some fundamental datings at Babylon are now being revised.

In Germany, during the early years of the German Oriental Society with its declared aim of taking part in 'the great task of discovering and recovering the earliest Orient through more extensive systematic excavations', a damaging debate arose. Owing to the evident connections between cuneiform texts and biblical texts – places such as Babylon, Ur, and Erech

(Uruk), and stories such as the Flood and the Tower of Babel – the claim that the Hebrew religion arose from Babylonian sources was put forward in several stages by Professor Friedrich Delitzsch. He gave a series of lectures to influential audiences including Kaiser Wilhelm II. The claim was taken up and exaggerated as evidence of anti-Semitism, a charge which has dogged that aspect of research to this day.[45] In France, the influential scholar Ernst Renan, who became a professor at the prestigious Collège de France in 1862, following current views on the cultural superiority of the Aryans, thought that the epic literature of Mesopotamia must be Aryan, not Semitic, because heroic epic texts supposedly originated among the ancient Greeks. He was the first to use the word 'Assyriologist', but in a different sense from that current today. The so-called science of phrenology was applied to a few sculptures that showed kings and officials with aquiline facial features, supposedly the mark of a 'Turanian' (Aryan) physical type.[46]

What new strategies and techniques have become available recently to help with the huge amount of work involved in Assyriology?

Enormous progress has been made in using the day-to-day texts to develop, overturn, or modify earlier understanding of royal inscriptions and the accounts of Greek writers. Dated administrative texts can be milked to sequence the careers of officials, whether governors, priests, goldsmiths, or members of the royal family, both male and female, by listing the names, professions, and dates of personnel for each city's records in each different period. This direction of research represents a major change of emphasis from the conduct of early Assyriologists, who often cherry-picked royal inscriptions, epics, and hymns, considering administrative texts unworthy of their attention.

As for the Babylonian language, now often called Akkadian, the great grammar by Wolfram von Soden in German, published in 1952, put linguistic analysis on a firm footing; his very fine dictionary, also in German, was published in fascicles between 1965 and 1981. The phenomenal *Chicago Assyrian Dictionary* consisting of twenty-six volumes was published between 1956 and 2010.

Another great step forward has come from the realization that even very broken tablets, some of them from texts with more than one copy, retrieved from the dusty drawers of museum basements could be pieced together and used to reconstruct major events and narratives. Sometimes a 'long-distance' join can be made from pieces in different museums, different

---

[45] See, e.g., Larsen 1995: I, 95–106.   [46] See Cooper 1991.

countries, even on different continents. By creating databases of digital photographs, scholars can reduce the need for expensive travel to look at particular tablets.[47]

Koldewey made careful records of his excavations. Those that were not lost in the confusion when the war brought digging to an abrupt end, allow new research to extract more information on the structures of Hammurabi's day. Not surprisingly, some of Koldewey's dating is now being revised; like other scholars of his generation, he assumed that Babylonian culture did not survive the tide of Hellenization, which was thought to have overwhelmed the country under Alexander's Seleucid successors. But recently it has proved possible to reassemble cuneiform archives of citizens from Hellenistic times.[48]

The writings of Babylonia were lost to the modern world for around 2,000 years. Unlike Greek and Latin texts, many of which survived in monasteries and libraries and were widely accepted and studied as part of European heritage at the Renaissance, Babylonian texts lay buried beneath the dirt of Mesopotamia until they were brought to light by archaeologists and looters from the mid-nineteenth century. Although some cuneiform inscriptions on stone would still have been visible or accidentally uncovered in early Islamic times, there is no record of ʿAbbasid caliphs collecting or exchanging rarities from their Babylonian past.[49] In Egypt, by contrast, there was no absolute break in the preservation of Egyptian monuments; the pyramids and the great temples, built sturdily in stone, were not swallowed up by erosion, and were only occasionally buried by a shifting landscape. Romans had taken back to Italy obelisks, columns, and smaller objects, many of them bearing finely chiselled hieroglyphs to intrigue the public; and the popular Roman cult of the Egyptian goddess Isis stimulated a trade in statuettes and figurines of the goddess. Glamorous stone ruins along the Nile were always visible throughout the centuries for inquiring travellers, whereas even the largest Assyrian and Babylonian stone inscriptions lay beneath the ground.

Now, a century and a half after the initial work of decipherment, we are still filling some of the many gaps in mythological and historical texts, using fragments that have come to light only recently, or major unexpected

---

[47] In particular digital photographs that can be manipulated on a laptop to change angles of surfaces and lighting.

[48] Pedersén 2005a.

[49] The absence of interest is deduced from the material collected in al-Qaddūmī 1996, and in the ninth/tenth-century *History* of al-Ṭabarī, translated by Rosenthal 1989.

discoveries from new sites and collections. An extraordinary variety of form and content for the written word in cuneiform has emerged.[50]

To establish reliable dates for the history of Babylonia and Assyria was one of the earliest preoccupations of scholars, once decipherment had begun. Even today a chronology of absolute dates for the third and second millennia is not agreed. The Middle Chronology is used in this book, for which an adjustment may eventually be required.[51] The basis for all dating schemes comes from the lengths of reigns in king-lists which are not quite complete, from inconsistent versions; different cities made their own adaptations. Some eclipses are known from texts, but as periodic events, they do not have a single occurrence. There are no coins to help; historical documents are seldom dated; inscribed bricks and dedications giving a king's name may be misleading because they were often reused and kept for many centuries. Carbon-14 dating is not sufficiently precise for the time spans required, and tree ring information is virtually absent because organic material is never well preserved.

The pace of discovery, research, and new understandings has been remarkable. Assyriologists, few as they are, have been very productive in publishing thousands of newly found texts as well as working through the old ones, stored in museums in their tens of thousands. This book, like all those that have gone before it, is therefore only an account of 'work in progress'. It ends with the latest dated cuneiform texts and the buildings associated with them.

To create a framework for connecting historical events with trends in art history, it has been traditional to assume that a new dynasty or a new invasion went hand in hand with innovation in art, architecture, and sculpture, from which the new men could stamp their own mark on the culture. This was a neat scheme for scholars, but oversimplification gave way to a different view as more material came to light and was studied more thoroughly. Usurpers, it is now realized, were so anxious to integrate themselves into the existing culture that they began by promoting very conservative styles. Only when the dynasty was well-established and new conquests celebrated did the new rulers feel confident enough to allow a certain amount of creative invention to take root within long-accepted canons of design. Loyalty to the king overrode all other considerations. A man who had bad luck and suffered ill treatment at every turn, despite his best efforts to live a good life, ended his complaints by recognizing that 'His

---

[50] Taylor 2011.

[51] This would give dates for Hammurabi 1784–1742. See Sallaberger and Schrakamp 2015: 303.

majesty is a shepherd, he looks after people like a god'.[52] As long as the king was supported by the gods, law and order would continue to maintain the prosperity of the people. Divination was used to show that the king was chosen in heaven, so his reign was not negotiable by men.

The archaeology of Achaemenid Persia, Greece, and Rome, in particular the empire won by Alexander the Great, exerted such a major influence on modern historians of the ancient Near East that until now written accounts of Babylonian history have ended either with Nabonidus in the sixth century, because he was regarded as the last indigenous Semitic king, or with the conquest of Babylon by Alexander in 332. The numerous cuneiform archives of the Achaemenid and Seleucid periods had not yet been studied for historical purposes, nor had fragmentary chronicles and the 'astronomical diaries' been pieced together. It was assumed that Greek culture swept over the land, superseding sad remnants of what was left from 2,000 years of Semitic literacy and scholarship; then pagan religion gave way to the religions of the book: Judaism, Christianity, the Manichean faith, and Islam. Even in the Islamic period, unexpected discoveries of treasures which were then collected or presented as gifts seem to date no further back than Alexander the Great.[53] However, cuneiform texts have proved that neither the conquest of Cyrus the Great in 538 nor the coming of the Macedonians in 332, nor the Parthians' invasion in 141 disrupted the continuity of literate culture, astronomy, and religious festivities in the great city; nor did they try to do so. The days of invoking Oriental despotism as a fossilized culture in which neither change nor progress was made for more than two thousand years, are long past. We have to thank those early excavators and scholars who struggled through enormous difficulties, and those in recent decades who have continued to persevere in finding order amidst extreme complexity.

[52] Oshima 2013: *Theodicy* line 297.
[53] al-Qaddumi 1996: §§ 98 and 99 (Alexander), 176 and 256 (Sassanian).

3 | First Kings to the End of the Great Rebellion, c. 1894–c. 1732

Babylon, which establishes Kingship.

(*Tintir* 1.34)

Amorite kings of Babylon and some contemporaries.

Babylon	Larsa	Mari and Hana
Sumu-abum (1894–1881)		
Sumu-la-El (1880–1845)		Yapah-Sumu-abum
Sabium (1844–1831)		Iṣi-Sumu-abum
Apil-Sin (1830–1813)	Warad-Sin	
Sin-muballiṭ (1812–1793)		Yahdun-Lim
Hammurabi (1792–1750)	Rim-Sin	Zimri-Lim (1775–1762)[1]
Samsu-iluna (1749–1712)		
Great Rebellion (c. 1742–1731)		Yadih-abum

Babylon played a small part in the history of Mesopotamia before its first dynasty took control and was recorded in king-lists. It was subordinate to whichever great city controlled the heartland of Mesopotamia. The earliest rulers were surrounded by many other kings who ruled in the extraordinary number of cities clustering in the region later known as Babylonia. Some of those cities had lost the importance they enjoyed in the third millennium, but many others, notably Sippar and Kish to the north, Larsa, Uruk, Ur, and Isin to the south, and Eshnunna to the east, were particularly important at this time,[2] each with its own local king, its own patron deity, and its own sequence of month-names. Much of Babylonia's population, however, was essentially tribal, probably lived in tents, and was not urbanized.

---

[1] Dates follow Barjamovic, Hertel, and Larsen 2012: 36. Main sources for the dynasty are: year-names which briefly give the main military or other event of the year or the previous year, and are used to date documents (see Horsnell 1999); chronicles and king-lists (see Glassner 2004). Official correspondence (not dated) is mainly found in the contributions of Frankena, Kraus, Stol, Van Soldt, and Veenhof to the Altbabylonische Briefe series; administrative and legal records (dated) are widely scattered in publications. Literary and lexical texts are very rarely dated.

[2] See the comparative chart of the major dynasties in Frayne 1990: xxx–xxxi.

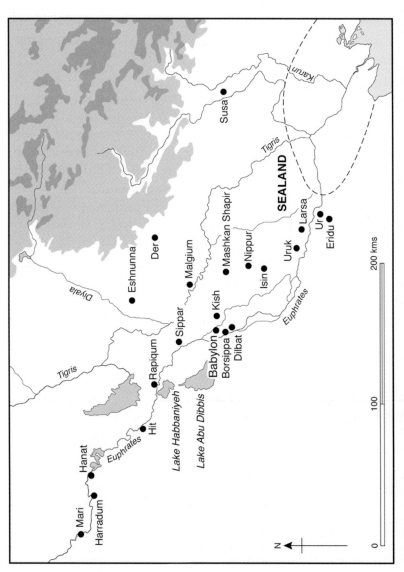

Figure 3.1 Sketch map of Lower Mesopotamia showing major cities, approximate river courses, and ancient shoreline, around the time of Hammurabi. Credit: Alison Wilkins and author.

Babylon's status as a relative newcomer is emphasized by comparison with Uruk, a huge city of spectacular architecture, home of the legendary Gilgamesh, which had flourished for more than 2,000 years before Babylon's first dynasty began. Uruk then maintained its prestige for the next 2,000 years, continuing to rival Babylon. Other ancient cities, each with its own proud traditions from the era of early city states, also challenged Babylon from time to time in the fields of architecture, literacy, festivals, and finance. A century after Babylon's first kings began the dynasty, the great Hammurabi, author of the famous law code, established a fame that was still remembered throughout Mesopotamia 1,200 years later, but other cities had their own, similar law codes at an earlier time. How did Babylon meet the challenge and manage first to supplant and then to outshine those cities?

On three sides Babylon was closely connected to much older cities that took water from branches of the river Euphrates. Each had an illustrious past, and a patron deity of high prestige. Each was linked with Babylon at the hub, by the river and by canals. Although a temple to the god Marduk may have been built in Babylon some 500 years before its first dynasty was founded,[3] two other early temples built there were not dedicated to him. Eventually Marduk was raised from an insignificant god to the highest status as patron god in the city of Babylon, becoming known simply as Bēl ('Lord').

Babylonia thrived on a busy network of waterways. In the nineteenth century, when Babylon became a city ruled by its own acknowledged kings, two other cities, first Isin and then its rival Larsa, both south of Babylon, were leaders of a wider region. The long canal that Hammurabi dug to Larsa from the Euphrates brought many southern cities into more direct contact; further north, other canals linked the two great rivers. Larsa's position allowed for easy contact with Susa, royal city of the Elamites.

Kish became a military base for Babylon during the reigns of Babylon's early kings. At a much earlier date its divine patron, the war-god Zababa, had become famous for oracles predicting the success of campaigns, or warning against precipitate action. In Borsippa the god Tutu had an early close association with Marduk and with Nabu, god of scribes, who later supplanted him. In Sippar, the Sun-god held a supreme role in ceremonies in which he took the lead as enforcer of justice throughout the land. Marduk emulated those gods without displacing them, and gradually rose

---

[3] See Lambert 2011. The reading of the early city name as Babylon is likely but not certain.

to supremacy not only in the city of Babylon but also far beyond, in ways that will be shown in the following chapters.

Under the deeply centralized administration of the Third Dynasty of Ur, Babylon city had been important enough to have its own governor, about 100 years before it had its first kings. Hardly anything is known of the city's political, commercial, or religious life until then. The city's name, *Bāb ili*, was understood to mean 'gate of god' long before there was a royal throne to claim.

When Babylon's first king came to the throne, a Sumerian lamentation mourning the downfall of the Third Dynasty of Ur over a century earlier kept the memory of the tragedy alive. In poetic terms, the disaster was blamed on invasion by an eastern kingdom allied with Elam which besieged, sacked, and looted, but did not take the kingship. From then onwards, as Babylon's kings built up their wealth, Elam and its eastern allies, described as 'like locusts', were the greatest enemy.

Some of the royal and other personal names of this time are West Semitic Amorite, so the period is sometimes labelled the Amorite period. But others had Sumerian or Babylonian names. At this time scribes in particular were keen to connect themselves to the legendary past of the Sumerian heartland, to anchor their power with claims to continuity and authority. The *Sumerian King-List* represents pre-Amorite times, when founding fathers had the names of constellations and legendary heroes,[4] whereas the early Babylonian king-lists represent Amorite links to a recent tribal past, employing cultural memory selectively to show progress towards city rule. The Amorite and Babylonian languages were close enough to be mutually intelligible at a basic level, which was useful for integration that included mixed marriages and business arrangements. During the First Dynasty a simplified use of the script over a wide area, by comparison with earlier times, allowed people to interact with contracts, administration, and correspondence. They could all rely on similar techniques of divination to evaluate risk and to advise on future success or failure, helping them to have confidence in their actions.[5]

Although the linguistic analysis of the personal names of this period gives an idea of ethnic groups in the population, people would freely translate their names from one language into another, and often gave their sons and daughters names in a language different from that of their own name. Also, sons could be adopted from other families, and the word

[4] See Steinkeller 2003, for a version dated to the Third Dynasty of Ur, and references to later, better-known versions.
[5] Maul 2018.

'son' itself could be honorific, expressing a close relationship that need not be genetic. So choice of names is not a simple guide, nor can members of the various Amorite tribes be identified by parental choice. This flexibility shows that particular languages and personal names did not necessarily express national or tribal loyalty. When a king's name was taken as part of a person's name, clearly that person was expressing his loyalty to the king; but he may have changed his name on succeeding to high office, or at the death of the ruler he had served.

Early kings dated their documents by briefly naming a recent event, whether of victory, dedication, or construction. Some lists of such year-names have been found, giving a chronological sequence to events. Each year's name was decided by royal officials, and tablets were sent out to inform people in other cities of the decision, giving the complete year-name rather than terse abbreviations such as are found on many records.[6] The year-names are basic and invaluable sources of information for the First Dynasty.

This period, dubbed the Middle Bronze Age by archaeologists to emphasize a second phase of the use of metals rather than stone, saw tin and copper in universal demand for alloying to make bronze. More than 32,000 written records of this period are now known, along with a wide variety of archaeological material excavated in the great cities, which were the centres of more-or-less-independent city states for the period of Babylon's first six kings.[7] Local trade went by boat; long-distance trade overland was conducted by caravans with donkeys, the main beasts of burden then. Tough and hardy, donkeys were so cherished that they have been found buried in prestigious tombs, even found inside temples of major cities. Amorite tribesmen from the margins of Mesopotamia were characterized as wreckers of civilized life, who lived in tents, had too many children, copulated like animals, ate forbidden things, had no priestesses or temples, and did not sacrifice to the gods.[8] But city dwellers relied on them for many services: pastoral, agricultural, military, and the supply of foreign luxuries from distant lands, and intermarriage between Babylonians and Amorites soon eroded cultural barriers.

Many clay tablets from Babylonia show that some cities had business contacts in Syria and the Levant. On the Middle Euphrates, Sippar and Mari were the two ancient cities dominating trade routes up through a

---

[6] They are known as promulgation documents; see Horsnell 1999: I, 149–72.

[7] For a wise approach to questions of the basic economy, advocating an open mind on diversity and flexibility, and emphasizing the lack of hard evidence, see Larsen 2015: 273–80.

[8] See Brisch 2007: appendix 5, a letter-prayer of Sin-iddinam to Utu, lines 24–9.

network of towns and small cities westwards, sometimes using Assyrian intermediaries for exporting into Anatolia. Assyrian cities on the Upper Tigris benefitted from routes up through the Tur Abdin and into Anatolia. Assyrian merchants are far better known than those from northern Babylonia, but Babylonians too joined in the activity, producing foods and textiles for export, sending on surpluses of Omani copper, and tin from a source still not identified.[9] Afghani lapis lazuli was very profitable as a transit trade.[10] Babylonian-style seal impressions are found on clay tablets recording the businesses of an Assyrian merchant colony at Kanesh in central Anatolia, showing that Babylonians were involved in the trade there.[11] But they were restricted to certain products: a law promulgated in the city of Ashur forbade Assyrian traders to deal in gold with Babylonians, though they could do so with Elamites; moreover, textiles produced in Anatolia were not allowed to be traded:

> From the king to the Kanesh colony. The tablet with the verdict of the City, which concerns gold, which we sent to you ... that tablet is can-celled. We have not fixed any (new) rule concerning gold. The earlier rule concerning gold still obtains: Assyrians may sell gold among each other, but in accordance with the words of the stela, no Assyrian at all may sell gold to any Akkadian, Amorite, or Shubarean.[12] Anyone who does so shall not stay alive.[13]

As far west as the Aegean Sea, Minoans on Crete conducted their own administration by writing on clay tablets, and with clay sealings, as Babylonians did, but in their own script and language. Minoan-style impressions on clay seals are known from Anatolian trading stations,[14] and hinges from a writing-board found in Mycenean Greece that perished long ago[15] imply that an organic material was also used for writing. This likelihood is supported by a list from Kanesh recording 'a tablet of wax'.[16] At that time, polished clay *bullae* (sealings) similar to those found on Old Babylonian sites come from many Minoan sites.[17] Coincidence can be excluded, for Minoan trade is known from Babylonian tablets: Hammurabi, the most famous king of the First Dynasty, received the gift of a pair of Minoan sandals.[18] Despite such links in the Aegean and

---

[9] Yener 2000: 72–5; Dercksen and Pigott 2017 for eastern sources.
[10] Walker 1980; Michel and Veenhof 2010; Hertel 2013: 74–5.
[11] See Teissier 1994: 63. The site of Kültepe is the ancient Kanesh.
[12] 'Akkadian' may refer to Babylonian and Assyrian here; 'Shubarean' may refer to Hurrian.
[13] Kt 79/k 101, see Hertel 2013: 73 n. 316.   [14] Veenhof 1993.   [15] Shear 1998.
[16] Barjamovic and Larsen 2008: 153. See also Volk 2014–16.   [17] Dalley 2005a: 9–10.
[18] Barrelet 1977: 57–8 n.

contacts with cities in Palestine, no traces of regular contact with Egypt have been found in Babylonia at this time.

Various groups of Elamites must have been determined to control and benefit from the trade in the most valuable goods that passed through their lands from east to west. Tin may have been brought from the north or east.[19] Copper from the mountains in modern Oman and Abu Dhabi, via the islands of Dilmun (modern Bahrain and Failaka), was vital for tools and weapons, and as a store of wealth, so the king began to exploit a second source in the west, from Cyprus 'the copper island', causing a decline in the prosperity of Dilmun.[20] Lapis lazuli, deep-blue symbol of the sky, often embedded with gold and silver specks which twinkle like stars, was brought from the mountains of Afghanistan to adorn temples and divine and royal statues, and to make luxury goods in Babylonia. Carnelian 'red stone' from the Gujarat area of India was especially fashionable for jewellery. Those gemstones would have reached Babylon via the seaport at Ur, for that city with its harbour temple lay about 45 km (28 miles) up a tidal flow from the shore of the Gulf. Silver, symbolizing the skull of the gods,[21] was used to plate the faces of divine statues, and precious silver vessels and decorations in temples pleased the gods. It was also a vital import for use as currency. The city of Babylon shared in the wealth derived from that trade, regulated by law and by written contracts. The rarity value of precious metals, stones, and timbers, combined with wealthy patrons in palaces and temples, gave the incentive to artists to create works of outstanding beauty and technical excellence.

Systems of credit and financial contracts for investing capital were already quite complex. Contrary to the common modern assumption that coinage is necessary for sophisticated transactions, the Mesopotamians and their trading partners used silver and copper by weight, made into handy objects, such as rings, miniature axe-heads, and little ingots, to facilitate transactions without the need for direct exchange of goods. The correct weight could be clipped off an ingot or ring, and scrap was easily reused. Different types of contract had special vocabulary, and variable rates of interest were carefully calculated.

The early kings of Babylon were tribal leaders who shared territory for pasture and trade routes. Some were Amorites who took Babylonian names, some worshipped the Moon-god or the Storm-god as leader of their pantheon, others promoted Marduk to be the patron of Babylon. Two concurrent kings began the dynasty, **Sumu-la-El** and **Sumu-abum,**

---

[19] See, e.g., Bardet et al. 1984: 556, and Klengel 1990. Recent analysis shows Devon and Cornwall in the UK were also sourced at this time.

[20] See Magee 2014: 176–7.   [21] Livingstone 1986: 94–5, line 12.

representing different tribes presumably with access to the same grazing land. Sumu-abum's name was incorporated into the names of two kings in the kingdom of Hana – a sign not just of approval in his lifetime, but of lasting fame.[22] His influence to the east is apparent from the text of an Elamite ruler who dated one of his own texts to the reign of Sumu-abum.[23] Sumu-la-El made a throne of gold and silver for Marduk: the first mention of the great temple Esagila, which would be improved, repaired, and extended over the next 1,500 years. Those early kings also built citadel walls and city gates. Sumu-la-El built or rebuilt six forts which formed a protective ring around Babylon, and claimed to have 'destroyed' nearby Kish and the city wall of Kazallu – both deeds presumably accompanied by profitable looting and capture of a labour force. His daughter Shallurtum ('Plum'), married the king of Uruk, the famous ancient city to the south, no doubt intending to cement an alliance; the arrangement is known from impressions made from her seal with an inscription: 'Shallurtum daughter of Sumu-la-El the king, wife of Sin-kašid her beloved one'.[24] Her high status as an individual is indicated by this inscription: as owner of her own seal, she would have been entrusted with responsibilities and command of officials within the palace at Uruk.

Already the custom was established by which some of a king's daughters would live in another city as *nadītu*-priestesses dedicated to the Sun-god. They were allowed to marry but not to have children, and could trade. Sumu-la-El and Sin-muballiṭ both sent daughters to Sippar, where the earliest and most prestigious group of such women was based in a 'cloister' (*gagûm*). Sumu-la-El's daughter Ayyalatum ('Doe'), a *nadītum*-priestess of the Sun-god at Sippar,[25] raised the status of Babylon in that way. This meant that many princesses earned wealth for their father through trade instead of needing dowries that would dissipate his wealth. They made payments with their own silver in the form of spiral rings from which the appropriate weight could be clipped off; and they possessed their own cylinder seals which were often made from the most valuable stones, such as agate or rock crystal.[26]

In imitation of the famous 'cloister' in Sippar dedicated to the Sun-god, Babylon set up a *gagûm* of *nadītu*-priestesses[27] dedicated to Marduk. Some

---

[22] Podany 2016: 69–98. Kings in cities on the Middle Euphrates were named Yapah-Sumu-abum and Iṣi-Sumu-abum as late as the reign of Samsu-iluna.

[23] Potts 2016: 153 discusses this ruler, whose name was Atta-hušu.   [24] Frayne 1990.

[25] Barberon 2012: 66.   [26] Barberon 2012: annexe 2, pp. 251–2.

[27] The exact roles played by the *nadītum* and the *entum* are not fully known, and may have varied from city to city.

of them lived in other cities and were associated with the cult of Marduk that was established as a 'branch' from Babylon's main temple, to promote the political and economic power of the home city.[28] Those institutions continued for several centuries.

Although no detailed royal inscriptions of the first four kings of Babylon's First Dynasty survive, remains of some business archives record the transactions of several previous generations to demonstrate rights of ownership.[29] There were so many cities with semi-independent rulers that cuneiform records of this period are confusing and hard to date, not least because each city used different names and orders for the months, as well as its own year-names.[30] Conquerors of particular cities did their best to impose their year-names and month-names for purposes of business and administration, but it was a slow process to change the habits of established cities. Not until the reign of Hammurabi did dating practices begin to follow that of Babylon beyond the city's immediate reach.

Agriculture, pastoral products, specialist manufacture, and trade all brought wealth. Prisoners captured in local campaigns were used to extend the canal network and bring a greater area of agricultural land into production; the main taxes went to the dominant city. Sumu-la-El's influence reached deep into the west: at Tilmen Hüyük, an elegant little Bronze Age 'city' to the south of modern Gaziantep[31] in Turkey, about 825 km from Babylon as the crow flies. An impression from a cylinder seal on a clay door seal, inscribed 'Lagamal-gamil son of Ibbi-Sin, servant of Sumu-la-El', has been found there, indicating with clarity that long-distance trade was not restricted to the Assyrians nor to eastern Anatolia.[32]

The third king, **Sabium**, continued the dynasty, beginning with a declaration of legitimacy recorded in his first year-name: 'Year Sabium entered into his father's house'. This statement identifies one of the great strengths of the whole dynasty: a publicly uncontested succession, with a smooth transition by a prince, chosen by the gods through careful acts of divination that acknowledged the importance of the stability of family-based inheritance.

Sabium's claim to have built Esagila serves to highlight an ambiguity in the language used to express building work, whether city walls or temples: the original act of building is often not differentiated from the act of repairing and rebuilding. Most buildings were made of mud bricks

---

[28] Barberon 2012: 30, 119, 123–5. [29] Pedersén 2005a: 11.

[30] For instance, 'Harvest' as a month-name might be appropriate for the north but not the south, etc.

[31] Antep, now Gaziantep, ancient ʿAinṭab. [32] Marchetti and Marchesi 2014.

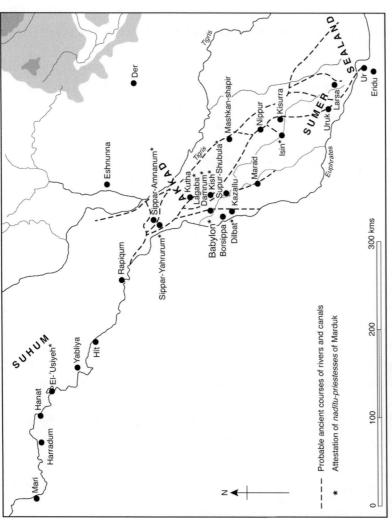

Figure 3.2 Sketch map showing sites where *naditu*-priestesses of Marduk are attested during the First Dynasty. Credit: adapted from Barberon 2012: fig. 2 by Alison Wilkins and author.

tempered with straw, and frequently needed repair. So it is usually impossible to tell from the wording whether a king built a structure for the first time, or added to the work of predecessors. When Sabium's successor recorded that he built the wall of Babylon, we are fairly sure that he either rebuilt or extended an existing wall; his claim to have built the temple for Ishtar in Babylon allows a similar ambiguity. Another misunderstanding may arise from the year-names in which a king claims to have 'destroyed' a city, sometimes on more than one occasion quite close in time. Although destruction undoubtedly took place, some of it was symbolic, and much of it was carefully targeted at a particular building or city gate, to make a breach that enabled entry and looting.[33] Mud brick does not burn easily, and it is simple to reuse debris to make new bricks for repairs, so revival may have been swift. Royal inscriptions sometimes include the claim that a king reduced an entire city to mounds of rubble, giving an image of an empty land which could be occupied legally by the conqueror with the support of its gods, who had deliberately deserted the inhabitants. In fact, the destructive victor often claims to have resettled scattered people there, and the same city is sometimes found to be flourishing a few years later, with local officials from the old regime now working for the new ruler. The language used should not necessarily be understood in a literal sense: an empty land is one that no longer has a ruler.[34]

During Sabium's reign, the balance of regional power shifted. The Elamites took control of the southern city of Larsa under a leader who was also backed by the Amorites, and exercised power from behind the throne without inserting his own name in the king-lists.[35] His name, Kudur-mabuk, is Elamite like that of his father, but his two 'sons', who were officially kings of Larsa, have Babylonian names. One of Kudur-mabuk's official residences was to the east, on the Tigris at Maškan-šapir.[36] He succeeded in keeping his 'sons' on the throne for some seventy-one years as vassals or clients of an Elamite emperor, and they received tribute, including gold vessels, from adjacent city rulers.[37] Larsa thus became an Elamite protectorate in the heart of southern Babylonia, where envoys from Elam arrived frequently at the court to

---

[33] Dalley 2005b; Samet 2014: 5–13.

[34] An example of a crucial word misunderstood is the verb *duākum* ('to do battle'), formerly translated 'to kill'. See also Barstad 1996.

[35] He was known as 'father of Yamutbal' – an Amorite word perhaps denoting an area of tribal rights. Emutbal/Yamutbal was the name of the area ruled locally from Larsa. See Stol 1976: 68.

[36] See Steinkeller 2004: 34–5, and Brisch 2007: 51–2. A small disc of stone bearing his inscription found at the site of Terqa near Mari may indicate authority there too; see Wilcke 1990.

[37] This is known from an administrative record found in Uruk. See Durand 1992.

check on its rulers and to dictate their alliances. Kudur-mabuk demonstrated his status by installing one of his own daughters as a prestigious *entum*-priestess in the temple of the Moon-god at Ur, a deed of extreme piety that was still remembered a thousand years later. Both sons installed statues of their father in temples.

The tentacles of Elamite power extended in all directions. To control goods from the east passing westwards through the Zagros Mountains into Mesopotamia, the Elamites needed a network of authority both in Babylonia and in Assyria. One main route into Mesopotamia came north-westwards from the Elamite royal city of Susa along the foothills of the Zagros Mountains, then down the valley of the river Diyala to its junction with the Tigris. This route gave access which enabled them to control the tribal territory of Yamutbal and its chief city, Der, as well as other cities in the vicinity.[38]

Susa was closer to Lower Mesopotamia than to the Diyala river valley, and there were tributaries which flowed into the Tigris near the shore of the Gulf, giving access not only to some of the great old cities such as Larsa, but also to the islands of Bahrain and Failaka in the Gulf, and on towards the mountains of Oman. Larsa was a focus of particular attention: water from a branch of the Tigris may have joined water from the Euphrates there.[39] If so, one could travel between Susa and Larsa all or most of the way by boat, when conditions of spate or drought allowed. The emperor of Elam was thus in a good position to mediate a dispute that arose over water rights between Eshnunna and Larsa, two cities over which he exerted control.[40]

The structure of Elamite power has been described as trucial or segmentary; several of their 'rulers' were contemporary.[41] The overlords remain shadowy figures, seldom named as individuals, referred to only as 'Grand Vizier' (*sukkalmah*). The Elamites did not attempt to rule cities directly through their own governors, but sent envoys and agents, backed by military force if need be, which makes them hard to trace in Babylonian texts.[42] But their shadowy presence has been found at Larsa, Eshnunna, and Shehna (Tell Leilan). When the relationship between a Babylonian overlord and a loyal ruler is expressed in correspondence, it is that of father and son, and local rulers of equal rank refer to each other as brothers, using the

---

[38] Der is close to modern Badra, at Tell ʿAqar. Clay tablets written at Der have been found in late Babylonian Uruk. Medieval Bādarāya/Bayt Darāyā in Syriac literature was a seat of learning. See Longrigg 1960: I, 870–1.

[39] Steinkeller 2001.   [40] Charpin and Durand 2013.   [41] Potts 2016: 145.

[42] For envoys see, e.g., Sulaiman and Dalley 2012; for an agent, see Eidem and Ristvet 2011: 2 and 25–6.

language of the family. But when the Elamite 'Grand Vizier' ruling from
Susa wrote, he ignored such conventional niceties, giving an impression of
impersonal superiority and arrogance.

Some groups of Elamites were invaluable to the Babylonians for their
expertise as archers; the terrain of their mountainous homeland made them
hardy and energetic, qualities that made them attractive as guards and
militias for hire to the comfortable city dwellers on the flat river lands, but
much feared as enemies. They may have been independent of Elamite rulers.

Subsequent early kings of Babylon built more walls and temples, and
dedicated thrones to their gods, filling the city centre with temples and
treasures, establishing the main buildings that would remain there for the
next 1,500 years. They dug new canals, and constructed forts including
the 'harbour of Apil-Sin's fort' at Sippar.[43] **Apil-Sin** took direct control of
the great city of Kish by conquest, and **Sin-muballiṭ**, father of Hammurabi,
installed governors in some cities that had formerly enjoyed the status of
client, beginning a move towards a more centralized authority. In Kish,
where a temple of Marduk was now to be found, the archive of a governor
responsible to the king in Babylon is one example of closer control;[44]
another is a group of letters found in excavations at Sippar, relating to
long-distance trade in copper, tin, and textiles.[45] Sin-muballiṭ sent his
daughter Iltani ('our goddess'), to the cloister in Sippar as a *nadītum*-
priestess of the Sun-god, to promote his interests there, following the
tradition established by earlier kings of Babylon.

Some avenues of trade with Anatolia were disrupted: the fire that
destroyed the Assyrian merchant colony excavated at Kanesh is now
thought to date to this time, although the houses were soon rebuilt, and
trade with Assyria resumed at a more restricted level.[46] Babylonian trade
with various cities to the north and west was flexible enough to allow
business to continue.[47]

In Babylon, remnants of an archive were found recording the activities
of a merchant/creditor named Kurû; his business began in Sin-muballiṭ's
reign and continued to the end of the dynasty. Its letters, dated contracts,
and various other types of text represent the lifespan of his business
organization, revealing activity covering seven reigns and several

[43] Roughly 40 km north-east of Sippar. See Gasche and Tanret 1998: 20 and map 6.
[44] Archive of Tutu-nišu. See also Blocher 1988: 42.
[45] Al-Rawi and Dalley 2000: nos. 97, 98, 106, 115, and 123.
[46] The burnt level is known as level II; the succeeding level is known as level Ib. See Larsen 2015: 40–1 and 75–9.
[47] Larsen 2015: 97.

generations in a family firm that benefitted from stability and loyalty to the dynasty.[48]

Military alliances changed frequently despite attempts to give them legal impact by means of treaties enforced by rituals. These involved killing an animal, blood-bonding between the leaders of the two sides, and the swearing of loyalty oaths; the participants ate food that was believed to turn against a perjurer:[49] 'They disregard the oath of their gods, they eat things that are taboo for them but their troops are still healthy', exclaimed an indignant king.[50] To persuade an ally to join a coalition, there was a price to pay, initially in the exchange of precious diplomatic gifts including carefully weighed and recorded works of art in silver. The Elamites bene-fitted from Marduk's temple treasury on one occasion when Hammurabi enlisted their help, and had to pay.[51] This marks a practice that continued throughout Babylon's history: banking wealth, especially in the temples of Babylon, allowed kings to hire foreign soldiers – Amorites, Elamites, Kassites – to protect them, leaving the indigenous citizens prosperous and content with a sedentary life.

The arrival of an ally's troops ostensibly for protection could quickly become an invasion of a rival under false pretences. Babylon's attempts to constrain the power of Rim-Sin of Larsa through alliances with other cities were not successful enough to throw off the power of Elam. A long letter of 149 lines, written by Anam the independent ruler of Uruk to Sin-muballiṭ, records his delicately worded suspicion that the arrival of Babylon's troops, supposedly as allies, was not well-intentioned:

> Speak to Sin-muballiṭ, thus says Anam. About the army of Amnan-Yahrur ... When the army arrived at the city gate, the fathers of the troops who go ahead of the army came before me and gave me their report, saying: 'At the time when our master gave us instructions, ... it was not ordered that the troops be brought into the city ...'. Truly Uruk and Babylon are one house and should speak openly ... But the report of Abdi-Ami is: 'Why did this huge army come here? Will they not load Uruk into a basket and go away again?' ... Ever since the time of Sin-kašid (his predecessor) and since the time I myself witnessed until now, the army of Amnan-Yahrur has arrived here two or three times for military aid to this house. One, two, five or ten thousand, with all their equipment, have come here and stayed for one, two or three years in this city. Even Sabium ... came here with a thousand troops ... God knows that I truly trust in you![52]

---

[48] Pedersén 2005a: 37–53.   [49] See the discussion in Eidem and Ristvet 2011: 311–20.
[50] Brisch 2007: appendix 5, Sin-iddinam to Utu, line 29.   [51] Charpin 1988: no. 371.
[52] Falkenstein 1963: 56–71, English translation van Koppen 2006: 127–30.

Sin-muballiṭ's long reign, and the power revealed in this letter, are indicators of strong rule, but seal inscriptions impressed on contracts show that not far away, high officials with Babylonian names were the servants of another Elamite ruler[53] who continued to oversee the rulers of many Mesopotamian cities when Hammurabi succeeded Sin-muballiṭ.[54] From correspondence found at Mari we catch occasional glimpses of intercepted letters, and of the Elamite emperor setting enemy allies against each other by spreading false reports. Messengers and messages were vulnerable to hostile interception.

The success of military campaigns depended on how many men could be mustered among a group of allies, and how well-armed they were. Manpower was carefully controlled: a farmer could provide a substitute to work on his field, or to maintain canals, but not for military service. Soldiers were paid with silver and with textiles, as we know from lists itemizing payments to them. Most were foot soldiers who used boats for transport wherever possible. In contrast, it was in the interest of leaders to capture important men and hold them to a ransom[55] which a king could order a particular temple to pay.[56] When Larsa was attacked by Hammurabi's coalition, it defended itself with 40,000 men, a figure which suggests that it relied on its own coalition; bands of foreign soldiers could be added to levies from vassals or loyal farmers.[57]

Hammurabi succeeded his father on the throne, ruling within a highly literate court, but constrained by cities under Elamite protectors until late in his long reign of forty-three years. Upstream along the Euphrates, the kingdom of Mari-and-Hana was sometimes an ally, sometimes a rival. Hammurabi was using Kish as a military base where his Hanean troops paraded in the 'garden of Zababa', an arrangement that was furthered by his successor.[58] There were clear advantages to keeping troops and weapons outside Babylon, not least at Kish because the oracle of Zababa the war-god could be consulted for prophesying on the likely outcome of a military expedition. Much further to the west, the kingdom of Yamhad, centred on Halab (Aleppo), was a powerful ally that sent troops in times of need and co-operated in trade with the Levant, giving Babylon access to east Mediterranean goods including Minoan luxuries.[59]

---

[53] At Malgium on the Tigris. He was named Kuduzuluš. See van Dijk 1970: 63–5, also de Boer 2013.
[54] Charpin 1985: 52, texts TIM IV, nos. 33 and 34.   [55] Durand 1988: no. 25.
[56] Stol 1981: no. 32.   [57] Eidem and Ristvet 2011: 19–22.
[58] Kraus 1985: no. 37; Heimpel 2003: 507; Moorey 1978: 175–7.
[59] Klengel 1990: 163–75. For the early spelling 'Halam', see Archi 2010: 3 n. 1.

Early in his long reign, Hammurabi claimed to have conquered three major southern cities, Uruk, Isin, and Ur, where a seal impression of the archivist and priest of the Moon-god, inscribed 'servant of Hammurabi', has been found. Those conquests gave Babylon control over major cities on the Lower Euphrates, although Larsa, still ruled by Rim-Sin, remained under the thumb of Elam until near the end of Hammurabi's long reign. Control of Ur would have allowed direct access to the Arabian Gulf.[60] At that time the island of Bahrain was ruled by kings with Amorite and Babylonian names. One of them had a large statue of which only one big, leather-clad foot has been found, perfectly inscribed in cuneiform.[61] It has become clear that Hammurabi was not a king of top rank until quite late in his reign.

In addition to the invaluable year-names, Hammurabi's scribes produced building inscriptions written in Sumerian or Akkadian or both; some are known from copies made after his death, to perpetuate his fame. By building or rebuilding a wall for the cloister of *nadītu*-priestesses at Sippar, which now included at least one of his own daughters, Hammurabi maintained a close relationship with that city, vital for profiting from trade up the Euphrates.[62] He restored the temple of the Sun-god there, a pious deed which was remembered 1,200 years later when king Nabonidus uncovered one of Hammurabi's foundation inscriptions. The king's various roles were not only expressed in epithets such as 'law-giver', 'warrior', 'shepherd of the people', or 'suppliant in prayer', but were also related to a particular pose or gesture in works of art including cylinder seals and stone and bronze sculptures. Some of those objects were on public display, long-lasting memorials to the greatness of the king and the craftsmanship that he and his successors promoted. One such memorial was the monumental stela inscribed with Hammurabi's laws, now one of Babylonia's most famous objects, discussed in detail in the next chapter. Hammurabi's title 'King of Justice' may have been claimed at a time when he made a particularly significant change.

Less imposing than the great law code stela, but more immediate, were the practical legal measures: the edicts recorded on clay tablets.[63] Known as *mīšarum* ('justice/right behaviour'), edicts were enacted by every king, including Hammurabi's predecessors, usually soon after accession, also sometimes at other points during a reign, each time with updating and revision. Proclamation was signalled by the raising of a golden torch in Sippar, publicizing Sippar's role as the centre of worship for the Sun-god as

---

[60] See Magee 2014: 166.   [61] See Hammond 2017.   [62] Barberon 2012: 67.   [63] Kraus 1984.

I. SKETCH OF STONE DISCOVERED BY CAPᵗ DURAND.
(2 Fᴛ. 2 IN. LONG).

2. PALM BRANCH OVER INSCRIPTION.

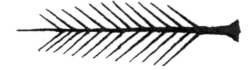

3. FACSIMILE OF INSCRIPTION ON STONE.

Figure 3.3 Black basalt stone foot from a giant statue of king Rimum found on Bahrain. Inscribed with cuneiform signs matching those of Hammurabi's time: 'Palace (of) Rimum servant of the god Inzak of Agarum (Failaka island)'. Credit: Durand 1880: 192.

lord of justice. In one instance the event is described with a picturesque metaphor as the occasion for 'washing the unkempt hair of the land', which was an act of mourning, probably referring to an edict following the death of the old king.[64] A main purpose was to release people from debt, to avoid a build-up that might cause debtors to abandon their land or face a lifetime of servitude and thereby weaken the economy, diminishing the food

[64] Van Soldt 1990: 172: 8'–10'.

supply, and decreasing revenue from tax.[65] Another purpose was to pro-
hibit trading with certain groups of outsiders, to protect profits.

When a king of Eshnunna captured both the Assyrian royal city
Ekallatum on the eastern bank of the Tigris and Ashur on the opposite
bank, the king of Assyria, Samsu-Addu I, fled, and it was Hammurabi who
gave him asylum. Samsu-Addu regained his kingdom, reconquered Ashur
three years later, and eventually captured Mari. He reigned in Assyria for a
total of thirty-three years, dying in 1776. Thus he became a powerful
Amorite king in northern Mesopotamia, and eventually claimed to rule
'the four regions', with influence from the eastern Mediterranean in
Lebanon to Bahrain in the Arabian Gulf; but the succession was weak.
Hammurabi took over from him some of Assyria, claiming among his
conquests Nineveh, which had previously been under the control of
Samsu-Addu.[66]

The relationship between the Assyrian king and Hammurabi had been
changeable. Samsu-Addu posted his own men as officers in cities to the
north and west, including at least two of his own sons. One son became
viceroy in Mari and married a daughter of the king of Qatna – one of the
greatest western cities of the time, just east of the river Orontes near Homs
in central Syria. The link was arranged by his father, who insisted on
displacing another wife from top rank.[67] This shows that royal marriages
could be overturned on the advantage of diplomatic opportunity.

The link of Mari with Qatna shows the extent of relationships with
western cities, as well as the power of Elam far from its base at Susa, for
on another occasion a group of Elamites received assurance that they would
have safe passage if they went to Qatna:

> When the Elamite messenger came towards Halab, he sent on from Emar
> to Qatna two of his servants. When Hammurabi learnt of it, he sent
> guards (?) to his border and they seized those men on their return, and
> asked for their news, and thus they spoke, saying: 'The man of Qatna had
> written to us to say: The land is given over to your hand. Come up to me! If
> you come up, you will not be attacked'.[68]

The importance of this letter is to demonstrate how close the links were, not
only between cities of Babylonia and Assyria, but also beyond
Mesopotamia to the Levant and Canaan, encouraging ambitious kings to
have a vision of empire far beyond regional triumphs. In pursuit of that

[65] Charpin 2000: 185–211.
[66] Nineveh was also called Ninet at this time; see Wu 1994: 198–200.   [67] Durand 1990: 291–3.
[68] Durand 1990: 40–2, text A.266; Charpin and Durand 2013: 341–53.

goal, alliances changed according to immediate needs. Eshnunna was under particular pressure to balance the ambitions of Susa and the Elamites with alliances in anti-Elamite Babylonian cities, since it lay on a major route between Susa and Babylonia.

As the letter above shows, another great power at that time was Halab, whose ruler gave a daughter in marriage to Zimri-Lim (1775–1762 BC), king of Mari and Hana. Halab is the ancient name of Aleppo, the royal city where the Storm-god Addu was a powerful patron and giver of oracles. Such was the temple's importance that Elamite leaders planned to donate to the god an Elamite bow, symbol of their military power, and Zimri-Lim dedicated a statue of himself there. The king of Halab's involvement in western affairs reached at least as far as Ḥaṣor, known from early books of the Old Testament as a royal city in Canaan, where a remarkable variety of Babylonian cuneiform texts written on clay tablets of this time has been excavated.[69]

Samsu-Addu's expansion to the Middle Euphrates might have challenged Babylonia for control of trade up that river; but even he seems to have been under the influence of the Elamite emperor, and may have lost control over Mari and other cities due to Elamite interference.[70] After Zimri-Lim had restored the old dynasty at Mari, he made an alliance with Hammurabi against Elam, an ill-advised move as it turned out. A draft for a treaty found at Mari declares:

> Swear by the Sun-god of Heaven! Swear by the Storm-god of Heaven! Those are the gods that Hammurabi son of Sin-muballiṭ king of Babylon invoked (when he swore): 'From now on, as long as I live, I shall indeed be enemy of Siwe-palar-huhpak (the Elamite ruler of Anshan). I shall not let my servants or my messengers mix with his servants, and I shall not dispatch them to him. I shall not make peace with Siwe-palar-huhpak without the approval of Zimri-Lim son of Yahdun-Lim king of Mari and the land of Hana' . . . What I have sworn by my gods, the Sun-god and the Storm-god, to Zimri-Lim son of Yahdun-Lim king of Mari and the land of Hana I will faithfully fulfil, happily and in complete sincerity.[71]

But another letter shows that the Elamite ruler had placated Zimri-Lim by giving him certain towns. When Hammurabi met two ambassadors of Zimri-Lim in Sippar, they sent back a report in which Hammurabi's own words were reported:

---

[69] Bonechi 1991; Cohen 2019.

[70] Information chiefly from Mari and Shemshara. See Eidem and Laessøe 2001: no. 64; Tell al-Rimah, ancient Qaṭṭara, see Dalley, Hawkins, and Walker 1976; Langlois 2017: 29–31, 43–4.

[71] Sasson 2015: 98–9.

> We arrived in Greater Sippar, and my lord's servant delivered my lord's message to Hammurabi. As he did so, Hammurabi kept listening without objecting during the entire message . . . but then addressed us, saying: 'Has this House, then or now, ever transgressed against Mari? Indeed, has there ever been a single conflict between Mari and this House? Mari and Babylon, then as now, are one house . . . Ever since Zimri-Lim moved to support me and began to communicate with me, no transgression or attack on him has been instigated by me. I have been entirely beneficial to him and he is deeply aware of how beneficial I have been to him.'

The ambassador from Mari declared his full agreement, and then said:

> Now then, matching the favours my lord has bestowed on you and the way he has honoured you, give him satisfaction: put yourself under oath regarding the towns that the Grand Vizier of Elam your 'father' has given my lord, and may complete sincerity prevail.[72]

It then emerged that they disagreed over whose troops should continue to man the garrisons there, and under whose command. The speeches reveal that the emperor from Susa was openly acknowledged at that point as the overlord of Hammurabi, being named as his honorific 'father'. At some point, when Hammurabi and Zimri-Lim were still allies, the Elamites planned to besiege the city of Babylon until a battle forestalled the attack.[73] But Elamites were everywhere: the king of Qaṭna requested Elam's help against Yamhad.[74] East of the Tigris, in the mountains of Kurdistan, one among a confederation of Elamite rulers was in a position to demand envoys, and to send a general with 12,000 men into the area of the Lower Zab to enforce the request.[75] In the pecking order of kings at that time, Elam and Yamhad were the two leading powers. Addu the Storm-god of Halab was credited with bestowing kingship upon the dynasty of Zimri-Lim at Mari, and was worshipped beyond the core kingdom of Yamhad, notably in towns up the river Khabur.[76] Second in rank were Larsa, Babylon, Eshnunna, Assyria, and Mari. Larsa was still ruled by a 'son' of the Elamite Kudur-mabuk.

Elam's domination over such a wide area left one spectacular mark upon the design of great temples. In Elam, grove temples or sacred groves were commonly places of worship.[77] In Babylonia and Assyria, cities that had

---

[72] Sasson 2015: 85–6.

[73] Charpin 1988: nos. 327, 328, 376, and 384. The battle took place at Hiritum, probably on a northern branch of the Euphrates above Sippar, in Zimri-Lim's tenth year.

[74] Kupper 1954: no. 19.

[75] Širuk-tuh, who ruled concurrently with Kuduzuluš. See Eidem and Laessøe 2001: no. 64.

[76] Durand 1993; Schwemer 2001: 211–31.   [77] Henkelman 2008: 443–5.

come under Elamite influence appear to have imitated grove temples at this time by giving their own buildings moulded brick façades resembling rows of date palms. The design, which consists of either a spiral (representing the male tree) or scallops (representing the female), has been found on many sites from southern Mesopotamia to cities east and west of the Tigris, and more distant ones on the Upper Khabur. The new style was a significant departure from traditional façades of oblong niches that go back to early Sumerian times, but it survived for many centuries, partly because this was a time of ambitious but quite sturdy temple building. It suggests that the influence exerted by Elam was cultural as well as political and military.[78] Although in the city of Babylon no temples survive from the First Dynasty, several cities that came under Elamite influence, including Larsa and Ur, built huge temples to this design, and it is likely that Hammurabi and his predecessors followed the fashion. Apil-Sin, a great builder of temples in Babylon, was contemporary with Warad-Sin of Larsa, whose palm-tree façade at Ur would have been admired, along with the huge temple of the Sun-god at Larsa with its internal courtyards and shrine designed to represent palm groves.

The discovery that Elam was a superpower at this time, with influence spreading at least as far as Qaṭna on the river Orontes in Syria, and probably as far as Haṣor in Palestine,[79] has made it fruitful to reinvestigate an old idea, that the story of Kedor-laomer king of Elam (whose name is Elamite) in Genesis 14:1–16 contains a core of historical information from this period.[80] He marched into the far south of Palestine, and ruled the locals for twelve years until they rebelled. Then he amassed an international alliance which was eventually defeated and driven out. The names of Kedor-laomer's allies are preserved in the Hebrew text, giving some striking similarities with men known from the time when Hammurabi ruled Babylon. Some of the likenesses have come to light recently. If they are significant, they contribute a political and military background, chiefly the wide reach of Elam that was such a surprising discovery in excavated texts, to the archaeological evidence of the palm-façade temples. Details of the question are given in the Appendix at the end of this volume.

Hammurabi, Babylon, and the cities of Lower Mesopotamia are not mentioned in the biblical passage. We now know they were subservient

---

[78] Dalley 2014.   [79] See Bonechi 1991; Potts 2016: 155–60.

[80] See Weippert 1976–80: 'Kedor-laomer' for previous attempts to date the episode; for recent work, see Durand 2005; Charpin 2004: 225. For the texts once associated with Kedor-laomer, see Foster 2005: 369–75.

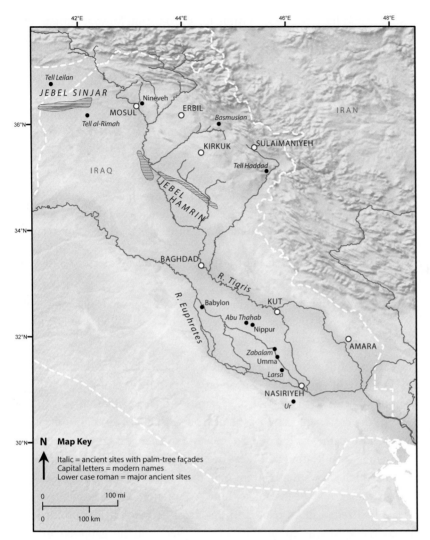

Figure 3.4 Sketch map showing distribution of temples with palm tree façades. Credit: Scott Walker. Reproduced by permission of the Hardt Foundation, Vandœuvres near Geneva, Switzerland.

to the Elamites until late in Hammurabi's reign. Babylon's subsequent rise is all the more impressive, therefore.

In Palestine, a few cuneiform texts have come to light in excavations, dated to the same Amorite period. Among them are lexical texts used for teaching cuneiform to apprentice scribes, some of them trilingual: Babylonian, Sumerian, and the local West Semitic language. Those trained scribes would have been responsible for introducing Mesopotamian texts to Canaan during the time of Hammurabi and his successors.[81]

Late in his reign Hammurabi built up a power base among the cities of Babylonia. Larsa seems to have been the only major city in Lower Mesopotamia that did not join his coalition against Elam, presumably because the pressure from its overlord was too strong. So Hammurabi's conquest of the Elamites, recorded in his thirtieth year-name, cleared the way:

> The year Hammurabi the king, the powerful one, beloved of Marduk, by the supreme power of the greatest gods, overthrew the army of Elam which had mobilized Subartu, Gutium, Eshnunna and Malgium en masse from the border of Marhashi; thus he made firm the foundation of Sumer and Akkad.

The conquest of Larsa took place the following year:

> The year Hammurabi the king with the help of Anu and Enlil, went before the army. By the supreme power which the greatest gods had given him, he conquered the land of Emutbal, and its king Rim-Sin.[82]

The capture of Rim-Sin, once thought to be the main event that made way for Hammurabi's rise, was of secondary importance, as Rim-Sin at Larsa was one of several puppets of the Elamite emperor. Hammurabi's treatment of the conquered city was lenient: he installed two high officials in Larsa whose names and extensive correspondence are known.[83] At least one member of a leading family in the city stayed on and accepted the new regime, which shows that Hammurabi did not entirely get rid of existing elites if they could be useful to him.[84] This merciful treatment of the defeated citizens can be related to the claim he made in the prologue to his law code, discussed in the next chapter, that he gathered up the scattered people and returned them to their homes. New field registers were drawn up to clarify ownership or tenancy, and to record grain yields for taxation, under the authority of the registrar, the 'scribe of fields'. A king-list of Larsa's own rulers began with its governors under the control of neighbouring Isin, continued with its own kings, including the sons of the Elamite Kudur-mabuk, and ended with Hammurabi and his son, to show the kings of Isin and Babylon as legitimate heirs to Larsa's throne and maintain the fiction of uncontested succession.[85] This shows how each city

---

[81] Cohen 2019.　　[82] Horsnell 1999: II, 139–43.
[83] On Sin-iddinam, Šamaš-hazir, and Balmunamhe; see Kraus 1968.　　[84] See Dalley 2005a: 4.
[85] Wilson 1977: 105.

was free to manipulate the genealogy of local rulers. Hammurabi's thirty-eighth year-name records with literary hyperbole that he 'destroyed Eshnunna with a very great flood'; but the event did not bring the city to an end; subsequent local rulers are attested.[86] The image of a flood may be metaphorical – even in our days expressions such as 'wave after wave of soldiers flooding into a city to overwhelm it' use the same metaphor.

By altering branches of the rivers and their canals, lines of communication could be changed. Rim-Sin I of Larsa had undertaken canal works to prevent fresh water from the two great rivers flowing straight to the sea, to make more water available for fields around Larsa.[87] Hammurabi describes a new canal named 'Hammurabi is the abundance of the people' which brought water through Nippur and Larsa down to Uruk, Ur, and Eridu.[88] This may be the time when the Lower Tigris was coaxed into an easterly branch, connecting Babylon directly to Larsa.

Babylon emerged at last as a superpower from Hammurabi's thirtieth year onwards, ranking alongside the still-powerful kingdom of Yamhad. Weak rulers in Assyria after the death of Samsu-Addu, followed by Hammurabi's defeat of the Elamite leader, the conquest of Eshnunna, Mari, and Larsa, paved the way to a sudden, rather unexpected, success.

The fate of Mari is curious: texts from the previous administration in the palace of Zimri-Lim were packed into containers and labelled.[89] This may imply that Hammurabi intended to keep the city viable under loyal administrators, as he had done at Larsa. But he returned two years after the initial conquest to tear down the city walls, perhaps finding that he could not control local dissidents. Hammurabi may have taken from Mari the life-size statue of a distinguished earlier governor named Puzur-Eshtar, which was recovered from Babylon, the head and the body separately, as well as another, unidentified governor (see Figure 8.5).[90] Mari itself never again became a major seat of power, although its fame lived on for a thousand years.[91] Soon afterwards the nearby city of Terqa seized the initiative and established its own dynasty of kings ruling the kingdom of Hana, which had previously been paired with Mari in the royal title 'king of Mari and Hana'. They took up the mantle of Mari's fame and established a kingship that lasted for the next 500 years.

---

[86] Frayne 1990: 591–2.   [87] Frayne 1990: 290–3.
[88] See Abraham and van Lerberghe 2017: 4–7.   [89] Charpin 1995.   [90] Sallaberger 2006–8.
[91] For a local dynasty at Mari in the Middle Assyrian period, see Kupper 1987–90, Maul 1992, and Zadok 2017.

Zimri-Lim's fate is unknown; he must have stayed outside Hammurabi's coalition until it was too late to switch, relying perhaps on a prophecy predicting the defeat of Babylon with its allies, and wealth for Zimri-Lim:

> The oracle-transmitter of Dagan god of Tuttul rose up and spoke as follows: 'O Babylon, why do you not cease making (trouble)? I shall gather you up in a net ... I shall deliver the houses of the seven companions (allies of Hammurabi?) in full to the power of Zimri-Lim'.[92]

Was this simply what the king wanted to hear, or was it a deliberate attempt on the part of Tuttul to sabotage Zimri-Lim's prospects, now that he had detached himself from Hammurabi's coalition? As if to show the latter, Hammurabi's Code asserts that he was 'the leader of kings, who subdues the settlements along the Euphrates according to the sign of Dagan his creator, who showed mercy to the people of the cities of Mari and Tuttul'. A Sumerian hymn records some of Hammurabi's actions at Mari after he had 'demolished' the city walls:[93] he installed a stone base for a bronze drum, 'fine of voice', and made offerings to Meslamta-ea, the god who travels up and down between Earth and Underworld, who tears the heart out of those who arrive in the Underworld, a war-god who causes plagues.[94] Does this belong to a ritual of capitulation? Hammurabi's son and successor Samsu-iluna, as part of a much wider promotion to preserve his father's fame and to discourage rebellion, had copies made of his father's text.

Hammurabi fell ill at the end of his long reign, and Samsu-iluna took up the kingship before his father died. The succession was well-planned. This we know from a short letter in which the new king also refers to his edict, his first act of debt remission on his accession:

> Speak to Etel-pi-Marduk: thus says Samsu-iluna. The king my father is ill, and I have just now ascended the throne of [my father's] house in order to guide the land aright. And in order to support the producers of state revenue, I have exempted the arrears of ... field managers ... I have broken the tablets with debt obligations of soldiers ... I have established 'justice' in the land ... When you see this tablet of mine, you and the elders of the region that you administer must come up and meet me.[95]

At all periods of Mesopotamian history the success of a king can be judged from the titles he took: 'great king', 'king of the four regions', 'king of the world', and the epithet 'he who unites the land between the

[92] Durand 1988: no. 209.

[93] Sollberger and Walker 1985: 257–64. The hymn is seventy-four lines long.

[94] See Katz 2003: 420–8.   [95] TCL 17, 76; translation van Koppen 2006: 130.

Tigris and the Euphrates'. The terms 'world' and 'four regions' are probably used to indicate a sphere of influence only roughly defined, perhaps related at this period to the extent covered by cities named in the *Sumerian King-List*.[96] The concept of world mastery may not necessarily refer to military victory, but may imply that a distant ruler sent diplomatic gifts in recognition of the king's fame, and engaged in trade with him. Hammurabi's extensive conquests and contacts late in his reign qualified him to take the highest titles. One might think that the main title *lugal*, translated into English as 'king', would be significant, but there are nuances and ambiguities. In earlier times each city had its own word for its top man.[97] This inconsistency sets traps for those who rely on translations.[98]

Half a millennium earlier, one of the kings of Agade had claimed to be divine. The claim may have had its basis in an oracle, and is visible to us in two ways: the sign for a god, the so-called 'divine determinative', is written before a king's personal name; and images of the king may wear a horned crown. Subsequently some Elamite rulers and some local Semitic rulers wrote their names with the divine determinative, showing an intermittent claim to divine status, presumably at a lower level than that of the great gods.[99] Some Amorite kings did not claim divinity, presumably lacking whatever qualifications were needed, but Hammurabi made his claim late in his reign, having made exceptional conquests.[100] On the law code stela (see Chapter 4) he referred to himself as 'a god among kings, acquainted with wisdom',[101] although he stopped short of showing himself wearing a horned headdress. He made the highest claims to the top rank of rulers:

---

[96] Wilcke 1989: 561.

[97] The term *lugal* means only 'big man' and may refer either to the king or simply to the owner of a field; the term *lú* means only 'man' but in conjunction with a city name can mean the ruler of the city. Elsewhere it can refer to any man, or may be used more specifically to denote a free man of high social standing. The ruler of Eshnunna was referred to sometimes as 'man of Eshnunna', but also, on his own royal inscriptions, as *rubûm* ('prince'). Elamite rulers could be called *sukkalmah*, which in Mesopotamian terms might be interpreted as 'great vizier', but seems to have the connotation of 'emperor' or 'grand regent' in Hammurabi's time; later, and further to the west, the title *sukkal* ('vizier') can mean 'scribe'. The *énsi* of a city may be its ruler, sometimes translated as 'governor', or may be used with its basic meaning of 'ploughman'.

[98] Further discussed by Horowitz 1998: 193–8, 298–9.

[99] In a year-name for his forty-second year three examples are known in which the divine determinative preceded his royal name. On the kings of Simashki, Malgium, Eshnunna, and Der, see de Boer 2013: 19–25.

[100] Horsnell 1999: II, 164; Dalley and Yoffee 1991: no. 278:11.   [101] Winter 2008: 75–101.

> Hammurabi, the god of his land, the one whom the sky-god Anu has covered with the aura of royalty, whose great destiny has been fixed by the god Enlil, the obedient one who fervently prays to the great gods.[102]

By referring to 'the great gods', his inscription implies that there was more than one level of divinity.

Hammurabi's posthumous fame is evident over a wide area for more than a thousand years after his death. His use of script and language extended beyond his political reach. His Code continued to be copied and studied. Copies of the whole text contained deliberate variants; for instance, a version found at Nippur replaced the names Babylon and Marduk with Nippur and its main god Enlil.[103] Great cities other than Babylon felt free to alter the text, just as cities had their own version of the king-list. In later royal inscriptions and literary texts, various lines of the prologue and epilogue were reused, or alluded to; for instance, almost identical curses are found in a treaty of the ninth century.[104] A Sumerian translation of the epilogue has been recognized; and a commentary was written in the late Babylonian period.[105] Those later uses of the text linked subsequent rulers to the prestige and authority of a distant past.

Hammurabi's name was taken by various kings along the Euphrates and all the way to the Mediterranean coast in subsequent centuries – in Halab, Alalakh, Ugarit, and Terqa – and he himself was proudly claimed as a distant ancestor by a king on the Middle Euphrates in the mid-eighth century BC, long after anyone else had taken an Amorite name.[106] Later in the same century the Assyrian king Sargon II proclaimed his own greatness in a way that implied he was the new Hammurabi,[107] and in the sixth century the last indigenous king of Babylon, Nabonidus, who restored, as Hammurabi had done, the temple of the Sun-god in Sippar, took Hammurabi's title 'King of Justice', and referred to the first five laws of Hammurabi's Code in one of his royal inscriptions. In these ways Hammurabi received the homage of his successors.

The cult of Marduk, in addition to having fine buildings in Babylon, gained a reputation as the seat of an oracle, which gave a particular importance to Babylon.[108] His cult branched out into other Babylonian cities. Using the prosperity accumulated from agriculture, conquest, and trade, the early kings of Babylon succeeded in building the city into one of the most prosperous in the world. Hammurabi 'made the four regions live

---

[102] Frayne 1990: 344, no. 10.   [103] Borger 1979: I, 7 (BM 34914).
[104] For details, see Hurowitz 2013: 89–100.   [105] Frahm 2011: 242.   [106] Frame 1995: 295.
[107] Hurowitz 2013.   [108] Charpin 1988: no. 371.

in peace' – a general statement encompassing clients and vassals to north, south, east, and west.

Taking the reins of power before his father died, **Samsu-iluna** made a smooth transition to kingship. Subsequently he came through serious rebellions, retaining Hammurabi's experienced general for at least the next twenty-seven years.[109] Although it has been supposed that the kingdom went into a steep decline that continued for more than a century to the end of the dynasty,[110] this interpretation, referred to here as the 'hypothesis of abandonment and refugees', has been refuted by new evidence, and a very different interpretation is now generally accepted.

Epic narratives proclaim the heroism of the king.[111] In a long, poetic inscription Samsu-iluna claimed that Marduk, authorized by the great gods Anu and Enlil, had chosen him to govern the whole country, entrusting him to keep it in peace and prosperity.[112] Many letters, some written by the king himself, are known; but all are undated and most are badly damaged. One significant change: rather than building temples and installing statues of deities, as Hammurabi and his predecessors had recorded doing in year-names, Samsu-iluna and his successors installed many statues of the king in temples in various cities, as well as furnishings and adornments. The temples themselves had been magnificent in design, and so well built, that some at least are known to have stood for a thousand years.[113] The time had come to concentrate first on statues of the gods with their thrones, and then on appropriate symbols for them, such as golden sun-discs for the Sun-god, lightning bolts for the Storm-god, and statues of the king paying homage in various poses corresponding to his epithets, such as offering a lamb, uttering a prayer, running, as leader of troops, or as king of justice. None of them survive.

Acts of piety and works of irrigation document the new king's energies within Babylonia. With Elam pushed back into its homeland, with Eshnunna and Mari no longer in a position to contend for power, one might suppose that Samsu-iluna could have relaxed in the palace where his famous father had lived. Sippar remained a most important partner of Babylon, just as it had been under Hammurabi. On the Euphrates to the north-west he had taken from Eshnunna's control the fort Harradum, 'the

---

[109] Durand 1988: 365–6; Lambert 2007: 141.
[110] See, initially, Charpin 1986; Stone 1977: 266–89. A similar but less extreme view was given by Gadd 1973: 220–7.
[111] They are written on four bilingual inscriptions. See Frayne 1990: 374–91, nos. 3, 5, 7, 8.
[112] Frayne 1990: 380–3, no. 5.   [113] See, e.g., Blocher 2012.

place where one stands guard', where taxes were collected at the quayside, before traders were given access to the west.[114] Having passed the border there, they continued upstream through the newly established kingdom of Hana, then on to Halab. Trade was conducted as before, but in Anatolia the Hittite kingdom began to dominate an ever wider area, reducing the autonomy of city states, diminishing trade at Kanesh, and eventually taking control of Halab. During his long reign Samsu-iluna promulgated four edicts, each one cancelling the debts of certain groups of people that had accumulated during roughly a decade, long enough for a debtor or a member of his family to work as a slave for his creditor.[115] He began a huge project to cut through mountain rock a channel that would divert water from the Euphrates near modern Ramadi into the Habbaniyah depression that could be filled to produce a lake. A second phase of the work, carried out nearly three decades later, tackled an even steeper cutting to channel water from the far side of that lake into another depression on the west side of the Euphrates, no doubt to control floods that threatened Borsippa and Babylon.

The Great Rebellion, which lasted for about eleven years, began around 1742, coinciding with the formation of the fiercely militaristic Hittite kingdom in Anatolia, and with an uprising of some Kassite troops in the Babylonian homeland. Ur and Larsa led rebels in southern Babylonia in the Sealand, a term that became common as a general reference to the area with its marshy terrain, which was apparently centralized under its own semi-independent kings. Although various parts of the uprising lasted perhaps as long as seven years, its long-term consequences, once thought to be disastrous for southern Babylonia, can now be presented in a different light, and allow a new assessment of the kings who ruled Babylon from then until the end of the First Dynasty. This is described in Chapter 5.

---

[114] Kepinski 2012: 149–50; Magee 2014: 165–6, 176–7.
[115] One fragment is extant; others are inferred from the year-names referring to an edict.

4 | Law, Education, Literature, and the Path to Supremacy

> Babylon, the city that loves stability,
> Babylon, the city of stability and justice,
> Babylon, which hates injustice.[1]

Hammurabi's Code, written towards the end of his reign in 1750, is an exceptionally famous text from ancient Babylonia.[2] It was written on a polished black stone,[3] not found in Babylon as one might have expected, but in excavations at the Elamite royal city of Susa. Elamites looted it from a Babylonian city and took it to Susa – some four tons transported without a breakage – as triumphal booty in the twelfth century BC,[4] and it is now on display in the Louvre in Paris.

The choice of a stone resembling diorite was significant according to lines in the Sumerian myth *Ninurta and the Stones* (*Lugal-e*).[5] Written down around the same time as the Code and widely circulated, it is a story of cosmic action telling how various stones were defeated by the god Ninurta in a terrible battle in the mountains. One by one Ninurta then decreed different fates for each. This is a curious tale for the modern reader, but can be better appreciated when one recalls that the Sumerian language has two classes of noun: animate and inanimate. The animate category includes not only trees and minerals, but also objects such as doors made of timber, mace heads made of stone, and gongs made of copper. After the battle, Ninurta fixed the fate of diorite, saying:

> The ruler who would establish his name for all time,
> Who has fashioned that statue for future days,
> Who will place it in the mortuary chapel in the splendid Eninnu-temple,
> You shall be made suitable for that.

---

[1] George 1997a.   [2] Roth 1995: 71–142.   [3] See Ornan 2019.
[4] It was probably installed originally in Sippar, city of the Sun-god, 'Lord of Justice'. Ornan 2019 has suggested that significant alterations were planned by the Elamites at Susa to 'rebrand' the monument, but were not completed.
[5] Black et al. 2004: 163–80.

In the same myth, basalt is called 'contemptible and valueless' and 'a bad lot in the Land', so unsuitable for royal statues. Whether the Sumerian word currently identified with the English 'basalt' covers the same type of rock is, as ever, uncertain.

At the top of the tall stela, a scene is beautifully sculpted. It shows the king standing in a posture of pious greeting in front of the Sun-god Shamash as if they are meeting in a temple. Both are in profile, according to the Mesopotamian convention that lasted for two thousand years. The god's seat resembles a temple façade of a traditional geometric kind which has frame-like vertical niches throwing a pattern of shadows to relieve the glare of plastered brick walls. The temple represents heaven as the god's home. Rays of light attached to the deity's shoulders identify him as the solar god and remind his worshippers that he sheds light on everything: nothing escapes his gaze, no criminal can avoid justice. The god holds two symbols of law and order: the 'rod and ring', as if to remind the king of his divinely appointed duty to maintain and improve his people's behaviour. They are probably surveying tools: the ring is sometimes shown as a looped rope, perhaps the 'surveyor's shining line' as described in the Sumerian myth *Inanna and Her Gardener Shukaletuda* for laying out straight lines, applicable for walls, canals, roads, and field plots, protecting and recording the boundaries of property, and metaphorically for 'going straight', leading an orderly life.[6] The names for them, 'reed' and 'rope', are also words for standard measures used by quantity surveyors and mathematicians, thus representing the allocation of land for fields. In one account of creation, when the gods created humans, their purpose was decreed: 'To mark out field by field', and to ensure 'that canals be maintained'.[7]

The king, dressed in a simple robe and hat, stands before the god, raising his right hand in homage. He carries no sceptre. Hammurabi's sculptors took as their model the monuments of Ur-Namma, who had founded a new and highly successful dynasty at Ur in 2112 BC and had composed his own law code in Sumerian.[8] The scene was so powerful that it continued to be used for at least a thousand years: in the mid-ninth century BC a fine stone tablet of polished grey schist with neat wavy edges from Sippar shows a similar scene of the king[9] before the Sun-god, installing a great sun-disc in his temple, no doubt in homage to great ancestors.[10] The two similar representations, so far apart in time, demonstrate that the Sippar temple's main statue of the Sun-god looked very similar to the earlier one even after

---

[6] Slanski 2007: 37–69 suggests that the meaning of the symbol changed over time.
[7] Lambert 2013: 356–7: 'A unilingual/bilingual Account of Creation, Old Babylonian period'.
[8] Civil 2011: 221–86.   [9] Woods 2004: 49.   [10] Seidl 2001. See Figure 7.2.

Figure 4.1 The top part of Hammurabi's stela showing him receiving the 'rod and ring' of kingship from the Sun-god of Sippar. Credit: Scheil 1902: pl. 3.

the intervening period; perhaps one of the stelas from Hammurabi's time had survived there and was still to be seen in public.

The text beneath the image is written in an elegant archaic cuneiform script that demonstrates the skill of scribes and engravers, showing their knowledge of sign forms that were already several centuries old. By using that script Hammurabi was linking himself to great rulers of the past, giving the Babylonians a feeling of continuity, stability, and a valuable heritage. The whole text consists of three distinct parts: a prologue proclaiming the king's titles and achievements among the many cities of

Babylonia; the laws themselves; and an epilogue which declares the king's purposes, adding curses on anyone who damages the monument.

Several earlier rulers of other Babylonian cities are known to have had their own codes, but they are mostly fragmentary, and are briefer.[11] Hammurabi's Code superseded them all, and its highly literary prologue and epilogue became central parts of the scribal curriculum for around 1,500 years. Found at the beginning of the twentieth century, the whole monument with its text was published promptly in 1902, stimulating tremendous interest in western Europe and America, not only for the text's own sake but also for its anticipated relationship to biblical Hebrew law and to individual legal documents. Many of the latter had already been found in Babylonia written on clay tablets, and from many different sites of the eighteenth century BC. But it has been surprising to identify almost no overt or implicit use of the laws in those documents,[12] and fresh discoveries bring new, unanswered questions of exactly how they related to legal decisions. Biblical comparisons were immediately drawn, but attempts to prove a close relationship with Mosaic law, as recorded in the Hebrew book of Deuteronomy, have not been convincing, even though cuneiform Akkadian was studied and written in Palestine around the time of Hammurabi. One Deuteronomic law, concerning the goring ox, has a close parallel, not in Hammurabi's laws but in a cuneiform school exercise text in Sumerian, dated around 1800 BC, in which a small collection of laws relating to oxen is written. But the form in which the Babylonian laws are couched, 'If a man … ', is different from that of the Deuteronomic laws. The main form of biblical laws is 'apodeictic', beginning: 'A man who … '; this is the form used in a different kind of legal text in cuneiform, the royal edicts, described in the previous chapter, which were frequently issued and updated by kings of Hammurabi's dynasty, and were explicitly referred to in letters and legal records written on clay tablets.[13] By contrast, there are no such references to the Code in those individual texts. The first lines of the prologue set the scene:

> When the lofty Sky-god (Anum) king of the (primeval) Anunnaki-gods,
> the Enlil (head of the pantheon), lord of heaven and earth,
> who determines the land's destinies, determined for Marduk the first-
> born

---

[11] Roth 1995: 13–70.

[12] Good expositions of how to understand the so-called law code are given by Otto 1994 and Hurowitz 2013. The divergent opinions of Westbrook are explained in Wells and Magdalene 2009: xi–xx.

[13] See Kraus 1984; Veenhof 1997–2000; Charpin 2000.

son of Enki, made him greatest among the (later) Igigi-gods,
gave Babylon its pre-eminent name, made it supreme in the world,
established eternal kingship within it, whose foundation is as solid as heaven
    and earth,
                        At that time
Anum and Enlil spoke my name, me, Hammurabi, pious prince, god-
    fearing,
to make justice apparent in the land, to destroy the bad and the wicked,
that the strong might not harm the weak,
to go out like Shamash to the black-headed people, to light up the land,
    to please people's flesh:
I am Hammurabi, the shepherd named by Enlil, who heaps up prosperity and
    plenty.

One of the words for 'justice', *kittum*, has wider meanings such as truth, stability, and loyalty, for law-giving was considered vital for order and cohesion in society. Omens were formulated in the same way as individual laws: 'If such-and-such an omen is observed, the result is such-and-such', and they implied that the gods would take a decision that was a legally binding contract.[14] Just as crucial as formal laws to ancient Babylonian society was the Sun-god's role in foretelling the future through divination, a process which was understood as an aspect of his judicial role. Thus the divination priest, sacrificing a lamb and examining its liver for particular shapes and markings supposedly 'written' by the gods, expressed his request for a clear result in the language of law-giving:

O Shamash, you opened the locks of heaven's gate,
You ascended the staircase of pure lapis lazuli,
You raise and hold up in your arms a staff of lapis lazuli for the cases you
            judge . . .
On the right of this lamb place a true/reliable verdict, on the left of this
    lamb
Place a true/reliable verdict![15]

In Hammurabi's time, every kingdom had many diviners, independent of palace and temple, who were consulted to find the likely outcome of, for instance, an expedition or an illness, so that preventative measures could be taken, disasters avoided. Each act of divination could be checked against

---

[14] Maul 2018: 33–4.
[15] Starr 1983: 30 and no. 37. The predicted result could be averted by rituals, allowing an element of choice or free will.

different types of divination – oil on water, birds, sprinkling flour – and the results could be discussed by impartial experts. Omens were eventually collected in manuals, for they relayed the words of heaven, and were studied. Since important decisions such as appointments of rulers and priests were made and confirmed by these careful methods, they were seldom challenged by mortals, but accepted as decisions taken by the great gods. The procedures ensured stability.

The three parts of the Code's inscription, prologue, laws, and epilogue, conform to a general pattern found in other types of text written on stone, but as with so many cuneiform compositions, there is much overlap between different types of literature; for instance, the poetic style of the prologue bears quite a strong resemblance to 'praise poems' written in Sumerian for the great kings of Ur, Isin, and Larsa several centuries earlier.[16] In 290 short lines it proclaims the king's right to rule by virtue of his selection by the great gods of heaven and earth, who had promoted Babylon's city god Marduk and the city itself to pre-eminence. Hammurabi, 'the lord adorned with sceptre and crown', then describes the improvements he has made to all the major cities of his kingdom. He declares himself to be 'a god among kings, acquainted with wisdom'. Boasting his conquests within Babylonia, 'a fighter without peer', he makes it clear that wealth, accumulated from successful wars and from extending agricultural land with new irrigation canals, is dedicated to beautifying the great temples and 'providing sumptuous banquets' for the many great gods. In this way his victories are presented as pious deeds that benefitted conquered cities; his successes were ordained by the gods, who transmitted their support through oracles and divination. He admits to putting down revolts, but implies that he has rescued people from anarchy and increased the prosperity of their gods.

Some aspects of Hammurabi's policies towards conquered cities, as declared in the prologue of his Code, are not mere posturing. As we have seen, his conquest of Larsa appears to have left the city and its people relatively unharmed; Hammurabi is 'the warrior king who shows mercy to Larsa'. So other statements may contain elements of truth, such as: the wise king 'shelters the people of Malgium in catastrophe ... founds their settlements in abundance ... makes the four regions obedient'. At Eshnunna, after it was conquered, and later damaged deliberately by a flood, the city remained viable. At Mari, after the initial conquest it appears that the original intention was to tidy up and restore order. By looking

---

[16] For example, see Black et al. 2004: 304–10.

carefully at the wording of Hammurabi's year-names we can see that he subjected, literally 'made to kneel', the conquered peoples. Not until he marched up into the vaguely worded 'mountains of Subartu' in the north did he use a word for slaughter. The conclusion to be drawn from this is that he aimed to accumulate more wealth for Babylon by allowing cities, even those who had shown enmity, to remain viable and productive. By publicizing his achievements together with the laws in writing on such imposing monuments as the law code stela, and by integrating the study of them into the curriculum for apprentice scribes, Hammurabi ensured that his personal claim to fame, and his ability to inspire a sense of loyalty to the kingdom of Babylon, would endure for more than a thousand years.

Since the prologue refers to the king's many conquests, it must have been written in its final form towards the end of the king's long reign, when he had pushed the Elamites out of Mesopotamia, having conquered their puppet kings in Eshnunna and Larsa. The whole text marks Hammurabi's ascent to overall domination, but the three sections were not necessarily all composed at the same time.

Although Hammurabi's Code is commonly referred to as a 'law code', in fact it is a literary collection of laws – between 275 and 300 of them (there is a short gap due to damage) – founded on principles entirely different from those of more recent law codes in western countries. The disconnect between Hammurabi's written laws and individual cases can be explained on the basis that there was no centralized institution from which jurisprudence, establishing legal principles in the abstract, could be disseminated to judges at a local level.[17] Civil law, criminal law, and contract law are not separated in the law code, which was authorized by the gods. Actual contracts were drawn up locally by local men; judges were perhaps locally appointed, and written documents served only as an aid to memory.[18] This explains, for instance, why witnesses listed on a tablet and repeated on the clay envelope in which it was wrapped[19] are not always identical; omissions and additions are frequently found. Each city had its own traditions, maintaining a degree of independence. The various customs of different tribes also had to be taken into account. In some cases, inconsistencies and downright contradictions may acknowledge the traditions of semi-nomadic tribes alongside the different traditions of city dwellers. For instance, two laws, §§ 196 and 197, follow the principle of *lex talionis*, an

---

[17] Wilcke 2007. [18] Wilcke 2007: 76.

[19] Envelopes are very rarely found. Their clay was probably reused for later documents, or to patch a hole in a roof.

eye for an eye, a tooth for a tooth, but three others, §§ 198, 199, and 202, state different kinds of punishment for exactly the same types of injury.

After the first publication of the text, many excerpts or copies of it on clay came to light – at least fifty-seven of them so far – emanating from a range of later periods covering more than a thousand years. Some of them have important variants and omissions, not just trivial mistakes and corruptions. There was no single standard text. This is true for many other kinds of literary text in the Bronze Age; the age of individual, named authors and 'standard' texts had not yet arrived.

To be effective, justice was dependent on several procedures which are mentioned in some of the laws: on people telling the truth under oath, on the assumption that the gods named in the oath would punish perjury; on the use of a river ordeal, 'sink or swim', to prove guilt or innocence, in which the river acted as divine judge; on witnesses agreeing to support a contract; and on producing a written record to uphold a claim. This last was crucial for maintaining business relationships, and is stated most clearly in two laws, §§ 122–3:

> If a man wishes to give silver, gold or anything else to another man for safekeeping, he shall show to witnesses the full amount that he wishes to give, arrange written contracts, and only then commit it to safekeeping. If he gave it for safekeeping to another man without witnesses and contracts, and they have denied it at the place where he made the deposit, that case is not subject to claim.

Many laws offer a view of Babylonian society's social structure consisting of court, temple, free men, slaves, and an intermediate class of dependents known as *muškênum*. This is the best information we have for the lives of the lower classes as well as prosperous people; the lower classes are seldom represented in the results of excavation on citadel mounds. Family relationships were important: contracts were essential for proof of marriage (§ 128), a wife must be careful to protect her reputation for the sake of her husband (§ 132), and adultery, if proven, was punishable by the death of both parties unless the husband wished to spare his wife (§ 129). A man could take a second wife if the first was barren or fell ill (§§ 138, 148), and a wife could take a second husband if her first was absent for so long that she risked penury (§ 135), but more general polygamy is not attested. The giving of dowries and marriage gifts, and their return in cases of particular problems, are carefully described, with special attention paid to protect women from poverty and to secure the rights of children in inheritance. It was normal for the eldest son to inherit a double portion, presumably because, as head of the family, he was responsible for providing twice-monthly offerings to his deceased father and ancestors as well as bride money for his brothers and sons, and dowries for his sisters and daughters. Adoption was common, of babies by childless couples, sometimes of the offspring of temple personnel, who did not keep their own babies; sometimes, as in § 188, of an older child for apprenticeship, or at various ages with a contractual obligation that the child maintain his adopters while they were alive and provide regular funerary offerings after their death. One of the bonds that held families together was the need to placate ancestors for fear of malign influence. 'I shall raise the dead and they shall outnumber the living' was a threat made by the goddess Ishtar in *The Descent of Ishtar*. Various situations in which the arrangements proved unsatisfactory carried punishments such as cutting out the tongue or an eye of a child who rejected its adoptive parents; but such harshness can be balanced by the permission for an adopted child to leave if he became desperate to find his birth parents, or if an apprenticeship was unsatisfactory. Hammurabi set out a general policy:

> So that justice may be ensured for the orphan and the widow in Babylon
> . . . to ensure justice to the oppressed . . . the wronged man who has cause
> should come into the presence of my image as king of justice, and read
> carefully my inscribed stela.

Land tenure was a major preoccupation and laws show that the palace 'gave' land to a man who could pass it on to his sons; but if he neglected it or had no offspring, it reverted to the king. Such a system was crucial to ensure that the networks of canals were kept in working order and taxes collected. Tax was assessed according to the area of land and the previous year's harvest. The edicts described in the previous chapter, entirely separate from the Code, show that a creditor could buy land from his debtor, but that this was not, as once thought, a freehold sale, for the debtor had the right to regain his property when his fortunes improved, sometimes as a result of working for the creditor. Attempts to prove that such transactions were freehold have been undermined by the discovery that a phrase on a title deed (of a later period), translated as 'forever', may mean 'for no fixed term', so land could revert to the king if an official who had been rewarded with an estate fell out of favour or died.[20] Some contracts establishing the subdivision of houses, at first thought to indicate oppressive debt, have since been found to represent binding agreements between members of a

---

[20] See Paulus 2014: 175–9 and her note on pp. 578–9.

single family according to their changing needs, to avoid squabbles within the family. Interpretations depend on establishing the relationships of the participants named on the record, which is often impossible.

The protection of property and merchants' contracts is notable in the Code, whether in the context of loans, safekeeping and storage contracts, inheritance, or neglect of obligations on agricultural land. Punishments vary according to status, with three clear divisions – a free man, a dependent 'serf', and a slave – as well as certain categories of women attached to temples according to their status. Injuries caused by brawling and domestic violence, treatment of slaves, the punishment of careless builders, boat hire and responsibility for damage to property, the hiring of oxen for ploughing, negligence or fraud on the part of shepherds – all these areas were the subject of written laws.

An important part of ensuring stability and social order was to record legal entitlement to land. One of many aspects of scribal training involved the arithmetic and basic geometry needed for calculating areas and the tax due on them.[21] Another involved the conversion of weights and measures from one system to another.

The epilogue of the Code consists of 331 short lines. Some of the general principles are stated for the laws, as they represent the ruler's obligations to the gods as shepherd of his peoples, to protect the weak from the strong, to care for the widow and the orphan, just as a shepherd cares for his flock. The king exhorts future men to remain faithful to the laws inscribed on the stela, and so to guide the people wisely on the path to which the Sun-god had directed Hammurabi, so that future kings' rule may be as successful and long-lasting as that of Hammurabi. This implies that his reign was coming to an end, anticipating the king's death. A long sequence of imaginative curses on whoever might damage the stela concludes:

> May Enlil the Lord who determines destinies, whose commands cannot be altered, who made my kingdom great, incite revolts against him in his abode which cannot be suppressed, misfortune leading to his ruin! May He fix for his destiny a reign of misery, days few in number, years of famine, darkness without light, sudden death! May He command by His powerful word the destruction of his city, the dispersal of his people, the transfer of his kingdom, the vanishing of his name and memory from the land!

The curses invoke each of the great gods in turn, calling on them to punish anyone who violates the stela and the laws written there. A similar list of

[21] Høyrup 1990.

curses was often inscribed on memorial stelas erected by a king's successor, probably with input from an aged ruler anxious to secure his legacy. Therefore it is possible that Hammurabi's son and successor Samsu-iluna was responsible for a part of the inscription to promote the fame of his dying father.[22]

What kind of education inspired the composition of such a magnificent text? Many school texts have survived from around the time of Hammurabi, allowing a penetrating view into the curriculum, showing how scribes were trained through many years and stages of intense instruction. The tradition continued through subsequent dynasties and was used far beyond Babylonia.[23]

Teachers had very small classes, often including young members of their own family, and held instruction in their own homes, usually located close to temples and palaces. They were specialists of high prestige, often with Sumerian personal names that reflected a veneration for the past and their attachment to an old language seldom spoken but often written. They regarded knowledge of the past as essential for understanding or representing the present. Patronage came from the king, from temples (especially for hymns and rituals), from merchants, and from wealthy people who required written legal documents. Pupils were mostly male, but female scribes were also trained. Much later, an appreciative description of the Babylonian system was given by Diodorus Siculus, who wrote in the mid-first century BC when early Arsacid kings ruled Babylon, a time when scribes were still trained in cuneiform Babylonian:

> The scientific study of these subjects is passed down in the family, and son takes it over from father, being relieved of all other services in the state. Since, therefore, they have their parents for teachers, they not only are taught everything ungrudgingly but also at the same time they give heed to the precepts of their teachers with a more unwavering trust. Furthermore, since they are bred in these teachings from childhood up, they attain a great skill in them, both because of the ease with which youth is taught and because of the great amount of time which is devoted to this study.[24]

The curriculum was vast, and was revised according to the need for change and modernization. First, trainee scribes had to learn to write cuneiform signs accurately and neatly, not only the forms current at the time, but also forms from long ago so that they would be able to read and copy old inscriptions. There were lists compiled for the purpose. Similar

[22] Lewis 1980: 93.   [23] See, e.g., van Soldt 2011.
[24] Diod. Sic. II.29.3–4, mainly referring to divination of different kinds. Trans. Oldfather.

lists were used to familiarize trainees with the different ways in which each sign could be read. Unlike the system for alphabetic writing, in which a couple of dozen linear letters each have a single reading (though with a few significant exceptions and combinations – compare *t + h* in English), cuneiform signs had almost inexhaustible possibilities, allowing some very clever, esoteric manipulation which began to develop among scholars. When the Kassites ruled in Babylon, they updated vocabulary lists, and showed extreme prowess by writing inscriptions with very rare sign values, emphasizing the role of divinely inspired sages who had lived before the Flood. In order to extend the scribe's vocabulary and enable him to translate and to produce bilingual texts in Sumerian and Babylonian, there were synonym lists and bilingual lists of various kinds that included nouns and verbs, and specialist lists of the technical phrases needed for drawing up legal documents. To provide records for palace administration, trainees had to learn how to write, for instance, lists of kitchen supplies and records of work done in jewellery and textiles. Popular personal names could be written in various ways, which a scribe had to master (compare Jane and Jayne, Elisabeth, Elizabeth, and Liza in recent times). So there were lists of personal names, lists of kings; lists of all kinds formed the basis of scholarship. Even the study of astronomy began with lists of stars and lists of observations taken from the night sky. To survey fields accurately and make tables of acreage from which taxation would be calculated, there were exercise texts giving a problem to be solved, requiring the under-standing of arithmetic and geometry. Model contracts were composed for teaching, and templates were practised in the composition of fictional letters from famous kings and courtiers, sometimes mistaken by modern scholars for genuine correspondence. Wisdom literature, which included Hammurabi's code, fables, proverbs, and dialogues, helped to instil a sense of ethics.[25]

Every city ruler kept musicians at court, trained from an early age not just in the mastery of an instrument, but also in music theory, which was written in cuneiform as part of the study of lexical texts. Those texts included technical words for the strings of seven-stringed harps and lyres of different sizes, and how to retune them for different modes. The man in charge of music had such high status that he could accompany the queen and represent the king as his envoy abroad; and he took charge of ensembles of female musicians, *šitrum*. Some of them were captives from foreign courts where different types of music – Amorite or Hurrian – were enjoyed.

---

[25] Cohen 2018.

Dancers and acrobats were involved in performances, but how words were sung or recited with music is not known.[26]

Copying and writing from dictation were regular means of making sure that pupils engaged fully with the material. Extensive manuals for various kinds of divination; extracts from famous literary texts, chronicles, astronomical observations – all these types of instruction had to be mastered by the best pupils to qualify them to become the expert authors striving to make and adapt the best compositions for the king and the gods. Omen manuals had a considerable influence on other types of literature, which were studied alongside them. Sumerian and Babylonian literary texts and royal letters written on clay may all be school exercises; if so, no official, complete versions have been recognized, raising the possibility that they were written on organic writing-boards and have not survived.[27] So it is sometimes impossible to decide whether a royal letter is genuine, or a rhetorical fiction with a pseudo-historical background.

Trainees were allowed to compose and practise humorous texts that mocked officials and asked awkward questions. Was piety to the gods a sure road to success compared with keeping the favour of the king? Could a poor, downtrodden man outwit a powerful official with impunity? A court jester could ridicule the court. In these ways the composition of texts was free enough to act as a safety valve for tensions, and might alert the king and his counsellors to dissent. Alongside this form of flexibility was another: alternative explanations were acceptable for how the world was created and what role was played by the gods – there was no need to argue for any one theory in preference to another. Poetic analogy, metaphors, and similes gave a wide scope for different descriptions.

Each city might have its own version of great texts, so flexibility ran alongside a great respect for tradition. The most obvious example is the *Sumerian King-List*, by which particular cities promoted their own idea of the past before the rise of Babylon. Kingship, according to that tradition, descended from heaven to each great city in turn, in contrast to the later tradition of Babylonian king-lists which promoted succession through a family line, but nevertheless claimed that the kings were chosen by the gods, with wording that refers to careful acts of divination. Thus Hammurabi referred to himself as chosen:

> Anu and Enlil named me to promote the welfare of the people ... the descendant of Sumu-la-El, the powerful son and heir of Sin-muballiṭ, the ancient seed of royalty.

[26] See especially Ziegler 2007.   [27] Michalowski 2011: 47; Llop and George 2001–2.

In the case of legends about Gilgamesh, too, details were flexible. In one version the archetypal king and hero who built the walls of Uruk was imitated by Hammurabi's near-contemporary Anam, 'who restored the rampart of Uruk, the ancient work of Gilgamesh'. That did not exclude the hero Gilgamesh acting as king of Ur in a version known later: the two traditions could exist side by side. Some of the writings that refer to past events cannot be understood as attempts to record the past accurately even though they were written at royal instigation. The past was manipulated by the king and his counsellors for specific purposes: to learn lessons from the past in the face of present needs, and to formulate a heroic history that would inspire people for the future.

In certain cases the king's exploits required a change in a traditional legend that would echo his achievements or his fate. In stories about Gilgamesh, the change of location from the Zagros Mountains to the Amanus range in the Lebanon reflects a new focus for expeditions around 2000 BC; the death of Sargon II is alluded to in Tablet XII of the *Epic of Gilgamesh* as known in a version of the eighth century. In the episode of the Deluge, the place where the boat went aground as the waters receded varied according to the interests of a particular patron and his audience. In this way there was no single author, no single version for such texts. Early texts did not have acknowledged human authors, but were attributed to legendary sages (*apkallu*) who were only partly human and had some divine attributes.

During their long period of rule, the early kings of Babylon made the first moves to put Babylon at the centre of Mesopotamian culture. Hammurabi's Code outstripped all earlier codes, and was incorporated into a fairly standard educational curriculum; new king-lists updated or replaced the *Sumerian King-List*; quite extensive literary compositions were linked to recent events and were written in a language and script close to that of daily correspondence; and Marduk began his ascent from the level of a parochial god to the pinnacle of power as king of the gods, equal to Enlil the great god of Nippur.

Warfare in the time of Hammurabi can be described from the Code, from historical records, and from official correspondence. A social category of men was bound by feudal obligations known as *ilku*. Their tasks included not only maintaining canals, in return for working a plot of land, but also fighting on behalf of the ruler, perhaps with armour (shields and helmets) and basic weapons (lances, axes, nets) provided by the local landowner. At this time, before horses were bred for warfare and to draw chariots designed for the battlefield, fighting was carried out mainly by foot soldiers with equipment derived from hunting and working the land. Militias of foreigners guarded forts. Raiding and capturing prisoners for ransom, or to increase the local workforce, were common. Elite troops were augmented by soldiers contributed by allies, who might defend cities in danger of capture. Groups of fighting men, whether elite troops or semi-nomads variously equipped, were numbered in their thousands and tens of thousands. A law in the Code specifies the death penalty for an officer who exploits his superior status, or a man who attempts to avoid service by supplying a substitute; other laws protect the family of a soldier who does not return from a military campaign. Several of the laws make it clear that a primary aim was to keep land under cultivation and to protect its ownership.

One strategy involved diverting canals and branches of rivers to create floods that would cause havoc for the enemy, especially in southern Babylonia, so river boats and their crews took part in many campaigns; one type of soldier was the fisherman, and captured enemies are sometimes depicted enclosed in nets.

Diviners travelled in groups with armies, and took frequent omens to determine which courses of action were likely to be successful, taking omens not only from the liver and other organs of sheep but also by dropping oil on water or sprinkling flour, or observing the flight of birds. Thus each omen could be checked swiftly, and a confirmed result could be relied upon, which was good for morale when going into battle or predicting recovery from illness. Although diviners reported directly to the king, they were not specifically employed by the palace or the temple. Written versions of important examples were collected, studied, and preserved for centuries.[28] Hammurabi, planning to attack the city of Kazallu, consulted:

> Shamash lord of judgement, Adad lord of the inspection, concerning the soldiers of the palace, the soldiers of the palace gate, the chariot[29] soldiers, the foot soldiers, the elite soldiers, the desert soldiers, ... soldiers that Marduk rules, as many as Hammurabi king of Babylon summons, organizes, and leads off: should he select and choose ... infantry? Should Adanšu-likšud son of Sin-nahrari, who supervises the infantry, take control? ... should he take the eastern route along the bank of the Tigris and go to Kasalluhhu? Will they then, on the border of his land, by speaking disinformation(?), by every kind of skilled tactic, and by all available kinds

---

[28] Jeyes 1989: 4–6, 20; Maul 2018: e.g. 103.

[29] Chariots, perhaps wagons drawn by donkey-onager hybrids at this time, may have played a largely ceremonial role.

of battle equipment, take that city of Kasalluhhu? Will they then return
safely with a share of abundant profit and spoils of that city?[30]

This oracle question became famous, copied into an anthology in the
Seleucid period, a millennium and a half later, helping to perpetuate a
victory won by Hammurabi but showing his careful reliance on the support
of the gods, obtained through divination.[31] The gods 'wrote' their decision
on the liver, and the movement of celestial bodies at night was involved in
the process.

   Such heroic victories as Hammurabi won over so many powerful
enemies required triumphal ceremonies for which one may assume an
appropriate epic song was composed. Such compositions are known for a
few other kings, though not for Hammurabi himself. The educational
process by which vivid narratives could be created has been pieced together
from a variety of school texts. From the archives excavated at Mari we know
that a celebratory poem with some resemblances to later epic was composed for Hammurabi's contemporary Zimri-Lim,[32] in which the king is
associated with the Storm-god in defeating the forces of Chaos. Several
types of royal inscription contain epic-style passages glorifying a god or
king as a successful leader in a battle against evil enemies, and they are
thought to come from victory songs composed for public celebrations of
triumph.[33]

   A text of this epic type is the *Myth of Labbu*, which sets the action
entirely in a heavenly sphere where the gods themselves wage war. It
features Tishpak the patron god of Eshnunna as the conquering hero,
and probably alludes to Hammurabi's victory over Eshnunna in his thirtieth year. The victory of Babylon's god over that of Eshnunna was marked in
Babylon when Hammurabi adopted for his own city god Marduk the
emblem of Tishpak: the raging, red snaky lion-dragon *mušhuššu*, who
formed the snake throne on which Tishpak sat. The snake-god, shown on
early cylinder seals from Eshnunna, is linked to Elamite depictions of gods
on snake thrones.[34] In the prologue to his laws Hammurabi called himself

> the pious prince who brightens the countenance of Tishpak,
> who provides pure banquets for Ninazu,[35]

[30] Lambert 2007: 24–5; my translation. It is uncertain why Kasalluhhu is the form of the city name;
     the word is close to that of the profession 'courtyard sweeper'.
[31] See Lambert 2007: 141.   [32] Guichard 2014a; see also Wasserman 2015.   [33] Villard 2008.
[34] Snake thrones are depicted on seals from Susa and on rock sculptures in south-west Iran. For
     snake thrones in Elam, see Potts 2016: 169–75 and 182.
[35] Ninazu was also a god of Eshnunna who sat on a snake throne.

who sustains his people in difficulties, who establishes a base for them in peace in the middle of Babylon.[36]

In other words, he set up a cult in Babylon to the defeated gods of Eshnunna and gave asylum to refugees, so the cult was extended to reflect the king's victory over the ruler of Eshnunna and his Elamite overlords. Thus Marduk, as the patron god of Babylon, took divine support away from Eshnunna, which had been a major base for Elamite expansion, by appropriating the symbol of its god. From then onwards the *mušhuššu*-lion-dragon remained firmly under Marduk's control; from a much later text we know that Marduk's sacred bed was adorned with a lion-dragon, where it was best placed to protect him while he rested: the defeated god became a servant to the victorious god. The creature was to remain Marduk's associate into the latest period of Babylon's history, continuing to commemorate the conquest of Eshnunna, and by extension the Elamites, as a most significant victory in Babylon's long history.

Tishpak's combat with a dragon is a story that can be traced back across several centuries, so his city Eshnunna represented not only the contemporary power of Elam as an invader, but also the fame of the great Sargonic kings who had ruled from nearby Agade.[37] The *mušhuššu*-dragon was incorporated into the *Epic of Creation* as one of the conquered host of Chaos.[38] The ruler of Eshnunna had promulgated a law code written in Babylonian only twenty years or so before Hammurabi, having defeated the city, and upstaged it by writing his own law code, which was a fuller and more literary composition.[39] Hammurabi's text supplanted the king of Eshnunna's text, showing that he was now in control of law and order, just as Marduk supplanted Tishpak.

Another text with a god as hero is *Girra and Elamatum*, which was perhaps composed to celebrate Hammurabi's triumph over Elam. It tells how the fire-god Girra rescued the land from the wicked 'Elamite woman/ goddess', setting the action in the sky, where the gods themselves wage war. Elamatum became a constellation, the Bow Star. The composition was linked to a festival as a regular event in the cultic calendar, and the name of the fire-god Girra became an epithet for Marduk as 'the powerful one'.[40] Thus the patron god of Babylon as a fire-god was the hero who defeated the city's most powerful enemy, Elam.

---

[36] Lewis 1996; Ornan 2005: 49.

[37] Many different attempts to locate Agade have not yielded consensus.

[38] Lewis 1996; Cooley 2013: 120–4. The *mušhuššu*-lion-dragon later became the horned dragon.

[39] Roth 1995: 57–70.   [40] Girra is found in year-names of Hammurabi's successors.

Although Hammurabi's Code describes the king as a fighter who pro-
tects the cities and temples of Babylonia from wicked enemies, it also
emphasizes his role as shepherd, merciful protector of vanquished people,
the king who restores stability to conquered cities, enhances their prosperity and pacifies warrior deities. The time of the heroic soldier, the elite
charioteer, and the aristocratic glory of battle, had not yet arrived. The
Poem of Aguŝaya, expressly written in Hammurabi's reign, may intend to
convey the message that warfare is not heroic; as a recent interpreter has
expressed it, 'wisdom shows that valour carried to excess is brutal, indiscriminate and stupid. True bravery knows restraint and dignity as well'.[41]
The poem relates how the aggressive goddess Ishtar – warfare was a game
for her as she whipped warriors into a frenzy in the mêlée of battle – was
brought under control by Ea god of wisdom. Appealing to her vanity, he
showed her an image of her hideous counterpart, Battle, formed out of dirt
from his fingernails mixed with spittle. The composition is linked to a
festival that involved dancing of a whirling kind.

Some of these works, with no named authors, date to Hammurabi's
reign. A much later text names the 'sage' of Hammurabi,[42] possibly referring to an author of parts of the Code; five centuries later, another sage
claimed descent from him. Sages in general, part divine, were claimed to be
the authors of great works, to explain the origin of early literature. Only a
few famous rulers had a sage, so Hammurabi stood in the company of the
greatest kings both before and after his own time.[43] To have an acknowledged sage at court was to promote an image of an intellectual ruler whose
brilliance was recognized long afterwards. Only towards the end of the
second millennium did authorship begin to be attributed to named mortals, and even then their role may have been to reshape earlier material for
new purposes.

As we have seen, the early kings of Hammurabi's dynasty selected
Marduk as the patron god of Babylon, built his temple Esagila and his
holy mountain E-temen-anki in the middle of the city, and created a
gorgeous throne on which a statue of the god sat. Marduk's prestige was
enhanced in other ways, too: by taking on the names and powers of other
gods, by setting up 'branch temples' or shrines in other cities, and by
building a reputation as giver of oracles. The stages by which he achieved
supremacy are relevant for dating the 'standard' text of the *Epic of Creation*,
which elevates Marduk to the head of the pantheon and to a primeval role

---

[41] Foster 2005: 97.
[42] Asalluhi-mansum, whose Sumerian name means 'the god Asalluhi has granted'.
[43] Finkel 1988.

as lord of creation – a far cry from his origins as a lowly god of the hoe and a doorkeeper. The idea of a particular date for the written composition is disputed, and presupposes a single author, but questions of authorship are important because the 'standard' *Epic of Creation* describes not only the rise of Marduk, but also the rise of Babylon to become the world centre for religion, the first city in creation, built to house all the deities of Mesopotamia.[44] Marduk addresses his words to the gods his fathers, telling them that he has built a dwelling for himself over the Apsu – the underground waters that he had defeated:

> Whenever you come up from the Apsu for an assembly,
> Your night's resting place shall be in it, receiving you all.
> Whenever you come down from the sky for an assembly,
> Your night's resting place shall be in it, receiving you all.
> I hereby name it Babylon, home of the great gods.
> We shall make it the centre of religion.[45]

Can this elevation be attributed to the First Dynasty of Babylon, or later? Was it a gradual process, or a single move?

The Babylonian *Epic of Creation* has been called the sacred text of ancient Mesopotamia. It was recited at the great rituals of the New Year Festival in Babylon at the spring equinox, developing and revising a collective memory of a mythological past, replacing the *Sumerian King-List* by describing how Babylon was the first city ever built by the gods on earth, rather than older versions which named Kish or Kuʾara or Eridu as the first. One of Babylon's quarters was named 'Eridu', another 'Kuʾara', to assimilate an older tradition, in order to represent Babylon as the first city to receive kingship.

As the *Epic of Creation* developed to take a central role in Babylon's ceremonies and its educational curriculum, it tapped into a rich reserve of earlier art in which composite creatures were depicted: the scorpion-man, the lion-dragon, and the fish-man became popular on cylinder seals and other carvings. Some of them were identified with constellations. The arch-enemy was Tiamat ('Sea'), mother of the gods; but she also personified Chaos. Marduk defeated her in a cosmic battle, split her into two equal halves to form heaven and earth as mirror images, built Babylon, and organized the heavenly bodies. Following his victory over Chaos, Marduk received the insignia of kingship by agreement of all the

---

[44] Abusch 2019 has shown that sections of the text dealing with the construction of Babylon city and related themes are secondary additions, but not datable.

[45] This extract comes from the much later-known written version of the *Epic of Creation*, Tablet V.

great gods.[46] Then he invited all the gods to come to Babylon, saying, 'Indeed, Babylon is your home too!'[47]

Marduk does not feature in any early Sumerian or Akkadian myths. He became a god of water supply, canals, and irrigation agriculture, symbolized by the hoe that later represented him as his symbol on cylinder seals and monuments. He was the canal-controller of heaven and earth,

> the one who directs rivers in the midst of mountains,
> The one who opens springs in mountainous regions,
> The one who pours out the spate of plenty for all dwellings,
> ... who sends dew down from the udders of the sky.[48]

Surprisingly, none of the First Dynasty kings took the name Marduk into their royal name.[49] Marduk's rise up the hierarchy of gods had begun when he took on the name of a god whose qualities were very different from his own, in order to extend his own rather limited sphere. At a time still unknown he began to take on the name and powers of Asalluhi, 'the exorcist of the great gods', a southern Sumerian god of magic and incantations with healing powers, a god fathered by the great creator-god Ea, through whom Marduk-Asalluhi was linked to Eridu, the first city in which kingship began according to a Sumerian tradition. Power resided in the name.

A myth known as *The Founding of Eridu*[50] claimed that Babylon and Eridu were essentially the same city, which allowed Babylon the key role as first city:

> No city had yet been built, no living creature had been placed there.
> Nippur had not been made, Ekur had not been built,
> Uruk had not been made, Eanna had not been built, ...
> All the lands were sea ...

---

[46] The *Epic* allows Anu the title 'king of the gods', as well as proclaiming that the Bowstar (Ishtar) is the highest of all the gods, perhaps implying that Anu and Enlil belonged to an older generation and could retain their titles. A flexible understanding is explained by two lines in the *Epic of Creation*: 'Even though the black-headed people have separate gods, / As for us, whatever name we call him by, let him be our god!' Thus the individual character of cults in each city was recognized, without prejudicing the tendency to assimilate great gods with Marduk in Babylon. Other cities could give their top god the title 'king of the gods', as we know happened with the Sun-god, the Moon-god, and others.

[47] Tablet VI 72.   [48] Oshima 2011: 240–1.

[49] A letter-prayer naming Marduk as 'divine king of Babylon' may date to late in the reign of Hammurabi, rather than its ostensible setting in the reign of an earlier king in Larsa. See Brisch 2007: 75–81. A literal view is taken by Oshima 2011: 45.

[50] See Lambert 2013: 367–8, for extant sources Neo-Assyrian and Late Babylonian, but probably composed much earlier. See also Streck and Wasserman 2008.

> At that time Eridu was built, Esagila was created,
> Esagila, which the King of the Holy Mound, Lugal-Dukuga (Marduk)
>   erected in the midst of the Apsu:
> Babylon was built, Esagila was perfected.

Other assimilations gradually raised Marduk's status until eventually he became Bēl ('Lord'), and accumulated the powers of all the other great gods. One of the texts known as *Hymn to Marduk*, written around the time of Hammurabi's successor, shows how the assimilation was expressed:

> King of all the Igigi (later gods), lord of mountains,
> Magnificent among the Anunnaki (primeval gods): of Marduk I sing! ...
> In the pure Apsu (fresh water underground) his name is Asalluhi, in
>   the sky
>   Anu-sky-god is his name.[51]

In the 'standard' composition of the *Epic of Creation*, Marduk the young hero-god defeats the watery forces of Chaos, which the older gods cannot face, and is proclaimed ruler of the gods, followed by a long list of divine names by which he can also be known. One of those names is Asalluhi, another is Tutu, 'lord of the scribal arts', the powerful god of purification and renewal, and the patron god of Borsippa, where Hammurabi built a shrine to Marduk.[52] As son of Ilurugu, god of the river ordeal of 'sink or swim', Marduk associated himself with the execution of justice.

The 'standard' version of the *Epic of Creation* is not known to have been written on clay until the thirteenth century. It was found in Assyria, not Babylonia, after the Assyrian king Tukulti-Ninurta I, having conquered Babylon, took tablets and writing-boards back to Assyria and had copies made from them.[53] The myth was presumably adapted from older epic literature and moulded to a new purpose. This can be seen from the *Epic of Anzu*, an early tale of a cosmic battle which shares its basic theme with the *Epic of Creation*. The hero-god Ninurta is proclaimed ruler of all 'because you made all foes kneel at the feet of Enlil your father' and he is proclaimed to be shepherd of all peoples; two other names are significant: 'In Elam they give your name as Hurabtil, they speak of you as Shushinak in Susa'. This extract implies that a victory over Elam, a specific event, inspired a version

---

[51] Al-Rawi 1992, probably written in the time of Hammurabi's successor Samsu-iluna.

[52] Eventually the youthful god Nabu, son of Marduk, took over the role of Tutu both as lord of the scribal arts and patron god of Borsippa, a city that came to be known as 'a second Babylon'. Frayne 1990: 354–5; Barberon 2012: 84–5.

[53] Lambert 2013: 3 quotes Köcher's opinion for the ninth century; Farber 2014: 16 thinks most are from the loot of Tukulti-Ninurta I in the late thirteenth century.

of the story, and shows that the defeated gods became servants of the victor whose father had been a great god. Two tablets with the story have been found at Susa, copies of Anzu texts probably dating from the First Dynasty of Babylon.[54]

Options for dating the 'standard' *Epic of Creation* are based largely on inconclusive inferences; already before the reign of Hammurabi, the cult of Marduk had been established at Kish, with a throne dedicated to him.[55] For instance, some of the epic's archaic features of literary style are found in hymns written before the end of the Old Babylonian dynasty. A characteristic of the text is its unusual vocabulary and grammar, giving an impression of an artificial, highly literary use of language, the so-called 'hymnic-epic dialect'.[56]

Kings used the hallmarks of much earlier times to anchor their power in the authority of tradition, so certain texts were perhaps written much later than their content suggests, devised to resemble early compositions. This is true of the fictitious royal letters such as the Weidner 'Chronicle', supposedly written by one nineteenth-century king to another. It gives a backdated pseudo-prediction for the reign of Sumu-la-El, one of Babylon's founder kings who had made a throne for Marduk. Recalling the deeds of even earlier legendary and historical kings, the chronicle claims that Marduk 'king of the gods' and his temple Esagila had been controlling events since the beginning of history, and would continue to do so in the future.[57]

In the heroic battle described in the 'standard' *Epic of Creation*, Amorite (West Semitic) elements have been detected, as well as signs of inspiration from Babylonian and Sumerian myths featuring the hero-god Ninurta. It is certain, therefore, that the composers of the 'standard' version of the epic made use of existing material that came from other Mesopotamian cities, and it is possible that it was written or adapted to celebrate a major victory for Babylon.[58] Oral versions are likely, among them a story of the Storm-god Addu of Halab battling the Sea, written by the chief of musicians at Mari explicitly for the king's accession, in the time of Hammurabi, but known only from a brief

---

[54] See Annus 2001: xxxviii. Other literary texts from Susa come from the latter part of this period, so the events of Abi-ešuh's reign may be preferred to those of Hammurabi.

[55] Or nearby Elip; see Rutten 1960: 25–6, no. 30:14; also Kupper 1959: D 11 line 6.

[56] Lambert 2013: 34–44.

[57] The chronicle may date from the reign of Xerxes. See Glassner 2004: 263–9 no. 38; also Schaudig 2009.

[58] See Kämmerer and Metzler 2012: 13–21. Perhaps Halab's forces played a major role in the victory over Elam, see Jean 1950: nos. 21, 71, 76.

reference in a letter.[59] Samsu-iluna celebrated an *akītu*-festival for Addu (the West Semitic form of the Storm-god's name) in Babylon. In the standard epic, Marduk took the West Semitic name Addu, one of his 'fifty names'. More than a thousand years later, Nebuchadnezzar II took a fine stela representing the Storm-god of Halab to display in Babylon, as if to remind the Babylonians of their debt to a great city in the west.[60]

A battle against the Sea could suggest a Levantine origin, but both Halab and Babylon are inland cities. To the Babylonians, however, marshland was 'sea' no matter where it was located: 'Sealand' could be found to the west of the Euphrates on the same latitude as Babylon, or in the vicinity of Nippur, or around the city of Larsa. Marshland represented disorder, a failure of canal and drainage systems, the obliteration of boundaries. So the concept of water as Chaos would have been meaningful to Babylonians.

A hymn from Samsu-iluna's reign assigns to Marduk the role of hero as a Storm-god controlling the winds, clutching the sacred rites in his right hand, in words that may prefigure the standard *Epic of Creation*:

> Who makes the seven winds intermingle in tempests, . . .
> Blazing one who overthrows . . .
> Dominating, powerful god, master of battle, . . .
> Every one of the sacred rites he holds in his right hand![61]

Marduk is highly exalted in a hymn of Abi-ešuh, Samsu-iluna's son:[62]

> Leader of the Igigi, strong one of the Anunnaki,
> Anu, your grandfather, king of the gods,
> Has imposed your lordship on the hosts (?) of heaven and Underworld,
> Has given you the control over the great exalted decrees of heaven and
>   Underworld,
> The sceptre of the land . . . he has put in your hand.
> He has exalted you among the great gods,
> He has added to you control of the royal sceptre and regulation of the
>   gods.
> Enlil has decreed as your destiny kingship of the whole of heaven and
>   Underworld,
> Allowing you no rival.

---

[59] Durand 1993: 41–61.
[60] Hawkins 2000: vol. 1, ch. VIII: BABYLON 1; and vol. 3 pl. 209. See Figure 8.3.
[61] Oshima 2011: 191–7.
[62] His reputation as an intellectual king is guaranteed by a reference to him having two sages. See Chapter 5, n. 75 below.

These two poems strengthen the argument that forerunners of the 'standard' *Epic of Creation* existed during the First Dynasty of Babylon. The process of revision, both in oral versions and in the written text, may have been frequent, since pressures to use it in support of political and religious changes would have overcome tendencies towards fossilization.[63]

Before the written text of the epic is known, certain events may have caused changes to forerunners, through which one can trace the elevation of Marduk to supreme status. In the sixteenth/fifteenth century the Kassite king Agum-kakrime described new doors for Marduk's temple with decoration that seems to refer to an early version of the *Epic of Creation*; details are given in Chapter 6. Another event to consider is one that inspired Kurigalzu I in the fourteenth century to describe Babylon as the primordial city, *āl ṣāti*, as if it had been one of the earliest, to be compared with, or to replace, Eridu, Ku'ara, and Kish, which are all named as the first city in particular versions of the *Sumerian King-List*. Nebuchadnezzar I in the twelfth century is favoured as author of the 'standard' text because he brought back to Babylon a statue of Marduk from captivity in Elam, and had a fine epic composed to narrate his victory over Elam,[64] but there are no allusions in any of his inscriptions to suggest a connection with the 'standard' version of the *Epic of Creation*.[65] A candidate for authorship or revision in the eleventh century is Simbar-šipak, in whose reign a fuller assimilation of Marduk with Enlil of Nippur was proclaimed.[66] In the seventh century the Assyrian king Sennacherib certainly produced a revised edition of part of the epic, with Aššur replacing Marduk as hero, after he had looted a statue of Marduk from Babylon in 689 BC; this version may have been partial and short-lived.[67] In the third century a version of the *Sumerian King-List* was known to Berossus that put Babylon as the first city ever created.

The city of Nippur, lying on a branch of the Euphrates about 85 km south-east of Babylon, never claimed kingship.[68] No palace was built there,

---

[63]	It is misleading, therefore, to use the term 'standard' for the composition at any stage. See Frahm 2010.

[64]	It was once thought that Marduk did not take the top titles until this reign, but those titles are now known to have been used for Marduk at earlier dates. See Kämmerer and Metzler 2012: 16–21.

[65]	Streck and Wasserman 2008.

[66]	See Hurowitz 1997. For Ninurta equated with seven other great gods, see Streck, 1998–2001: §12.

[67]	Grayson and Novotny 2014: nos. 160–1.

[68]	Tenney 2016. Lambert 2013: 458 and 465 thought that the *Epic of Creation* was composed as a deliberate insult to Enlil and Nippur, perhaps to suppress deviant myths, a view that perhaps underestimates the acceptable plurality of Mesopotamian traditions.

no kings of Nippur were listed on clay. But the city had enormous prestige as a centre for Sumerian and Babylonian cuneiform literacy in the time of Hammurabi, and for the worship of Enlil, the head of the Sumerian pantheon, and his son the mighty warrior-god Ninurta. Enlil's temple at Nippur was the place where heaven and earth were linked, and where the gods assembled to take decisions, in the Court of Assembly (*ubšukkinakki*) where thrones for the seven great gods who determine fate were placed on the Dais of Destinies. Therefore it was of prime importance for Marduk to assimilate to Enlil, and to show respect for Nippur by linking Babylon to it. Ninurta, like Tishpak of Eshnunna, had defeated the *mušhuššu*-dragon in the cosmic battle that resulted in control of Chaos, and he put the fabulous creature to work as his servant, the fierce protector of his conqueror.[69] Marduk's appropriation of the *mušhuššu*-dragon thus had a very early and prestigious antecedent in Nippur.

Aspiring to assimilate to Enlil, Marduk took the titles 'Enlil of the gods' and 'king of heaven and earth', and the city of Babylon took on the epithets 'the creation of Enlil' and 'the bond of the heavens'. Babylon also created its own assembly place of the gods, and incorporated an *ubšukkinakki*-chamber into the building of Babylon, representing one of Nippur's most central religious functions without supplanting them:

> Nippur is Bēl's city, Babylon is his favourite,
> Nippur and Babylon have but a single mind![70]

Exactly when these moves took place is uncertain. But within the great temple Ekur in Nippur was the shrine of Enlil called 'House of Life' (E-namtila), from which Babylon took the epithet 'the seat of life' when it had its own 'House of Life', built and embellished during Hammurabi's dynasty. Much later, in the eleventh century, a king of Babylon installed a throne for Ninurta which was placed within the Ekur temple at Nippur, inscribed to emphasize that Marduk and Enlil were identical:

> When the god Marduk – the great lord, Enlil of the gods, supreme deity – sits upon this throne, may the king's destiny be favourable![71]

One of seven statues of Marduk as a manifestation of Enlil 'king of the gods of heaven and earth', made of alabaster, was installed in Babylon's 'House of Life' temple. Thus Nippur and Babylon had counterpart shrines and

---

[69] Images of its predecessor, the *ušumgallu*-dragon, lion-headed with eagle feathers and claws, guarded the threshold of the Ekur, the temple of Enlil and Ninurta, in the time of the Sargonic kings who had ruled around 2334–2218 BC. Westenholz 1987: 42, no. 17.
[70] Foster 2005: 879.   [71] Frame 1995: 73.

Figure 4.2 *Kudurru*-stone fragment showing the horned *mušhuššu*-dragon, symbol of Marduk. Credit: www.metmuseum.org/art/collection/search/327048.

statues for Enlil-Marduk.[72] In a variant of Hammurabi's Code found at Nippur, the name Enlil is substituted for that of Marduk.[73] That Nippur accepted Marduk's role is indicated in a myth, the *Defeat of Enutila, Enmešarra, and Qingu*, where Ninurta, having defeated the wicked leader of rebels, seizes the crown of kingship and dashes to Marduk with it.

Babylon also associated itself with Nippur in other ways. The names of the walls of both cities were virtually interchangeable: Nemetti-Enlil/ Marduk and Imgur-Enlil/Marduk,[74] suggesting that town planning in Babylon was modelled to some extent on the layout of Nippur.[75]

---

[72] Another stood in the shrine of Ninurta within Esagila. George 1997b; Hurowitz 1997.

[73] Borger 1979: 7–8, for col. v.15 (end of prologue).   [74] George 1993a: 46.

[75] George 1993b: 737. He suggests a link with the putative composition around the thirteenth century of *Tintir*, the compilation of names of temples, streets, etc. in Babylon. See Chapter 8 below.

To refer to the *Epic of Creation* as a sacred text, or as a 'canonical' composition, tends to imply a single, rigidly conserved text. That model comes from modern ideas of single authorship with copyright, but very many cuneiform compositions, such as the *Sumerian King-List* and the *Epic of Gilgamesh*, show that it is mistaken. What mattered was the version of the text that was accepted by a particular community at any one time.[76] Flexibility and revisions according to circumstances certainly allowed the epic to change over time, even if scribal curricula tended towards conservatism. If early versions were written down rather than oral, waxed writing-boards were the most likely medium for such a prestigious text.

Variant versions of the *Epic of Creation* existed with a different hero. A text describing a ritual for a New Year Festival refers to the goddess Ishtar as the victor receiving palm fronds as tokens of her triumph.[77] Quotations found in some Neo-Assyrian texts refer to at least one other version.[78] Tablet VII, which lists many extra names and epithets for Marduk, has long been recognized as an appendage to the main text. The 'standard' text we now have may be the one selected from among others for study in schools in the first millennium BC.[79]

The Code of Hammurabi, and versions of the *Epic of Creation* that put Marduk and Babylon at the centre of world history, are the two great cuneiform Babylonian texts that set the reputation of the city above all the rest. They far outlived their creators and continued to support and inspire subsequent rulers. Grander and more impressive than most other compositions, they showed why the king deserved the loyalty of his people and how he was supported by the great gods to the benefit of his subjects. They set an example to the rest of the world. Neither the Egyptians nor the Hittites could rival them.

These two great texts are shown in a clearer light by contrast with another epic of this time, that of Atrahasis, in which neither Babylon nor Marduk play a role, for its inspiration surely comes from the alluvium of southern Mesopotamia. The *Sumerian King-List* is linked by naming the father of Atrahasis as king of Shuruppak immediately before the Flood:

> At Shuruppak Ubar-Tutu was king: he reigned 18,600 years; one king reigned 18,600 years.
> (Summary line including previous cities named before Shuruppak):

---

[76] See Lim 2017: xviii, referring to biblical and extra-biblical texts.
[77] Çagirgan and Lambert 1991–3.   [78] Kämmerer and Metzler 2012: 26–36.
[79] For a list of extracts in school texts, none of them datable to the second millennium, see Kämmerer and Metzler 2012: 37.

Five cities; eight kings ruled 385,200 years.
The Flood swept over.

One of the most entertaining, thoughtful, and humorous epics in the Babylonian repertoire was composed around the time of Hammurabi in southern Mesopotamia: the *Epic of Atrahasis*.[80] It tells the story of the world's creation by the gods who tired of the labour involved in digging canals and riverbeds, so they created mankind to serve them. Failing to appreciate that humans, unlike the gods, needed to have a limited lifespan, they soon found that overpopulation made the world too noisy, so they were unable to sleep. At first they sent disease, which reduced the population so excessively that the gods deprived themselves of food offerings. A rare survivor, Atrahasis, son of Ubar-Tutu king of Shuruppak, advised the survivors to placate the plague-god with a food offering, but to withhold offerings from the other gods. The gods relented; but within a few centuries the problem of overpopulation recurred. This time the gods sent famine. Again, Atrahasis survived to give advice to a tiny remnant, and the gods relented; but again, after many centuries the problem recurred. Then the gods decided to send the Flood and make sure there were no survivors; but one of the gods surreptitiously made the divine decision known in advance to Atrahasis, who built a boat in time to survive the Flood, for which he was granted immortality. Finally the gods realized their lack of foresight in giving mankind an indefinite lifespan, and ordained a natural, inevitable death for all people. In addition, categories of infertile and celibate people, as well as infant mortality in the charge of the 'Eradicator' *pašittu*-demon 'to snatch the baby from the lap of the woman who gave it birth', kept the population within acceptable limits. It is remarkable to discover that the Babylonians recognized how excessive population had caused disaster in the past, and it is unexpected to read of the gods' decision to control female fertility. The three categories of women who are to be celibate include the *nadītu*-priestesses. Also remarkable is other textual evidence for 'medicinal plants and medicaments needed for conception, abortion and fertility control', showing a responsible and practical attitude to procreation.[81] The end of the *Epic of Atrahasis*, where these three categories of celibate women are specified, is fragmentary however; in the previous three or four lines the creator god is speaking to the birth-goddess, instructing her on how to limit births.

---

[80] See George 2009: nos. 2 and 3. For some alternative views, see van Koppen 2011: 140–66.
[81] Böck 2013; Biggs 2000.

This story, with its archetypal plague, famine, and flood, transferred the recent experiences of Babylonians into a long-term view of social and environmental problems. Although Marduk and Babylon play no part in the story, it remained widely popular in variant versions at Ugarit in the Levant,[82] Assyria, and Late Babylonia. Its widespread and long-lived popularity shows that while promoting its own version of creation, Babylon did not attempt to suppress others.

[82] See Darshan 2016.

5 | From the Great Rebellion to the End of the First Dynasty, c. 1732–1592

In future days, forever, may any king who emerges in the land guard the words of justice which I wrote on my stela. May he not alter the law of the land which I enacted.

(Code of Hammurabi, epilogue, 59–74)

Babylon	Sealand[1]	Hana	Hittites
Samsu-iluna (c. 1749–1712)	Ili-ma-ilum	Yadih-abum	
Abi-ešuh (c. 1711–1684)		Kaštiliaš	
Ammi-ditana (c. 1683–1647)	Damiq-ilišu	Šunuhru-Ammu	
Ammi-ṣaduqa (c. 1646–1626)	Gulkišar	Ammi-madar	Hattusili I
Samsu-ditana (c. 1625–1592)	Gulkišar[2]		

The city of Larsa was the main leader of the Great Rebellion, which lasted from about 1742 to 1731. Hammurabi's conquests, impressive though they had been, and Samsu-iluna's smooth succession, did not prevent a protracted struggle.

The last five kings of the Amorite First Dynasty have been neglected by recent historians because they were all thought to be unsuccessful following their supposed defeat in the Great Rebellion. This chapter shows to the contrary how stable kingship was, and how creative the period was in producing literature, up to the end of Samsu-ditana's reign. Among archaeologists the period is known as the later Middle Bronze Age, coinciding with the continuation of the Minoan Palatial period in the Aegean and the rise of the Hittite kingdom in Anatolia.

When Rim-Sin 'II', acting as a king in southern Babylonia for at least two years, led the Great Rebellion, Larsa tried to wrest power back from Babylon. He had taken his name from the long-lived Rim-Sin I of Larsa conquered by Hammurabi. It was the start of a major uprising. Later list makers left Rim-Sin II's name out of the king-lists of Larsa, but in

---

[1] See Glassner 2004: 132.
[2] The synchronisms are based on the *kudurru* of Enlil-nadin-apli, BE 1/1, no. 83, late twelfth century. See Paulus 2014: ENAp 1; and Zomer 2019: 28–37. See also Chapter 6, nn. 8 and 102.

Babylon he was regarded as ruler of Larsa, accepting kingship also from the great goddess in Kesh, which lies less than ten miles east of Babylon, dangerously close; and he also claimed the title 'king of Ur'. Anxious to get the support of the king of Uruk, he sent envoys there in a flurry of activity just before Babylon struck. At that time Uruk took advantage of the situation by taking refugees from Larsa to work in its textile workshop.[3] As we have seen, Larsa had been governed well by subordinate officials, not by its own king, after its initial conquest by Hammurabi. Now Eshnunna, ruled by its own local king, having survived its 'total destruction' by Hammurabi, was an early ally of the rebels. It had extended its influence westwards for a while over the town Harradum on the Middle Euphrates.

A letter written by Rim-Sin 'II' while he was still full of hope, reveals his ambitions:

> Speak to Amurru-tillati, thus says Rim-Sin. The great gods established the foundation of my throne in Kesh, city of my creator, in order to bring light to Yamutbal[4] and to gather its dispersed people. Just as the entire country has heard and rejoiced and has come and met me, you too must come and meet me. As soon as you have read my letter come and meet me. Then I will raise you to high rank . . .[5]

In the same year that Samsu-iluna claimed victory over Rim-Sin 'II' and many other great cities, the rule of local city kings in each of them came to an end. The first Sealand king named in the king-lists, Ili-ma-ilum, presumably benefitted from the defeat of Rim-Sin 'II'.[6]

Shortly before the Great Rebellion, Samsu-iluna had received a petition from the people of Uruk in the form of an oracle. It presented a request from the goddess Nanaya to relieve the city of the *sūtu* grain tax, revealing discontent with the current level of taxation, and flattering the king as a faithful shepherd when he visited the ancient temple, assuring him that his presence there would bring him good fortune and long life if he remitted the tax.[7] The oracle emanated from the palace in Uruk, and shows that the economy was of central concern.

After the Great Rebellion was quelled, clay tablets are no longer found in the cities of southern Babylonia, nor have foundation inscriptions been retrieved from temples and palaces in the south. Such a striking absence, by

---

[3] Rositani 2014: 35–64, with earlier bibliography.
[4] Here 'Yamutbal', variant 'Emutbal', refers to regions dominated by Larsa.
[5] van Soldt 1994: no. 53.   [6] See Dalley 2005a: 5.
[7] A draft of the text came to light in the palace at Uruk. See Dalley 2010.

comparison with the wealth of finds for the period before the rebellion, has led to the inference that the southern cities were abandoned for the following two centuries or more. Were they abandoned? Did refugees flood into the northern cities, bringing the remnants of their cults?[8] Or can the gap in evidence be explained in other ways, as some recent discoveries appear to show?[9]

The adoption in the south of organic materials, including wooden writing-boards, may provide part of the answer. Much earlier, as we have seen, a clay record from the Assyrian colony at Kanesh refers to a 'wax tablet';[10] and bronze hinges from Minoan and Mycenean sites tell a similar story.[11] In the Amarna period (fourteenth century BC) treaty texts are known from stone monuments, but not from clay tablets, as final versions of treaties were written on writing-boards or on metal. A large, solid bronze tablet of the thirteenth century, inscribed with a long treaty text, has been unearthed in the Hittite capital.[12] Those examples are later, but show that clay was by no means the only material on which texts were written in the Bronze Age. Clay was perhaps primarily for drafts, school exercises, and copies for filing, of documents sent elsewhere.[13]

The lack of clay tablets and royal foundation inscriptions from southern cities has encouraged the view that official communications from there with Babylon ceased, but that is not necessarily a sign that southern cities such as Larsa, Isin, Nippur, Ur, and Uruk were abandoned. Ten years after the end of the rebellions, the king of Babylon received a letter from a man in Larsa requesting help in the resolution of a legal dispute, which indicates that Larsa was still under the jurisdiction of Babylon with official contact by clay tablet.[14] A tablet that originates from Larsa listing year-names up to the end of Samsu-iluna's reign shows that scholars were still at work on behalf of the city.[15] Other clay tablets, recently discovered, show that Nippur and Dūr-Abi-ešuḫ, an outlying fort closely connected with it, still had literate administration almost to the end of the First Dynasty around 1592.[16] These clear pieces of

---

[8] The hypothesis is maintained in the publications of Stone 1977; Charpin 1986 and 2004; Pientka 1998; Pientka-Hinz 2006–8. The suggestion goes back to Birot 1974b: 271–2. Reservations have been expressed by Richter 2004: 280–1.

[9] See Dalley 2019; van Lerberghe and Voet 2009.   [10] Barjamovic and Larsen 2008: 153.

[11] Shear 1998: 187–9.   [12] See Bryce 2005: 268–9.   [13] See also Chapter 6, p. 136.

[14] Spar 1988: no. 50, concerns an attempt in the twenty-fourth year of Samsu-iluna, to reclaim silver borrowed from the palace in Hammurabi's thirty-fourth year. An Old Babylonian text from Isin is dated three years later. See also Kaniuth 2017: 492 n. 3.

[15] Horsnell 1999: I, 192.   [16] van Lerberghe and Voet 2009; Abraham and van Lerberghe 2017.

evidence undermine the suggestion that the cult of Nippur's gods had been transferred to Babylon at a much earlier date. The lack of foundation inscriptions in the south may be because anonymous local governors and client kings dared not appear to usurp their overlord's prerogative by writing a formal inscription when they repaired and modified major buildings. Samsu-iluna's later year-names lack direct information about military events in southern Babylonia perhaps because such events were recorded only if they commemorated a king's imposition of direct control.[17] At this time the early kings of the first Sealand Dynasty may have been client kings of intermittent loyalty to Babylon.

A hypothesis of 'abandonment and refugees' has been backed by assumptions drawn from a lack of archaeological evidence. For instance, at Nippur and at Larsa the discovery of some sand dune deposits on top of buildings at the relevant level of occupation does not indicate that a whole site was overwhelmed by sand.[18] At Ur, archaeological evidence, though slender, shows continuous though impoverished occupation through to the Kassite period.[19] These are all huge, sprawling sites, only a very small proportion of which has been excavated. The opinion of David Oates, an experienced excavator, is appropriate here:

> I do not believe that 'breaks in occupation' of a well-favoured site are as common as the evidence of incomplete excavation often seems to suggest, and it is worth emphasizing that excavation is always incomplete. Anyone who has observed local building practice in a mud-brick village will know that occupation oscillates from one end of the general site to the other, simply because it is easier to build a new house on the site of one abandoned many years before, and consequently levelled by the natural process of decay, than to undertake the labour of levelling a newly abandoned building. Obviously the excavation of a part of such a village would reveal many levels of apparently intermittent occupation, which do not give a true picture of the history of the site as a whole.[20]

Some defenders of the abandonment theory have also made an argument from breaks in style within pottery sequences.[21] This argument is

---

[17] Horsnell 1999: II, 35–6.   [18] Armstrong and Brandt 1994.   [19] Brinkman 1969.

[20] Oates 1968: 30 n. 5.

[21] Gasche, Armstrong, Cole, and Gurzadyan 1998. In general, pottery types from one site do not necessarily match those of other sites. For example, at Harradum pottery of the eighteenth to seventeenth century was comparable with that of Bahrain rather than central Mesopotamia. See Kepinski 2012: 149–50.

questionable if there is regional diversity, or differences between areas within a single city.

If the south had been abandoned, refugees would supposedly have flooded into northern cities. Personnel attached to the cult of Inanna of Uruk have been identified in Kish following the Great Rebellion, their presence interpreted as the result of Uruk supposedly being deserted. But one cannot tell whether the new arrivals were impoverished as opposed to being the staff required for a 'branch' cult, as happened for the cult of Zababa set up at Ur,[22] and for a 'branch shrine' of Marduk in Kish, both established before the reign of Hammurabi. A cult at Borsippa had been set up expressly by Hammurabi.[23] Such 'branch shrines', installed for major deities in times of relative peace, presumably had appropriately trained staff to serve the cult in a new city. It may be no coincidence that these three deities: Inanna-of-Uruk, Zababa-of-Kish, and Marduk-of-Babylon, are all known for their oracles giving divine support for kings.

That some cities of southern Babylonia remained depressed after the Great Rebellion was quelled can hardly be doubted. Depopulation and a fall in revenue would have discouraged their citizens. To encourage its people not to desert their land, the city of Larsa enjoyed continued exemption from grain tax according to edicts, which are described below.[24] Uruk's oracular request for relief from the grain tax may have been granted. If there was a recession, contributory factors may have included the disruption of trade in Anatolia linked to the rise of the Hittite kingdom, as well as changes that Hammurabi and Samsu-iluna made to the rivers and canals, causing damage by flooding that got out of control.

Samsu-iluna's reign represents a change when individual city states began to coalesce through conquest, taxation, and near-standard literacy, leading to the concept of Babylonia as a region. Southern Mesopotamia had previously been known as Sumer, the north as Akkad, but now, represented by the *Babylonian King-List* rather than the *Sumerian King-List*, the concept of a united kingdom under Babylon's rule began to emerge.

The kingdom of Hana, based on the cities of Tuttul and Terqa around the Middle Euphrates and the river Habur, had taken up leadership of the area left vacant by Mari's downfall. Its rulers leaned towards Babylon rather

---

[22] Frayne 1990: 247–78.   [23] Frayne 1990: 354–5.

[24] Kraus 1984. Charpin 2010 supposes that the reference to Larsa in the edict of Ammi-ṣaduqa was a fossilized item that was no longer current; but, as described below, the edicts were updated and immediately applied at each act of debt remission.

than towards Halab or the Hittites.[25] Hana acted as a buffer state protecting Babylonian cities on the Euphrates from Hittite raiders. By then Marduk of Babylon was influential enough to be invoked in oaths on legal contracts written on clay in Terqa. Two Amorite tribal elements: 'sons of the North' and 'sons of the South' as easily distinguished as 'white ants' and 'black ants', inhabited the land.[26] Hana's scribes continued to follow the conventions of Babylon in their records for more than six centuries.[27] Samsu-iluna's contemporary, the Amorite-named Yadih-abum, used Babylonian year-names and Babylonian month-names, which implies close contact, perhaps a client status.[28] The name of his predecessor, Iṣi-Sumu-abum, is significant for incorporating the name of Sumu-abum, one of the founders of Babylon's first dynasty, as a public show of historic allegiance. Kaštiliaš, Yadih-abum's successor, has a name that points to a new development: it is a Kassite name, and would be used centuries later by several non-Semitic rulers of Babylon. During his reign, the kingdom of Hana maintained its close relationship with Babylon.

The Kassites were famous as horsemen. Their appearance in Babylonia marks the period when horses began to take on importance in battle as well as ceremonies, eventually transforming the nature of warfare. The mobility afforded by new equestrian skills may be one factor behind the rise of Kassite troops employed as guards in fortresses and garrisons by Babylonian kings. They gave their horses personal names; and they used metal bits.[29] Some Kassites were regarded as an enemy by Samsu-iluna, who 'ripped out the foundation of an army of Kassites at Kikalla', a place perhaps close to Babylon; Rim-Sin 'II' also saw them as a threat when, probably referring to the same episode, he called them 'the evil Kassites from a barbarian land who could not be driven back into the mountains'.[30]

Elamites also served Babylon as guards, often as archers. In Susa they continued to acknowledge Babylonian culture, despite their defeat by Hammurabi: excavations at Susa have yielded fragments of literary texts as well as contracts and mathematical texts written in Babylonian cuneiform.[31] This shows that the scribal traditions of Babylonia remained in use in Elam, despite overt hostilities.[32] Kings in Babylon continued to refer to the Elamites as wicked enemies.

In the aftermath of the Great Rebellion, Samsu-iluna's successes were exaggerated with the rhetoric of triumph: he 'destroyed the great walls of

---

[25] The Hittite dynasty ruled from Hattusha to the west of the old royal city Kuššara.
[26] Durand 1997–2000: no. 733.   [27] Podany 2016.   [28] Podany 2002: 41.
[29] Weszeli 2003–5.   [30] A year-name of Rim-Sin II. See Rositani 2003: 16.
[31] Potts 2016: 161.   [32] De Graef 2013.

Ur, Larsa, Uruk, and defeated the army of Akkad[33] for a second time'. The next year he defeated 'the armies of Sumer and Akkad which had rebelled again'. Subsequently he 'brought the region of Kisurra and Sabum[34] under control'. Finally, he 'slaughtered the rebellious enemy kings who had caused Akkad to rebel, with their own weapons'. His poetic description of those events, recorded in the Sumerian-Akkadian text known as *Bilingual B*, has the ferocity of epic style:

> I turned cities hostile to me into mounds and heaps;
> I tore the foundation of the enemy and the wicked from my land.
> I settled all the land under my command.

In that same year, his father's inscription describing the fate of Mari was copied, perhaps relevant as an example of a city's dire fate if it continued to resist.

Having killed Rim-Sin 'II', Samsu-iluna held a victory celebration at Kish, his military base near Babylon.[35] For reasons unknown, this triumph was not narrated for another decade, during which one suspects further measures had to be taken to suppress further uprisings and to capture their ringleaders. However, it is clear that much of the southern lands was under control, for the king authorized an energetic programme of restoration: he restored the wall of Isin and the great fortresses of Emutbal around Larsa. To the north of Babylon he built the wall of Sippar and rebuilt the six forts around Babylon erected by Sumu-la-El, 'my great forefather, my fifth-generation ancestor' more than a century earlier.[36] Although he 'slaughtered the entire army of the land of Eshnunna',[37] and built a fort named after himself near Eshnunna, the city had its own named ruler again within a few years.[38] Two years after defeating Eshnunna he rebuilt or renovated the ziggurat in Kish for Zababa the war-god and for Inanna, and had sixteen statues made. These works show that he had profited from his success and had a large workforce at his disposal for taking steps to secure key locations, including areas that had previously been rebellious, and to strengthen his military base in Kish. These are the deeds of an energetic, confident, and wealthy king who had not lost his nerve while quelling the rebellions.[39]

---

[33] Perhaps this referred to Eshnunna and its vicinity, or to Babylonia more generally.

[34] The problems of locating Sabum are discussed by Stol 2006–8.

[35] 'A vital military outpost in the time of Samsu-iluna': Moorey 1978: 176.

[36] Frayne 1990: 382, no. 5.   [37] Year-name twenty.

[38] Dur-Samsu-iluna, identified as the archaeological site Khafage mound B in the Diyala river region.

[39] Richardson 2005: 306 points out that there is no real evidence for economic distress in the aftermath of the Great Rebellion.

Bilingual C, composed in Sumerian and Akkadian, narrates what happened when the period of rebellions came to an end:

> Half of the year had not yet passed when he (the king) killed Rim-Sin who had caused Emutbal to rebel, and who had been raised to the kingship of Larsa. In the land of Kish he heaped up a burial mound over him. Twenty-six rebel kings, his enemies, he killed, destroyed all of them. He defeated Iluni the king of Eshnunna, one who had not heeded his decrees, led him off in a neck-stock and had his throat cut. He made the whole land of Sumer and Akkad peaceful, he made the four regions abide by his decrees.

The war-god Zababa in Kish could be relied upon to give oracles predicting the feasibility of campaigns:

> 'O Samsu-iluna, eternal seed of the gods. We will go at your right side, kill your enemies, and deliver your foes into your hands!' Samsu-iluna the able king who heeds the great gods, had confidence in the word that Zababa and Inanna spoke to him; he prepared his weapons in order to vanquish the enemies and made a campaign in order to destroy his adversaries.[40]

Samsu-iluna aimed to rehabilitate damaged cities once the rebellions had been quelled. Like his father, he set many of the cities he conquered back on track, rebuilding their walls as a positive incentive to settle, prosper, and pay taxes. No doubt his extended and ruthless crushing of the rebellions caused a downturn in the economy of some great cities in the south,[41] but the Babylonian policy of selective punishment followed by rehabilitation contrasts with early Hittite campaigns which followed a policy of 'attack, destroy, withdraw'.[42]

As Assyrian power weakened, Samsu-iluna was still sufficiently sure of his base to conduct a campaign to the north-west. He attacked the city of Shehna (modern Tell Leilan) on an eastern tributary of the Upper Khabur, a site where a well-preserved palm-façade temple reflects earlier Elamite influence.[43] Shehna had been a major centre of Assyrian power when Samsu-Addu made it a royal city; and its king had wined and dined envoys from Babylon, but generous hospitality did not save him.[44] Samsu-iluna

---

[40] Translations: Frayne 1990: 384–8. The text was written to record events of the king's twenty-fourth year.

[41] Mashkan-shapir, an important city once thought to have been abandoned at this time, is now known to have subsequent continued settlement. See van Lerberghe and Voet 2016.

[42] See Bryce 2005: 81.

[43] Also spelt 'Shahna'. As Samsu-Addu's capital, it had been named Shubat-Enlil, in the kingdom Apum.

[44] King Yakun-šar, see Eidem and Ristvet 2011.

'destroyed' Shehna along with other towns to the west of it within its kingdom.[45] Archaeologists once attributed to this event the violent end of the place, but clay records from elsewhere show that close contacts with Babylon continued into the last two reigns of the Old Babylonian dynasty.[46] In other words, that kingdom seems to have remained a loyal client of Babylon after Samsu-iluna's punitive action.

To the north, Assyrian merchants in Kanesh still continued to trade with central Anatolia,[47] backed by a weakening succession of Assyrian kings, until around 1720, Samsu-iluna's twenty-seventh year, when cuneiform records of their trading colony came to an end. Although the network may have continued through other colonies into the reigns of the next two kings of Babylon,[48] the leading city of Kanesh had been conquered by Pithana, ruler of a nearby city.[49] Assyrian traders, if they got into difficulties, could no longer count on strong backing from their rulers in Ashur.

To take part successfully in trade up the Euphrates and into Syria, the merchants of Babylon needed good relations with Halab and the towns in its orbit, as can be seen plainly from a letter Samsu-iluna sent to the king of Halab, requesting permission for a major shopping expedition: 'Speak to Abban, thus says Samsu-iluna. Now, I am sending Siyatum ... with a purse ... to Halab to make purchases. Let him make purchases!'[50]

The need to fraternize with Halab had an effect upon the cults in Babylon. By his twenty-eighth year, having settled affairs in the south, Samsu-iluna turned towards the west, for he had received an oracle from the Storm-god-of-Babylon 'his lord of oracles' in the previous year, and made an offering to the deity for his New Year Festival.[51] The basalt stela showing the Storm-god found in Babylon is very likely connected with this relationship.

Another five years on, and Samsu-iluna went up the Euphrates and along the Khabur to Saggaratum in the kingdom of Hana, a town well known from letters of Hammurabi's time found in the palace at Mari for its role in giving advance warning of river floods.[52] The action shows that the Babylonian king could still intervene directly in the affairs of Hana. In the

[45] Guichard 2014b: 154.
[46] Five years later, after a rebellion in Hana, a year-name mentions the king of Hana Yadih-abum; but there was no sign of destruction: records from his and later reigns have been excavated at Terqa in the kingdom of Hana, and at Harradum. A raid by Hittites cannot be ruled out.
[47] This final period corresponded to the final phase of Kültepe 1B.
[48] Barjamovic, Hertel, and Larsen 2012: 40 and n. 140 with references.
[49] Lacambre and Nahm 2015. Pithana's presence marks the prelude to the rise of the Hittite Old Kingdom, which was founded by his son Anitta.
[50] Kraus 1977: no.1.   [51] Horsnell 1999: II, 219.   [52] See Birot 1974a.

same year Samsu-iluna built a new palace in Babylon, displaying the wealth and status that resulted from his success. He was sufficiently sure of his prowess to take the top title 'king of the world'[53] and to have an epic poem written for recital of his heroic deeds.[54] Only a fragment of the poem survives, but it is a copy written by one of his successors to prolong the knowledge of his fame, which gives it particular significance: it shows how Samsu-iluna's successors demonstrated their loyalty and admiration, just as Samsu-iluna had done for his father Hammurabi.

Rim-Sin I at Larsa had had the benefit of fresh water supplied from both of the great rivers; the main branch of the Tigris had then flowed to the west of its present course, connecting many of the earliest cities.[55] Then a change took place: Samsu-iluna may have suffered unintended consequences of Hammurabi's great canal project, called 'Hammurabi is the prosperity of people', recorded in his thirty-third year-name, which brought water and silt to Nippur, Larsa, Uruk, Ur, and other cities – evidently a very long canal and a very ambitious scheme.[56] Letters written by Hammurabi (or his scribe) had given orders to clear the watercourse of detritus and to divert water into marshy depressions around Larsa:

> Speak to Sin-iddinam: thus says Hammurabi … As soon as you have finished the digging out that you are engaged in, clear out the detritus from the Euphrates, from Larsa to Ur, take the rubbish away, and put it in order.[57]

In times of flooding, Larsa city was protected by filling natural depressions nearby with excess fresh water, creating marshland at the expense of farmed fields. Another letter from Hammurabi to his official in Larsa describes this situation:

> If the water for Larsa and Ur has emerged, you are not to deposit anything at the 'gate of the watercourses' (sluices or regulators); the water must emerge in Larsa and Ur.[58]

But then:

> The river is making the flow, but the water is too much. Open the irrigation canals in the direction of the marsh, and fill the marshes beside Larsa.[59]

North of Hammurabi's long canal, the Euphrates brought danger from flooding to Sippar and Babylon. Probably at this period as in later times a

---

[53] Jeyes 1989: 47–50 and no. 4.   [54] See Frayne 1990: 372.   [55] Steinkeller 2001.
[56] Van Lerberghe and Voet 2016: maps 1 and 2.   [57] Frankena 1966: no. 4.
[58] Kraus 1968: no. 80.   [59] Kraus 1968: no. 85.

branch of the river ran through the centre of Babylon, and a new canal was required to protect it. Samsu-iluna diverted floodwater from Ramadi, upriver of Babylon, into the Habbaniyah depression. When rebellions had been brought under control, he extended the canal's effect by cutting through a stone ridge, a natural barrier which he called 'the great mountain of Amurru' that divided the Habbaniyah depression from that of Abu Dibbis. This was an ambitious work of engineering that changed the landscape forever:

> Samsu-iluna the king split the great mountain in the land of the Amorites into stone slabs without comparison, (measuring) eighteen cubits long, four cubits being their depth and side; he diverted the overflow of the canal 'Samsu-iluna is the source of abundance' into a reed swamp, and made it flow forth along a broad course; he enlarged the fertile fields of Babylon.[60]

There would have been sluice gates in a structure of baked brick and bitumen, or a temporary dam wall.[61] Meanwhile to the east the Tigris was augmented, above the point where it changed to a more easterly course, by two channels which diverted some water from the Euphrates above Sippar right across to the other great river – good for transportation and for adjacent fields, good for reducing the risk of flooding to Sippar, but also depleting the flow in the Euphrates' main course.[62]

These ambitious changes to watercourses, and the likelihood of unforeseen consequences, should be taken into account when evaluating the question of what happened to southern Mesopotamia after the Great Rebellion against Samsu-iluna.

Samsu-iluna's legacy is clear from many testimonies. The king's name is sometimes preceded by the sign for 'god', showing that he claimed divine status. He was venerated by his successors: his grandson put statues of him in temples. Personal names from the reign of his successors indicate high regard: 'S-is-the-light-of-the-land', 'S-is-equal-to-a-god', and 'S-is-a-conqueror'.[63] No omens of disaster refer to his reign. A new technique for cutting intricate miniature designs on cylinder seals was introduced, accompanying a wider choice of stone, including harder, more precious ones.[64] Four great bilingual texts, in Sumerian and Babylonian, composed

---

[60] For a discussion of its dimensions, see Horsnell 1999: II, 218 and 399–403.
[61] Ionides 1937: 71 gives a description of how this was done in recent times.
[62] Gasche and Tanret 1998: 11–13.   [63] Arnaud 2007: 42–59, tablet from Dur-Abi-ešuh.
[64] Teissier 1994: 63.

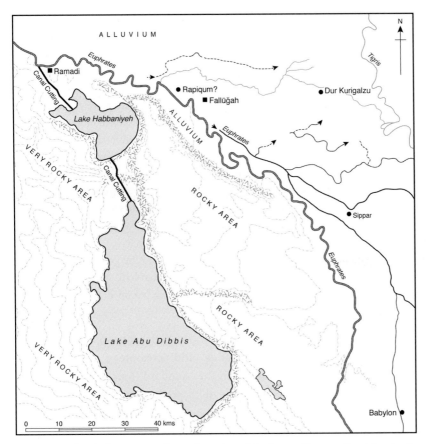

Figure 5.1 Sketch showing canals cut through rock by Samsu-iluna to divert floodwater from the Euphrates into the Habbaniyah and Dibbis depressions as it enters the alluvial plain, to protect Babylon and other cities. Credit: Alison Wilkins and author, after Ionides 1937: fig. 16 and Gasche and Tanret 1998: map 8.

at different stages of Samsu-iluna's reign, record his deeds in epic style. The one that focuses on Kish and its war-gods proclaims their oracles of victory on which he relied:

> Enlil whose lordship is supreme among gods, the shepherd who decrees fate, turned his holy face towards Zababa and Ishtar, valiant ones among the Igigi, and truly set his heart to build the wall of Kish the foremost city, their lofty dwelling, to raise its top higher than before; and Enlil the great lord whose utterances cannot be changed, whose decrees cannot be altered, looked with a joyous face at Zababa his mighty son, the agent of his victories, and at Ishtar his beloved daughter, the lady whose godhead is second to none, and he spoke favourable words to them:

'Be a shining light to Samsu-iluna my strong, indefatigable messenger, who knows how to fulfil my wishes. Let there be for him a favourable omen from you. Smite his foes, deliver his enemies into his hand, so that he build the wall of Kish, make it grow higher than before, and install you in a dwelling of happiness!'

The hearts of Zababa and Ishtar, noble lords, almighty among gods, rejoiced jubilantly at the words which their father Enlil had spoken to them, and they lifted their radiant, life-giving faces towards Samsu-iluna the mighty king, valiant shepherd, their handiwork, and they spoke to him with elation:

'O Samsu-iluna, of eternal divine lineage, O jewel of kingship, whose fate Enlil has exalted: he instructed us to be the guardians of your well-being. We shall march at your right, we shall smite your enemies, we shall deliver your foes into your hand. Build the wall of Kish our august city, make it grow higher than before!'

Samsu-iluna the able king who pays heed to the great gods, put much trust in the words which Zababa and Ishtar had spoken to him. He prepared his weapons to smite the foes, he led an expedition to crush his enemies.

The king continued to advertise the rise of Marduk to supreme status by invoking him as 'the Enlil of lands' and 'creator of wisdom' (*bāni nēmeqim*), titles later emphasized in the 'standard' *Epic of Creation*. As a pious king who perpetuated the fame of his predecessors, he raised the wall of Nippur, which his grandfather had built, surrounding it with a moat filled from the Euphrates:

He caused the people of Sumer and Akkad to dwell in peaceful abodes. He made them lie down in pastures. He made the name of Sin-muballiṭ his grandfather eminent in the lands.[65]

Abi-ešuh promulgated at least one edict for remitting debts, and for regulating the financing of merchants, shortly after his own succession and probably again at intervals throughout his reign. Fragments of business archives dating to his reign have been found in Babylon. Several letters that he wrote to the merchants and judges of Sippar concern fields and barley, inspecting equipment, and the purchase of donkeys,[66] for Sippar was still a most important city for Babylon, and the king took an active and personal interest in its welfare. Early in his reign an 'army' of Kassites is mentioned, showing that a militia or a group of bandits was at large in the Babylonian homeland.[67] Lists of Kassite soldiers who were stationed at forts in the

---

[65] Frayne 1990: 374.   [66] van Soldt 1994: nos. 50–2.
[67] See Horsnell 1999: I, 51–81 for the ordering of the year-names.

heartland of northern Babylonia confirm that Kassite militias continued to guard Babylonian territory.[68] Not all relations with the Kassites were hostile: Abi-ešuh wrote to the harbour officials and judges of Sippar to tell them that Kassite messengers and chariots were on their way from Babylon, and ordered them to put 300 jugs of beer at their disposal.[69]

Hostile Elamites on the border of Babylonia were still the main enemy, however. Around his seventeenth year, Abi-ešuh routed troops of Eshnunna, very likely to discourage Elamite incursions, and seized their king.[70] Perhaps two years later, the king recorded that he had dammed the Tigris.[71] A much later Babylonian chronicle records that this was done in the hope of capturing the Sealand king, an action which was not successful;[72] so the dam may have been a temporary tactic for military purposes, rather than a construction intended to be permanent. At the time, the deed was enormously important, however, and knowledge of it was perpetuated for the next thousand years, copied into a late Assyrian collection of oracle questions:

> Sun-god lord of the judgement, Storm-god lord of the inspection! Should the soldiers of the palace, the soldiers of the palace gate, the soldiers of the military wings, the elite soldiers, the desert soldiers, the assembly soldiers, the Sutean soldiers and the ... of the country, the craftsmen-soldiers, the hod-carrying soldiers, soldiers whom Marduk rules, as many as Abi-ešuh king of Babylon, son of Samsu-iluna, harnesses and provides for, within this month until the thirtieth day, a day he identified, consulted about, and kept looking for, the day his face was set towards, his heart induced him:
>
> On the far side of the Tigris, to the east, should they open the barrage, should they set it at right angles? Should reeds and soil be heaped up and should they make the closure? As soon as it (the river) flows, should it flow, or should they cross back and on the side to the west should they make fast a barrage opposite the 'cheek', should they set it at right angles, should reeds and soil be heaped up? ...
>
> (damaged section)
>
> Thus I deal with this lamb with (my) right hand, with the right hand I bless, on its right may there be right judgement.[73]

Such oracle questions were the business of the diviner, *bārûm*, who was closely involved with planning military campaigns. It was he who carried

[68] Abraham and van Lerberghe 2017; Van Lerberghe and Voet 2016.
[69] Frankena 1966: no. 67.
[70] King Ahušina. Horsnell 1999: I, 62 and II, 259, a year-name not previously known.
[71] Horsnell 1999: II, 260–1, around year nineteen.   [72] Glassner 2004: no. 40: rev. 8'-10'.
[73] Lambert 2007: no. 3.

out the ritual of sacrificing a sheep, examining its entrails for a decision on whether an enterprise was likely to succeed. The diviner on this occasion was almost certainly the owner of a fine chalcedone seal inscribed with his name which has come to light.[74]

Abi-ešuh's literary productions were so splendid that he is the only king in Mesopotamian tradition to have had two sages acknowledged for his reign.[75] One of the finest compositions describes waterworks, a very Mesopotamian concern, fit for epic verse. It originally consisted of a long epic hymn to Ishtar as Mistress of the Gods, preserved only at the beginning and end of its eight columns, and it seems to refer to the same operation for damming the Tigris as his year-name. It puts the goddess at the centre of the action, guiding her heroic champion, the king, to success:

> She took hold of her champion, she bolted the Tigris with locks of copper,
> With locks of copper and bronze bolts she bolted the Tigris.[76]

A fragment of a clay cylinder calls Abi-ešuh 'king of the Tigris river ... who built a gate against the rebellious land'.[77] The fort Dur-Abi-ešuh was connected to Nippur by a canal deep enough to take heavy barges, and probably stood at the junction of the canal with a branch of the Tigris.

The goddess was not only a heroic dam-builder, she is presented as an irresistible lover in fragments of Sumerian poems that name the king. In an Babylonian love lyric, in which she appears under her alternative name Nanay, she declares her well-requited passion for the god Muati, connecting it to her command that Abi-ešuh live a long and fruitful life:

> She looked upon Babylon with her approving eyes,
> She blessed it, she ordered good fortune for it,
> Daily she [commanded] vigour for the king who dwells there,
> Nanay [commanded] vigour for king Abi-ešuh ...
> Love-charms will rain down like dew ...
> O Muati, your love-making is honey,
> The charm of your love is all one could want of honey ...
> May the king live forever at your command,
> May Abi-ešuh live forever [at your command].[78]

---

[74] Moortgat 1988: no. 494.

[75] Named Gimil-Gula and Taqīš-Gula, they were fully incorporated into a later list of all sages, who would claim to be descended from an earlier sage, a genealogy, comparable to a king-list, known chiefly from a list of the Seleucid period. See Lenzi 2008: 137–69 esp. 141. A 'chain of authenticity' for transmitting works of scholarship, it is ancestral to the *silsila* of Sufi tradition.

[76] Horsnell 1999: II, 260–1 n. 94, translating CT 15 nos. 1–2, col. vii.

[77] Frayne 1990: 406–7 no. 1001.

[78] See Foster 2005: 96, with bibliography; Streck and Wasserman 2012.

Abi-ešuh's claim to be 'the king who makes the four regions be at peace',[79] identical to the claim of Samsu-iluna, was based upon real successes. In the reign of his successor, a man bore the name Abi-ešuh-ili, meaning 'Abi-ešuh is my god', which evidently shows that the king had been regarded as divine.[80] He had been an energetic and successful king during his twenty-six years of rule in Babylon.

Abi-ešuh's son **Ammi-ditana**, who as crown prince had impressed a fragment of an edict with his own seal, took the throne as an experienced statesman.[81] He traced his legitimacy back to Sumu-la-El as founder of the dynasty, in an inscription copied a thousand years later by a doctor in Babylon.[82] Acknowledging his debt to his grandfather, he rebuilt Samsu-iluna's palace, and installed a heroic statue of him in Enlil's temple, the 'House of Life' (E-namtila).[83] He renovated Hammurabi's great canal, dedicated a statue of himself as leader of the troops, and dedicated a weapon to Urash, a great warrior-god, implying gratitude for a successful campaign. At the end of his reign, he 'destroyed' the wall of Udinim (near Ur) which the Sealand king had built.[84] That event required a campaign from Babylon to the southernmost limits of Mesopotamia, to control the power of the client king of the Sealand.

A fine hymn to Ishtar, composed during Ammi-ditana's reign to win divine favour, describes the goddess in her many aspects, beauty, allure, sweetness, wisdom, as the queen who surpasses the great gods of heaven, an effective speaker in the divine assembly:[85]

> Sing of the goddess, most awe-inspiring goddess!
> May she be praised, mistress of peoples, greatest of the Igigi-gods!

Paired with the Sky-god, she received Ammi-ditana's offerings of cattle and fatted lambs. In return she requested of the Sky-god long life and success for the king:

---

[79] Frayne 1990: 405.   [80] VS 22, 29:35. See Klengel 1983.   [81] Charpin 2010.

[82] Frayne 1990: 404–5, no. 1.

[83] Either the temple in Nippur or its namesake in Babylon. George 1993a: 130–1 and 325–6 maintains that all the royal statues of this period were in Babylon's Enamtila, where Hammurabi had built a warehouse for Enlil as 'lord of the lands'. The statue for year-name twenty-eight showed the king presenting a *mašdaria* tax, such as was commonly supplied to Nippur in the Ur III period; see Horsnell 1999: II, 309; Bahrani 2017: 143, 146. Spycket 1968: 86 assumed that the Enamtila in question was in Nippur.

[84] See Frayne 1992: 33–6. On reading Udinim, perhaps like Edina, as Kissik, see Horsnell 1999: II, 319–20 n. 176.

[85] Foster 2005: 85–8.

> By her command she gave him
> The four regions in submission at his feet.
> She harnessed to his yoke the whole inhabited world.

These lines suggest that the hymn celebrated a military victory. A prayer ends the poem:

> O Ishtar, grant long life forever to Ammi-ditana,
> The king who loves you. Long may he live!

The king's explicit and implicit military deeds, along with the top titles 'king of the world' and 'king of the four regions', suggest that military expeditions were wide-ranging. As 'king of all the Amorite land', he presumably held sway over parts of Assyria and Hana. As further evidence for his greatness, beautifully produced legal records from his reign, impressed with the seals of judges and others, have been found at several of the great Babylonian cities. An edict promulgated by his son refers to the end of his reign as the time from which debts causing constraint are to be refunded on pain of death, a clause suggesting that the terms of such edicts were duly enforced.

The king took personal responsibility for funerary offerings to ancestors. Ammi-ditana wrote to one of his officials:

> Milk and ghee are needed for the funerary offering in the month Abu. As soon as you have read this letter, have one of your officials take thirty cows and sixty quarts of ghee and come to Babylon so that milk will be available until the funerary offerings are completed. He must arrive here quickly without delay.[86]

This emphasizes the importance of succession through direct ancestry under Amorite kings, contrasting with earlier times when the city itself rather than its kings had been the focus of the succession in the *Sumerian King-List*.

Ammi-ṣaduqa was one of Babylon's greatest kings. He had two exceptionally powerful contemporaries: Hattusili I in Anatolia and Gulkišar in the Sealand. Ammi-ṣaduqa was regarded as a god among the Hittites and in Syria.[87] In the confident words of his first year-name, he 'went forth like the sun for the sake of his country and caused the people, in their totality, to prosper', with the support of Enlil, chief god of Nippur. A clay tablet records a series of appeals for justice over an inheritance, addressed to judges of Nippur, in a prolonged lawsuit that began in the sixteenth year of

---

[86] Veenhof 2005: no. 7.   [87] Haas 1994: 113–15.

Ammi-ditana, continued through the reign of Ammi-ṣaduqa, and was finally resolved only in the fifth year of Samsu-ditana – forty-seven years of great expectations.[88] It confirms that legal process continued in Nippur at a time when scholars had wrongly supposed that the city suffered centuries of abandonment.

As the son of the previous king, Ammi-ṣaduqa was the key figure in a remarkable ritual, found in a text showing how piety towards ancestors was expressed in the hope of bringing good fortune to the living king. The *Genealogy of the Hammurabi Dynasty*, composed to accompany a ritual for naming and nourishing the spirits of ancestors, included not only kings of Babylon but also eponymous founders of tribes. It continued with current groups described as *bala* (a term for a period of office), namely Amorites, Haneans, Gutians, and any other who might be offended by accidental omission – 'not recorded on this tablet, including any soldier who fell while on his lord's campaign(?), princes, princesses, any of mankind from east to west who has nobody to make (funerary) offerings and to tend (his grave): "Come! Eat this, drink this, bless Ammi-ṣaduqa son of Ammi-ditana"'.[89] Many of the kings' names occur in an Assyrian king-list that incorporates part of the genealogy without bothering to adapt it to fit. The match suggests that Assyria and Babylon regarded their heritage as a shared one at this time, perhaps ever since Hammurabi took control of Nineveh.

As a divinized ancestor residing in the Underworld, Ammi-ṣaduqa was later remembered in texts of the fourteenth and thirteenth centuries found in the Hittite capital Hattusha and the Syrian city Emar on the Middle Euphrates.[90] At both sites cuneiform literacy for local scribes had been promoted by scholars from Babylonia and Assyria. Contemporary kings who showed their respect for Babylonian literacy by adopting it included the king of Elam. In Susa the Elamite ruler wrote his formal inscriptions in Babylonian rather than Elamite.[91] Fragments of the Babylonian *Epic of Etana* found at Susa probably date to this time, along with school texts that show a typically Babylonian curriculum was in use for training local scribes;[92] Elamites and Kassites are mentioned in administrative texts, as before, among groups of guards working in Babylonia.[93]

---

[88] George 2009: no. 15.

[89] See Wilson 1977: 93–114. There are some major differences in the spelling of royal names between this text and other sources.

[90] See Wilhelm 2009: 59–75 and Ornan 2012: 15–16. A domestic version of a funerary ritual for ancestors is found in an incantation: Abusch 2014: 1–10 esp. 2–3.

[91] Vallat 1993: text VS vol. 7, no. 67.   [92] De Graef 2013: 272.

[93] Van Lerberghe and Voet 2016.

In southern Babylonia, the local dynasty of Sealand kings may have acted as a buffer against Elam, for its king Gulkišar ('destroyer of the Earth'), reigned for fifty-five years and was memorialized by his successors in the divine name 'Oh Shamash, bless Gulkišar!', a protégé of the Sun-god who received offerings.[94]

In Hattusha, the Hittite king Hattusili I (c. 1650–1620) authorized bilingual inscriptions, known only from later copies, produced in Babylonian and Hittite.[95] After the Hittite king's early years, in which he established a power base in his homeland, Hattusili began to campaign in northern Syria, but the kingdom of Yamhad with its international temple at Halab, still a major power, resisted successfully, and remained strongly independent until near the end of Babylon's First Dynasty, two generations later. Very likely it was during Ammi-ṣaduqa's reign that the Hittites adopted Akkadian cuneiform and adapted it for writing the Hittite language.[96] Cultural rather than military fame would account for why, in many Hittite texts from Hattusha and in Akkadian texts from north-west Syria at Emar, his name, in the forms Ammizadu/Amaza, is included in a group of Mesopotamian deities.[97] The deification suggests that Ammi-ṣaduqa was far from being 'a rather undistinguished Babylonian king'.[98]

Determined to perpetuate his name and fame, Ammi-ṣaduqa dug a new canal named after himself, built a new fort also named after himself, and dedicated statues of himself to the gods of several major cities including Babylon, and Sippar where he rebuilt the ziggurat and the cloister of the *nadītu*-priestesses for the Sun-god.[99] Some fabulous statues are described as 'objects of wonder', boasting the king's pride in displaying their beauty and skill, which reflected his greatness in the artistic sphere and his ability to command precious materials.

At least twice during his reign he promulgated an edict of debt remission, and we are fortunate to have a fairly full text of one of them with only a few damaged passages. Here is a paraphrase of some excerpts:

---

[94] Dalley 2009: no. 83:15'.

[95] Bryce 2005: 662–4. There is growing evidence that the Hittites took their primary education in cuneiform from a centre in Syria.

[96] Bryce 2002: 59–60. The primary stage of learning cuneiform may have been organized for Hittites in a Syrian city, perhaps Emar. Some features of Old Babylonian dialect have been found in ritual and incantation texts excavated at the Hittite capital. See, e.g., Watkins 2004: 552; Beckman 2014: 6.

[97] Haas 1994: 83, 110, 113, 115, and 571.   [98] Gurney 1977: 15.

[99] Janssen 1991. It is difficult to evaluate the complaints made in letters written by women, who often complain of neglect!

> Tablet of the edict which the land was ordered to obey at the time the king invoked a *mišarum*-act of justice for the land ... The market of Babylon, the markets of the country ... their arrears dating from the year (year twenty-one) in which Ammi-ditana remitted the debts which the land had contracted until the month of Nisan of year one of Ammi-ṣaduqa the king, because the king has invoked the *mišarum* for the land, the collecting officer may not pursue the [debtor] for payment. Members of a debtor's family who have been taken in lieu of other means of payment are to be released.[100]

In some clauses the debt is incurred directly to the palace. The markets in cities whose names are preserved in a fragmentary passage show a wide network, from north-west Syria to the Lower Tigris, also including Isin and Larsa – Sealand cities that still had viable economies.[101] In the client kingdom of Hana, certain legal documents were dated by the Babylonian king rather than the local ruler.[102] Debts incurred by tenant farmers in Suhu country, just downstream from Mari, were to be cancelled, implying that the area was under direct rule from Babylon:

> Written records of interest-bearing loans of barley or silver made to an Akkadian or an Amorite for certain periods of time are to be invalidated; if the interest has already been collected, it is to be refunded. He who does not make a refund in accordance with the royal edict shall die.

The text seems to imply that all Akkadians and Amorites were obliged to obey this Babylonian edict. Elamites and Kassites are not mentioned, however, perhaps implying that the only work available to them in Mesopotamia was soldiering or banditry, that they were excluded from some of the benefits enjoyed by Semitic people. Nor were they included in the genealogy quoted above.

By this time celestial observations were being recorded in writing. The name of Ammi-ṣaduqa is attached to some of them, a recognition not found for any other king. The moon's phases were crucial. If it was evident that a month could have twenty-nine, thirty, or thirty-one days, other lengths might be possible in theory, so schemes were taken to impossible extremes on either side of the ideal of thirty days. In practice, variation away from the ideal signified danger, which required confirmation or

---

[100] For a full translation, see Pritchard 1969: 526–8.
[101] They include Borsippa, Isin, Larsa/Emutbalum, Idamaraz, Kisurra, Malgium, Mankisum, and Shitullum.
[102] E.g., Podany 2002: 56.

otherwise from divination, followed by appropriate rituals if necessary, to avert harm.[103]

Since the lunar year did not align with the solar year, an intercalary month was added from time to time, but not necessarily in all cities at once. Babylonian scholars collected and interpreted observations and supplied them for the king, who made the decision to add an intercalary month. The month-names on written records that prevailed in Babylonia from Hammurabi's time onwards were mainly those of Babylon, putting the city and its king in control of the calendar. Lunar phases also dictated when offerings to ancestors should be made. In medicine, potions were exposed to the light of the Moon because it made them more efficacious.[104]

For the timing of festivals and the order of prayers in rituals, astronomers needed detailed and regular observations of the night sky, particularly the appearance and disappearance of particular celestial bodies. They probably kept continuous records from an early date, so that timing could be known in advance. Much more difficult was to predict eclipses of the sun and moon, for they were not regular. Since eclipses did not conform to an ideal scheme, they were regarded as a significant warning from the gods, portending harm to the king. That gave a firm link between astronomy and celestial divination, which eventually became more important than other forms of divination for assessing risk to the king. The astronomer's role overlapped with that of the 'lamentation priest' who could control the risk when statues of deities were obliged to leave their temples during festivals or when temples needed repair. Thus astronomy and astrology were inseparable and had equal value, so their observations took the same written format: 'If such and such is seen (in the sky or on a liver, etc.), the consequence is danger to the king'.[105] Some of their technical terms were the same: *manzazu* can mean 'station of a planet in the sky' or 'depression mark on a liver'; *tarbaṣu* ('halo') can mean 'horizon' or 'a particular mark on a liver'.

The power and movements of the sun, which cast light on all activity and dictated the timing of solstices and equinoxes, were self-evident. They were easily found by using a shadow clock; other instruments available to astronomers were the water clock and the sand clock, the latter of which is mentioned in the *Epic of Atrahasis*. Observations were recorded regularly, and from them arithmetical tables and lists were drawn up.

---

[103] See Steele 2011: ch. 22; Cooley 2013: 124–9.   [104] Reiner 1995: ch. 8.

[105] Earlier records of celestial observations may not have had the same format.

Celestial observations were used in rituals and in myths. The seven celestial bodies affecting human affairs were the moon, the sun, Venus, Mercury, Jupiter, Saturn, and Neptune, each linked to a major deity. Stars and constellations, and their relationships in the sky, played a part in myths where they were woven into the actions of the gods.[106] The *Prayer to the Gods of Night* shows that some names of planets were those of major deities, and the names of constellations such as the 'Bow', the 'Yoke', the 'Wagon', the 'She-goat', and the 'Dragon' were therefore already assigned when the first text was written.[107] The purpose of the prayer was to plead for a favourable result from extispicy, one of the earliest known links between astronomy and divination.

The huge compilation *When Anu and Enlil* (*Enūma Anu Enlil*) served as a handbook of celestial and meteorological observations and as a guide to divination. It is best known in a fairly standard version from later times, but incorporated earlier material. It included a section, tablet 63, now known as 'The Venus tablets of Ammi-ṣaduqa', which links the king by name with scholarship in astronomy. The intervals between successive first and last visibilities of the planet Venus were recorded during his reign, in order to forecast possible lunar eclipses.[108] The planet Venus remained invisible for much longer than expected in Ammi-ṣaduqa's twelfth year, departing dangerously from the ideal.[109] A ritual by purification for averting evil portended by an eclipse was written during his reign.[110]

Omens from extispicy, written in southern Mesopotamia and compiled into manuals, also date to Ammi-ṣaduqa's reign.[111] This implies that the older works were still available in cities such as Ur, where the great ziggurat would have allowed astronomers to give authoritative sightings of the

[106] See, e.g., Cooley 2013.   [107] See Horowitz 2000.

[108] The first twenty-two tablets in the later, standard compilation concern lunar observations and meteorological events, then planets and stars follow. See Reiner and Pingree 1975. Some of the material later compiled for *When Anu and Enlil* dates from around this time, but it probably belongs to forerunners; the eventual compilations known in several slightly different versions from the end of the second millennium were extensive. The complete scheme is still not certain. For many other types of astronomical text, and commentaries on some of them, see Hunger 2011–13.

[109] This may be linked to the volcanic eruption at Santorini in the Aegean: in the tephra deposited by that huge explosion, an olive tree branch was found, datable by a combination of tree rings and C-14 to around 1627 BC. If the link is correct, it establishes the Middle Chronology for the dynasty. See Chapter 2, p. 46 above.

[110] Tablet CBS 563 with colophon, which is a forerunner of a much better known ritual of exorcism through physical purification, known as *bīt rimki* ('bathhouse'). See Ambos 2013: 188–91.

[111] Older material is recognizable where characteristic orthography and phonetics show the text was 'edited using southern originals', implying input from the Sealand cities. See Jeyes 1989: 8.

moon. Ammi-ṣaduqa would have been able to access them in order to begin the process of producing manuals for use in Babylon and the northern cities. Babylon was taking the lead from the southern cities in keeping records of observations, and its astronomers had access to the specialist scholarship of the Sealand.

Ammi-ṣaduqa took measures to organize extra protection against marauding Kassites in the vicinity of Sippar. In his twelfth year a detachment of Sutean troops (presumably classed as Amorites) warned of an impending attack on Sippar, so the king wrote to the authorities warning them not to open the city gate before sunrise, nor allow the watchmen to come down from the city wall.[112] Three years later 1,500 Kassite troops were advancing to raid herds and flocks in the vicinity, according to a letter which the king himself wrote:

> The city gate is not to be opened before sunrise!
> The troops are not to leave!
> The guards are to be strengthened![113]

The danger seems to have consisted of frequent if intermittent raids upon livestock, so that fairly standard warnings were sent out by the king to keep the local authorities alert.

Ammi-ṣaduqa's reign was significant in so many ways that one cannot doubt the continuing prosperity of Babylon, embellishing its temples with works of art, spreading his fame through Hana into the Hittite kingdom under Hattusili I, and collecting the fruits of cuneiform scholarship from southern Mesopotamia. Disturbances in the countryside do not necessarily mark the approach of the end of the dynasty, for urgent precautions were surely needed from time to time.

Samsu-ditana his son inherited the kingship. The First Dynasty of Babylon came to an end under his rule, but not for another thirty-three years; there is no evidence for decline until the last few years. A reference to an edict in a letter indicates that rules concerning debts and trading continued to be revised.[114] Samsu-ditana's donation of a mace for Marduk 'the hero/warrior' may have been a thanks offering for a profitable campaign; and the statue of himself leading soldiers nine years later, followed by an offering to the warrior god Uraš, 'who made him attain his heart's desire', alludes to military success. His use of much gold for

---

[112] Kraus 1985: no. 150.

[113] Kraus 1964: no. 2; Kraus 1977: no. 47, also written by the king, refers to the same threat, as do other, less well-preserved letters.

[114] Klengel 1983: VS vol. 22, no. 20.

statues made of various deities shows that he was not short of that most precious metal.

Documents from Terqa in the kingdom of Hana were still being written in Babylonian style, one of them dated to Samsu-ditana's reign;[115] and some seal impressions show that he remained closely connected with that kingdom.[116] He was not, therefore, confined to a shrinking realm. But the *Epic of Gulkišar* contains a ferocious speech in which the Sealand king threatened to fight Samsu-ditana and to make his troops drink poison, a threat which abandons the heroism of face-to-face combat.[117] Poisoning as a weapon of war is found in two other epic texts of this period, and is implied in the *Epic of Creation* IV, in which the hero-god grasps a herb to counter poison.

An increasingly dangerous situation in the countryside may be reflected in an oracle, but the text is not closely dated.[118] It bore the title 'Oracle Question concerning the Safety of the City', and is exceptionally long, consisting of sixty-nine lines. It was later incorporated into a series found preserved in the late Assyrian period, probably because it was linked to the end of the dynasty.

> O Shamash lord of judgement, Adad lord of extispicy: within this month until the thirtieth day, and the following month until the second day, according to the procedure of divination, will this city be safe? Will it remain quietly settled and fully secure? Elamite troops, . . . Kassite troops, Idamaraz troops stationed in Idamaraz and foreign troops with them, the Samharu army and foreign troops with them . . . who have rebelled against Marduk and Samsu-ditana son of Ammi-ṣaduqa king of Babylon, and keep seeking hostile action . . . Will they, by day or at night, against this city, by . . . trickery, by siege, by sweet talk . . . (about twenty-five other possible actions are listed) . . . turn it into a ruin heap? . . . O Shamash lord of judgement, Adad lord of extispicy, this lamb: with my right hand I offer, with my right hand I bless, with my right hand may truth obtain.[119]

Although a few damaged signs prevent complete readings, the Hittites, who raided Babylon towards the end of the reign, appear not to be included by name though may be subsumed in the expression 'foreign troops'. The Elamites precede the Kassites as rebellious troops within Babylonia. A letter from Samsu-ditana to one of his officers warns:

[115] Podany 2016: 69–98.   [116] Colbow 1994: 61–6.   [117] Zomer 2019: 35.
[118] See, e.g., Richardson 2005.
[119] Lambert 2007: 24–9. Samharu is the name of a Kassite tribe; Idamaraz probably refers to the north-western part of Hana.

> Concerning what you wrote to me: 'In view of the enemy troops it is not
> right to leave the barley that became available in the territory of Sippar-
> Yahrurum in a store outside the city. Our lord should order an instruction
> to be sent to us to open the Shamash Gate so that that barley can enter the
> city'. (In answer to what you wrote to me:) As soon as all the barley of the
> city's cultivation belt has been harvested, open the Shamash Gate ... and
> do not fail to guard that city gate.[120]

This situation did not necessarily apply to other cities; Nippur still had
judges at work there, who could travel by boat to a neighbouring fort.[121]

The archive of Kurû the merchant, found at Babylon, had begun in the
reign of Sin-muballiṭ and continued into this reign. It records loans of silver
made for journeys on the Euphrates. One letter refers to extispicy to
establish whether the omens were good for travelling to Babylon.[122]
Another refers to silver entrusted to Hittite troops, implying that now
Hittites, like Kassites and Elamites, were serving the Babylonian king, at
least on that occasion. This confirms that silver was still the main metal for
currency, which had not been debased to copper as it would be in later
times of hardship.

Given the circumstances documented for Sippar, a Hittite raid on
Babylon cannot have come as a surprise, though some historians have
called it 'a bolt from the blue'. The event is known only from the much
later *Babylonian Chronicle of Early Kings*, which simply states: 'In the time
of Samsu-ditana the Hittites [marched(?)] against Akkad'.[123]

A different text does not mention Hittites, but says:

> When the battles of the Amorite land, the attacks of Haneans, and the
> army of Kassites changed the borders of Sumer and Akkad under Samsu-
> ditana, and made the ground plans (of temples, etc.) unrecognizable ...
> Kadašman-Harbe chased Suteans out of the land from East to West.

But this is far from being a contemporary record. Kadašman-Harbe, ruling
a couple of centuries later, may have been claiming credit by reference to an
earlier event that supposedly resembled one of his own time.[124] Neither the
city of Babylon nor the end of the Babylonian dynasty is mentioned in a
contemporary text.

So what actually happened? The route taken by the attackers is not
known, although a march through Hana has been assumed. The only
other source of information was composed a century later: the Hittite

---

[120] Veenhof 2005: no. 8.   [121] van Lerberghe 2008.
[122] Kraus 1983: text VS 22:83–92, no. 91.   [123] Grayson 1975b: 156, chronicle 20.
[124] Paulus 2014: 296–304.

Proclamation of Telepinu names the Hittite king as Mursili I (c. 1620–1590) and claims that he marched to Babylon, 'destroyed' it, defeated Hurrian troops, and brought captives and possessions from Babylon to Hattusha.[125]

This event may have been a brief and marginally destructive affair, exaggerated as a boast from Hittite tradition, so its significance is not clear. No statue of Marduk was seized, no violation of shrines is recorded. Hittites did not take the kingship of Babylon. No mention is found of Elamites, who might be expected to have joined the fray. A text now labelled the *Marduk Prophecy*, written by a Kassite king Agum, claims that Agum retrieved a statue of Marduk from Hana, repaired and embellished it and reinstalled it in Esagila, which he had restored; but whether that statue was ever looted from Babylon by the Hittites, or had been installed long ago in a 'branch shrine' in Hana or elsewhere, is unknown. The event may not have been catastrophic enough to bring an immediate end to the dynasty, but may have been a signal for attacks and treacheries. The terrifying conditions envisioned in the *Oracle Question* for the city – its population reduced to shrieking and losing their minds – are unambiguous, but a realistic assessment of the oracle's dramatic language is impossible.

Samsu-ditana's rule may have lingered on for several years, but it is sure that the dynasty came to an end. The big question is, what happened to Babylon? Who took up the reins of power?

---

[125] Bryce 2005: 98–9 gives an uncritical assessment of these sources.

6 | The Next Six Centuries

Kassite, Sealand, Isin, and Elamite Kings, c. 1592–979[1]

> Wherever land is settled, skies extend,
> Sun shines, fire blazes,
> Water flows, wind blows,
> Those whose clay Aruru pinched off,
> Living beings who stride,
> As many as exist, praise Marduk!

(Ludlul IV 77–82)

1 Early Kassites and the First Sealand Dynasty, c. 1595–?
(a provisional scheme that begins by showing synchronisms of Gulkišar)

Babylon	Sealand[2]
Ammi-ṣaduqa (1646–1626)	// Gulkišar (Gulki) (55 years)
Samsu-ditana (1625–1595)	// Gulkišar (continued)
(end of First Dynasty)	
(hiatus?)	
	Pešgaldarame (Pešgal) (50 years)
Pešgaldarame (for his last 3 years?)[3]	
Ayadaragalama (Ayadara) (for his first 15 years?)	Ayadaragalama (28 years)
Agum II kakrime (22 years; placing very uncertain)[4]	
(6? uncertain Kassite kings)[5]	
Burna-Buriaš I (? placing uncertain)	
(4 uncertain Kassite kings)	

---

[1] The chronology is still unclear; see Brinkman 2017: 1–44.

[2] In one king-list, the names of three Sealand kings are abbreviated: Gulki, Pešgal, and Ayadara. These short forms are used in this chapter for the two who reigned in Babylon. The names are Sumerian.

[3] The Sealand tablets from Tell Khaiber near Ur are dated to the same time span as the Schøyen texts (Dalley 2009), based on which the lengths of reigns in Babylon are suggested. See Calderbank et al. 2017.

[4] Alternatively, Agum II may have reigned soon after Samsu-ditana.

[5] They may include the rulers attested on tablets from Tell Muhammad, see Al-Ubaid 1983; or those rulers may be local city rulers.

When Samsu-ditana's reign came to an end, several groups might have aspired to take over kingship in Babylon. Babylonian king-lists relating to this period do not indicate when a dynastic line won control of Babylon.[6] This contrasts with the First Dynasty, which maintained an unbroken line of descent and accession. After that, for a dynasty to qualify for complete inclusion in the Babylonian king-lists, it was only necessary for one or more of its kings to have ruled in Babylon, but the lists do not specify which ones.[7] In the case of the First Sealand Dynasty, two of its early kings, Iluma-ilu and Damiq-ilišu, who troubled contemporary kings of Babylon are included in Babylonian king-lists even though they never ruled from Babylon.[8] The concept of a dynasty may have widened, but the ideal was still dominant. Two later kings did rule in Babylon: Pešgal and Ayadara. But where do they belong in a chronological sequence?

This chapter covers six centuries and six different dynasties of which by far the longest-lasting has kings all with non-Semitic, Kassite names, clearly distinct from earlier rulers. About 15,000 texts are known from this period, most undated, unpublished, and fragmentary, and many refer to local administration.[9] Literary texts often cannot be dated more precisely than within a period of around 800 years or more, making it impossible to link them to a historical context.[10] The use of informative year-names was abandoned in favour of laconic dating by simple year numbers.[11]

The geopolitical frame widens now to include the Egyptians on the Nile and the Hittites with their powerful kingdom in Anatolia, forming a network of royal correspondence and exchange of gifts. Several objects datable to this long period have been found far from Babylonia: in Palestine, in Egypt, in the Arabian Gulf, in Armenia, and in the East Mediterranean, tantalizing for any attempt to assess Babylon's power

---

[6] They include the names of ancestors who did not rule in Babylon, they ignore overlaps, and perhaps count extra years in short-lived attempts to begin a new era. See Boiy 2012.

[7] The long period covered in this chapter begins around the end of the Middle Bronze Age, shading into the Late Bronze Age, and ending in the Early Iron Age, in archaeological terminology.

[8] Although some historians have assumed that Sealand kings took the kingship of Babylon at the death of Samsu-ditana, the synchronism from the *Epic of Gulkišar* probably precludes that option.

[9] Most of these texts are from Nippur and Dur-Kurigalzu, few are from Babylon.

[10] See Brinkman 2017: 31–2.

[11] The change was gradual and inconsistent: there was no clear-cut shift. See Horsnell 1999: I, 124 ff.

when indigenous sources are so sparse.[12] Changes of dynasty from Samsu-ditana to Kassite and Sealand did not necessarily impoverish Babylon, and they hardly disturbed the continuity of literary and educational traditions from earlier times. Trade was not necessarily disrupted.

The Sealand king Gulkišar, found in a list of deities, was clearly regarded as a key figure in the First Sealand dynasty. The *Epic of Gulkišar*, in which he plays the hero, gives a boastful account:

> I will darken the day for Samsu-ditana's troops . . .
> I will drench all enemies in venom![13]

A later text gives another synchronism, of Gulkišar with Ammi-ṣaduqa, who preceded Samsu-ditana as king of Babylon.[14] There may have been a hiatus in the kingship of Babylon, which came to an end through the accession of either a Sealand or a Kassite king.

From Sealand literary texts it is clear that Ur, in the Sealand, was still a centre for scholarship in literature in which, for example, the legendary hero Gilgamesh was king of Ur rather than Uruk.[15] The Sealanders were literate in Sumerian and Babylonian cuneiform; they followed traditional methods of administration and religious practices, and they referred to Ur as 'the holy city'.

Where did the Kassites come from? They were foreigners, not Semitic people, perhaps from the mountains of the western Zagros in modern Iran, where horse breeding in the many valleys was known to be a speciality in later times. They had no known royal cities in their own homeland. Their only non-Mesopotamian gods were two mountain gods named Shuqamuna and Shumaliya, on whom they relied to support their kingship in Babylon. But they were not new to the country: as we have seen, groups of Kassite military horsemen with chariots were already working in Babylonia, manning forts, during the latter half of the First Dynasty of Babylon, and were described as 'evil' only at the beginning of their appearance in texts, long before they took the throne in Babylon.[16] They would have been well-placed to take Babylon's kingship. Subsequent dynasties bear no trace of hatred of Kassites as wicked foreigners, nor of expulsion. Never did the Kassites present themselves

[12] Tell en-Nasbeh near Jerusalem, Tell el-Amarna in Egypt, Bahrain in the Gulf, Metsamor in Armenia, Thebes in Greece.
[13] Zomer 2019: obv. 7' and 25'.
[14] *Kudurru* of Enlil-nadin-apli, BE 1/1, no. 83 (Paulus 2014: 521–4), a much later, twelfth-century text.
[15] See Dalley 2020.   [16] See Brinkman 1976–80.

as victors who had swept away the traditions of the past, nor as new rulers in a land cleared for their occupation, although the new name Kar-Duniaš was often used for Babylon and Babylonia.[17] Their exclusion from trading, explicit in the late Old Babylonian edicts, surely ended. Their use of archaic cuneiform script in their stone inscriptions, their compositions including bilingual (Sumerian-Akkadian) texts, confirm that their culture was hardly distinguishable from that of their Amorite predecessors and the Sealanders. Agum II's long text describing in detail the new gate for Marduk's temple (see below), shows how thoroughly the Kassites inserted themselves into the religious and literary traditions of the country.

In offering their services as militias to the urban Babylonians, manning their fortresses and protecting their trade routes, some Kassites may have moved westwards, including into the kingdom of Hana, where its king Kaštiliaš and an important man named Agum[18] both had their names taken later by Kassite kings in Babylon. Hana, having taken the lead on the Middle Euphrates and Lower Habur after the destruction of Mari, remained a client kingdom of Babylon, acting as a buffer between Babylonia and the Hittites for half a millennium. Hana may have supported the Kassites in taking over the kingship of Babylon.[19]

Agum II was possibly the first Kassite ruler after Samsu-ditana.[20] Although Gulkišar in the Sealand, with his long reign of fifty-five years, had played a major role in weakening the power of Samsu-ditana, he himself may not have won Babylon. Even when Pešgal succeeded Gulkišar in the Sealand, his fifty-year reign was limited to southern Babylonia until his final three years. During the early years of Pešgal's reign in the south, Agum II[21] is likely to have taken the kingship of Babylon, and celebrated by restoring the gates of Marduk's temple. Pešgal perhaps took control of Babylon in the last three years of his long reign. His successor Ayadara, taking advantage of several short-lived, weak Kassite

---

[17] An alternative reading is *Kar-(an)duniaš* ('Quay of Duniaš'). No god named Duniaš has been recognized elsewhere.

[18] Podany 2002: 43–51. Although a much later cuneiform text equates the land of Hana with the Kassites, its rulers never claimed to conquer any part of central Babylonia, nor are they included in the Babylonian king-lists.

[19] Eventually conquered by Assyria, Hana remained recognizable as a kingdom for at least a thousand years: from around 1750 to the seventh century. See Podany 2016. Variations on the name include Hanigalbat and Habigal.

[20] A later ruler named Agum may be the king whose tablets have been excavated on Bahrain.

[21] His epithet *kakrime* is presumably a Kassite word of unknown meaning.

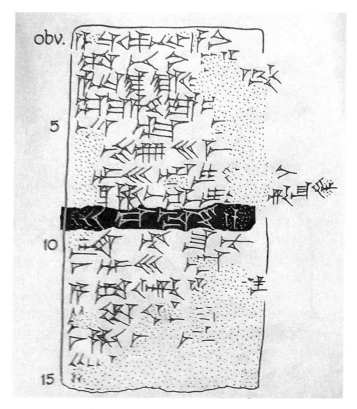

Figure 6.1 Handmade copy of a cuneiform Babylonian letter mentioning in line 9 thirty wooden sticks to be delivered as written records. Sixteenth/fifteenth century BC. Credit: Dalley 2009: pl. IV, MS 2200-7.

kings, seized the throne in Babylon for the first fifteen years of his reign and was then edged out, but ruled the Sealand for thirteen years more.[22]

As for the Sealand kings, their very existence as rulers of a kingdom with traditional high literacy has only recently come to light. In addition to keeping their records in cuneiform on clay, they also wrote an early alphabetic script,[23] which is found nowhere else at this time, and implies that an organic medium was used alongside cuneiform on clay, perhaps wooden tally sticks made of palm-frond midribs, as well as waxed wooden writing-boards: a letter dating to one of the Sealand kings

[22] The name Burna-Buriaš is found in a Sealand text, and could be the same man as the Kassite who became king. See Dalley 2009: 9, note following no. 16.

[23] The script is known only as an addition incised on an edge of a very few cuneiform clay tablets, only one of which is readable. See, e.g., Hamidović 2014. For the south Arabian alphabetic order identified in Egypt in the reign of Thutmose III, see Fischer-Elfert and Krebernik 2016.

mentions thirty 'sticks' or writing-boards entrusted to two men who are on their way to the addressee.[24] This may be the explanation for why clay tablets have not been found from this time in many of the great cities of the south. The word *mehrum* ('copy'), written as a subscript on many of the Sealand administrative texts, suggests that clay tablets were copies, probably from wooden media, and kept in the files as official records available for checking.[25]

As inhabitants of marshland, most Sealander settlements would have consisted of dwellings built from reeds rather than brick, and would have decayed, leaving no trace, neither would skins and gourds have survived, only pottery. Those two Sealand kings in Babylon, Pešgal and Ayadara, took the top title 'king of the world', implying influence over a wide area, and they made rich donations to the gods; for instance, in the 'Year Ayadara the king installed wooden statues overlaid with red gold for Enlil and Enki'. A few Elamites and men with Kassite names can be identified in Sealand texts, indicating that non-Semitic people were not expelled from the administration; but scribes do not have Elamite or Kassite names, which suggests that Babylonians continued their scholarly work without serious interruption or interference. After the Great Rebellion, Ur no doubt suffered but it was not abandoned. Inhabitants may have fled from the attack by Samsu-iluna

Figure 6.2 Linear alphabetic inscription incised on the edge of a cuneiform tablet of the First Sealand Dynasty, MS 2200-435. Sixteenth/fifteenth century BC. Credit: Photograph by Bruce and Kenneth Zuckerman, and Marilyn Lundberg, West Semitic Research. Courtesy of the Schøyen Collection.

[24] See Dalley 2009: no. 7. The term used is ambiguous.
[25] For clear instances of this usage from other cities, see CAD s.v. *mihru* A 1 a).

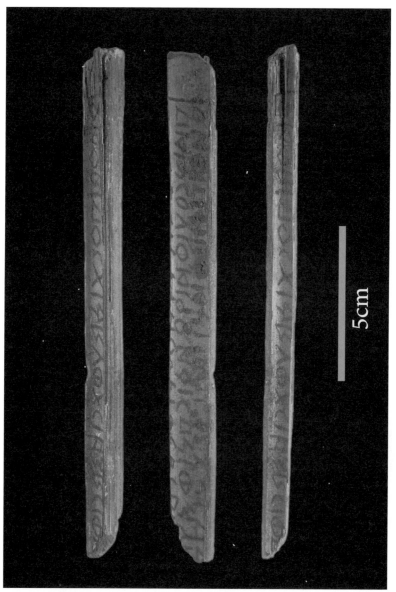

Figure 6.3 Date palm frond midribs from Yemen incised in minuscule alphabetic Arabian writing. Eleventh/tenth century BC. Credit: Leiden University Libraries: Yemeni palm stick no. 24; Drewes and Ryckmans 2016: no. 24.

but they returned and restored the ancient temples, though with work of poor quality.[26]

Babylonia's wealth, already well established through trade, was enhanced at this time by an indigenous industry for producing glass-like compounds and synthetic basalt.[27] In southern Babylonia local knowledge of soil and plants allowed the creation of new products. One industry's connection with the First Sealand Dynasty is known from a tablet giving a recipe for making glass, which was written by a priest of Marduk and dated to the reign of Gulkišar.[28] A glass-making industry is alluded to by an earlier text from Larsa, dated around the time of Hammurabi, mentioning a 'meadow of *anzahhu*', a type of glass perhaps used as an imitation of rock crystal.[29] Fragments of vessels made of glass cones, producing a millefiori effect, have been found in a Kassite palace at Dur-Kurigalzu and in north-western Iran.[30] Together with faience vessels and miniature glass axes,[31] they became fashionable in Babylonia and beyond, a valuable export. Parts of the city of Babylon would surely have shone with colour at this time.

Babylonian coloured glass was widely exported as a raw material in disc form, and can be identified by new techniques of analysis: raw discs and beads made in Mesopotamia have been found as far afield as Romania, northern Germany, Scandinavia, Mycene in Greece, in the cargo of a ship wrecked at Ulu Burun off the southern coast of Turkey, as well as in Tutankhamun's tomb on the Nile.[32] Glass cylinder seals and glazed stone seals came into use. Eye-stones of banded agate could be created chemically from plain brown agate to give one or more concentric bands of white.[33] Kassite kings were also manufacturing artificial lapis good enough to send as diplomatic gifts at the highest level. These new materials and techniques created wealth through luxury exports, enticing the Assyrian traders who are recorded in texts from Dur-Kurigalzu, a city about 100 km from Babylon.[34] All this evidence shows that Babylonians became expert in the chemistry

---

[26] Woolley 1965: 1–2.

[27] From Mashkan-shapir on the Tigris.; see Stone et al. 1998; Campbell et al. 2018: 226.

[28] BM 120960, and VAT 16453 found in Babylon, see Oppenheim, Saldern, and Barag 1988. The priest from Eridu may indicate either the primeval southern city, or a quarter of Babylon that was named after it.

[29] Dalley 2005a: no. 7.   [30] Marcus 1991.   [31] Clayden 2011.

[32] Results announced June 2016 on Agade Bulletin by Moesgaard Museum and the National Museum of Denmark.

[33] Oppenheim 1966; Sollberger 1987.

[34] Brinkman 2001: 73. It was built as a new administrative centre by Kurigalzu I on the site of an earlier town named Parsa.

needed to produce imitations of precious stones.[35] Trade down the Tigris to the Gulf, notably with the island of Failaka, also prospered at this time.[36]

Agum II kakrime was rich enough to build an imposing shrine with splendid doors in Babylon.[37] It was constructed to house statues of Marduk and his consort Zarpanitum and to furnish them and the shrine with valuable possessions.[38] Some extracts of his long and detailed text are given here:

i.1–10 'I, Agum kakrime son of Uršigurumaš, pure seed of Shuqamunu, named by Anu and Enlil, Ea and Marduk, Sin and Shamash, strong young man of Ishtar the goddess-warrior of the gods'.

i.31–43 'I, king of the Kassites and Akkadians, king of the wide land of Babylon, who settled the widespread peoples of the land of Eshnunna, king of the land of Padan and Alman,[39] king of the Gutians – stupid people! – king who has brought to submission the four regions, favourite of the great gods'.

i.44–52 'When the great gods spoke with their pure speech ordering the return to Babylon of Marduk the lord of Esagila and Babylon, Marduk then set his face to Babylon . . .'.

ii.1–7 'I planned, I took trouble, and I set Marduk's face to bring him to Babylon, I went into partnership with Marduk who loves my reign'.

ii.8–23 'I questioned his majesty Shamash through the lamb of a diviner and then I sent off to a distant land, to the land of the Haneans, and I took the hand of Marduk and Zarpanitum, and I returned Marduk and Zarpanitum, who love my reign, to Esagila and Babylon,[40] to the (divine) dwelling as Shamash had decided by extispicy, and I settled craftsmen there'.

A sculptor, goldsmith, and seal-maker are listed, then three lines are too damaged to read. Agum goes on to describe the precious gold and gemstones used for the gods' clothing, the horned crown, the red/raging *mušhuššu*-dragon, and Marduk's seal of authority:

---

[35] Moorey 1999: 160; Dalley 2019.   [36] See Calderbank et al. 2017.   [37] See Paulus 2018.

[38] It is Agum's only extant inscription, known from two copies kept in the library at Nineveh of the Assyrian king Ashurbanipal nearly a thousand years later; a long text written in eight columns, each with about fifty-five lines, not all well preserved.

[39] Two towns near the Upper Diyala, on the road leading through the Zagros Mountains into Iran; see Fuchs 2017.

[40] The assumption that the statues were looted is not backed by evidence. The *Marduk Prophecy*, of much later date, claims that Marduk travelled abroad to facilitate trade.

iv.2–9 'I set him upon his seat, a seat of cedar wood, while the craftsmen worked to prepare the shrines of their divinity . . . (nine lines damaged)'.

iv.36–54, v.1–13 'Great door-leaves, twin doors of cedar wood I had made and I set them firmly in the cult rooms of Marduk and Zarpanitum. With long bands of bronze I bound them, I enclosed their pivot-poles with straps of cleansed copper. I filled them with a *bašmu*-snake, a *lahamu*-bull-man, a *kusarikku*-bison, an *ugallu*-storm-demon, a wild dog, a fish-man, a goat-fish, of lapis, rock crystal (?), carnelian, and alabaster . . .'.

vii.11–21 May the days of Agum the king be long, may his years be long, may his reign be mingled with goodness, may the ropes of the wide heavens be opened for him, may the clouds send down rain.

Other gods are invoked to support the king, 'who built the shrines of Marduk and freed the craftsmen'.[41] The composition establishes the Kassite king's legitimacy as king of Babylon. The specified tax exemption for Babylon's craftsmen would be followed by the city's general privileges and exemptions under Kurigalzu I.[42]

The list of monsters depicted on the bronze bands of the temple doors are not quite identical to those named as spawn of Tiamat (the 'Sea', representing Chaos) in the later-known standard Babylonian *Epic of Creation*. In that text they form the army of the enemy in the cosmic fight between chaos and order, in which Tiamat is eventually defeated: *bašmu*-snakes, red/raging dragons, *lahamu*-bull-men, *ugallu*-storm demons, wild dogs, scorpion-men, vicious storms, fish-men, *kusarikku*-bison, many or all of which are the names of constellations.[43] This episode thus reflects a literary interest in celestial observation. The three paths of the sky named after Anu, Enlil, and Ea in the standard *Epic of Creation* are also found as a group in Agum's text.[44]

Other compositions mark a deep interest in astronomy. One of Marduk's decrees in the standard *Epic of Creation* is to assign the regulation of months to the Moon-god Sin, in a poetic account of lunar phases. The details show how important the moon and the calendar were in Creation, and Marduk's ultimate control over them:[45]

---

[41] The text ends with a colophon that assigns that copy to the reign of Ashurbanipal in the seventh century BC.

[42] *Autobiography/Donation of Kurigalzu*, two later copies, have sometimes been considered to be fictional compositions. See Brinkman 2017: 32 and Paulus 2018.

[43] Tablet I lines 141–3 in the edition of Kämmerer and Metzler 2012: 145–6.

[44] Likewise in a brief text of Ulam-buriaš king of the Sealand, whose inscribed serpentine (?) mace head was found in Babylon.

[45] Steele 2011: ch. 22.

He made the crescent Moon appear, entrusted night to it,

and designated it the jewel of night to mark out the days:

Every month without fail he raised it up in a corona.

'At the beginning of the month, to glow over the land,

Shine with horns to mark out six days;

On the seventh day the crown is half.

The fifteenth day shall always be the mid-point at the half of each month.

When the Sun looks at you from the horizon,

Gradually shed your visibility and begin to wane.

Always bring the day of disappearance close to the path of the Sun.

And on the thirtieth day, be in conjunction, rival the Sun'.[46]

The goat-fish (*suhurmašu*), although he plays no part in the *Epic of Creation*, recited the bravery of Marduk in a different composition, giving the image an importance central to Babylon:

Marduk, most exalted of the great gods,

Who has no equal among the gods his fathers,

Lord of the heavens and underworld, light of the world regions,

Who resides in Esagila, lord of Babylon, Marduk the exalted,

Your cuneiform writing was fixed in earlier time,

The utterance of your mouth cannot be altered!

I, Goat-fish, proclaim your heroism.[47]

His name is also that of a constellation.

2a   Kassite Independence in Babylon
Selection of 13 from 36(?) early Kassite kings in Babylon[48]
to the conquest by the Assyrian king Tukulti-Ninurta I

Babylon Kassites[49]	Contemporaries Egyptians, Assyrians, Hittites, Elamites
Burna-Buriaš I	// Thutmoses III (1457–1424) // Puzur-Aššur III

---

[46] Translation adapted from several others.

[47] *Defeat of Enmešarra*, Lambert 2013: 294–5, rev.v.7–13.

[48] The Kassites repeated names for various kings, so we are unsure, for lack of detailed information, how many kings were called Kaštiliaš, Agum, or Kurigalzu, and which of the early names in the *Babylonian King-List* represent rulers of Babylon rather than pre-conquest ancestors. Numbers for years of reigns may be misleading. See Boiy 2012: n. 1.

[49] Dates for Kassite kings from Kadašman-Enlil onwards are taken from Brinkman 2017: 36.

(4 or 5 uncertain kings)

Kara-indaš (floruit c. 1413)	// ? Aššur-bel-nišešu // Tudhaliya I
Kadašman-Harbe I	
Kurigalzu I (floruit c. 1385)	// Amenophis III
Kadašman-Enlil I (c. 1374–1360)	// Amenophis III (c. 1386–1349)
Burna-Buriaš II (1359–1333)	// Akhenaten // Aššur-uballiṭ I // Untaš-napiriša
Kurigalzu II (1332–1308)	
Nazi-maruttaš (1307–1282)	// Ramesses II (1290–1224) // Adad-nirari II
Kadašman-Turgu (1281–1264)	// Hattusili III (1267–1237) // Ramesses II
Kadašman-Enlil II (1263–1255)	// Hattusili III // Ramesses II
Kudur-Enlil (1254–1246)	// Hattusili III // Ramesses II
Šagarakti-Šuriaš (1245–1233)	// Hattusili III // Ramesses II
Kaštiliaš IV (1232–1225)	// Tukulti-Ninurta I (1225–1217) // Tudhaliya IV (1227–1209)

Respect for earlier traditions is striking during this period of Kassite kings: some royal inscriptions were written in Sumerian; images on seals and *kudurru*-stones are mainly derived from older motifs; and no new deities were introduced, with the exception of the two mountain gods to whom a few inscriptions attribute rulers' kingship. During three or four centuries of more or less peaceful rule, works of literature continued to be copied, read, adapted and updated, or newly composed.[50] One of the most famous men who contributed significantly to this process was Arad-Ea, who was claimed as an ancestor by ambitious scribes in several cities for many centuries.[51] Of the thousands of clay tablets from this period, most were found at Nippur, where conservative scribal activity flourished alongside scurrilous compositions in schools. By the fourteenth century, if not earlier, the worship of Marduk was embedded in Nippur, where an *akītu*-festival of the New Year honoured Babylon's patron god. Marduk owned a temple, a field, and a garden there.[52]

After Ayadara was expelled from Babylon, rulers in the Sealand would have been vassals or clients of the Kassite kings in Babylon. Interference from Elamites may have been deflected by several generations of diplomatic marriages that eventually resulted in a forceful claim to the throne of Babylon by an Elamite king. The text that indicates these events was found, badly damaged, at Babylon. Its haughty rhetorical tone has aroused a suspicion that this is a literary royal letter composed by irreverent scribes

---

[50] It is often impossible to distinguish undated literary texts of the late First Dynasty of Babylon from those of early Kassite times and even later. See, e.g., Farber 2014: 9–10.

[51] The king Marduk-zakir-šumi II, who ruled for only a month in 703, may have been a descendant of Arad-Ea, the famous scribe of Kurigalzu II. See Brinkman 1980–3b.

[52] Tenney 2016.

in a school environment, with a pseudo-historical background;[53] certain problems with the chronology also support that possibility. But such royal marriages were certainly arranged, not only by Elamite rulers but also by Assyrian kings, each one presumably hoping eventually to put a descendant on the throne of Babylon and enjoy its wealth. An extract from the best-preserved part gives the flavour:

> Why do I, who am a king, . . . descendant of the oldest daughter of mighty king Kurigalzu, not sit on the throne of the land of Babylonia? I sent you a sincere proposal. You, however, have granted me no reply. You may climb up to heaven, but I'll pull you down by your hem! You may go down to the Underworld, but I'll pull you up by your hair! I shall destroy your cities, demolish your forts, stop up your irrigation ditches, cut down your orchards, pull out the locks at the mouths of your canals! . . . Send me a favourable answer![54]

A significant change in methods of warfare, from local 'pitchfork soldiers' to horsemen and charioteers, gave birth to a heroic aristocracy, justifying new structures in society. Warfare became an elite pursuit worthy of celebration in epics. The Kassite connection with horses and chariotry, known from the reign of Samsu-iluna onwards, resurfaces in the records of this period when Babylon supplied Egypt with horses, chariots, and trappings in the hope of eliciting gold in return. Superior equine stock, expertise in training and upkeep, with all the panoply of glamorous gear, gave new opportunities for king and court to shine in public processions.[55] A functionary who in earlier times had been a minor official mainly connected with donkeys, the groom (KIR$_4$.DAB *kartappu*, literally 'nose-rein holder'), was a high court official. Also now the trainer, LÚ.KUŠ$_7$ (*kizû*), held one of the highest offices at the Kassite court, 'personal attendant of the king, the groom whose counsel has always been preferred, who was placed in the front ranks'.[56] The Kassite word *šakrumaš* ('rein-holder') – one of very few Kassite words found in cuneiform texts – was also used for a top royal official. Although boats on canals were never superseded in the south, nor donkeys and donkey hybrids as the main mode of transport in

---

[53] Brinkman 2017: 33; Devecchi 2017: 122. Chronicle P, much later than the events of this period, which it supposedly records, may have incorporated pseudo-history from such sources. For a major inconsistency, see Llop and George 2001–2: 1–23.

[54] Translation of lines selected from the Berlin Letter adapted from Potts 2016: 199 and 223.

[55] The word for charioteer, *marianni*, once thought to have been brought by Indo-Iranians around this time, has since been found two centuries before Indo-European Mittani rulers are attested, in an Old Babylonian text from Shehna (Tell Leilan). See Eidem and Ristvet 2011: no. 142.

[56] Paulus 2014: 538–42.

northern Babylonia and further afield, their status was downgraded when horses and chariots rose up the scale of social status.[57]

Although all the kings (and their horses!) bore Kassite names, showing that they remained proud of their different ancestry, their dynasty was as much accepted in the *Babylonian King-List* as if they had been Semites originating in one of the ancient cities of Mesopotamia. This indicates a change of attitude from the time of the edicts, when Kassites were among those excluded from certain trading activities.

Around the time that the Kassite kings settled in Babylon, the great pharaohs of New Kingdom Egypt under Ahmose I (c. 1539–1514) and his successors expanded from the Nile Valley into Palestine and Syria. They would have found that the rulers of city states there were trained in Babylonian cuneiform. The city rulers had been using both script and language since at least the time of Hammurabi; Babylonians and Assyrians presumably went abroad to train local scribes attached to courts in some of those cities.[58] The Egyptians would have found that the Hittites and the people of Ugarit were also using Babylonian cuneiform, as well as their own languages in the same script, on clay tablets. Even the king of Alashiya (Cyprus) used the Babylonian language and script for correspondence with the pharaoh. So it is not surprising that the pharaohs used Babylonian cuneiform to communicate with the great rulers around the Near East in the royal correspondence found at Tell el-Amarna on the Nile. These are the famous Amarna Letters. They were written on clay in cuneiform, mainly in the Babylonian language or Canaanite adaptations of it, and they were found with lexical and literary texts used in the training of scribes.[59]

The 350 royal letters and school texts found at Amarna in Egypt are not dated, but two letters mention that good relations between the pharaoh and Babylon began with Kurigalzu I, marking direct contact between the rulers even before the city at Amarna was developed. Because Amarna was a new royal city built by Amenophis IV, son of Amenophis III, housing both kings' cuneiform archives, and abandoned after less than thirty years, the question whether its international archive of correspondence belonged within a wider time span of cuneiform use in Egypt can now be confirmed

---

[57] Mitchell 2018: 100–7.   [58] Cohen 2019.

[59] On the circumstances of their discovery and retrieval, a shocking tale, see Sayce 1923: 251–2. For lexical and literary tablets, see Izre'el 1997. For examples in the Hittite language, see Beckman 1999. For an English translation of the letters, see Moran 1992.

from subsequent finds at other sites, in Egypt, Palestine, Anatolia, and Babylonia. These discoveries show that Babylon was far from a weak land trying to recover from a long period of disruptions, but was regarded as one of the world's greatest powers.

Long before the time of the Amarna Letters, at the capital city of the Hyksos rulers in the Nile Delta, Avaris (modern Tell ed-Dab'a), a single fragment of a cuneiform clay letter was discarded in a well, along with a tiny clay seal impressed with part of a cuneiform inscription of Old Babylonian type.[60] Small though they are, these two finds provide proof of direct communication in Babylonian cuneiform between Hyksos and rulers who employed trained scribes, but they do not necessarily prove direct contact between Babylon city and the main cities of the Nile.[61] Later, in the mid-fifteenth century, the *Annals of Thutmoses III* note that a 'Goodwill gift of the chief of Sangar (Kassite Babylonia): lapis of Babylon, true and man-made', that is, blue glass, was sent to the pharaoh on two separate occasions, for Babylon controlled supplies of the most precious and fashionable gemstone of that time, as well as the artificial kind.[62]

The letters on clay tablets found at Amarna are thought to be copies of the ones that were actually sent, and presumably were kept for reference in a royal archive. Likewise the Hittite kings' correspondence on clay found at their capital city Hattusha may be copies kept in the archives, corresponding to texts written on other, perishable material, which were therefore not found in the palaces of the recipients.

The pharaohs who feature in the correspondence are Amenophis III, Akhenaten, and Tutankhamun, with whom several Kassite kings of Babylon corresponded as equals: they were 'brothers' between Nile and Euphrates. The letters give a rich and detailed picture of diplomatic exchanges in the middle of the Late Bronze Age. Kurigalzu I's son received from the pharaoh a gift of furniture for his new palace at his accession in

[60] Known between the reigns of Hammurabi and Samsu-ditana; van Koppen and Lehmann 2012–13; Radner and van Koppen 2009: 108, TD 9420, measuring 2.0 x 1.1 x 1.1 cm.
[61] Not necessarily contact with Babylon itself, because a Syrian or Canaanite king, those as are known to have written such letters, for example at Qaṭna, Pella, or Hazor, is another possibility. The deduction of Radner and van Koppen 2009, that Babylon must have been involved, is too bold. The site of Avaris was occupied between about 1783 and 1550 BC, but the chronology of the Babylonian kings cannot yet be linked accurately with that of the Hyksos kings.
[62] See Redford 2003: 51, 75, 250. 'Chief of Sangar' is the title used for Kurigalzu I, found inscribed in Egyptian hieroglyphs on the carnelian seal discovered at Metsamor in Armenia. See Leclant and Clerc 1989: 350.

Babylon.[63] Burna-Buriaš II, grandson of Kurigalzu I, also corresponded from Babylonia, while during his reign the king of Ashur city, Aššur-uballiṭ, cast off foreign overlords and corresponded likewise with the pharaoh. At the same time, the Assyrian king began a relationship with the Babylonian king that would eventually result in competing with Babylon for domination.

About a century after the Amarna Letters, the thirteenth-century correspondence of the Hittite king Hattusili III, found at his royal city Hattusha and at the Kassite administrative centre Dur-Kurigalzu, shows that Hattusili and two Kassite kings exchanged letters.[64] Pudu-Hepa, the redoubtable wife of the Hittite king, boasted that two of her sons were married to Babylonian princesses.[65] Although most other Hittite letters are written in the Hittite language, Babylonian was used for letters written from Hattusha to Babylon.

All these texts from the seventeenth to the thirteenth century show that Babylonian, written in cuneiform script, was the main diplomatic language throughout the Near East. International exchanges were not restricted to the 'Amarna period'. They show that Kassite kings in Babylon were among the top world leaders of their day, not by conquest, but through cultural and commercial contacts. School texts, including parts of Babylonian literary texts such as the *Epic of Etana*, show that training in the Babylonian language and script took place in Amarna,[66] just as at Susa and in Palestine at an earlier period, and show how Egypt may have been able to use scribes living at Amarna to incorporate knowledge of the great Babylonian astronomical compendium *When Anu and Enlil* (*Enūma Anu Enlil*).[67] They also show that the elite of Hana (under its extended name Hanigalbat) ranked equal with Babylon, Egypt, and the Hittites, perhaps rather briefly, until the Assyrians expanded westwards.[68] By this time Marduk the god of Babylon was acknowledged in the Hittite pantheon, even though Babylon had never invaded Hittite territory in Anatolia.[69]

The great kings exchanged experts, notably diviners and men with medical knowledge. The Hittite king Hattusili III (1267–1237) requested a sculptor from his contemporary in Babylon:[70]

[63] Moran 1992: nos. 1, 3, 5, 9, 10. See also Finkel 2006 for a tablet found at Sidon.
[64] See Bryce 2005: ch. 11.   [65] KUB 21,38 rev. 7 ff. See de Roos 2006.   [66] Izre'el 1997.
[67] Ossendrijver and Winkler 2018.
[68] The elite, known as Mittanians, appear to be Indo-Iranians ruling a population consisting of a mixture including Hurrians and East Semites. See, e.g., Wilhelm 2004: 96.
[69] See Kammenhuber 1987–90: 371–2.   [70] Hoffner and Beckman 2009: 137, no. 23, para 16.

[Furthermore, my brother]: I want to make [images] and place them in the family quarters. My brother, [send me] a sculptor. [When the sculptor] finishes the images, I will send him off, and he will go home. [Did I not send back the previous] sculptor, and did he not return to Kadashman-Turgu?[71]

The same letter requests horses, preferably younger and taller than those sent earlier; also better quality lapis lazuli, and silver. The emphasis on sculpture is especially interesting because the only evidence we have for a Kassite royal sculpture consists of fragments from the feet and the inscription of a life-size (or larger) diorite statue of Kurigalzu found at Ur. So the Hittite letter suggests that the quality of Babylonian sculpture was exceptional, although the Babylonian king expressed to the pharaoh admiration for Egyptian sculpture too.[72]

The reputation of **Kurigalzu I** ('shepherd of the Kassites'), shows why that king was able to establish his credentials with the pharaoh.[73] He allowed tax exemptions for Babylon and Nippur. His fame as a warrior king is reflected in the invitation he received from some Canaanites to join a campaign to plunder Egyptian territory. By this period Babylonia had amassed enough gold to use that metal rather than silver for currency, a situation that lasted until the reign of Šagarakti-Šuriaš, around 1245 BC, when the use of copper for payments suggests that Babylon's economic situation had deteriorated.

Kurigalzu I's relationships with Elam evidently involved the same top-level marriage alliances that are a strong theme in many letters found at Amarna. At all periods of Babylonian history until Darius I it was customary for a king to cement his alliances by sending a daughter in marriage to another king, regardless of ethnicity. Although the hope may have been that the girl would succeed in becoming the official queen and produce an heir to the throne, in many instances she joined the ranks of other girls who had been sent by other kings for similar reasons. In Babylonia, Assyria, and the Hittite kingdom, a foreign wife could give birth to the heir to the throne, or could be sidelined for failures of fertility or character – the Babylonian wife of the Hittite king Suppiluliuma I, his third official consort, was banished for bad behaviour. In Egypt, however, the pharaoh made it clear that the son of a foreign daughter-in-law could not expect to inherit

---

[71] Veldhuis 2008.   [72] Moran 1992: no. 10.

[73] Owing to confusion caused by using particular royal names, such as Kurigalzu, for several kings of the dynasty, it has only been a recent breakthrough to attribute many particular inscriptions and the deeds they record to the correct king.

the Egyptian throne. No such reservations existed in western Asia, but differences of custom may not have been appreciated by all parties.

Kurigalzu's new administrative centre had a fine ziggurat built in mud brick interleaved at intervals with layers of reed matting and bitumen. He named it Dur-Kurigalzu ('Kurigalzu's Fort'):

> The princely Igigi-gods assembled and exalted . . .
> In the land of Karandunias̆[74] the great gods built Dur-Kurigalzu . . .
> In Babylon, the seat of the Kassite king, the primeval city, the firm foundation,
> In the temple of Shumaliya and Shuqamuna, great gods,
> They exalted his authority, adorned him with splendid aura, rites of kingship, (proclaiming:) Kurigalzu, king of the world, wise king!

Important as this new foundation was, the inscription makes it clear that Babylon was the true seat of royalty, founded in the earliest times.

In recent times the ziggurat at Dur-Kurigalzu was still so prominent that some early travellers thought it was the biblical Tower of Babel and that the ruins of the city were those of Babylon itself. A major building included a huge complex of courtyards surrounded by many oblong rooms, presumably a palace. Administrative texts reveal a wealth of craftsmanship in rare materials and textiles, and fragments of letters indicate an international correspondence. It was part of a building boom which is a hallmark of Kurigalzu's reign, signifying that he had accumulated much wealth for the purpose. Other building work was largely focused on the southern cities, likewise his predecessor had built a temple at Uruk. But no evidence for his building work or endowments has been found in Babylon itself.[75] In Babylon, some of the monumental buildings of the Amorite kings may still have stood, piously preserved; some Kassite buildings may lie directly below the huge constructions of Nebuchadnezzar II, but all are likely to have suffered subsidence from time to time.[76] Building and other activities in Babylon itself are poorly attested, but Nin-mah 'the Great Goddess', invoked in a curse on the mace head of Ulam-Burias̆, had a fine temple known from a much later date. It was excavated in the central complex at Babylon, named E-mah, the 'Great House', after Early Dynastic temples dedicated to the same

---

[74] Babylonian scribes enjoyed inventing elaborate versions of names.   [75] Bartelmus 2010.
[76] Longevity in mud-brick buildings is known: at Larsa, for instance, the great temple of the Sun-god, built before the time of Hammurabi, appears to have lasted for well over a thousand years. See Blocher 2012.

goddess elsewhere.[77] It lay close to the later-known Ishtar Gate on the Processional Way. In its earliest form it may have been built long before the Kassite period. Private houses and some burials of this general period have been identified in the Merkes district of Babylon.[78]

The prestige enjoyed by Babylon's Kassite kings on the world stage in the fourteenth century shows that Mesopotamia was richer and more powerful than one might have expected from the scant evidence found within its territory. Although there are no year-formulae to indicate military events, nor royal inscriptions that boast of victories, many bronze arrowheads inscribed with royal names, and sometimes dedications too, presumably relate to successes or narrow escapes on campaigns. The Kassites surely did not give up their fighting capabilities, and a few Assyrian inscriptions show that periodic clashes took place with Assyria and Elam, especially to the east of the Tigris where fertile border zones and trade routes were coveted by all three powers.

To the south on the island of Bahrain in the Gulf, a Kassite governor of Dilmun, 'brother' of the governor of Nippur, had a palace as an administrative centre using clay tablets for records.[79] Although Agum II kakrime may not be the man of this name whose clay tablets were found on Bahrain, control of trade through the Gulf would have been a source of wealth enabling the king to make valuable contributions to Babylon's wealth.[80] On the nearby island of Failaka the presence of cuneiform inscriptions, glass, and cylinder seals in Kassite style, testifies to Kassite control.[81] Although copper from Oman was undoubtedly still important, further to the west there were other mines to satisfy demand from Egyptians and Myceneans.[82] Towards the end of the Amarna period a rich new source of information is available: excavations at Nippur have yielded a prodigious quantity of administrative texts that cover about a century, ending around the time of the city's conquest by Tukulti-Ninurta I in the late thirteenth century. One published group shows the wealth and complexity of textiles and dyes

---

[77] E.g. at Adab and Kesh, both major cult centres for Nin-mah in the third millennium.

[78] Sternitzke 2017.

[79] In the reign of Agum III (?); see Magee 2014: 177–80. But the existence of a third Agum (III) is contested.

[80] The great-grandson of Kurigalzu I's (or II's) governor of Bahrain owned an inscribed cylinder seal. See Porada and Collon 2016: 74, 1K 35.

[81] Magee 2014: 180–2.

[82] E.g. at Timna in the Negev, those dispersed through the Wadi Faynan east of the Dead Sea in Jordan, and on Cyprus; but individual mines are still difficult to date with precision.

at this period, an industry for which Babylon remained famous into Roman times.[83]

Assyria was emerging as a major power. A sequence of events began with a diplomatic marriage between an Assyrian princess and the Kassite king's son. The child of that marriage became king in Babylon but was soon killed by rebels, whose chosen usurper was executed by Aššur-uballiṭ in revenge for his murdered grandson. Kurigalzu II, installed as king by Aššur-uballiṭ, and related to him, thus ruled as a client king to the Assyrian. The episode makes clear that the Assyrian king, whose daughter had produced a promising son, expected his grandson to inherit the throne of Babylon. Perhaps around the same time exceptionally fine cylinder seals made of lapis lazuli, other valuable stones, and glass, were sent (perhaps indirectly) to Boeotian Thebes on the Greek mainland. Some of the dedicatory inscriptions name Marduk, bringing the name of Babylon's god to Mycenean Greece.[84] The dowry for a princess is a likely cause for such a collection of precious objects.

Kurigalzu II was the grandson of an Assyrian king and won the throne with Assyrian help: a daughter of Aššur-uballiṭ had married Kara-indaš, whose lovely temple at Uruk, with a sculptured brick façade representing the waters of the twin rivers, gives a tantalizing idea of what fine buildings may have enhanced Babylon at this time. When Aššur-uballiṭ invaded Babylonia to put his blood relative on the throne, he authorized a branch temple and a gate to be built for Marduk and Zarpanitu within the precinct of the national god Aššur in Ashur city, the heartland of Assyrian tradition, signifying co-operation and perhaps also submission of Babylon's gods to Assyria's national god. Inevitably there were tensions and rivalries in Babylon as well as in Assyria: a master scribe fled from Babylon to escape 'treachery' and built himself a house adjacent to the shrine, putting himself in a position to promote Babylonian culture at the highest level:[85]

> The house which I built in the shadow of the temple of the god Marduk my lord . . . may Marduk my lord look upon that house . . . may he allow it to endure in future for my sons, my grandsons, my offspring and the offspring of my offspring. May Marduk my lord grant to Aššur-uballiṭ,

---

[83] Aro 1970.

[84] Brinkman 1981–2: 74 no. 26. The naming of Marduk may imply that the Babylonian king was directly responsible for making the deposit; an official of Burna-Buriaš II is named in one of the inscriptions. See also Aruz, Benzel, and Evans 2008: 281–7.

[85] His name was Marduk-nadin-ahhe. See Grayson 1972: 43 and Wiggermann 2008: 203–34.

who loves me, king of the world, my lord, long days together with abundant prosperity.[86]

Many of that scribe's descendants are known to have been famous scribes in later centuries. Just over a century later, another Babylonian scribe, Burruqu ('Blondie'), with a full staff accompanying him, took up residence in the new royal city built on the Tigris by the Assyrian Tukulti-Ninurta I, strengthening the links between Babylon and Assyrian literary activity. Kurigalzu's most famous author-scribe was named Arad-Ea from whom great scholars claimed direct descent for the next thousand years.[87]

Towards the end of the Amarna period, Kurigalzu II proved a worthy inheritor of the royal name, and a doughty campaigner: he made many rich donations to the fine temples built by his namesake, and twice fought against the successor of Aššur-uballiṭ, presumably to restrict or escape Assyrian control. He defeated an alliance that had massed at Der; and he took booty from Susa in a campaign against the Elamites.

Der, located at modern Badrah, had become much more than just a border fort: it was a city with temples to its several gods, a centre for the production of scholarly literature,[88] and the main rallying point for campaigns, whether for Babylonians defending against Elamite attacks or for Assyrians joining Elamites. Each group hoped to gain and control territory east of the Tigris, to raid Babylonia from down the Diyala Valley, avoiding the marshes further south, and to protect or raid caravans travelling along the great Khorasan road. In the time of Hammurabi, the focus had been on Eshnunna, but events were now played out further to the south-east on the border at Der. Significantly, Der is one of the few cities named on the famous Babylonian World Map. From Der, Elamite troops coming down into Mesopotamia along the road from Susa were easily spotted before reaching the fertile plains of the Diyala headwaters, or were punished as they retreated clutching their spoils. Kurigalzu dedicated a sword to Ninurta, and thanked the war-god for punishing men from Der who had killed men of Nippur.[89]

To the reign of **Nazi-maruttaš**, 'king of the world', were ascribed several major literary compositions.[90] One famous poem composed in his reign is

---

[86] Grayson 1972: 43.   [87] Robson 2008: 175.

[88] Some of its tablets have been found at Uruk. In Christian and Islamic times, like Bet Deraya and Badurayya, it was a seat of learning. See Longrigg 1960.

[89] George 2011: no. 61.

[90] On the Assyrian copy of a hemerology, ND 5545, see Livingstone 2013.

Ludlul bēl nēmeqi ('Let Me Praise the Lord of Wisdom (Marduk)'), now commonly known as *The Poem of the Righteous Sufferer*. It is a monologue spoken by a man whose unusual name may identify him as a top official in the reign of Nazi-maruttaš.[91] Like the biblical Job, he met with endless misfortune despite good behaviour and acts of piety; he complained that life was unfair until Marduk and his consort Zarpanitu relented and his fortunes improved. The message of the poem is clearly stated:

> Who but Marduk would have revived him from his deathly condition?
> If not Zarpanitu which goddess would have given him life?
> As many people as exist, praise Marduk![92]

Following the reign of Nazi-maruttaš, the Assyrian empire expanded to include Hana. This caused a realignment of powers that must have affected Babylon, but the main evidence suggests that disruptions from Elam and from incursions of semi-nomads were more damaging to Babylonian interests.

As before, no echoes of a distinctive Kassite culture have been traced in any medium.[93] In texts the wholesale integration of Mesopotamian traditions may be linked to continuity in scribal practices and the promotion of earlier literary works. It is exemplified in a cuneiform manual known as *Hemerologies* for which copies of older texts were sought out in seven great cities of the day and selected for the new composition, written down at the behest of Nazi-maruttaš.[94] That group of texts is attributed to the seven legendary Sages from before the Flood, giving favourable days linked to the phases of the moon for avoiding losses, begetting children, and many other endeavours.[95] Various other kinds of text – medical, lexical, and mythological – were also attributed to sages, who took the form of sacred carp known from myth and sculpture. As authors, sages endowed texts with extreme antiquity to give them the authority of primeval wisdom from before the Flood. On cylinder seals of the Kassite period, fish-men were introduced into the repertoire perhaps for the first time.[96] Some fine cylinder seals inscribed for Kurigalzu appear to have been designed with the sculpture on top of

[91] Šubši-mešre-Šakkan. See Oshima 2014: 3–77.   [92] Oshima 2014: tablet IV 73–4, 82.
[93] See, e.g., Bahrani 2017: 204.
[94] Named as Sippar, Nippur, Babylon, Larsa, Ur, Uruk, and Eridu.
[95] Livingstone 2013: 179.
[96] The tradition itself may be older rather than an invented pseudo-tradition. The 'Sage canal' attested from the Ur III period onwards, written ÁB.GAL, NUN.ME, *apkallatu*, and *pallukkatu*, is the earliest, and isolated, reference to a sage tradition, if the word did not change meaning later. See Edzard and Farber 1974: 252–3. For examples of fish-men sages in glyptic art, see e.g.

Hammurabi's Code stela in mind, deliberately using an archaic, traditional design alongside an archaic script on the lower part of the stela better known for writing inscriptions on seals in an esoteric style of Sumerian.[97]

Characteristic sculptures from around 1400 BC and continuing long into the following periods are the small inscribed stones known as *kudurrus*.[98] Most are irregularly shaped boulders of black bituminous or beige limestone inscribed with the record of a juridical act whereby the king donated land to one of his favoured officials. This represents a change from locally resident landlords to absentees who were holders of prebends in the great temples. A prebend holder had the right to supply a temple with, for example, beer, or bread, or musicians, presumably a lucrative privilege. During the First Dynasty of Babylon, most land had been held by individuals in return for services to the state including military and manual labour, and could be sublet to a substitute; taxes were due on the crop. Five hectares was the area required on average for one man's family. That land could be inherited if an heir was available; if not, or if the land was neglected, it reverted to the king. But many *kudurru* texts show that huge areas of land, averaging 1,239 hectares, not necessarily all in one place, were donated to a single official by the king in return for faithful service. That official was the landlord of the farmers, but did not necessarily live in their vicinity. Some land was owned by temples which likewise served as institutional landlords to tenant farmers. In some cases, the new owner was exempt from taxation, and was a prebend holder who could subcontract by providing substitutes to do the work.[99] The change in land ownership appears to mark a shift from a relatively egalitarian society to one with an elite consisting of powerful owners of vast estates.

Each stone and the act it recorded were protected by symbols, carved in low relief, representing the gods – mainly those named in curses on future malefactors. The curses were inscribed at the end of the legal text. They were not always effective: many of the *kudurru*-stones were captured in raids on temples by Elamites and taken to Susa; many

Matthews 1990: nos. 129, 135, 136, 137, 140, 141, 144. Two of those seals were found in Boeotian Thebes.

[97] Porada 1948: 229–34.

[98] See Paulus 2017. They are sometimes misleadingly called 'boundary stones'.

[99] For differing interpretations of land tenure in texts, see Paulus 2014: 205–15.

referred to lands east of the Tigris where Elamite influence was strong and skirmishes frequent. A group of three horned helmets, frequently depicted at the top of the stones, represent Anu, Ea, and Enlil, corresponding to the three zones of heaven created by Marduk in the *Epic of Creation*, and some motifs are connected to the known names of constellations. Some of the stones have a domed top on which the symbols, seen from above, show a scheme for the gods in heaven and the lower levels of the cosmos (see Figures 2.1, 2.2, 6.4, and 6.5).[100]

Kudurru-stones sometimes state that the text had been recorded on a wooden writing-board; and when the Assyrians conquered Babylon, taking Babylonian texts into Assyria to make their own copies on clay, they sometimes note that they made their copy from a wooden writing-board. Occasionally a clay tablet must be turned from side to side rather than top to bottom, as if in imitation of boards with hinges down one side. A copy of the legal section of *kudurru*-texts, lacking an introduction and curses, would have been written on clay or on a wooden writing-board.[101] Duly sealed, it was kept by the new owner when he took possession, as the text on stone specifies. Land sales and donations sometimes show a knowledge of ownership reaching back for centuries. A *kudurru* dated at the end of the twelfth century records that a certain boundary had been established by the Sealand king Gulkišar, contemporary with Ammi-ṣaduqa some 400 years earlier.[102] This shows how carefully old legal records were kept for future reference.

The structure of society, especially in the royal court and among top military men, cannot be described clearly, for interpretations vary widely. In particular, did the elite in Babylon include eunuchs? Does the term *LÚ.SAG/ša rēšē*, literally 'head man', mean 'eunuch'? Are some men shown beardless because they are eunuchs, or for other reasons of fashion, youth, or status? The question, hotly contested, concerns not only Babylonia but also Assyria, Ugarit, and the Hittites.[103] In the case of certain Babylonian kings, the term refers to a 'son of the king' who succeeded his 'father'.

Inevitably there were causes of disruption in Babylonia. The Suteans were a branch of Amorites known as 'people of the wind', tent dwellers who had been named as invaders towards the end of the First Dynasty of Babylon. They were demonized as destructive warriors, people with an

---

[100] Hinke 1907; Seidl 1989.   [101] Paulus 2014: 102–4 and n. 269.   [102] Paulus 2014: 521–4.
[103] See Groß and Pirngruber 2014, showing that there is no unambiguous evidence. For Babylonia in this context, see Dalley 2001 and Paulus 2014: 112–13.

evil reputation, opportunistic raiders, generally troublesome outsiders. Like other groups of semi-nomads, they had formed military groups and served as auxiliary contingents in Hammurabi's time, but eventually some of them became involved in landholding and became literate. During the later second millennium they were tribal warriors often named together with the semi-nomadic Ahlamu, who made incursions into the settled areas, causing damage even in the great cities.[104] Their reputation induced terror: the horrible demoness Lamashtu was specified as a dangerous foreigner, whether a Sutean, an Elamite, or an Amorite.[105] Having been thrown out of heaven by her Sky-god parents, she was held responsible for killing babies and pregnant women. Groups of refugees known as *hapīru*, who lacked tribal support and sought refuge in cities, were also troublemakers.[106]

One might suppose that Lower Mesopotamia with its irrigation agriculture was immune to drought. Nor was it in a major earthquake zone. But trade networks were definitely disrupted by earthquakes and drought elsewhere, and the water table did not keep to a reliable level. Much further to the north at Ashur, an unusual inscription of Aššur-uballiṭ I in the fourteenth century tells that the king ordered a well to be filled in, because its ten-cubit depth (approximately 5 m) was no longer 'suitable for the requirements of an orchard. In future, a king who wishes to use that well can remove the earth and reach the water again'. It is clear that the groundwater level alongside the Tigris had changed, and that the matter was sufficiently serious to require a royal inscription.[107] Babylon on the Euphrates would have suffered similar inconveniences from fluctuations in water supply.

In the reign of **Kadašman-Turgu**, Babylon was still powerful enough to offer infantry and chariots to the Hittite king in his struggle against Egypt when the pharaoh was expanding into the Levant. A sequence of inscriptions from a large cylinder seal of lapis lazuli was impressed on a clay tablet found at Nineveh: originally it belonged to 'Šagarakti-šuriaš, king of the world'; then 'Tukulti-Ninurta, king of the world, son of Shalmaneser I king of Assyria' seized it as 'booty of Karanduniaš', and 600 years later, the Assyrian king Sennacherib, finding it had been returned to Babylon, looted it for a second time and added his own inscription to the seal.[108]

[104] Heltzer 1981. For a possible link of Ahlamu with Halab, see Owen 1993; Archi 2010.
[105] Farber 2014: 7–9.   [106] Veenhof and Eidem 2008: 201.   [107] Frame 1987: 111–18, no. 3.
[108] Radner 2005: 187–90; Grayson and Novotny 2014: 215–17.

2b   Later Kassite Kings and Conquest by Assyria
(6 of 9 kings listed)

Babylon	Assyria, Hittite, Elamite	Egypt
Kaštiliaš IV (1232–1225)	// Tukulti-Ninurta I (1225–1217)	? // Merneptah
Adad-šuma-iddina (1222–1217)		
Adad-šuma-uṣur (1216–1187)	// Ninurta-apil-ekur (1192–1180)	
	// Aššur-nirari III (1202–1197)	
	// Suppiluliuma II (Hittite)	
Meli-šipak (1186–1172)		
Marduk-apla-iddina I (Merodach-baladan) (1171–1159)		
Enlil-nadin-ahi (1157–1155)	// Šutruk-Nahunte I (Elamite)	

The dynasty of Kassite kings in Babylon was interrupted by the Assyrian king **Tukulti-Ninurta I**, who conquered lands in Syria and Anatolia before turning to Babylon. **Kaštiliaš IV** was captured and taken to Assyria, Babylonians were deported to Assyria, valuable loot was seized, but most remarkable of all, literary tablets were taken, which indicates that Babylon was still recognized and admired in Assyria as the centre for high literacy. Tukulti-Ninurta took the title 'King of Dilmun and Meluhha', implying that Kaštiliaš had inherited from his predecessors the earlier governance of Bahrain and places further east. The Assyrian king may simply have taken those trading stations as part of his conquest in Mesopotamia, without having to extend a campaign there.

The *Epic of Tukulti-Ninurta* was written to celebrate the triumph. It was probably composed with the help of the king's Babylonian scribe, 'Blondie'. Enough of the work survives to show that this was a splendidly heroic composition, originally containing as many as 850 lines.[109] The Assyrian king referred to predecessors who had come to blows with earlier Kassite kings, and justified his cause in terms of oaths broken, land pillaged, soldiers unjustly slain with the result that god had deserted the great cities of Babylonia. Terrifying dreams afflicted Kaštiliaš, omens foretold defeat and disaster.

The Assyrian king, by contrast, had treated captured Babylonian merchants well and released them. On hearing of the impending attack, Kaštiliaš 'jumped from his chair . . . he flung away the meat . . . he could not swallow a bite . . . he mounted his chariot'. Envoys from each side made fine speeches, relayed verbatim: 'This is the day your people's blood will soak pastures and meadows, and like a thunderstorm I will

---

[109] Machinist 2014; for a translation, see Foster 2005: 298–317.

make a flattening deluge flood over your camp'. Various ruses were deployed as troops gathered, espied by the Assyrians, before the great battle in which the Assyrian troops, having torn off their breastplates and their clothing, 'charged furiously into combat, like lions, ... the fierce, heroic men danced with sharpened weapons'. The great gods fought for Assyria: 'The god Aššur went first, the conflagration of defeat burst out upon the enemy'.[110] He was accompanied by seven great gods, each playing an individual role: the Sun-god to blind the enemy, the Storm-god to deploy wind and flood, Ninurta to smash the Kassites' weapons. The composer of the text used motifs from the *Epic of Creation* and myths of Ninurta. He altered the sequence of actual events recorded in royal inscriptions.[111]

Tukulti-Ninurta proudly listed the booty, 'the rich haul of the Kassite king's treasure' including tablets of scribal lore, exorcistic texts, prayers, divination manuals, medical texts, and 'the muster lists of his ancestors'. By this act he could claim to have ingested the high culture and prestige attached to Babylonian scholarship.

Tukulti-Ninurta's hymn to Aššur contains some unexpected lines of self-pity, giving insight into the king's character. He addressed the god saying:

> The lands of one accord have surrounded your city Ashur with a noose of evil,
> All of them have come to hate the shepherd [king] whom you named, who administers your peoples,
> All regions of the earth, for which you had produced generous aid, held you in contempt ...
> Vilely they plot evil against their benefactor,
> They trespass against the ordinance of the lord of the world.[112]

His sentiments can be compared with those of the sufferer in *The Poem of the Righteous Sufferer*, in which the high-ranking official complains:

> Courtiers were plotting malicious speech against me,
> They gathered together, they were inciting calumny ...
> I, who had walked about as a lord, learned to slink by.
> I was once dignified but became as a slave ...
> My brother became a stranger,
> My friend became an enemy and a demon.

[110] Radner 2005: 187–90; Grayson and Novotny 2014: 215–17.
[111] Michalowski and Rutz 2016.   [112] Foster 2005: 318–23.

Assyrians controlled Babylon indirectly for the next few years, allowing Tukulti-Ninurta to hold the titles due to a Babylonian king, 'king of Sumer and Akkad', 'king of Sippar and Babylon' but devolving responsibility to three short-lived vassals. Marduk continued to be worshipped in Esagila, and the customary rituals and ceremonies were performed. Elamites did not raid there. When Tukulti-Ninurta died, killed by one of his own sons, the Kassite dynasty resumed in Babylon, presumably somewhat impoverished by the earlier looting; the wealth that Tukulti-Ninurta had taken from Babylonia to pay for new temples in Ashur and for his new royal city on the Middle Tigris must have taken its toll on Babylon. But the Assyrian king's piety and respect for Babylon suggests that the city was not necessarily badly damaged and trade networks were still accessible to those Babylonian merchants who had been released from captivity. An ingot of copper in the shape of an ox hide found at Dur-Kurigalzu represents copper imported from Cyprus in the twelfth century, suggesting that trade with the eastern Mediterranean still flowed.

When the Kassite kings became independent again, they appear to have resumed life in moderate prosperity as before, without major attacks and invasions. Fragments from the *Epic of Adad-šuma-uṣur* narrate a victory over an Assyrian king in which he apologised for breaking Babylon's exempt status, *kidinnūtu*.[113] Records of his son Meli-šipak have been found from Ur to Emar. Meli-šipak did restoration work on the main temples at Nippur and Isin and granted lands to his daughter and his crown prince.[114] His son **Merodach-Baladan I** repaired the great temple at Borsippa, traded in textiles with Assyrian merchants, and granted many lands to the north and north-east to his magnates. But the good times did not last: the belligerent Elamite king Šutruk-Nahunte I and his son, who claimed to rule both Anshan and Susa, the two great royal cities of Elam, hoped to add the throne of Babylon to their empire. They were eventually thwarted by Nebuchadnezzar I.[115] This defeat brought to an end a remarkable era

---

[113] This exemption freed the city of various taxes, duties, the prohibition on the bearing of arms, and military obligations.

[114] See, e.g., Roaf 1996: 425; Matthews 1990: 64–5.

[115] Potts 2016: 176–7. Early attempts to uncover the background to the episode of 'Kedor-laomer' in Genesis 14 are no longer accepted. See Chapter 3, above, and the Appendix, below. For the *Epic of Kudur-nahunte*, son of Šutruk-Nahunte, see Foster 2005: 369–75.

Figure 6.4 Symbols sculpted on the top of a *kudurru*-stone of king Meli-šipak
recording a donation to his son who succeeded him as Merodach-Baladan I. Beneath
the symbols are 390 lines of cuneiform text. Black limestone. Twelfth century BC.
Found at Susa, now in the Louvre. Height of whole stone: 68 cm. Credit: Hinke 1907:
no. 32.

of stable rule, prosperity, and impressive cultural achievements in
literature, art, and architecture.

The end of the Kassite dynasty was dire for Babylon. Šutruk-Nahunte,
who considered that he had a right to put his son on the throne because
of his descent from an earlier dynastic marriage, invaded Mesopotamia
in 1158 and got rid of **Enlil-nadin-ahi**, the short-lived king of Babylon.
He took an extraordinary quantity of loot back to Susa, including not

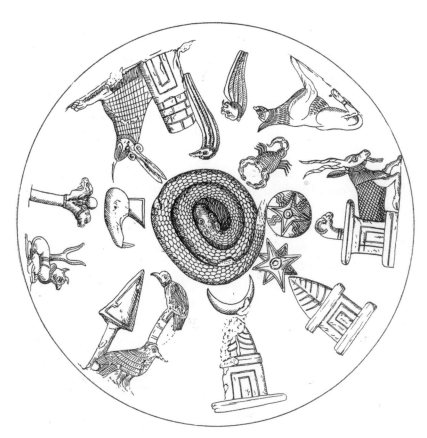

Figure 6.5 Symbols sculpted on the domed top of a *kudurru*-stone of Merodach-Baladan I confirming a grant made to Munnabittu by king Meli-šipak. Black limestone. Twelfth century BC. Found at Susa. Louvre. Height of whole stone: 46 cm. Credit: Hinke 1907: fig. 10.

only masses of gold and silver, but also the great law code stela of Hammurabi, and other stone stelas and statues from previous Mesopotamian kings.[116] He rubbed down a small panel on the surface of some of the monuments in order to insert his own name, claiming for himself the prestige of Babylonian royalty. Nevertheless, he failed to install his son on the throne of Babylon. It was a Babylonian from southern Mesopotamia who claimed the throne and ended the Kassite dynasty three years later, when, according to king-lists, the 'Second Dynasty of Isin' began.

---

[116] Potts 2016: 213, 225–8. Many of the details of Elamite relations with Babylon are still unclear.

3   The Second Dynasty of Isin and Nebuchadnezzar I
1157–1026 (3 of 11 kings listed)

Babylon	Egypt, Assyria
Itti-Marduk-balāṭu (1139–1132)	
Nebuchadnezzar I (1125–1104)	? // Ramesses X
	// Tiglath-pileser (1114–1076)
Adad-apla-iddina (1068–1047)	

Fourth and foremost among the new line of rulers was **Nebuchadnezzar I**, undoubtedly one of the greatest of Babylon's kings.[117] Secure in his claim to his father's throne, he was followed in turn by three successive relatives. At that time the collapse of Hittite and Mycenean powers, and the fading of Egypt's Ramessid dynasty, would have given new opportunities to Babylon in the north and west.[118]

Although the southern city of Isin, with its temple to the healing goddess Gula and her dog cemetery, has its name attached to this dynasty in the king-lists, little is known of the background that produced one of the most illustrious kings of Babylon. Isin did not become a royal city at this time, and could be considered part of the Sealand. The kings who ruled in Babylon all had Babylonian names.[119] *Kudurru*-stones began to record not only royal but also non-royal land grants. This could have been the result of delegation of power, or the reward of loyal subjects for exceptional service. Like Hammurabi, Nebuchadnezzar had at his court a famous sage, the 'chief scholar of Sumer and Akkad' Saggil-kīnam-ubbib whose name means 'O Esagila, keep the just man pure!'[120] He composed, sometimes compiling and amalgamating earlier works,[121] such as texts known from later copies including the *Exorcist's Manual*, which lists the corpus of texts needed for that profession; and the *Diagnostic Manual* (*Sakikku*) for a range of medical conditions. He also composed the *Theodicy*, one of the greatest texts of Babylonian wisdom literature, putting the syllables of his own name into an acrostic in the opening lines of the text, which reads: 'I am Saggil-kīnam-ubbib the incantation priest who praises god and king'. The work, nearly 300 lines of it, takes the form in alternating strophes of a dialogue between a sufferer who questions divine justice, the efficacy of

---

[117] References to this reign are to be found in Frame 1995: 11–35; Brinkman 1998–2001a; Frahm 2018.

[118] See Cline 2014.   [119] See Frame 1995: 5.

[120] Oshima 2013: xiv–xvii and 2014; Frahm 2018: 29–33.

[121] Heeßel 2017. Many such texts are known only from copies made long after their original composition.

prayer and pious acts and a wise companion who attempts to reassure him, ending with the line: 'May the shepherd his majesty (the mortal king) turn the people to the god'.[122] Saggil-kīnam-ubbib commemorated in many ways the greatness of a king whose works were studied four centuries later by Assyrian kings at Nineveh. Much of the sage's work is credited to him in the reign of Adad-apla-iddina, by which time he would have matured towards old age.

Such was Ashurbanipal's admiration that he had copies made specifically to be read to him in his palace at Nineveh in the seventh century. One of his astrologers relayed a celestial omen that related to Nebuchadnezzar's triumph over Elam, half a millennium earlier:

> If a meteor [flares up] from the rising of [the north wind] to the rising of the south wind, and its train has a tail like a [scorpion], ... This omen is from the mouth of a scholar, when Nebuchadnezzar broke Elam.[123]

Although Nebuchadnezzar's dynasty bears the name of the city of Isin, he claimed descent from a legendary king of Sippar, which indicates that Sippar was as important then as it had been in the time of Hammurabi:

> Nebuchadnezzar king of Babylon who administers correctly all the cult
>   centres and confirms the regular offerings,
> Distant descendant of kingship, seed preserved since before the Flood,
> Offspring of Enmeduranki king of Sippar ...[124]

His successes in the north, achieved in triumphs against 'Amurru', before the redoubtable Tiglath-pileser I came to the Assyrian throne in 1114, provided a buffer against the rise of Aramean kingdoms to the west. Those upstarts soon included the kingdom of Damascus. In the east, Nebuchadnezzar and his general set off from the key city of Der in the stifling heat of summer to fight the 'wicked Elamite' in a heroic battle. That campaign, evidently his most glorious conquest, is described in detail in several inscriptions. The Storm-god, 'powerful lord', had given him an oracle of victory; in the fighting Marduk took charge: when enraged, he could empty a country and then resettle it when appeased. In one account of the expedition, the army departed from Der to fight on the banks of the

---

[122] Cohen 2015 shows that sceptical attitudes are found also in much earlier literature, and cannot be linked to historical events. The crucial last line can be translated in different ways, e.g., 'His majesty guides mortals like a god'.

[123] Hunger 1992: no. 158.

[124] This text is known as *The Seed of Kingship*. See Foster 2005: 376–80.

river Ulaya, emphasizing the exceptionally harsh conditions as water ran short at the height of summer. Many details of Nebuchadnezzar's heroic actions are described on very fine *kudurru*-stones, linking donations of land to military success, and giving a rare glimpse of Babylon at war. He wrote a prayer to Marduk admitting his self-doubt, imploring the god to strengthen his weapons. He inscribed bronze daggers and hatchets with his own name, either to request or to celebrate victory, and donated them to the god. These campaigns justified his title 'king of the world'. As a great ruler, he was the model chosen by the king who took his name more than 500 years later: Nebuchadnezzar II. But none of his extant inscriptions contain allusions to the *Epic of Creation*. This is surprising because many scholars think the main version of it was composed during Nebuchadnezzar I's reign.[125]

Elam had revived more than a century earlier under the visionary Untaš-napiriša, who built a great sanctuary at the site of Choga Zambil in western Elam. An enormous ceremonial complex 40 km south-east of Susa, it included several temples and a 12 m central ziggurat, all decorated with colourful glazed baked bricks. It was dedicated to the Elamite patron gods of Susa and of Anshan, and to the Babylonian Nabu.[126] Its destruction and pillaging may be attributed to Nebuchadnezzar, whose general, the hero of the hour, was rewarded with estates.[127]

During his reign Kassites still held high positions, and the population of Babylon, whom Nebuchadnezzar addressed in a letter, comprised professional experts, merchants, and commercial agents, making it clear that the city's prosperity still rested on its trade rather than on its military strength. Donations made to the Moon-god at Ur helped to keep the loyalty of the Sealand people under Nebuchadnezzar's control; and there he made a special dedication of his daughter as a priestess. In Nippur, he dedicated a throne to Enlil and a powerful governor kept control over the country's ancient centre of religion and culture.

The *Marduk Prophecy* is an unusual text that begins by narrating past events in which Babylon was conquered by three named kings from the past: a Hittite, an Assyrian, and an Elamite king in turn, thus implying that Marduk had left the city.[128] Then it switches from past events to the future, prophesying success for an unnamed king, who may be Nebuchadnezzar

---

[125] See now Abusch 2019.   [126] Seidl 1998–2001: 'Nabu B' § 3.1.   [127] Paulus 2014: 503–10.
[128] Mursili, Tukulti-Ninurta, and Kudur-nahunte I.

late in his reign.[129] Marduk relates that he, the god, had travelled among the Hittites, staying for twenty-four years to promote trade.[130] Later, he went to Assyria, where he helped its king to victory, and travelled to Elam, where he caused diseases and starvation. Returning to Babylon, he predicted the rise of an unnamed king who would restore its temples, double the height of Marduk's temple, and lead the god into it in a glorious procession. Prosperity would ensue:

> The watercourses will bring fish.
> Field and acreage will be full of produce.
> Winter crops will last till the summer harvest, summer crops till the
>   winter.

Then total victory over Elam is predicted:

> Finally, I and all the gods will be reconciled with him.
> He will smash Elam, he will smash its cities, he will dismantle its fortresses.

The text ends with a list of offerings required in exchange for this favourable prediction. Clearly the unnamed king was encouraged, through this pseudo-prophecy, to use the profits from trade and triumphs to improve the sacred buildings and increase offerings in Babylon, enhancing the prestige of Marduk. His reign is presented as marking Marduk's return after a long period of absence, to be celebrated with better donations than previously. The style resembles omens as if to persuade the donor with a prophecy derived from past events.

Nebuchadnezzar's character may be seen in several of his actions: he was generous to Šitti-Marduk, his named general, whose success in battle was rewarded with a huge grant of land. As a lover of horses, he was proud of his thoroughbreds, and worried that many were dying of an undefined problem attributed to the *kattillu*-demon.[131] The king recorded the difficulties of the campaign: his fear of death and his depression when faced with superior forces are reminiscent of the epic hero Gilgamesh, whose courage almost failed him at moments of extreme danger, a man who did not claim invincibility but would persevere through terrible conditions with the help of loyal companions. He was proud of Babylon as a multicultural city where

---

[129] The text is known from tablets found in Assyria, but it states that they originate from a Babylonian writing-board. See Neujahr 2012: 27–41; but note that there is no good evidence that Nebuchadnezzar I 'successfully took Susa' (p. 39). Only Der is named in Nebuchadnezzar's own royal inscriptions. A Neo-Assyrian date for the composition of the text is also possible.

[130] Foster 2005: 388–91.   [131] The *kattillu*-demon took the form of a predatory animal.

people prayed to the city god Marduk in many languages: 'People of all different tongues pray to him who has no rival'.[132] The king himself set an example to people who had taken to godlessness and treachery, with his declarations of piety and his emphasis on retrieving a statue of Marduk and another city god from Elam, bringing them back to Babylon in triumph for great celebrations. Evidently this occasion is a possible one for which the standard *Epic of Creation* was either written down for the first time, or expanded from an earlier written version.

Although the earliest mention of one of the two great defensive walls of Babylon (named Imgur-Enlil, 'Enlil agreed') dates to around this time, hardly anything is known of building work in the city or dedications to its temples because of the gigantic changes made to all the public buildings in the seventh and sixth centuries, described in Chapter 8. The great five-tablet text known as *The Topography of Babylon* (*Tintir*) may date from around this time. It lists the names of the city, its temples, streets, and gates, some of them match names of features in *The Topography of Nippur*.[133] An inspiration to Babylon's architects was surely Choga Zambil with its lofty arched gateways and shining coloured façades using local technology in glazes on high brick walls.[134]

After the triumphs of Nebuchadnezzar, the years were punctuated by various incursions, including a Babylonian raid on Assyria in which the statues of two gods were snatched from Ekallate, Tukulti-Ninurta's old royal city on the Tigris. A few decades later a strong Assyrian king, Tiglath-pileser I (1114–1076), retaliated by sacking Babylon and burning a royal palace. But an invading surge of Arameans from the west threatened both countries, a shared danger which induced Assyria and Babylon to conclude a treaty of alliance. At this time Aramaic is presumed to have been the spoken language of some groups of western Semitic semi-nomads. Their intermittent incursions into Babylonia over several centuries may be connected with crop failures and famine reported in a chronicle.[135] However, **Adad-apla-iddina**, another who identified as 'son of a nobody', formed a strong alliance with Assyria, sending a daughter for marriage to its king – a surprising achievement considering that he did not claim noble lineage. Despite all the difficulties that beset his reign, he managed to repair temples in several Babylonian cities, and probably 'rebuilt' the walls of Babylon.[136]

[132] Frame 1995: 30.   [133] George 1992.
[134] See the recent studies Mofidi-Nasrabadi 2018 and Potts 2016: 214–23.
[135] Walker 1982: 400 line 17.   [136] Frame 1995: 50–63.

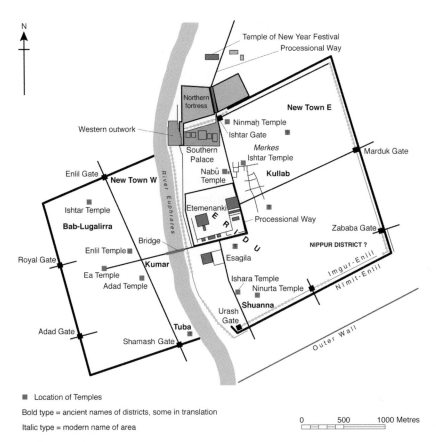

Figure 6.6 Sketch of Babylon's main citadel. Credit: Alison Wilkins and author, after Koldewey 1931 and others.

Around this time a new impetus for trade was opening up. The domestication of the camel for transport across deserts gave opportunities for greater interaction with Arabian tribes for trade and soldiery. Although wild camels had long been herded for their milk, wool, and leather, the tricky problem of designing harness, saddle, and panniers for that wobbly hump had now been solved. Camels could also cope with sand dunes and store water to sustain them between oases.[137] The main route up through north-west Arabia continued into Sinai, Palestine, Syria, to Mesopotamia skirting the worst of the desert, a very long way using donkey hybrids; a shorter route across the northern desert into southern Mesopotamia required camels that could also use the longer route.

[137] Magee 2014: 237, 256, 261.

4   Second Dynasty of the Sealand, 1025–985
(1 of 3 kings listed here)

Simbar-šipak (1025–1008)

Unexpectedly bearing a Kassite name despite founding a 'Sealand' dynasty, and the only king of the Second Sealand Dynasty with a reign of significant length, **Simbar-Šipak** is known for installing a sun-disc in the temple of the Sun-god at Sippar and a throne for Enlil at Nippur. Babylon's close relations with Sippar and Nippur were reinforced by such deeds, perhaps in imitation of Nebuchadnezzar's pious donations.

5   Bazi Dynasty, 1004–988(3 kings, no kings listed here)

This short-lived dynasty seems to represent a brief revival of Kassite power with kings who traced their origin to Bazi, the name of a deified hero with connections north of Mari, in the region of Hanigalbat.[138]

6   An Elamite 'Dynasty', c. 984–979

A brief 'dynasty of a single king' ensued. It is listed in the Babylonian king-lists with the name of king **Mar-biti-apla-uṣur**. By using in his throne name the name of Der's god Mar-biti, son of Nabu god of literacy, he indicated a particularly close link with that city as an intermediary with Elam, because Mar-biti was the chief god of Der. An inter-dynastic marriage of the kind that had given Elamite kings a hope of putting a grandson on the throne of Babylon may also lie behind the name of this dynasty. This is the only time that an Elamite ally took the throne of Babylon until Cyrus the Great, with his mixed Elamite and Iranian background, became king of Babylon almost 500 years later.

Mar-biti-apla-uṣur's reign saw the compilation of the fundamental compendium of Babylonian astronomy, *Plough Star* (*Mul.Apin*), which includes a catalogue of stars, astronomical and calendrical information, and associated mathematical schemes,[139] and an encyclopaedic

---

[138]   Perhaps an abbreviation of a Kassite tribal name, Bīt Bazi ('the house of Bazi'), harking back to the kingdom of Hana, where one ruler had a Kassite name. See Cohen 2012.

[139]   See Hunger and Steele 2018: 5. It may date from this time or later, possibly written by a single author.

compendium of astral omens, *When Anu and Enlil*.[140] Both were fundamental to Babylonian society, and their use continued to the end of cuneiform writing in the Parthian period, but difficulties of dating do not yet
allow a connection with a particular king.

A library in a private house excavated in the Merkes district of Babylon
was accumulated by diviners at some point during the Late Bronze Age –
the earliest library in Babylon so far discovered. It included two manuals
used for divination.[141] A collection of texts from the reign of Nazi-maruttaš
can be deduced from the compositions dated to his reign. Such texts, with
the accumulation of the next fifty years or more, would have been among
the literary treasures taken in triumph to Assyria by Tukulti-Ninurta I. The
great tradition of Babylon's libraries was already well-established, and was
envied by its neighbours.

---

[140] Koch-Westenholz 1995. It is of uncertain date, but clearly a composite work.
[141] Pedersén 1998: 110–12.

7 | In the Shadow of Assyria, 978–625

For the people of Babylon and Borsippa, his people, he (Shalmaneser III of Assyria) established protection and freedom under the great gods. He arranged for a banquet and gave them bread and wine. He clothed them in multicoloured garments and presented them with gifts.[1]

1 Rivalry and Cooperation: Babylon with Assyria[2]
(5 out of 12 kings)

Babylon	Assyria
Nabu-mukin-apli (978–943)[3]	
Mar-biti-ahhē-iddina (942–?)	
Šamaš-mudammiq (c. 905)	// Adad-nirari II (911–891)
	// Tukulti-Ninurta II (890–884)
Nabu-apla-iddina (c. 870)	// Aššur-naṣir-apal II (883–859)
Marduk-zakir-šumi I (c. 851–824)	// Shalmaneser III (858–824)
(then 5 short reigns)	// Šamši-Adad V (823–811)
	// Adad-nirari III (810–783)

This chapter describes how the relationship between Babylon and Assyria developed, with an emphasis on disputed control of land east of the Tigris. Not only was the region crucial for fending off invasions by Elamites, but it was also a zone watered by rivers that flowed from the uplands of the Zagros Mountains to the Tigris, excellent land for agriculture and

---

[1] Grayson 1996: 31. Grayson edits and translates almost all known Assyrian royal inscriptions from the period 858–745, often referring to relations with Babylon.

[2] This period corresponds approximately to that from Late Iron Age II into Iron Age III in archaeological terminology.

[3] Sources include Assyrian royal inscriptions; the *Synchronistic Chronicle*; the Assyrian *Eponym Chronicle* gives brief notice of major events including plagues. Some Assyrian official letters refer to Babylon, never dated, and usually damaged; Assyrian treaties, oracles, and prophecies. *Babylonian Chronicles* were composed in Babylonia, and Babylonian epics and myths were copied and perhaps revised; manuals and compendia of astronomy and divination were studied.

pasturage. Assyrian royal inscriptions increase in number, and include dealings with Babylon; Babylonian royal inscriptions are scarce; chronicles of several kinds continue as before. By the late eighth century a vast resource of Assyrian royal and official letters and very plentiful Assyrian royal texts often concern crucial events in the history of Babylon. Thus the history of this period is mainly known from an Assyrian perspective.

The founder of the dynasty who came to the throne of Babylon in 978 BC was able to pass the kingship on to the next two members of his family. But the instability that had impoverished the previous centuries continued, making it impossible in some years to celebrate the New Year Festival in the city. This was disastrous for the reputation of Marduk. The message of his supremacy in the world, so brilliantly conveyed in the *Epic of Creation*, was no longer valid, making way for the *Epic of Erra and Ishum*, composed to account for his impotence.[4] This highly original work describes with rhetorical passion the dire state of the country, and threatens an end to humankind with an apocalyptic vision. Erra, god of violence, had gone on the rampage, allowing a rabble to raid the great cities. Marduk was power-less to stop him. In other words, Babylon could not protect its territories. The city of Der, crucially situated between Babylonia and Elam, was especially vulnerable to attack as it defended the great cities of Mesopotamia: 'The king of gods has risen up from his dwelling, so how can all the lands stay firm? He has taken off his lordly crown'. Erra takes control: 'I promise to destroy the rays of the Sun; I shall cover the face of the Moon in the middle of the night'. All action and inaction is explicitly linked to the motions of planets and stars, allowing a fatalistic view of events. The horrors of war – disruption, poverty, misery – are portrayed much more vividly than the glories of campaigns and heroic victories. Injustices will prevail. Law and order will break down. Erra declares: 'I shall devastate public places, wherever people tread. I shall cut off the voice of mankind and deprive him of joy'.[5] Marduk is banished to the Underworld, wailing: 'Alas for Babylon, whose crown I made as luxuriant as a date palm, which the wind has shrivelled'. The text warns of the danger that the great city will finally lose its supreme status in the world owing to lack of power, with consequences for the whole world. War is not heroic: it wrecks the lives of people, and ruins cities.

The name Mar-biti god of Der appears in the name of the solitary king of the previous dynasty, and now again in the name of the second king of this

---

[4] Its date of composition is thought to be only approximately within this period. Frahm 2010.

[5] This anti-war, anti-heroism theme may have been present in the time of Hammurabi, according to one understanding of the Poem of Agushaya. See p. 94.

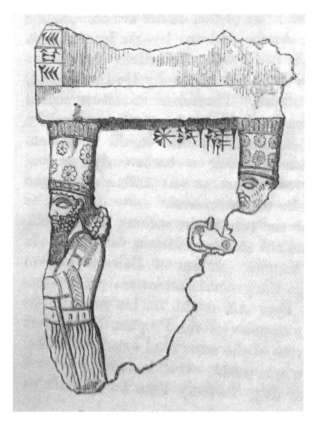

Figure 7.1 Stone fragment from a throne supported by Mar-biti god of Der, great vizier of Nabu, consort of goddess Nanay. Credit: Layard 1853: 508; British Museum WA N 2050.

dynasty, **Mar-biti-ahhe-iddina**. This links both kings with the city where control was vital for repelling Elamite aggression. In the *Epic of Erra and Ishum*, Marduk was responsible for turning Der into a wilderness, so presumably Babylonian forces were responsible for bringing that brief Elamite dynasty of Babylon to an end.[6]

Despite the mention of Der, the *Epic of Erra and Ishum* refers neither to Elamites nor to Assyrians as troublemakers. The ravagers are Aramean and Chaldean tribesmen who are found in records from the late eleventh century onwards,[7] sometimes referred to as Suteans. The Arameans are presumed to have spoken an early form of Aramaic. Many migrated into the cities of Babylonia, Assyria, and Syria; their main settled base was eventually established as the kingdom of Aram centred on Damascus,

[6] Tablet IV.   [7] Zadok 2017: I, 331–4.

'town of donkey-drivers' (*ālu ša imērišu*). Many others remained rootless. At least forty different Aramean tribes have been identified.

Chaldeans built fortified settlements in southern Babylonia as well as reed houses in the marshes. Their language is unknown, but they took Babylonian names, and their leaders became literate in Babylonian cuneiform, adopting Babylonian literature, administration, and sciences, becoming rivals for the kingship of Babylon, and were absorbed into king-lists as native rulers of Babylon.[8] But at this time they were not united; each tribal group followed its own alliances, often in opposition to its immediate neighbours. The three largest Chaldean tribes were Bīt Yakin in the east, Bīt Dakkuri near Borsippa, and Bīt Amukkani in the south-west. Usurpers from at least two of these tribes took the throne of Babylon. They were wealthier than the Arameans, trading especially in luxury goods such as ivory and elephant hide, metals, timbers, and incense – commodities that they offered as tribute when pressed. Their prosperity had increased partly because the domestication of the camel for transport allowed foreign goods, especially aromatics and gemstones, to pass more easily across the northern Arabian desert into southern Babylonia, and they were well placed to benefit from trade up and down the Gulf. Mules, a sterile hybrid of horse and donkey, fast and sturdy, were introduced for delivering official letters overland as well as for long-distance trade.[9]

The palaces and temples in Babylon and elsewhere continued in use throughout troubled times, so it was not a 'dark age' compared with the major changes that afflicted Greece and parts of Anatolia. The influx of Arameans allowed the Aramaic language to gain ground. Administrative records and correspondence are mostly lacking until direct Assyrian administration took over.

In the eastern Mediterranean attacks by migrating Sea Peoples and a probable long period of exceptional drought helped bring Hittite, Mycenean, and some Levantine kingdoms to an end.[10] More relevant to Babylonia were changes in the Arabian Peninsula where, around 1000 BC, a change of climate led to the formation of extensive sand dunes, driving unsettled people out towards fertile lands. Around this time the *falaj* (qanat) system of irrigation was developed in eastern Arabia, bringing water through underground tunnels from mountains into agricultural land, avoiding the labour of carrying water from wells. From then onwards

---

[8] Strabo, 16.1.6, trans. Jones 1961: 203, wrote in Roman times that 'the Chaldeans . . . are concerned mostly with astronomy', but this is not necessarily valid for much earlier times, before the Chaldeans came into Mesopotamia.

[9] Mitchell 2018: 26 and 95–100.   [10] Cline 2014: 170 stresses the non-linear series of factors.

villages and towns multiplied, and a common material culture emerged throughout the peninsula.[11] Various Arab groups were already semi-settled and literate by the eighth century, and incense entered Mesopotamia along several desert routes.

As early as the thirteenth century, ironworking for making tools, machinery, and weapons developed in cities in Anatolia and towns in Arabia,[12] although we still call the period the Late Bronze Age.[13] Expertise may have developed not only from alloying, but also from working meteoric iron, which is known from records of the early second millennium: 'the falling of iron which impacts the ground'.[14]

The discovery of a few top-quality objects suggests that the city of Babylon kept its hold on prosperity at the centre of a kingdom, preserving its trade and its skills. Cultural and artistic output for the king **Nabu-apla-iddina**, who enjoyed a long and successful reign in the ninth century, is known from an inscription on the plaque of grey schist, sculpted elegantly in low relief, on which a huge new sun-disc is shown being installed in front of the Sun-god at Sippar in the presence of the king. The enthroned god holds the rod and ring, as on the great stela of Hammurabi.[15] His throne is supported by two bull-men (*kusarikku*) whose presence here symbolizes the rising sun. The king recorded on the plaque his restoration of the cult and its privileges following disruptions by Suteans which had led to neglect and suspension of worship. That theme is reminiscent of the troubles narrated in the *Epic of Erra*; however, Marduk is named not as a powerless god, but as the king's divine backer, saviour of the land after recent desecration:

> the valiant man, well suited to kingship, bearer of a furious bow, who overwhelmed the evil Sutean enemy whose sins were very great; the one in whose hand Marduk the great lord placed the righteous sceptre to avenge Babylonia, to resettle cities, to (re)found shrines, to draw up plans, to restore cultic rites.[16]

Despite the tribulations of previous decades, the city of Babylon was still held in great esteem by Assyrian kings for having a more sophisticated and deeper culture than their own. Increasingly, Assyria and Babylonia shared the same gods and had similar rituals. Marduk was venerated in Assyrian shrines; in Babylon, a branch cult of the great Assyrian goddess of war

---

[11] Magee 2014: 44–5 and 214–22. See also Drewes and Ryckmans 2016.
[12] Magee 2014: 225–7.   [13] Kuehne 2017: 318–40.
[14] Fragment of Old Babylonian literature. See CAD s.v. *parzillu* 1b.   [15] Woods 2004.
[16] Woods 2004.

Figure 7.2 Upper part of schist plaque showing installation at Sippar of the Sun-god's rotating disc. The king is shown second from left. The two bull-men in the throne represent the sunrise. The god holds the rod-and-ring, the symbol of kingship bestowed on king Nabu-apla-iddina c. 870 BC. Credit: King 1912: pl. XCVIII.

Ishtar-of-Nineveh had long been in place.[17] But Babylonia and Assyria were kingdoms with very different environments and traditions. Assyrian kings had begun to incorporate warlike accounts of military expeditions and hunting exploits in their building inscriptions, but Babylonian kings shunned such boasts, displaying humble piety, while sometimes composing heroic royal epics and hymns in the tradition of their predecessors. Babylonian temples were much larger than Assyrian ones. For their royal libraries Assyrian kings continued to have prestigious Babylonian texts copied from Babylonian writing-boards on to clay tablets. As a significant mark of respect to Babylonian literacy, Assyrian kings composed most of their royal inscriptions in the Babylonian dialect with distinctively Babylonian forms of cuneiform signs. Official letters, however, were generally written in Assyrian dialect with Assyrian forms of cuneiform signs. Relationships between Assyria and Babylon were often friendly. The

---

[17] Da Riva and Frahm 1999–2000.

Chaldeans either tolerated Assyrian campaigns to Babylonia, sometimes fighting on their behalf, or joined opposition against them.

The few public buildings from this time that have been excavated in Babylonia use moulded and painted bricks, plaster, and sculpture on free-standing stone. Static heraldic ornament and abstract symbols represent gods. That type of design contrasts with the stone panels in low relief which became fashionable inside the palaces and temples of Assyria, depicting lively, energetic warring and hunting, moments of action, supported by gods in human guise.

Several kings of Babylon at this time recorded their piety to the god Nabu by including him in their royal name. In a remarkable rise through the hierarchy of gods, Nabu became a major focus of worship in Babylonia, Assyria, and Elam. During the First Dynasty the god had been called 'scribe of Esagil', and in the Kassite period he was named as Marduk's son, and then as Marduk's vizier. In Borsippa, Nabu displaced the erstwhile patron deity Tutu. At the great Elamite ceremonial centre Choga Zambil, a temple dedicated to Nabu with his statue had been installed. His cult was introduced or expanded into Assyria from the thirteenth century onwards; his branch temples throughout Mesopotamia were all named Ezida after the huge original in Borsippa. He became an equal of Marduk. 'Place your trust in Nabu, do not place your trust in any other god', wrote the Assyrian governor of Kalhu (modern Nimrud), who erected a great temple to the god in the centre of his city in the reign of Adad-nirari III.[18]

On the Middle Euphrates, the kingdom of Suhu still traced its royal lineage back to Hammurabi as a statement of long-standing loyalty to Babylon. The fact that Hammurabi had rescued Babylonia from Elamite overlords, more than a thousand years previous, would not have been forgotten. Assyria may have hoped to exercise control there through military actions, but did not dislodge the kingdom's ancestral loyalty to Babylon. Suhu was a lucrative prize: in addition to collecting tax from boats trading along the Euphrates, it had its own inexhaustible source of wealth derived locally from the bitumen wells at Hit, 'bitumen town', which were still famous when Herodotus described them four centuries later.[19] Benefitting from the recent domestication of the camel for transport, one of Suhu's kings records that he raided Arabian caravans arriving from Tayma in north-west Arabia, and from Saba (biblical Sheba, modern Yemen) in southern Arabia, where frankincense trees grow.

---

[18] Grayson 1996: 227.   [19] Zadok 2014.

In the ninth century, the great Assyrian king Aššur-naṣir-apal II fought the 'king of Karduniaš (Babylon)' in Suhu. In the mid-eighth century, kings of Suhu took the title 'governor of Suhu and Mari' and erected informative building inscriptions in stone. One such inscription found in Babylon was presumably produced after the kingdom had shaken off Assyrian control. Its king boasted that he had introduced honeybees and planted date palms around his palace; and he 're-established the regular offerings and festivals of the Storm-god according to the command of Hammurabi king of Babylon'.[20] He credited the great gods Shamash of Sippar and Marduk of Babylon with his own military success. Even though the kingdom had had an Assyrian governor in the previous century and had paid tribute to the king of Assyria, kings of Suhu wrote in Babylonian dialect and clearly looked towards Babylon as its traditional friend.[21]

To the east, despite Nebuchadnezzar I's epic campaign, Elamite rulers continued to aim to control Der, where they clashed not only with Babylon but also with Assyria. In Babylonia, the Assyrian king Adad-nirari II 'defeated' his Babylonian contemporary **Šamaš-mudammiq**, claiming also that he won control over cities east of the Tigris, including Der,[22] and had 'conquered the entire land of Karduniaš', probably exaggerating his territorial gains.

The king in Babylon remained on his throne. From now onwards the status of Babylon as a city can be recognized as separate from Babylonia in general, as an exceptional city state within a kingdom. Šamaš-mudammiq's successor in Babylon gave a daughter to the Assyrian king for a diplomatic marriage, and their grandson, **Marduk-zakir-šumi I**, was able to call on the powerful Assyrian king Shalmaneser III for help in quelling an uprising. The two kings are shown shaking hands on the magnificent carved throne base found at Nimrud.[23] As an iconic motif marking a famous *entente cordiale*, the same scene has been found decorating an alabaster urn.[24]

This accord did not clash, apparently, with Shalmaneser's claim, written on that same throne base, to have marched about justly in the extensive land of Karduniaš:

> I marched to Babylon, Borsippa and Kutha, and made sacrifices to the gods. I went down to Chaldea and gained dominion over Chaldea in its entirety. I received tribute from the kings of Chaldea in Babylon.[25]

---

[20] Frame 1995: 304.   [21] Suhu is not to be confused with Sutu and the Suteans.

[22] He names the towns Lahiru, Arrapha, and Idu, the latter of which is now identified as Satu Qala on the Lower Zab, not Hit on the Middle Euphrates. See Van Soldt 2008: 55.

[23] It was found at Nimrud in 1962, when I was working there in my gap year.

[24] Miglus 2000.   [25] Grayson 1996: 106.

Figure 7.3 Central scene from a long line of relief sculpted on the side of a throne base, from Nimrud, showing Assyrian king Shalmaneser III and Babylonian king Marduk-zakir-šumi shaking hands at the conclusion of a treaty, c. 845 BC. They stand beneath a fringed canopy. Yellow limestone. Height of this section c. 40 cm. Credit: British Institute for the Study of Iraq, Mallowan 1966: II, 447.

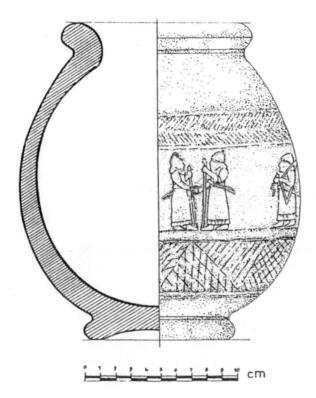

Figure 7.4 Copy of the central scene from the Nimrud throne base, etched on an alabaster urn, showing the Assyrian and Babylonian kings shaking hands. Credit: Abu Assaf 1992: fig. 5; Damascus Museum.

> Shalmaneser entered Babylon, the link between heaven and earth, abode of life, and Esagila, palace of the gods, abode of the King of All. He appeared reverently before Bēl and Bēlat, and correctly performed their rites.

He was acting as if he ruled Babylonia, not as king of Babylon city: he did not celebrate the New Year Festival there, which was the prerogative of full kingship in Babylon, and he did not try to depose its king. According to the *Synchronistic Chronicle*, an Assyrian text that recorded treaties and border agreements, 'the people of Assyria and Karduniaš were joined together'.[26] Marduk-zakir-šumi's donation of a very large cylinder seal, made of 'shining lapis lazuli and red gold', to put around the neck of Marduk's statue in Esagila, bore an inscription in which the king

---

[26] Grayson 1975b: no. 21.

claimed the title 'king of the world'. The relationship was that of a particularly respectful overlord with a unique client king. Recognizing the exceptional status of other great cities in central Babylonia, the Assyrians not only exempted Babylon from taxes, but also Borsippa and Kutha, due to their importance as religious and cultural centres in the orbit of Babylon.

The flexible relationship allowed Assyrians to campaign in Babylonia on behalf of the nominal king of Babylon as an ally – virtually as an Assyrian militia supporting the Babylonian king. Only a pro-Assyrian king could sit on the throne in Babylon, reduced to a restricted role as custodian of the holy city with the benefit of protection by an Assyrian army. Marduk-zakir-šumi made a treaty with Shalmaneser's successor in Assyria, Šamši-Adad V,[27] and during a period of weakness in which southern Babylonia asserted greater independence, it was the Assyrian army that came to help. The Assyrian king captured no fewer than eleven deities from Der, including two manifestations of Mar-biti, leaving the city without the support of its patron gods. He aimed to control lands east of the Tigris and to defend borders against Elamite incursions and territorial claims from Babylonia. Šamši-Adad took the title 'king of Sumer and Akkad', but not the title 'viceroy/governor of Babylon'. His name was not inserted into the *Babylonian King-List*, nor did he take part in the New Year Festival. But there was an iron fist inside the velvet glove: the Assyrian king removed two consecutive kings of Babylon and punished one of them by flaying him alive at Nineveh.

Adad-nirari III continued the Assyrian policy as overlord. Babylon, Borsippa, and Kutha presented him with remnants from temple offerings, an honour which implies that the indigenous king of Babylon was still his client. Like his predecessors, he did not take part in the New Year Festival, nor did he take a title as king or governor of Babylon city. He needed to keep good relations with Babylon while busily fending off the rising power of Urartu, a ferociously militaristic kingdom that was expanding towards Assyria from the north and east,[28] and he had to campaign in the west against powerful Damascus.

Der did not stay quiet despite losing its gods. Adad-nirari was obliged to campaign twice against it, eventually declaring peace between Assyria and

---

[27] Grayson 1996: 180.

[28] For instance, the Urartian king Menua (c. 810–785/80) took tribute from Melid (Malatya), and an Urartian fortress town was built on the Upper Euphrates at Kayalidere; the religious centre at Kumme was under Assyrian control but threatened by the Urartians. See Salvini 1993–7; Röllig 1980–3.

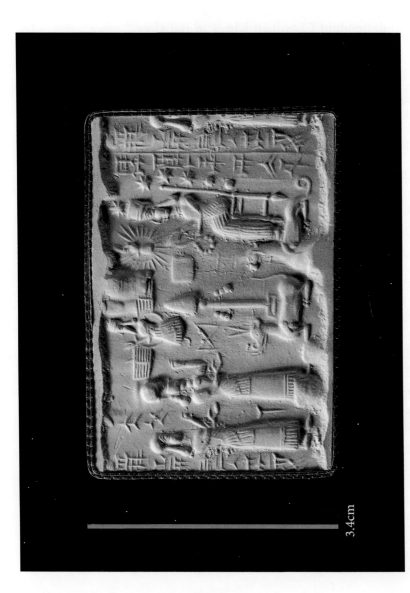

3.4cm

Figure 7.5 Impression from a banded agate cylinder seal of Nabu-šarru-usur, Assyrian governor of Talmussu near Nineveh c.786, bearded magnate of Assyrian king Adad-nirari III. The worshipper stands before the symbol of Marduk god of Babylon standing on a *mušhuššu*-dragon base and celestial Ishtar goddess of Nineveh enthroned. Above is the winged disc of Aššur. AM 1922-61. Credit: Ashmolean Museum/photo Ian Cartwright; see Buchanan 1966: no. 633.

Karduniaš (the old name for Babylonia), and fixing a boundary. The *Synchronistic Chronicle*, written in Assyria, asserts that 'the people of Assyria and Karduniaš were joined together, they fixed the border zone by mutual consent'. In southern Babylonia, Adad-nirari imposed new taxes and tribute on the Chaldeans as a conquered people. During the Assyrian king's control over Babylon, Marduk was invoked in Assyria alongside Assyrian gods, not as a captive god stripped of power, but as an equal of the great Assyrian deities.[29]

2   Independent Chaldean Kings in Babylon[30]
(8/9 out of 13 kings)[31]

Babylon	Assyria
Eriba-Marduk (c. 769–760)	// Aššur-dan III
Nabu-šuma-iškun (c. 760–748)	
Nabu-naṣir (747–734)	
Nabu-mukin-zeri (aka Mukin-zer, 731–729)	// Tiglath-pileser III
Tiglath-pileser III (Pulu) of Assyria (728–727)	
Merodach-Baladan II (721–710)	// Sargon II[*]
Sargon II of Assyria (710–705)[*]	
Sennacherib of Assyria (704–703)[*]	// Sennacherib[*]
Merodach-Baladan II (again, 703)	

* marks kings from Hanigalbat

A period of five or more short reigns in succession around the beginning of the eighth century, and a kingless interregnum, suggest a time of upheaval and rebellions in Babylon. From those troubled times emerged the first Chaldean king of Babylon from the Sealand tribe of Bīt Yakin, **Eriba-Marduk**, called 'king of justice' and 'the one who restored the foundations of the land'. Some scholars think that the *Epic of Erra and Ishum* was composed during his reign, alluding to his strength when the country was restored after hard times. He re-established Babylonian control over the Diyala region east of the Tigris. North of Assyria, the power and expansion of the Urartians, and to the west the increasing prosperity of Levantine and Palestinian cities, kept Assyrian rulers fully

---

[29] Frame 1999.

[30] For this and the subsequent period, two books are recommended: Brinkman 1984 and Frame 1992.

[31] See Fales 2014.

occupied, allowing Babylon, after two decades of struggle, to regain full independence.

As a Chaldean from Bīt Yakin, Eriba-Marduk was especially interested in promoting the southern city of Uruk, where he restored temples[32] and was responsible for introducing a statue of its goddess into Babylon. According to the *Uruk Prophecy*, a text composed or compiled many centuries later, an unnamed king, identified as Eriba-Marduk from allusions, was accused of replacing the statue with an improper substitute, an act which, from a later perspective, allowed him to be described as a 'bad' king.[33] The aim of the prophecy was to list a selection of good and bad kings from the past, to issue a warning, derived from past events, to an unnamed king in the present or future. Its written form contains features associated with omen texts and prophecy, avoiding names, which allowed the text to be reused and modified on future occasions. This format could be used to express dissent.

Eriba-Marduk's reign is noted for the record of the solar eclipse of 763 BC, a benchmark valuable to modern scholars in establishing absolute chronology. The great manuals of divination, medicine, and astronomy, and commentaries on them, were to be found in Babylon and Borsippa, written on waxed wooden writing-boards.[34] These included *When Anu and Enlil* (*Enūma Anu Enlil*) for astrological omens, which was continuously copied until at least the first century BC, 'If a City' (*Šumma ālu*) for terrestrial omens, and 'When the Moon Is Observed' (*Sin-ina-tāmartišu*) for lunar omens. The great compendium *Plough Star* (*Mul.Apin*) was widely used.[35] For the first time, texts calculating the distances between constellations are found.[36]

Eriba-Marduk's successor, **Nabu-šuma-iškun**, came from a different Chaldean tribe, the Bīt Dakkuri. He was vilified by later kings for he had been unable to control fighting in the vicinity of Borsippa and Babylon over

---

[32] George 2011: 171–7.

[33] de Jong 2007: 426–8; Neujahr 2012: 50–9. The text, still known in Seleucid times, may have been reused with reference to one of the Seleucid kings.

[34] Copied on clay by the Assyrians for their own collections. See, e.g., the activities of the scribe and scholar Nabu-zuqup-kenu: Baker and Pearce 2001. Assyria was particularly reliant on Babylonian expertise for divination and astrology. See Maul 2018: 135–6, 184–8.

[35] The earliest known copy of *When Anu and Enlil* dates to 718, see Fincke 2016. The earliest known astronomical diary is no longer dated to this time, but later, to early sixth century.

[36] Fincke 2016: 130 gives tables that display the known dates for the manuals. She writes that the untranslatable compilation *i.NAM.giš.hur.an.ki.a* 'calculates the dimensions of cultic spaces, astronomical phenomena, links between names and specific qualities of deities, mathematical rules including reciprocals, and calendrical tables'.

the ownership of fields, to such an extent that it became too dangerous for the statue of Nabu to travel to Babylon from Borsippa to take part in the New Year Festival.[37] By then the festival included ceremonial itineraries by boat from Borsippa to Babylon, on to Kish, and then back again. To cancel such a great event would have been a serious blow to civic morale. But such disruptions did not necessarily impede economic relations elsewhere. The archive of a Babylonian governor in Nippur shows a flourishing trade in slaves, wool textiles, iron, and horses, using as currency silver by weight. Nippur afforded opportunities to do business, and had profitable connections with Arabian traders.[38] A group of its records has provided evidence lacking from the city of Babylon.

Nabu-naṣir, who ruled in the mid-eighth century, was of origins still unknown to us, but his name comes first in the *Ptolemaic Canon*'s list of Babylonian kings. The earliest eclipse records transmitted in Greek by Ptolemy date to Nabu-naṣir's reign, and cuneiform tables of eclipses list eclipses from 747 onwards. The suggestion that he may have begun a new era is debatable.[39] A laconic, perhaps unbiased type of Babylonian chronicle which records the main events centred on each king's deeds, may have begun to be written during his reign. He is mainly known by his reputation for supposedly destroying all earlier historical records; but this slander, found only in much later texts, may be a Hellenistic atrocity story.[40]

Northern and eastern Babylonia were invaded by the Assyrian king **Tiglath-pileser III** (744–727), whose main intention in his three campaigns into Babylonian territory, similar to the policy of ninth-century kings, was to control the Arameans and Chaldeans, not to interfere with the city of Babylon.[41] He claimed to have deported almost half a million people from the Chaldean regions of southern Babylonia to break up pockets of resistance, and brought in people from central Anatolia. These actions may have met with approval in Babylon itself; several of the great cities were granted exemption from taxes.

At Nabu-naṣir's death, his son succeeded to the throne but was soon deposed by the infamous **Nabu-mukin-zeri**, commonly known as **Mukin-zer**, a Chaldean from the tribe of Bīt Amukkani, who took his opportunity to claim the throne of Babylon while Tiglath-pileser was fully occupied in

---

[37] Grayson 1975b: 130, line 22.
[38] Cole 1996. See also Magee 2014: 256; the archive mainly dates from c. 755–732.
[39] See Waerzeggers 2012; Boiy 2012.
[40] Brinkman 1998–2001b. For other atrocity stories, see pp. 233, 272, 284, 289, and 292.
[41] Tadmor 1994: 272.

the west. The Elamites spotted an advantage, too, and managed to capture and deport from Borsippa some Arameans including sons of Mukin-zer.[42] When Tiglath-pileser eventually returned to Babylonia, the Chaldean fled to his tribal capital Shapiya, where he was deserted by his Elamite allies, besieged, and killed.

Tiglath-pileser III was the first Assyrian king to take the throne of Babylon directly, a change that marks a shift in Assyrian policy towards Babylon. As a sign of welcome, he was given the remnants of offerings from the temples of Marduk, Nabu, and Nergal, the same honour as had been accorded to Adad-nirari III; and he acknowledged most of the great cities of Babylonia as unrivalled cult centres.[43] But, unlike Adad-nirari, he was inserted into the *Babylonian King-List* under a separate throne name, **Pul**, as if to emphasize that his role in Babylon was not simply an extension of his rule over the Assyrian empire, but was separate, acknowledging the exceptional status of the great city.

As king of Babylon, Tiglath-pileser fulfilled his royal obligation to celebrate the New Year Festival in two successive years – the last years of his reign over Assyria. He worshipped at Kish, the ancient city of which the warrior god Zababa was patron, and where a major Assyrian military base close to Babylon had continued or revived the role it had played in the time of Hammurabi's dynasty.[44] He reinforced control over territory east of the Tigris to ward off Elamite interference, and took tribute from some Chaldean tribes at a ceremony in their own city of Shapiya, including 'gifts' from the duplicitous Merodach-Baladan, local ruler of the Bīt Yakin and rival of Mukin-zer, who would shortly seize the throne in Babylon for himself as Merodach-Baladan II: as a client ruler of Chaldea, where he was the local king, he had made a treaty with Tiglath-pileser, but it did not ensure a lasting alliance. At the premature death of Tiglath-pileser's successor during the siege of Samaria, Merodach-Baladan took the opportunity and seized the Babylonian throne with Elamite help. As a 'son' of Eriba-Marduk, he could claim legitimate succession in Babylon. It would be eleven years before the next Assyrian king, Sargon II (721–705), was in a position to retaliate, for he suffered an early defeat in a battle at Der against the Elamites and their allies.[45]

Merodach-Baladan II, 'king of Babylon, governor of Sumer and Akkad, renewer of all the temples', also known as 'king of the Sealand', ruled for twelve years, and was among the most cultured and effective rulers of

[42] See Luukko 2012: especially xxviii–xxxiii, for an up-to-date account of this period.
[43] Tadmor 1994: 160–1, Sippar, Nippur, Babylon, Borsippa, Kutha, Kish, Dilbat, and Uruk.
[44] Moorey 1978: 22.　　[45] Melville 2016: 62–73; Fuchs and Parpola 2001: xiv–xxii.

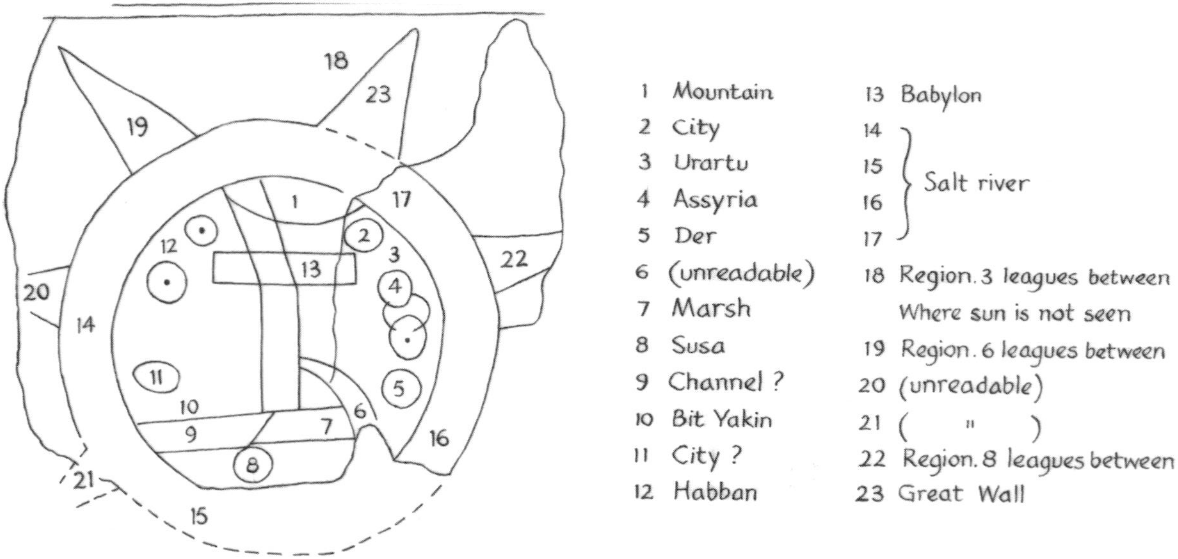

18
23
19
17
22
20
14
12
1
2
13
3
4
11
5
10
6
9
7
16
8
21
15
1 Mountain
2 City
3 Urartu
4 Assyria
5 Der
6 (unreadable)
7 Marsh
8 Susa
9 Channel ?
10 Bit Yakin
11 City ?
12 Habban
13 Babylon
14, 15, 16, 17 Salt river
18 Region. 3 leagues between
Where sun is not seen
19 Region. 6 leagues between
20 (unreadable)
21 (")
22 Region. 8 leagues between
23 Great Wall

Figure 7.6 World map incised on clay with cities and watercourses labelled in cuneiform; Babylon off-centre, Assyria nearby; encircled by salt water. Perhaps eighth century BC. British Museum BM 92687. Credit: author and Marion Cox†.

Babylon. He was probably a grandson of Eriba-Marduk, and he is known to have had at least five sons. According to the *Epic of Gilgamesh*, this meant that he, like the legendary hero-king, would get good treatment in the Underworld:

> Did you see the father of five? 'I saw him!
> Like a first-rate scribe he is open-handed,
> He enters the palace as a matter of course'.[46]

A father of seven sons would in death join the assembly of gods alongside minor deities – a major incentive to procreation.

Merodach-Baladan went to great efforts to harmonize relations between Babylon and its great rival Uruk. He was the model of an energetic, pious, and cultured king. He recaptured territories that Tiglath-pileser had taken away, and restored the exemptions formerly enjoyed by the citizens of Babylon, Borsippa, and Sippar. His inscriptions, mainly known from *kudurru*-stones, are beautifully inscribed using the archaic sign forms found on Hammurabi's Code stela; and the relief sculpture on one well-preserved *kudurru* is of the highest standard. Merodach-Baladan displayed his erudition by alluding to the great literature of Babylon: the *Epic of Creation*, the *Epic of Erra and Ishum*, and the *Plough Star* (*Mul.Apin*). He called himself both king and governor of Babylon and asserted that he owed his elevation to Nabu and Marduk, the gods of Ezida and Esagila. His highest officials, he claimed, looked on him 'as a god'. He is known as a gardener-king from an unusual cuneiform tablet inscribed with a list of the herbs and vegetables in his royal garden. His fine chalcedone cylinder seal was engraved, like the official royal seal of Assyria, with an image of the king fighting a rampant lion. The delegation he sent to Hezekiah in Jerusalem, recorded in 2 Kings 20:12–21, shows that he had international status. With hindsight, the event was understood in Judah to have caused divine wrath leading to the eventual exile of the Judeans to Babylon.[47] Hezekiah showed his armoury to the Babylonians as if to demonstrate his potential as a useful ally against Assyria. Political motives can only be guessed; but Babylon's need to trade through Judah with Egypt and with the Arabian principalities must have played a part.[48]

For the first eleven years of his reign in Assyria, **Sargon II** was unable to unseat Merodach-Baladan, who 'ruled against the will of the gods' in

[46] George 2003: I, 734–5; translation my own.   [47] See Cogan and Tadmor 1988: 253–63.
[48] Cogan and Tadmor 1988: 260–3.

Figure 7.7 *Kudurru*-stela of black limestone showing Merodach-Baladan II facing the governor of Babylon. The text on the back includes a prayer to Marduk as well as recording various landholdings of Babylonians. 715 BC. Provenance unknown. Berlin, Vorderasiatisches Museum VA 2663. Height 45 cm. Credit: Hinke 1907: fig. 20.

Babylon.[49] As a usurper who came from Hanigalbat to seize the throne of Assyria,[50] Sargon altered his lineage to claim descent from Tiglath-pileser.[51] His early defeat at Der showed that Assyria was vulnerable, so the Babylonian king broke his oath of loyalty to Assyria and made an alliance with Elam. Meanwhile Sargon was busy on other borders of his empire, exerting control and creating good conditions for trade, receiving gifts from the pharaoh in Egypt and from Arabian potentates. When at last Sargon turned towards Babylonia, he was unable to capture the wily Sealander Merodach-Baladan, who fled to his tribal base at Dur-Yakin where he flooded the surroundings and pitched his tent, sitting 'like a duck'. Sargon besieged Dur-Yakin 'like a flying eagle I caught him in a net' until his enemy fled to Elam in such haste that he left behind his tent, his sceptre, bed, golden parasol, and other personal belongings. Holed up in Elam, still supported by his tribal confederates, Merodach-Baladan bided his time. In the marshes of southern Babylonia the Assyrians, who depended for their mule express service[52] on well-maintained roads in the north, were unable to chase off the rebels. Sargon could only hope to succeed by other means to win over his enemy's allies, for instance by accusing Merodach-Baladan of removing divine statues from the cult centres of southern Babylonia.

For the second time an Assyrian king took the throne of Babylon. Having driven out Merodach-Baladan, **Sargon II** was promoted to rule in Babylon by Aššur, Nabu, and Marduk. Combining the support of Assyrian gods with those of Babylon, he was crowned in 710: 'At that time, the great Bēl-Marduk gave excellent judgement to Sargon'.[53] He described his joyful entry into Babylon at the invitation of its citizens in an account that created a precedent for subsequent foreign usurpers, most notably Cyrus the Great and Alexander:[54]

> The citizens of Babylon and Borsippa . . . said to me: 'Enter Babylon!' and gladdened my heart, so into Babylon the cult city of the Enlil of the gods (Marduk) I entered with joy of heart, and I seized the hand of the great Bēl-Marduk and Nabu king of all heaven, and I took him safely along the way to the temple of the New Year Festival.[55]

By celebrating the New Year Festival there, Sargon presented himself as a fully Babylonian king, accepted into the official king-list; taking the titles 'king of Sumer and Akkad' and 'king of the world', nevertheless he did not

---

[49] For a recent detailed account of Merodach-Baladan's actions and his relationship with Elam, see Potts 2016: 253–68.
[50] See Fales 2014.   [51] Fuchs 2011.   [52] Fuchs and Parpola 2001: no. 83.
[53] Frame 1995: 147.   [54] See Kuhrt 1990.   [55] Fuchs 1994: Annals lines 312–13, 320–1.

call himself 'king of Babylon', but rather governor (*šakkanakku*) of Babylon. Later Babylonians denied his legitimacy, calling his son 'son of a (male) house slave'. He liberated Babylon from those treacherous tent dwellers the Suteans. He made magnificent donations of precious metals, gemstones, robes, and perfumes to Bēl-Marduk and his consort Zarpanitu, presenting himself as a sympathetic liberator who released prisoners, improved roads, and put an end to banditry; he reinstated the tax-exempt status of Babylon and put all his subjects under the command of his benevolent kingship.[56] He stayed in Babylon for three years, and received homage and tribute from 'seven kings of Ya, a district of Adnana (Cyprus)', and the king of Dilmun (Bahrain): 'They sent to me in Babylon silver, gold, furniture of ebony and boxwood'.[57] He constructed a new quay wall by the Euphrates, and worked on the canal linking Babylon with Borsippa, because a change of course in a branch of the Euphrates around Babylon required considerable repair work and stabilization.[58] Sargon also did building work on the city walls, which would be a requirement for almost every subsequent ruler of the city.

To remove likely instigators of rebellion, he deported people from Babylon and Kutha to Samaria in Palestine.[59] Six centuries later, coins of Samaria bore the first syllable of the city's name written in cuneiform, as if proud of that part of its inheritance. On the inscribed bricks he used for building work at Uruk, Sargon allowed the divine determinative to be used in front of his name. He resisted the pressure to write official correspondence in Aramaic, insisting that cuneiform be maintained.[60] It is clear that writing-boards, which were suitable for both cuneiform and alphabetic writing, were used even for lists of names and could be sealed with clay *bullae*.[61] He did building work at Kish, where he reinforced the Assyrian military base; a library with literary texts was there too.[62] Adopting the *kudurru*, a distinctly Babylonian type of record, Sargon recorded land transactions in the region of Der which relate to continued efforts to hold Der secure against Elamite ambitions.

When a ruler tried to exert excessive pressure on Babylon, Nippur, or Sippar, he was warned against the danger of alienating those cities. The *Advice to a Prince*, a text in the tradition later known as the Mirror of Princes, was composed by advisers as a work of 'wisdom' literature, hoping to protect the tax-free status of the great cities. Once again, the text was

---

[56] See van der Kooij 1996.   [57] Radner 2010; Malbran-Labat 2004: no. 4001.   [58] Cole 1994.
[59] Or one of his successors; see Cogan and Tadmor 1988: 209.   [60] Dietrich 2003: no. 2.
[61] Luukko 2012: no. 103.
[62] See Pedersén 1998: 182; Moorey 1978: 178, but also Brinkman 1984: 53 n. 250.

couched in the language of omens and the ruler was not named, so the composition could be used for more than one occasion.[63] It begins by quoting an omen known from a manual, and appears to be directed at an unnamed Assyrian king:

> 'If a king had no regard for due process, his people would be thrown into chaos, his land would be devastated'. Ea king of destinies will change his destiny . . . If he disregards scholarly advisers, his land will rebel against him.

For example:

> If he took money belonging to citizens of Babylon and used it as his own, or heard a lawsuit involving Babylonians but dismissed it at trial, Marduk lord of heaven and earth will set his enemies over him and donate his possessions and property to his foe.
>   If he called up the whole of Sippar, Nippur, and Babylon to impose forced labour on those people, demanding service from them at the recruiter's summons, Marduk sage of the gods, thoughtful prince, will turn his land over to his foe so that the workforce of his own land will do forced labour for his foe.
>   Anu, Enlil, and Ea, the great gods who dwell in heaven and earth, have established the exemption of those citizens in their assembly.

While he was unable to be present in Babylon, Sargon put in charge his most trustworthy brother, who continued to act as governor there after his death.[64] Sargon's donations to various Babylonian temples were generous and well-publicized: 'He directed his attention to renovating the abandoned cult centres and sanctuaries of all the gods of the land of Akkad'. Nevertheless, after his unforeseen death in battle abroad, his astrologers, who were Babylonians, wondered whether the cause of such an evil fate was that he had placed the gods of Assyria above those of Babylon. The tragedy was interpreted as a deliberate act by Marduk, who 'had turned away in divine anger from the land of Akkad, so that the evil enemy, the Subarian (Assyrian), ruled over Akkad for seven years' before relenting, and much anguish lies behind a text known as *The Sin of Sargon*, trying to find out why diviners had failed to anticipate such a catastrophe.[65] In fact, Sargon had accorded great respect to Marduk, calling him the 'Enlil of the gods', and participating in the New Year Festival in Babylon.[66] But the possibility of accidental offence to the gods could not be excluded, and with it came

---

[63] As with the *Uruk Prophecy* mentioned above. Some scholars think it dates to this time; see Foster 2005: 867–9.
[64] See May 2012: 204–5; also Bartelmus 2007: 287–302.
[65] Tadmor, Landsberger, and Parpola 1989: 3–51.   [66] Brinkman 1984: 53–4.

the awful likelihood of inherited guilt: 'The father has eaten sour grapes, and the children's teeth are set on edge'.[67] The fear of delayed retribution is stated in the exorcistic compilation *Burning* (*Shurpu*)[68]: 'The *mamītu*-curse of seven generations seizing a man [of] the house of the father'.

In a heroic account, Sargon claimed to have besieged Dur-Yakin, the Sealand capital of the Bīt Yakin tribe, and to have 'allowed' Merodach-Baladan to take refuge in Elam. This inconclusive action caused trouble for his son and successor Sennacherib, who also besieged Dur-Yakin. Sargon's 'twin brother' directed the action against Merodach-Baladan and then stayed on in Babylonia, acting as regent with the title 'grand vizier', and continuing to serve Sargon's successor, for the next decade.[69] The Assyrian policy of mass deportations from Babylonia helped to increase the labour force for the construction of the great palaces and temples at Khorsabad, Sargon's new royal city, and at Nineveh, both in Assyria. The Assyrian king would have been far too busy to remain in Babylon for long, and his absence gave opportunities to plotters. Merodach-Baladan was waiting, and seized his opportunity.

3   Babylon and Late Assyrian Kings
(8 out of 10 kings, beginning with a kingless period)

Babylon	Assyria	Hanigalbat[70]	Egypt
Sennacherib (704, 703)*			
Merodach-Baladan II (721–710, 703)			
Bēl-ibni (702–700)	// Sennacherib	Sennacherib	
			Taharqa
Aššur-nadin-šumi (699–694)*			
Mušezib-Marduk (aka Šuzubu the Chaldean, 692–689)			
	// Sennacherib		
Esarhaddon (680–669)*	Esarhaddon	Esarhaddon	
			Taharqa
			Tantamani
Ashurbanipal (668)*	Ashurbanipal	Ashurbanipal	
			Psammetichus
Šamaš-šum-ukin (c. 668–652)* Ashurbanipal*	// Ashurbanipal		

[67] Ezekiel 17:2.   [68] Borger 2000: tablet III line 6.   [69] May 2012.
[70] See Grayson and Novotny 2012: 23; Fales 2014.

Kandalanu (647–627)	// Aššur-etel-ilani (c. 630–627)
	// Sin-šum-lišir (c. 627–626)
	// Sin-šar-iškun (c. 627–612)*
Nabopolassar (625–605)	// Sin-šar-iškun
	// Aššur-uballiṭ II (c. 611–609)

Note: asterisks mark Assyrian kings ruling in Babylon.

Sargon's unexpected death abroad in battle led to the well-planned accession in Assyria of his son **Sennacherib**, who had already gained experience as an able administrator for his father. Like his father, Sennacherib was regarded as a man of Hanigalbat extraction. But he did not acknowledge his paternity, perhaps because he hoped to avert inheriting a sin that had not been identified, yet might be inherited. He did not take the title 'king of Babylon'.

The difficulties encountered by Sargon trying to rule Babylon directly suggest that the Assyrian king could control neither the city nor southern Babylonia when he was obliged to fulfil manifold duties in Assyria and to campaign abroad. The way ahead may have seemed clear from the success of Sargon's brother, who had been put in charge while the king was still alive, and stayed to control the country when Sargon died and Sennacherib was crowned king in Assyria. Sargon and Sennacherib had had the foresight to educate in Assyria a native Babylonian, **Bēl-ibni**, 'who had grown up in my palace like a young dog', and who then ruled Babylon for three years on behalf of the Assyrians. But stability was undermined by the Chaldeans and Elamites: there were no fewer than seven changes of ruler in Babylon during the first fifteen years of Sennacherib's reign in Assyria.

Sennacherib briefly ruled Babylon, but soon a usurper seized the throne and ruled very briefly before being deposed in the same year by the resurgent Merodach-Baladan II, who in turn was driven out by Sennacherib. The Assyrian-educated Bēl-ibni was then put on the throne.[71] It may have been during this time that fine red brecchia stone was used to make great well heads and a water supply system in Babylon;[72] the same type of stone was used to pave the Processional Way with slabs bearing the simple inscription 'Sennacherib. King of Assyria'.[73] The appointment of Bēl-ibni was not a success: after a couple of years, the Chaldeans and Elamites conspired to put a

---

[71] The sequence of events is sometimes confusing in the royal inscriptions; see Grayson and Novotny 2012: 9–14.

[72] Frahm 1997: 191.   [73] Frame 1995: 154.

Chaldean on the throne in 702. Sennacherib soon drove out the new man, then chased Merodach-Baladan (who had managed to take the throne again and rule for nine months) into the marshes after a battle: 'He joyfully entered his palace in Babylon, and took possession of his treasury as well as his wife, his palace women, courtiers, and craftsmen'.

Sennacherib put his son **Aššur-nadin-šumi** on the throne in 699, and his six years of rule gave a short period of stability to Babylon. During that time, the Assyrians had boats built by Sidonian craftsmen to fight the Chaldeans in the marshes, but they were eluded with ease. Meanwhile the Elamites launched an invasion into northern Babylonia and succeeded in capturing Sippar. In 694 they carried off Aššur-nadin-šumi, who was never heard of again. A new king appointed by the Elamites in Babylon to replace Sennacherib's son was taken captive, and Sennacherib, bereaved and infuriated, campaigned against the usurper's supporters in Babylonia, and against the Elamites who had interfered to depose the Assyrian king's son. In 692 the traitors in Babylon took gold and silver from the treasury of Esagila and gave it to the Elamites to secure a wide range of allies. Sennacherib raged through the lands along the border with Elam, capturing forts and making the city of Der a command centre for Assyrian soldiers in the region, but he was unable to re-establish control in Babylon despite support from some of the great cities. Babylon virtually became a protectorate of the Elamite ruler in Susa. A ferocious battle took place in the following year at Halule,[74] described by royal inscriptions in an epic style that bears striking resemblances to the battle told in the eleventh book of Homer's *Iliad*.[75] The inscriptions describing the action begin with a list of twenty-four enemy contingents who

> gathered like a swarm of locusts in springtime, rising up together against me to do battle; the dust from their feet covered the face of the broad sky like a severe storm in very cold weather.

Then the narrative focuses on the Assyrian king donning his armour, mounting his chariot, and brandishing his bow to lead the action supported by all the great gods. The text spares no detail of the blood and guts – one might think that he had won a significant victory, with the few enemies that survived chased off the field of battle, and a son of Merodach-Baladan

---

[74] Halule was to the north of Babylon, on the Tigris near modern Samarra.
[75] See West 1995, who gives the *Iliad* a mid-seventh-century date of final composition.

captured.[76] But a Babylonian chronicle states clearly that the Elamite king won, forcing the Assyrians to retreat.[77] The comparison between these sources shows how an unreliable impression of triumph can be gained from such magnificent epic-style royal texts. At a later date, Sennacherib pursued Merodach-Baladan for the last time:

> Merodach-Baladan fled alone to the Sealand. Then he gathered up the gods throughout his land together with the bones of his ancestors from their tombs, loaded his people into boats, and crossed over to the city of Nagitu, which is on the far side of the bitter sea. There he disappeared.[78]

Although Sennacherib was able to recapture Babylon in 689, it was only after a siege of fifteen months, which caused terrible suffering in the city. Abandoning the respect due to its religious and cultural status, he treated it like any other enemy city, carrying off the main cult statue of Marduk, and ordering demolition on a scale described with rhetorical passion in rock inscriptions in the heart of Assyria. He claimed to have 'filled the city squares' with the corpses of its citizens, young and old, and smashed divine images:

> I blew in like the onset of a tempest . . . I destroyed, devastated, and burned with fire the city and its buildings, from its foundations to its crenellations. I tore out brick and earth, as much as there was, from the inner and outer city wall, the temples, and the ziggurat, and threw them into the Arahtu river. I dug canals into the centre of that city and levelled the site with water. I destroyed the outline of its foundations to make its destruction even greater than that by the Flood, so that in future the site of that city and temples would be unrecognizable. I dissolved it in water and reduced it to meadowland.[79]

One would expect from this dramatic passage that archaeologists would have found physical evidence at the very least for a layer of destruction by fire and water corresponding to the text. But not a shred of evidence for any kind of devastation has come to light on the main citadel mound,[80] leading one to wonder whether the event consisted mainly of symbolic acts of destruction: removing a token pot of soil, and token bricks from the

---

[76] Parts of this narrative bear comparison with book 11 of the Homeric *Iliad* (see West 1997: 375–6), and with a passage in the fragmentary Inaros Tale, found on papyrus fragments at Tebtunis in Egypt, in which Esarhaddon is named. See Hoffmann and Quack 2007: 64 and 107–17; and p. 206 below.

[77] See Grayson and Novotny 2012: 6.   [78] Grayson and Novotny 2012: 221–2.

[79] See Grayson and Novotny 2014: 316 for the full text.   [80] See, e.g., Frame 1992: 55–6.

Figure 7.8 Part of a black *kudurru*-stone showing Aššur-nadin-šumi, eldest son of Sennacherib, as king of Babylon. Divine symbols include the *mušhuššu*-dragon of Marduk. Height 15 cm. AM 1933 1101-c. Credit: by kind permission of the Ashmolean Museum.

ziggurat, and throwing the debris into the Euphrates.[81] However, the key act of subjugation was to remove the main cult statue along with the god's consort, his bed, and his throne, which Sennacherib carried off to Assyria in an act that deprived the city of divine support. Excavators found that the red brecchia paving stones on the Processional Way, inscribed for

---

[81] George 2005–6: 79.

Sennacherib, had simply been turned upside down and reused in the same place. Sennacherib does not mention the fate of the temple treasury, which may therefore have remained in place. Once again, an epic-style royal text gives a very misleading impression.

These events had a significant impact on literature, quite apart from the royal inscriptions. Sennacherib commissioned a new version of part of the *Epic of Creation* that put the Assyrian god Aššur in place of Marduk as the hero god who created the universe, composing appropriate commentaries to explain the changes.[82] A detailed scene related to the new version was publicly displayed on the gates of a New Year Festival temple which he built at Ashur: art in the service of politics. On the understanding that similar-sounding names had deep significance, he used the divine names Asarre (one of Marduk's names) and Anshar, which resemble the name Aššur, to enable the transition. A dais for one of Marduk's statues under the name Asarre at Babylon reflects this reinterpretation.[83] Sennacherib replaced the dedicatory inscriptions on the bed and throne of Marduk and his consort with dedications to Aššur and his consort.[84] An entirely new work, the *Ordeal of Marduk*, was composed in two different versions, Assyrian and Babylonian, to show Marduk as a criminal put on trial and imprisoned for sins against Aššur, then banished powerless to the Underworld; Ishtar-of-Nineveh was his nurse, and Aššur took control of the Tablet of Destinies.[85] These texts and commentaries show how recent events were considered from two complementary aspects, the one on earth and the other in heaven, intertwined in literary royal inscriptions. Words were used as weapons of power.

Regardless of political and military events, Sennacherib was attended by sage-scholars in the Babylonian tradition, following the practice of earlier Assyrian kings. This is a distinctive mark of Assyrian respect for Babylon's cultural eminence. Even a top Assyrian official might engage a Babylonian scholar to educate his own son. A letter to Sennacherib's successor and son, Esarhaddon, tells of such a situation:

> Parutu, the goldsmith of the queen's household, has, like the king and the crown prince, paid for a Babylonian and settled him in his own house. He teaches exorcistic literature to his son, extispicy omens have been explained to him, and he has even studied a collection of materials from *Enūma Anu Enlil*.[86]

---

[82] See Frahm 2011: 349–60 for a full discussion.   [83] See George 1992: 248.
[84] Grayson and Novotny 2014: no. 161.   [85] Frahm 2011: 352–8.
[86] Luukko and van Buylaere 2002: no. 65.

By this period, Aramaic was certainly the general vernacular in both Assyria and Babylonia, but texts emanating from the royal court were still written in cuneiform, and the Babylonian scholars who wrote for the Assyrian king continued to use Babylonian dialect and script.[87]

The great city had been terribly impoverished by the events of Sennacherib's reign, not least the long siege. The damage done was probably left unrepaired for about twenty years, with no government to take the initiative and no wealth to fund the work. The Euphrates may have changed course, inflicting further damage.[88] The main cult statue of Marduk stayed in Assyria, powerless to help his people; but his cult continued elsewhere, and Babylon's temples still stood. The Sealand region, including the city of Ur, was governed separately by two sons of the deposed king Merodach-Baladan II, with such a close relationship to Elam that an Elamite king claimed the Sealand belonged to Elam, not to Assyria.

Sennacherib was murdered by one of his sons in 681.[89] The instigator was Esarhaddon with the help of his powerful mother Naqia-Zakutu, who was the king's second official consort, and with support from a faction in Babylon.[90] The regicide resulted in a struggle in Nineveh against Esarhaddon's half-brothers including the previous crown prince, whom Esarhaddon had displaced.[91] Sennacherib's grandson, the great Ashurbanipal, later 'dedicated Babylonians as a funerary offering'[92] at the place where Sennacherib was murdered, thus implicating Babylon's citizens in the regicide. This reflects a shift in the blame: Sennacherib's son and successor had claimed that Marduk abandoned Babylon because its citizens had taken treasure from Marduk's temple to pay the Elamites for their help; essentially, Marduk himself was responsible for the awful state of the city.[93] But more than a century later, the Babylonian king

---

[87] For example, the sign *LUGAL* ('king') has an Assyrian form that is different from its Babylonian form; 'path' is *hūlu* in Assyrian, *harrānu* in Babylonian; the two dialects use verbs differently.

[88] Leichty 2011: 203.

[89] Knapp 2015: 310–31; Grayson and Novotny 2014: 26–9 questions the previous suggestion that Esarhaddon's half-brothers were responsible for the murder.

[90] The name of Semiramis and her location in Babylon in later legends may relate to deeds of Naqia in the seventh century BC; see Frahm 2016.

[91] For a change of dating Esarhaddon's inscriptions, see Leichty 2011: 6; Novotny 2015b, and 2015a.

[92] This may mean that he sacrificed them.   [93] Leichty 2011: 225, 229, 244.

Nabonidus claimed that Sennacherib was murdered because he had sacked Babylon.[94]

Babylon had no king for the next eight years of Sennacherib's reign and the twelve years of Esarhaddon's reign – a total of twenty years during which time the city's role as the great ceremonial centre of all Babylonia was discontinued. The New Year Festival was suspended. A huge number of Babylonians – as many as 208,000 are mentioned in one text – were deported to labour on the construction of new palaces at Nineveh and other grand projects in Assyria.

Esarhaddon came to the throne after a brief civil war in northern Assyria, and faced subsequent difficulties: the Elamites exploited the situation, and entered Sippar in his sixth year, where a massacre took place; a son of Merodach-Baladan besieged Ur; the *Babylonian Chronicles* record much beheading of foreign rulers who reneged on their oaths of loyalty.[95] Towards the end of his reign, Esarhaddon carried out a purge of many of his chief officials, presumably to forestall a major uprising. Although he took the titles 'king of Sumer and Akkad, governor of Babylon', the *Babylonian Chronicles* do not mention any restoration work in Babylon; there was no New Year Festival in which Esarhaddon could participate, and his name was not added to the king-list of Babylon. Ostensibly, he had some work done on the great Esagila temple and on the ziggurat, but some of his claims may record intentions rather than action.

Esarhaddon's grandfather, Sargon II, had died abroad in battle, a tragedy unforeseen by diviners. As a traditional memorial inscription, *The Sin of Sargon* begins, 'I am Sennacherib', but it was presumably composed by Esarhaddon since it refers also to Sennacherib's own premature death.[96] Had Sargon's grandson, now ruling in Babylon, inherited some unidentified guilt and brought its pollution into the city? Official versions of events changed over time. The sacking and destruction of Babylon by Sennacherib could be considered an atrocity because of the esteem in which the Assyrians held the city; but the memorial inscription describes how Sennacherib had revered Marduk, and from the grave urged Esarhaddon to complete repairs on the god's statue, which was still held captive in Assyria, exoncrating his father and implying that the work he had piously undertaken was unfinished.

[94] Grayson and Novotny 2014: 28 n. 94.   [95] Leichty 2011: 7.
[96] Tadmor, Landsberger, and Parpola 1989.

Babylon's tax-exempt status may have been eroded during the kingless years, provoking 'the people of Babylon' to write a formal letter to Esarhaddon:

> Ever since the kings our lords sat on the throne, you have been keen to confirm our protected status and our happiness . . . Babylon is 'the bowl of Enlil's dog' – its name is established for protection; even a dog that enters inside it is not killed.[97]

Impoverished though Babylon was, there was still a danger that the Elamites would take advantage of the situation and seize the city. Were their overtures of reconciliation to be trusted?

> Shamash, great lord, give me a firm, reliable answer to what I ask you. If Urtaku king of Elam has sent his proposal for making peace to Esarhaddon king of Assyria, has he honestly sent true, reliable words of reconciliation to Esarhaddon?[98]

If it is the case that Esarhaddon and his mother Naqia colluded in the murder of Sennacherib – his father, her husband – his nervous nature and an illness would have made him insecure, to say the least.[99] His mother, dominating her son, received reports about political matters, and was responsible for restoring the quay in Babylon.[100] As the owner of estates in Lahiru (biblical Laʾir) east of the Tigris, she was inevitably involved in events linked to Elamite insurgencies and Babylonian politics.

Like his predecessors, Esarhaddon employed Babylonian scribes and scholars who were no doubt responsible for his perfect expressions of piety,[101] and they wrote remarkably fine accounts of his expeditions far abroad. His royal inscriptions conceal his long delay in beginning to repair the damage at Babylon, by using an ambiguous term that can mean either 'at the beginning of my rule' or 'at the top of my rule'.[102] With the aim of leaving an impressive-seeming legacy for posterity, the ambiguity, masking the truth, allows the impression of a dynamic, successful ruler who was able to carry out major work in Babylon immediately on winning the throne. The sequence of events in Esarhaddon's reign is now better understood, showing that some royal inscriptions that described events leading up to the murder of his father were written not soon after his succession, but much later, just a couple of years before his death. His first attempt to

---

[97] Reynolds 2003: no. 158   [98] Translation based on Starr 1990: no. 74.
[99] Porter and Radner 1998: 146.
[100] Leichty 2011: 315–24, and for her correspondence etc., see Melville 1999.
[101] Bēl-ušēzib is one example among many.   [102] Frame 1992: 67; Leichty 2011: 6.

invade Egypt failed; on his second attempt he attacked from the desert of Sinai, and was briefly successful in conquering Lower Egypt and territory up the Nile as far as Memphis, driving the Nubian king Taharqa from cities of the Nile delta and installing grateful local city rulers, Egyptians who were bound by oaths of loyalty. He took the title 'king of the kings of (Lower) Egypt, Upper Egypt and Kush', having extracted widespread tribute as well as loot from Memphis to fund restoration work in Babylonia. But the Egyptian cities soon regained their independence, facing another invasion by the relentless Taharqa. Babylon, meanwhile, was left open to treachery. Esarhaddon's third attempt to invade Egypt was aborted when he died on the way; evidently the gods and diviners had failed to protect him.

The Lion of Babylon is a gigantic block of basalt roughly carved, and unfinished, to show a lion dominating a prostrate man. Found in 1852, it stands 1.95 m high, and 2.6 m long. It is still on the site of Babylon on a new pedestal block, too heavy to move. The lion may represent Assyrian royalty, as it does on Assyrian royal seals, and the man lying beneath it has only one parallel, on a pair of ivory plaques found in Assyria, on which he is usually identified as a Nubian.[103] This comparison suggests that the monument represents Esarhaddon's conquest of Egypt and remains unfinished because he died in 669 on the way there.

Towards the end of his reign, having at last received favourable omens, Esarhaddon claimed that he had returned a statue of Marduk and begun to restore the great temple Esagila and its ziggurat E-temen-anki, to great rejoicing. He also made shining baked bricks for the Processional Way. He claimed to have restored the exemptions and privileges of the great religious centres; he claimed also to have returned statues of deities to Der and to have 'rebuilt its temples', work which his son and successor Ashurbanipal claimed to his own credit, on the grounds that the images of Babylonian deities had been damaged by floods and storms;[104] he did not blame his father.

Ill omens may have delayed Esarhaddon's plans for Babylon, as well as an overflowing of the Euphrates, and the urgent need to raise sinking floors in the huge buildings on the citadel by about half a metre.[105] However, the king was able to carry out some repair work before the end of his short reign. But can we believe what was written? Doubts arise because although the few baked bricks stamped with his inscription, and quite detailed royal inscriptions, support Esarhaddon's claim to have repaired Marduk's

---

[103] Cf. Herrmann and Laidlaw 2009: 25–6 and 114–15.   [104] Leichty 2011: 198.

[105] See Bergamini 2013: 43–64.

Figure 7.9 Black basalt lion of Babylon suggesting Assyria triumphant over an enemy, unfinished sculpture on a modern pedestal; perhaps intended to celebrate Esarhaddon's conquest of Egypt, cut short by his death. c. 669 BC? Estimated weight 7,000 kg. Credit: OAID/thewanderingscot.

temple Esagila and the ziggurat E-temen-anki, most of them come from another part of the city, and none from the city walls he claimed to have 'rebuilt'.[106] He donated a very large cylinder seal of lapis lazuli to the Storm-god of Esagila, as the property of Marduk.[107] Late in his reign he recorded in some detail that he had restored the 'ruined' temple of Nabu-of-Vats, 'the temple that bestows the sceptre', which suggests that he now hoped to receive the blessing of Babylon's gods as their king, perhaps planned as a celebration for his conquest of Egypt.[108] A letter written to him by the chief temple administrator (*šatammu*) reveals that inscribed statues of the king were set up not only in Esagila but also in the other temples, so that the Assyrian king would be associated directly with the worship of Babylonian deities in Babylon.[109] He may never have entered Babylon in person, but perhaps relied on the priests there to carry out his orders.[110] Many prophecies have been found in which one or other of the

[106] Porter 1993: 53; Leichty 2011: 250–6.   [107] Leichty 2011: 249 and fig. 16.
[108] Leichty 2011: 229–30; Cavigneaux 2013.
[109] Cole and Machinist 1998: no. 178; Landsberger 1965.
[110] Cole and Machinist 1998: nos. 161–70 and 173–80.

Figure 7.10 Ivory plaque showing royal lion of Assyria triumphant over supine Nubian, from Kalhu (Nimrud). One of a pair perhaps celebrating Esarhaddon's conquest of Egypt c. 669 BC? Height 5 cm. Credit: Georgina Herrmann ND 2548 (Iraq Museum, missing).

great gods appears, frequently Ishtar of Arbela, who reassures a neurotic ruler that he would not be poisoned:

> Could you not rely on the previous utterance I spoke for you? Now, you can rely on this later one, too. I will banish trembling from my palace. You shall eat safe food and drink safe water, and you shall be safe in your palace. Your son and grandson shall rule as kings in the lap of Ninurta.[111]

When, the year before he died, Esarhaddon named his younger son, Ashurbanipal, as his heir in Assyria, and his eldest, **Šamaš-šum-ukin**, as his heir in Babylon, he dedicated the latter to Marduk: 'I gave Šamaš-šum-ukin my son, my offspring, as a present to Marduk and Zarpanitu'.[112] He

---

[111] Parpola 1997: no. 1.   [112] Leichty 2011: 114.

called upon all of his family and officials to swear loyalty to his two sons, on pain of horrific curses, invoking stars and planets to bear witness. The long text known as *Esarhaddon's Succession Treaty* is notable for including astronomical references, as if emphasizing that the study of the heavens was carried out at Nineveh and Nimrud by Babylonian experts.[113] Scholars are discovering that Assyria made substantial contributions to Babylonian astronomy around this time.

Esarhaddon's mother Naqia promoted the succession of her grandsons by drawing up a legal document calling upon the people to support her elder grandson as king of Babylon, and the younger as king of Assyria, swearing oaths of loyalty under threats of dire punishments. Despite these arrangements, six months elapsed between the death of Esarhaddon and the accession of Šamaš-šum-ukin, which suggests that the transfer of power was not straightforward.

Stimulated by Herodotus' account of the exploits and building works of 'Nitocris' in Babylon, it has been proposed that this was Esarhaddon's mother Naqia.[114] There is no evidence for such a link in Babylonian inscriptions.[115] According to the *Epic of Creation* (VI 63), Babylon's ziggurat tower had been built by Marduk as part of the original foundation of Babylon, when the gods still lived on the earth: 'They raised the top of Esagila, matching the Apsu, they created the high ziggurat of the Apsu'.

The tower was presumably built before the *Epic of Creation* was composed (with that line included), and the story of the Tower of Babel in Genesis 11:1–9 may have taken its inspiration from the well-publicized repairs of Assyrian kings in the seventh century, or from a version of the *Epic of Creation*.[116] Babylon's tower was named 'House, foundation of Heaven and Earth' (E-temen-an-ki), meaning the place where the sky and the Underworld were connected. The tower was a gigantic, awe-inspiring structure with a base measuring between 73 m and 90 m square. The Esagil Tablet, which contains sections giving the dimensions of the tower, is thought to be an academic work, a hypothetical ideal, perhaps composed during Esarhaddon's reign to show his interest when he did not in fact do the physical work.[117] It was **Ashurbanipal**, his successor in Assyria, who took credit for carrying out repair work in Babylon, by inserting his own inscribed bricks into particular structures.

---

[113] Parpola and Watanabe 1988: 28–58.

[114] The name Nitocris is that of an Egyptian princess, daughter of Psammetichus I, who lived c. 600 BC. Herodotus maintained that she had built the main bridge crossing the Euphrates in Babylon. See Streck 1998–2001.

[115] See Melville 1999: 3.   [116] Frahm 2011: 365–7.   [117] George 2005–6: 78.

Already in the second millennium the Babylonians had been ridiculed by the Hittites and Hurrians in the bilingual *Parable of the Tower*, which tells of a tower built to reach heaven, an excessive structure that fell down owing to the pride of its builders.[118] That tale presumably reflects the catastrophic collapse of one (at least) of the great ziggurats in Babylonia in the mid-second millennium, and reminds us that natural forces rather than enemy action could damage such a structure. A huge tower made of mud brick, even when it was clad with a skin of baked brick, would be prone to collapse. Such a tower would need frequent repairs. In the *Epic of Erra*, referring to a period when Babylon was weak, the god Erra points out to Marduk that he has lost his power:

> Why does the finery, your lordship's adornment, which is full of splendour like the stars of heaven, grow dirty?
>
> The crown of your lordship which made the Temple of the Secret of Heaven and Earth shine like E-temen-anki? Its surface is tarnished!

The reference in the last phrase may be to blue glaze on the surface of bricks, which lost their shine and needed to be replaced. Babylon had particular problems maintaining such a huge monument, because of subsidence which could lower the base level by several metres. That alone would have weakened the superstructure.

This period of Babylon's fraught relations with Assyria, attempts at military alliances with Judah and Egypt, and regicide, gave rise to dramatic storytelling which is known only from centuries later.[119] Several ancient novels circulating in Aramaic and in demotic Egyptian retell events with names easily recognizable from this period, perhaps from several different reigns. As in earlier, Babylonian, works of wisdom literature, it was a popular theme to give the advice that, despite extreme adversity, a man should remain loyal to the king.

The most famous is the *Tale of Ahiqar*. Ahiqar was the childless adviser and seal-bearer of Sennacherib and then of Esarhaddon. The story became highly popular in many different languages, spreading a subversive view of back-stabbing and forged documents among the Assyrian king's entourage. Ahiqar was falsely accused of treason by his wicked, dissolute nephew, who forged letters in his uncle's name. Threatened with death, Ahiqar fled

---

[118] Neu 1996: no. 14, a Hurrian/Hittite bilingual text that contains Babylonian loanwords for 'builder' and 'ditch'.

[119] Much of it is preserved in Aramaic or Egyptian demotic on papyrus in the dry conditions of the Egyptian deserts.

to Egypt, where the pharaoh appreciated his wisdom, expressed in the form of proverbs. Eventually pardoned by Sennacherib, Ahiqar returned to Assyria and resumed his former loyal service to the king. The wicked nephew swelled up and burst.[120] In cuneiform of the Seleucid period, Ahiqar was named as the sage of Esarhaddon; his name is also mentioned in St Jerome's prologue to the *Book of Tobit*, which he claimed was based on a Chaldean text.[121] Elements in stories of Inaros and Petubastis, known from a much later demotic Egyptian text describing battles in the Nile Delta, may refer to Esarhaddon's Egyptian campaigns.[122]

A story painted on the wall of a cave tomb in Egypt, known as the Sheikh Fadhl Inscription, may be a semi-historical fiction of later date.[123] Naming such key characters as Esarhaddon, Taharqa, and Necho, and adding a theme of unrequited love, it demonstrates the enormous interest in events leading up to the fall of Assyria, which persisted for many centuries through Achaemenid and Seleucid rule, and formed the core of early novels – a new form of literature.

'King of justice, wise governor for Shamash and Marduk, eternal seed of kingship' – **Šamaš-šum-ukin** king of Babylon,[124] the elder son of Esarhaddon, presented himself as the model of piety who purified and restored the temples, the 'twin' brother of Ashurbanipal, acknowledging Sargon his great-grandfather as his ancestor, omitting his grandfather Sennacherib. His coronation took place in Babylon with lavish ceremonies, and he performed at the annual New Year Festival. In his first year, statues and furniture of the gods, including a bed of ebony and gold, were brought back from Assyria to take up their proper places in the city's temples, though his younger brother, king of Assyria, claimed the credit. A treacherous judge of Babylon was taken prisoner and executed, an event of such importance that his name and fate were recorded in two Babylonian chronicles.

Early in Šamaš-šum-ukin's reign there was a lunar eclipse, very likely a bad omen interpreted to harm the king. For the occasion, a generic version of a prayer to Marduk beginning, 'I am So-and-so, son of So-and-so' was personalized by him and similarly by his brother Ashurbanipal, another example of a composition designed to be used flexibly according to particular needs:

---

[120] For an overview, see Schürer 1986: 232–9.
[121] In the prologue to his translation into Latin around AD 390. By 'Chaldean' he meant Aramaic.
[122] Hoffmann and Quack 2007: 64.   [123] Holm 2007: 193–224.
[124] A detailed account of sources for this reign is given by Baker 2011a.

> I am Šamaš-šum-ukin king of Babylon, whose god is Marduk, whose goddess is Zarpanitu.
> Due to the evil of the lunar eclipse which occurred on the fourteenth of Kislimu,
> Due to the evilness of the evil and the unfavourable signs
> Which came to be in my palace and my land,
> I am scared, I am afraid, I am fearful . . .
> By your just command
> May I live, may I be well, may I praise without end your divinity.[125]

Official correspondence found at Nineveh shows that Ashurbanipal restricted his brother's activities, taking for himself the titles 'governor of Babylon' and 'king of Sumer and Akkad', and treating his brother more like a local city governor than the independent ruler of a kingdom. As with earlier rulers in Babylon city, Šamaš-šum-ukin's power was chiefly restricted to the city of Babylon, allowing him to act mainly as custodian of the great religious centre where the cult of Ishtar-of-Nineveh, long established there, would represent Assyrian interests. Esarhaddon had been responsible for renewing statues in the temple of Ishtar-of-Nineveh in Babylon, and special attention was paid to distributing offerings for her.[126] Šamaš-šum-ukin seems to have had virtually no army to command, which may have been one intention behind the privileges granted to the great cities. Some of the witnesses listed on his *kudurru* records held distinctly Assyrian military offices. Governors of cities such as Ur and Nippur corresponded directly with the Assyrian king in Nineveh, and put their own name to building work in their cities 'for the good health of Šamaš-šum-ukin', showing that they, rather than Šamaš-šum-ukin, were responsible for their temples. Babylon had become virtually a separate state within Babylonia.

The way in which Babylon relied on allies rather than troops of its own can be seen from an oracle question posed to the gods of divination, asking whether a Sealand leader, who has turned against Assyria and mustered an army of Elamite archers endangering Babylon, will now attack:

> Will he fight and do battle with the men and army of Ashurbanipal king of Assyria, whether with Assyrians, or Akkadians, or Chaldeans, or Arameans who have grasped the feet of Ashurbanipal?[127]

As his grandfather had done, Ashurbanipal had boats built by Sidonians so that his governors in the Sealand could fish their enemies out of the

---

[125] Oshima 2011: 342–3.   [126] Da Riva and Frahm 1999–2000: 169–82.
[127] Starr 1990: no. 280.

marshes. Meanwhile he was amassing a massive library at Nineveh, sending scholars to collect and copy on to clay tablets the texts written on writing-boards in Babylonian cities. One such group of texts consists of oracle questions reaching far back in time to the dynasty of Hammurabi.[128]

For sixteen years Šamaš-šum-ukin held on to kingship in Babylon while the Assyrian army, true to form, exerted its military might both within Babylonia and beyond. The main needs were to prevent incursions from the Elamites, to keep control of cities east of the Tigris, including Lahiru, where the queen mother's estates were, and Der. A sequence of Elamite kings was pro-Assyrian when it suited, anti-Assyrian according to the interests of the moment. But the pressures eventually turned Šamaš-šum-ukin against his brother.

Ashurbanipal the Assyrian, the scholar-king who tucked a stylus into his belt in place of a dagger, had lost Egypt by 653 BC, which had regained its independence, and the revenue from it. Nevertheless, he took the military initiative against Elam, in one instance going so far as to kill king Te-umman and put his own candidate on the throne of Susa. The arrangement did not last, and Ashurbanipal's army, having campaigned there on at least three occasions, sacked Susa in 647 BC. In 652, major rebellion had begun in Babylon; after sixteen years of loyalty, Šamaš-šum-ukin gathered support from the Elamites, Sealanders, Arameans, Arabians, and citizens of Babylon, to fight against his own brother. To the citizens of Babylon, Ashurbanipal sent a letter:

> I have heard the false words which my unbrotherly brother said to you, everything he said. Lies! Do not believe him! By Aššur and Marduk, my gods, I swear that I have not plotted in my heart nor spoken out loud any of the bad things he claimed of me. That man has thought of nothing but trickery, thinking: 'I will ruin the reputation of the Babylonians who love him'.[129]

The situation was so dangerous that the New Year Festival was not celebrated in 651 or 650, Babylon being besieged by Assyrian forces. The cancellation was later interpreted in a chronicle as the cause of Babylon's tribulations.[130] Šamaš-šum-ukin was a traitor who had broken his oaths of loyalty: 'outwardly, his lips spoke of friendship; inwardly, his heart plotted murder'. But his plans were revealed to a man in a dream in which a pedestal of the Moon-god was inscribed with the following ominous words:

---

[128] Lambert 2007: e.g. nos. 24 and 25.   [129] ABL 301. See Moran 1991: 320–31.
[130] Waerzeggers 2012: 293.

> Whoever plans evil against Ashurbanipal, king of Assyria, and makes war
> on him, I shall bestow an evil death on him; with a swift sword, fire-fall,
> starvation, and plague I shall end his life.

Babylon's people, reported Ashurbanipal, were reduced to eating the flesh of their sons and daughters, and when the city capitulated at last, the gods threw the treacherous brother into the flames. The blockade had lasted for more than two years, around 650–648, by which time the price of barley had risen disastrously, from 3 shekels per litre to 180.

Ashurbanipal rounded up all the traitors, cut out their tongues, and gathered together all his brother's personal possessions. He left the corpses of other citizens for dogs and pigs to eat, throwing their bones over the city walls. Other inhabitants were dedicated as dead offerings, allowing dogs, pigs, jackals, vultures, and eagles to eat their flesh, in revenge for Sennacherib, presumably laying blame on Babylon's citizens for the death of Aššur-nadin-šumi and the city's sack by Sennacherib half a century earlier. In his palace at Nineveh a bas-relief panel shows the king of Assyria receiving the insignia of kingship that had belonged to his faithless brother: crown, royal seal, sceptre, and chariot.[131] Once again, the Assyrian king took direct control of Babylon.

The extent to which Babylon was damaged in the siege and final capture is unknown. As far as we know, Ashurbanipal was never blamed for committing sacrilege against the great city; its gods and temples remained in their proper places, and after one year, in which Ashurbanipal did just enough to be added to the list of the kings of Babylon, a new king, **Kandalanu**, presumably had an appropriate coronation and participated in the New Year Festival as befitted the ruler of Babylon. But Assyrian royal records cease around that time, and Babylonian chronicles are not preserved for most of this period, so the events of the following decades are barely known.

The death of Šamaš-šum-ukin in Babylon is thought to be the basis on which Ctesias, a Greek doctor of the Achaemenid period, wrote his story of the death of 'Sardanapalos'. The scurrilous story was widely quoted and reused in Greek literature because it had the popular appeal of a stereotype, showing easterners as effete and degenerate. The king was later compared with the Roman emperor Nero.[132] More in tune with historical characters was the Aramaic *Tale of Aššurbanipal and Šamaš-šum-ukin,* in which the sister of the royal brothers attempts unsuccessfully to mediate between them; dramatic dialogue and urgent journeys between Nineveh and

[131] Novotny and Watanabe 2008.   [132] See Röllig 2009–11.

Figure 7.11 Upper row of a sculpture panel from Nineveh showing Assyrian soldiers carrying off the royal insignia of Šamaš-šum-ukin as trophies after his defeat: from left to right his chariot, staff, cylinder seal, and crown. Credit: by kind permission of the Trustees of the British Museum (BM ME 124945).

Babylon are discernible in the fragmentary papyrus.[133] Like the *Tale of Ahiqar*, this story shows that the general population engaged with the drama and personalities of late Assyrian history, and remained fascinated for several centuries. Events of this time found their way into the biblical Book of Esther, a novel which was available not only in Hebrew but also in Elamite.[134] Some of its actions are modelled on Ashurbanipal's campaigns against Elam, and the main characters Mordecai, Esther, and Haman use the names of the gods of Babylon, Nineveh, and Susa.

The way in which his brother put his own name on the building works in Babylon would have been a source of aggravation for Šamaš-šum-ukin. It was thus Ashurbanipal who ostensibly restored many of the main temples, the ziggurat, and the great outer wall and gates of the city, continuing the work begun or intended by his father Esarhaddon. Ashurbanipal writes as if the work was all his own, mentioning his brother only 'in order that the strong might not harm the weak' (a quotation from the law code of Hammurabi):

> During my reign, the great lord Marduk entered Babylon amidst rejoicing and took up residence in Esagila the eternal. I confirmed the interrupted regular offerings for Esagila and the gods of Babylon, I established the privileged status of Babylon ... I decorated Esagila with silver, gold and precious stones.[135]

Inscriptions of Šamaš-šum-ukin have been found only in other cities, recording his renovation work at Sippar and at Borsippa. In support of his duty to enhance the New Year Festival in Babylon, he had a ceremonial boat made for Nabu the great god of Borsippa, who was also the divine scribe of Esagila 'who carries the Tablet of Fates of the great gods' and played a major role in the New Year Festival.[136] But his titles refer only to Babylon, not to Sumer and Akkad, nor to southern Babylonia.

Whether Ashurbanipal completed the work is uncertain; the loss of Egypt, his most lucrative province, and then the rebellion of his brother, must have stalled his plans. Stelas of each of the royal brothers carrying a basket for bricks on his head[137] have been found at Borsippa; where the face

---

[133] Inscribed in Egyptian demotic script, but in the Aramaic language. The copy on Papyrus Amherst 63 was probably made around 400 BC from an older text. For a translation, see Steiner 1997: 322–7.
[134] See Dalley 2007: 170 and 183.   [135] Adapted from Frame 1995: nos. B.6.32.1 and 2.
[136] Frame 1995: 256–7.
[137] The basket would have been made of silver and dedicated to the deity, according to a Kassite precedent. See Abraham and Gabbay 2013.

of Ashurbanipal is intact, the face of Šamaš-šum-ukin has been hacked away in a deliberate act of iconoclasm, blotting out his identity as if the image were animate, as if the punishments of gouging out eyes and cutting off nose, lips, and tongue were carried out on the man himself. Another intact block of stone showing Ashurbanipal similarly carrying a hod of bricks, but larger and finely inscribed, has been found at Babylon. It is possible that all traces of his brother were removed from Babylon immediately after the rebellion ended.

During the final phase of Assyrian power, a significant change has been detected in cylinder seals: deities in human form no longer appear, being replaced by symbols, such as the crescent moon for the Moon-god. This new fashion remained in Babylonia after the fall of the Assyrian empire.

Soon after Šamaš-šum-ukin died in 648, **Kandalanu** became king.[138] Virtually nothing is known of his origins.[139] No historical inscriptions from Babylon bear his name. But he ruled, according to Babylonian king-lists, for twenty-one years, long enough to suggest stability. Dated records bearing his name, and others bearing the name of Ashurbanipal, indicate that he, like his predecessor, was circumscribed by the Assyrian king, his power restricted to the city. Kandalanu seems to have died in the same year as Ashurbanipal, in 627. Even then the city benefitted from rich donations: a successor of Ashurbanipal dedicated an offering table and a gold sceptre to Marduk and carried out other pious works in various Babylonian cities.

Those royal deaths mark a period for which royal inscriptions from Babylonia and Assyria are lacking. Because its fall was only fifteen years away, the temptation to speculate that the Assyrian empire became unmanageable is almost irresistible, bolstered by the rhetoric of Hebrew prophets. In fact, Kandalanu was succeeded by two kings of Assyria, who are found together in the *Uruk King-List*:[140] **Sin-šum-lišir**, who acted as guardian for Ashurbanipal's son in Nineveh before taking his throne in Assyria and Babylon; and **Sin-šar-iškun**, whose seven-year reign in Babylon is documented by at least sixty dated records. His piety towards the great city is emphasized in a prayer to Marduk, god of Babylon, which he took directly from one written for Ashurbanipal, inserting his own name in the place of his great predecessor. He co-opted as a general a man named **Nabopolassar** to

[138] Problems in identifying Kandalanu are discussed by Frame 1992: appendix F, 296–306. His name, unusual for a king, is a word for a copper or bronze vessel.
[139] See Frame 1992: 296–306.   [140] Grayson 1983.

serve the Assyrians against rebel groups of Sealanders. But as a member of the elite in Uruk in the Sealand, Nabopolassar's loyalty was under pressure, and he soon turned traitor: he pushed Sin-šar-iškun out of Babylon back to Assyria, and in 625 seized the throne of Babylon for himself.

8 | Empire

Nabopolassar and Nebuchadnezzar II, 625–562[1]

Babylon was a golden cup in the Lord's hand.

(Jeremiah 51:7)

Babylon	Assyria	Egypt, Media, Judah
Nabopolassar	// Aššur-etel-ilani	
(Nabu-apla-uṣur, 625–605)		
	// Sin-šumu-lišir	
	// Sin-šar-iškun	
	// Aššur-uballiṭ II	// Necho II (610–595)
		// Cyaxares
Nebuchadnezzar II		// Jehoiakim
(Nabu-kudurri-uṣur, 604–562)		// Jehoiakin
		// Zedekiah
		// Psammetichus II
		(595–589)

Battles in the vicinity of Babylon made it too dangerous to perform the New Year Festival during the last years of Assyrian rule, but Babylon did not lose its special status after the end of Kandalanu's reign. Meanwhile the city of Uruk in southern Babylonia had powerful hereditary governors; the son of one of them, **Nabopolassar**, served as a military commander fighting on behalf of the Assyrian king Sin-šar-iškun.[2] When he rebelled against the Assyrian, on the first occasion he was beaten back to Uruk, but on the second he succeeded in defeating the Assyrian army, and took the throne of Babylon, inaugurating a new dynasty in 625. One of the titles he took was 'strong king', which had not been adopted before by Babylonian kings; it was an Assyrian royal title.

---

[1] The period is known as Neo-Babylonian to historians and archaeologists. Royal inscriptions have mainly been edited by Da Riva and Schaudig (see bibliography). Brinkman 1998–2001a gives a detailed summary of Nabopolassar's reign. The *Babylonian Chronicles* give key information.

[2] Jursa 2007b.

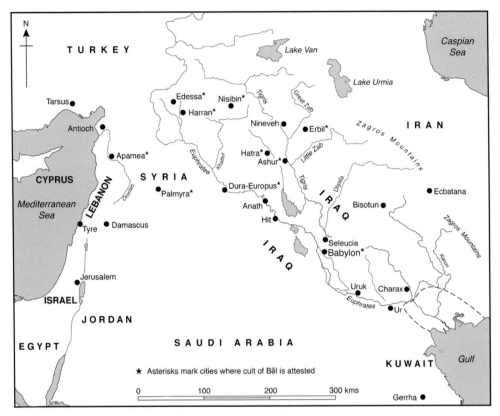

Figure 8.1 Sketch map showing sites of the late first millennium BC, including places where the cult of Bēl persisted into Late Antiquity. Credit: Alison Wilkins and author.

In referring to himself as 'son of a nobody', the king meant that he had no genetic connection with a previous Assyrian or Babylonian king; but since he belonged to an influential family from Uruk, his power base would have been well-established before he became king in Babylon. The Babylonian *Uruk King-List*, which is the only one to preserve the change from Assyrian appointees in Babylon to the accession of Nabopolassar, gives a continuous list without distinguishing between Babylon and Assyria. This gives the same picture as the Greek historian Herodotus, who wrote around two centuries later that:

> Assyria [was] a country remarkable for the number of great cities it contained, and especially for the most powerful and renowned of them all – Babylon, to which the seat of government was transferred after the fall of Nineveh.[3]

---

[3] Hdt I.179.

This suggests that he was unaware Nabopolassar came to the throne in Babylon some thirteen years before the fall of Nineveh and was not an Assyrian, but Herodotus' understanding would be a natural inference to draw from the *Uruk King-List*. At Harran, an inscription dated around 547 lists Assyrian kings from Ashurbanipal to Nabopolassar, giving the impression, like the *Uruk King-List*, that Nabopolassar's reign continued the Assyrian line.

At his accession Nabopolassar sent back to Susa those gods that the Assyrians had removed to Uruk, as part of his policy to dissuade Elam from trying to undermine the new regime in Babylonia. Due to his connections with Uruk, Nabopolassar was referred to as 'king of the Sealand', but in Babylon he took the modest title of 'governor' (*šakkanakku*).[4] As king of the Sealand, he founded a dynasty headed by an urban, literate Chaldean nobility. Various types of record, such as chronicles and oracles, describe individual kings as 'Chaldean,' but we are not certain what that implies in this period. The tribal grouping called Chaldean may already have developed into a specialized group of scholars and religious wise men, especially astronomers, 'magicians' (diviners and incantation priests), and astrologers.

The main events of the fall of Assyria are briefly recorded by year of reign in the *Babylonian Chronicle*, giving the sequence of events. From this reign onwards, no further tablets of that chronicle have been found.[5] In 623 Nabopolassar drove the Assyrians temporarily out of Der. They soon returned: the Assyrians did not give in easily. The city of Ashur resisted strongly with Egyptian help, but eventually fell. With Median help, Nabopolassar captured Ashur; the Medes had already marched much further north to take the town of Tarbiṣu near Nineveh, where Assyrian crown princes traditionally lived.[6] The Medes at this time were called Umman-manda, a vague term for a rabble of uncivilized outsiders, which implies that they were hard to control.

Aššur-etel-ilani, the late-born son of Ashurbanipal, had succeeded his father as a minor around 630. He ruled Assyria with the help of a guardian, a top military man who recommended that the young king grant land and tax exemptions to successful military commanders:

> Sin-šumu-lišir the chief of magnates who had had the confidence of my father who begot me, who had guided me constantly like a father, installed

---

[4] See Spar and Lambert 1988: no. 44. This account is from a letter of the second century found in Esagila, which may be a literary fiction.

[5] Waerzeggers 2012: 297.   [6] The Medes are first known by name from a text of 835 BC.

me safely on the throne of my father and begetter, and ensured that the Assyrian people, great and small, guard my kingship during my minority and respect my kingship.[7]

The guardian succeeded his ward as king around 626, and would have been an experienced and effective opponent of Babylonian forces had he not been killed in battle soon after.

Nabopolassar was unable to count on pro-Babylonian loyalties around the Middle Euphrates, where the people of Suhu rebelled against him, and he had to withdraw when he met an Assyrian army there. The *Babylonian Chronicle* reports 'a hard battle' within Nineveh in his fourteenth year, the death of Assyria's king Sin-šar-iškun, and extensive plundering before the Babylonian king accepted the submission of the Assyrian army. The *Chronicle*'s author, aghast at the damage, resorted to rhetorical language: 'They reduced the city to a heap of rubble'. But Nabopolassar, as the Babylonian conqueror, was able to receive submission from the former Assyrian province of Raṣappa[8] while he resided in Nineveh after the sack, presumably in one of the great palaces built by Sennacherib and his successors. Parts of these palaces continued to be occupied subsequently. Twenty-five letters written in Elamite found at Nineveh perhaps date from a time after the capture of Nineveh.[9]

According to Nabonidus, writing two generations later, Nabopolassar was so upset at the damage done to Nineveh that he lay on the ground, refusing a comfortable bed, stricken with remorse, and 'did not lay hands on the rites of the gods, but took over everything'. In the palaces, the carefully selective mutilation of the faces of Sennacherib, Ashurbanipal, and his queen (or his grandmother Naqia) on stone panels of sculpture in low relief probably dates to this time, and would not have been done while the chaos of looting prevailed. Help from the Medes had come at a great price in unnecessary damage, as the description of them as Umman-manda 'barbarians' indicates.

Aššur-uballiṭ II became king of Assyria based in Harran in the Hana region. Two more years of campaigning, fighting, and plundering ensued before Nabopolassar was able to capture that city, where the Egyptian army under Necho II was supporting the Assyrians. Again the plunder was stupendous. But the Assyrians returned with a large Egyptian army, and

---

[7] Kataja and Whiting 1995: 7–9 no. 36.

[8] Grayson 1975b: chronicle 3. Raṣappa (Rusapu), was located north of modern Nisibin.

[9] They may represent Medes writing in Elamite, rather than Elamites from the region of Susa. The Medes, who were immigrants into north-west Iran with their capital city at Ecbatana (modern Hamadan), may not have written their spoken language.

were able to drive a Babylonian garrison out of Harran. It was during this campaign that the progress of pharaoh Necho's army through Palestine was resisted by Josiah, who was killed at Megiddo (Armageddon) in 609.[10] Josiah's successor Jehoiakim paid a heavy tribute to Necho. A second attack by Babylonians and their allies was more effective, and ended his brief reign in Jerusalem. After their defeat, some Egyptians stayed on for a while to defend the area around Carchemish. Nabopolassar and his allies took control of the Assyrian empire, and adopted Assyrian military, administrative, and judicial practices.[11] He and his successors were military men. Assyrian terms for military professions in texts of his dynasty show that the Babylonians now had an army modelled on that of the Assyrians.[12]

The conquest brought vast new wealth to Babylon. It also introduced an ever-increasing number of Arameans, whose Aramaic language was written in an alphabetic script, usually on parchment. The use of cuneiform became ever more restricted, while the use of Aramaic spread ever wider; but much of it is lost to us because the organic writing materials used mostly perished long ago.

The total destruction of Assyria, as described with rhetorical gusto by biblical prophets, was supposed to be a historical fact until new evidence emerged to refute it. Surprisingly, clay tablets with cuneiform texts continued to be used in Assyria after the fall of its empire. Excavation at a formerly Assyrian city[13] revealed that Assyrian-style texts, composed in Assyrian dialect and with Assyrian versions of cuneiform signs, continued to be written, both in Babylon and elsewhere, long after the fall of Nineveh. The discovery shows that Assyrian scribes and their administrative habits survived the collapse of the Assyrian empire. This suggests that conditions after the fall were not unstable enough to stop all business, trade, and collection of taxes. It was as if cities in the Assyrian empire simply transitioned into the Babylonian empire. This was not the complete break described in Hebrew and Greek sources. Nabopolassar's description of his own rise to power is pious and self-effacing:

> When I was young, although I was the son of a nobody, I constantly sought the shrines of my lords Nabu and Marduk. My mind was committed to establishing their cultic ordinances and to the perfect performance

[10] For Megiddo as the seat of the governor in Israel's former territory after the conquest of Samaria, see Franklin 2019.
[11] Da Riva 2014.   [12] Da Riva 2013a.
[13] Kuehne 2002. The tablets, dated up to the thirty-fourth year at least of Nebuchadnezzar II, were found in a substantial, newly built 'post-Assyrian' building at Dur-Katlimmu, modern Sheh Hamad on the river Habur in Syria.

of their rituals. My attention was directed towards justice and equity. Shazu (a name of Marduk), the lord who knows the hearts of the gods of heaven and the Underworld, who regularly checks the behaviour of the people, noticed my 'heart' and set me, so young, who had not been noticed by the people, in the highest position in the land where I was born. He called me to rule over land and people. He made a favourable protective deity walk beside me and ensured that I succeeded in everything.[14]

In the nineteenth year of his reign, exhausted by so many hard campaigns, and keen to revive Babylon as a city of splendour, Nabopolassar returned early from a campaign, handing over sole military command to his son Nebuchadnezzar, the crown prince, who took part with his own army. Nebuchadnezzar gained invaluable experience from his early responsibilities.

In a long inscription dedicated mainly to the rebuilding of Babylon's Imgur-Enlil wall, Nabopolassar referred briefly and humbly to his expulsion of the Assyrians from Babylonia (named 'Akkad' here):

> He (Shazu, a name of Marduk) had Nergal, strongest among the gods, march at my side. He killed my enemy, he defeated my foe the Assyrian who had ruled Akkad because of divine anger, and had oppressed the people of the country with his heavy yoke. I, the weak one, the powerless one, who repeatedly seeks the lord of lords, with the mighty strength of my lords Nabu and Marduk, I chased them out of the land of Akkad, and I had them (the Babylonians) throw off their yoke.[15]

In this version of events, the cause of Babylon's occupation by Assyria had been the anger of the gods towards the city, so their relenting was due to the king's exceptional piety.

In his royal inscriptions,[16] Nabopolassar did not present himself as a warrior king; he did not use similes or metaphors involving aggressive wild animals as Assyrian kings had done. His emphasis on piety and justice mirrored the inscriptions of Hammurabi, whose archaic script he deployed, for those ancient forms were still studied and used by scribes and stonecutters. In no inscription does he mention any triumph other than that in Assyria. As 'king of justice', he restored the temples of the Sun-god, lord of justice, in Sippar and Larsa, the two great ancient cities where that god's worship was pre-eminent; and in the inscriptions written to record his deeds, he attributed his conquest of Assyria to the Sun-god, rather than to Marduk. The Elamites had previously removed a temple

---

[14] Da Riva 2013b: 94, col. i 7–24.   [15] Da Riva 2013b: 93–7.   [16] Da Riva 2013b and 2008.

library from Uruk to Susa, a city which, having recovered from Ashurbanipal's vengeful sack, was once again independent with its own appointed Elamite ruler. Nabopolassar brought the library back to Uruk, ensuring that his ancestral city resumed its status as leader among the sacred cities of the south.[17]

A different view of Nabopolassar's character and exploits is given in the very fragmentary *Epic of Nabopolassar*.[18] A clash is described between Assyrians and Babylonians in the city of Kutha, of which Nergal god of the Underworld was the patron: a fight took place at night with torches; drains and canals were filled with blood. The king's coronation in Babylon took place *after* the conquest of the Assyrians in this account; it reverses the order of events in order to match the sequence in the *Epic of Creation*, where Marduk slays the enemy Tiamat, before being proclaimed king of the gods. In the *Epic of Nabopolassar*, the king is presented with the royal seal at the triumphal ceremony, perhaps the same one as was delivered up to Ashurbanipal at the defeat of Šamaš-šum-ukin. His officials at the coronation entrust to him personally the avenging of Babylonia, just as the *Epic of Creation* describes how Marduk is promoted in order to avenge the gods. Differences between this literary text and other inscriptions show how restricted were the latter in their presentation of military prowess; but that prowess, transferred to a heavenly sphere, could be recounted in much more heroic detail in a literary epic. The coronation and participation in the New Year Festival at Babylon would have involved, according to custom, remission of sins and cleansing from pollution using two rituals: one in the Shower House (*bīt salā' mê*) which also involved the royal insignia, another in the Bath House (*bīt rimki*).[19]

Late copies of a fictitious exchange of letters between Nabopolassar and Šamaš-šum-ukin seek to justify the Chaldean takeover of the throne. They refer to the wicked removal of property from Esagila to Nineveh as the reason for Marduk's punishment of Nineveh, and trace blame back to Sennacherib, whose father Sargon is derisively described as a house slave.[20] One of these letters dates from the reign of Alexander the Great, about 270 years later. This shows how long-lived in Babylonia was the interest in events surrounding the fall of Assyria. The importance of finding causes, assigning blame, and the fear that guilt could be inherited, were still pervasive.

---

[17] Cf. Potts 2016: 283–5.   [18] Grayson 1975a: 78–86.   [19] See Ambos 2013: 1 and 155–211.
[20] Da Riva 2014.

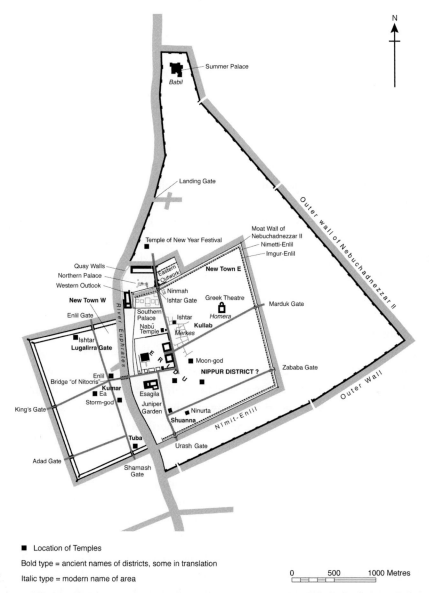

Figure 8.2 Sketch plan of buildings on the main citadel of Babylon, chiefly during the Chaldean Dynasty. Credit: Alison Wilkins and the author.

In Babylon, Nabopolassar undertook a great programme of construction. As well as his restoration of the city wall Imgur-Enlil, 'which with the passing of time had become weak and caved in, whose walls had been carried away by rain and heavy storms, whose foundations had heaped up and accumulated into a pile of ruins', he constructed an embankment of baked brick outside the walls. Both the wall and the embankment were addressed in the inscriptions placed within them, calling upon them: 'O wall, speak good words about me to my lord Marduk'. The king described the wall as 'the strong shield that bolts the entrance to hostile lands ... the stairway to heaven, the ladder down to the Underworld'. The work of rebuilding and raising the height of the wall was so enormous that Nebuchadnezzar continued it after his father's death. A branch of the Euphrates and various canals leading off from it were redirected to fill a system of moats that protected the palace area on the Kasr mound. This is clear on the ground plan of the city, although most phases of the work cannot be dated.

Unlike images of Assyrian kings in their own lands, no stelas or images of Nabopolassar and his son have come to light, nor is there reference to them in their texts. A change is apparent in the design of cylinder seals. Instead of depicting many deities in human form, symbols represented them; following a fashion of the late Assyrian empire, mentioned above, divine symbols were most commonly shown erected on plinths with a worshipper standing in prayer alongside them.[21]

One of Nabopolassar's greatest efforts was devoted to restoring the ziggurat E-temen-anki, located beside Marduk's temple Esagila in the enormous walled compound, stating specifically that he used wealth obtained from plunder. Notably, as with the city wall, he did not attribute its lamentable state of repair to damage done by Sennacherib in 689, nor to any other enemy action. Subsidence and buckling of the high structure are therefore likely causes of the damage he tried to repair. Due to these factors, and to the eventual complete ruination of the monument, no foundation cylinders survive to give the history of its construction. Subsidence of perhaps 12 m occurred during this period, which must have endangered the astronomers if they took their observations from the top of the tower; they may, therefore, have relocated at times to the ziggurat of nearby Borsippa.[22] The tower, the king wrote, was 'near collapse', so Marduk ordered him to rebuild it from the foundations, a stupendous task, 'to ground its foundation on the breast of the Underworld, to make its head equal heaven':

> May this work, my handiwork, endure forever. Like the bricks of E-temen-anki, firmly fixed forever after, establish firmly the foundations of my throne for distant days. O E-temen-anki, pray on behalf of the king

[21] Ornan 2005 and Altavilla and Walker 2016 provide many examples.
[22] See Bergamini 2013.

who renovated you! O House, when Marduk joyfully takes up residence within you, speak favourably on my behalf to my lord Marduk!

The king involved himself and his sons in the labour of creating a marvel:

> I bowed my neck to my lord Marduk, I rolled up my garment, my royal robe, and carried on my head bricks and earth. I had hods made of gold and silver, and I had Nebuchadnezzar, my first-born son, beloved of my heart, carry alongside my workmen earth mixed with wine, oil, and aromatic shavings. I had Nabu-šuma-lišir, his close brother, the child, my own offspring, the younger brother, my darling, seize mattock and spade, I had him bear a hod of gold and silver, and dedicated him to my lord Marduk.

Nabopolassar added a mantle of baked brick to the original structure, which is estimated to have involved between 32 and 36 million bricks in total. Dimensions of the ziggurat's base are given in the Esagil Tablet. This esoteric text may have been intended to relate to the great square of the constellation Pegasus, the *ikû* measurement (see below) which gave the city an alternative name, giving astral significance to the design; but the numbers do not correspond closely to most of those unearthed, and are probably symbolic and theoretical. They include archaic units of measurement alongside units current in Nabopolassar's time.[23] The only reliable measurement based on excavation is a 91 m square outline of the tower's base, but it is not datable. At least ten different reconstructions have been proposed for the complete tower.

Four gates gave access; on the summit, statues of Marduk and his divine consort may have been enshrined alongside an astronomer's table and chair. Modern estimates of the height of the tower range between 69 m and 90 m. The threshold of the excavated gates seemed to be some 7 m higher than the level of the earliest construction, an astonishing figure that gives some insight into the problems in the city centre caused by subsidence, flooding, and changes in the level of the water table.

Already adopted by the Assyrians and Elamites, a technique of glazing baked bricks for adorning public walls and gateways had developed from the Late Bronze Age onwards,[24] and was magnificently displayed in the streets and buildings of Babylon during this dynasty. Expertise in brickwork enabled façades to feature colourful figures in relief, largely taken from mythology, such as the *mušhuššu*-horned dragon. In contrast to the narrative style of Assyrian wall paintings and stone bas-reliefs, Babylonians

---

[23] George 2005–6: 77; Keetman 2009.   [24] Harper, Aruz, and Tallon 1992: 223–41.

favoured static and heraldic designs. Nabopolassar began to build a new palace for himself, probably on top of an older palace, but at a higher level to compensate for the sinking of the previous building. Nebuchadnezzar completed the work. The palace was located beside the great Processional Way on the main Kasr mound, close to the great temple Esagila and the ziggurat, both of which would have dominated the skyline.

Taking the throne at his father's death, **Nebuchadnezzar II** was already an experienced soldier who inherited the wealth taken from Assyria and the relative stability of its administrative methods, as well as the disruptions in Babylon of partly unfinished building work. In the traditional ceremony marking the New Year during the year of his accession, in the first month 'he took the hand of Bēl (Marduk) and the son of Bēl (Nabu), and celebrated the New Year Festival'. The newly crowned king had already gained administrative experience from his time as treasurer/bishop (*šatammu*) of Eanna, the great temple of the goddess at Uruk. One of his tasks as king was to maintain control over cities formerly ruled by Assyria, while pushing against Egyptian expansion in the Levant. Another was to complete the restoration of the city's great buildings: the walls, the ziggurat, the temples, and the palace. He extended the city, building on a new area, the Babil mound, protected with a wall of bitumen and baked brick which enclosed the Summer Palace. At that time Babylon was a huge city, reckoned at more than 850 hectares:

> In order that no merciless enemy should ever reach the boundaries of Babylon, I had the country surrounded by waters as vast as the expanse of the sea, so that to cross them was as difficult as crossing the heaving ocean [or?] a brackish lagoon. And in order that no dyke breach occurred there, I piled up a wall of earth around them, and surrounded them with quays of baked brick. I strengthened the defences skilfully, and I made the holy city of Babylon a fortification.

Fearful of raiding where so much wealth was heaped up to tempt an avaricious foe, Nebuchadnezzar II began to build two enormously long walls across the countryside beyond the city:[25] 'From the Euphrates to the Tigris I piled up a great heap of earth and strengthened its sides with a strong embankment'.

The southern wall, an embankment faced with bricks, ran for about 50 km from the Euphrates at Babylon, passed Kish, and went on to meet the Tigris' bank at the river harbour of Kar-Nergal. The northern one, about

---

[25] Da Riva 2012a. Remains of the wall at Habl es-Sahr were surveyed in recent times.

54 km long, stretched from Sippar on the Euphrates to Upe (later renamed Seleucia). These massive earthworks may relate to a name newly found at this period for Babylon: 'the dyke, a bank of earth surrounding a plot of land' (*īku*), which puns on 'the Field' (*ikû*), a name also given to the constellation Pegasus.[26] Nebuchadnezzar gave his motive in an inscription: 'I did not let any troublemaker prevent people dwelling inside from carrying the chariot pole of my lord Marduk'.

Thus the primary aim of the walls was to ensure that festivals were never endangered, and that the statues of gods, conveyed to Babylon from other cities for festivals, by boat and by chariot, did not risk attack. By constructing the two cross-country walls, by renovating and raising the two city walls, and by deliberately building no other royal residences outside Babylon, the king concentrated wealth in the capital. The city now lay enclosed within a rectangle, consisting of the Euphrates and Tigris to west and east, and the cross-country walls to north and south. The northern wall is still visible; bricks with Nebuchadnezzar's inscription have been found within the wall, and it is thought to be the wall built 'to keep out the Medes' mentioned by Xenophon.[27]

Nebuchadnezzar did not restrict his work on temples to Babylon; bricks stamped with his inscription have been found in many other of the great cities. Longer foundation inscriptions often specified the lavish offerings due to their deities. Various superlative creations – his palace and the city gates in Babylon, a cultic boat for Marduk, the temple to Nabu in Borsippa, and the temple of the Sun-god in Sippar – were all described as 'wonders for all peoples', using the expression that Assyrian kings had used for their finest works in previous times, equivalent to the Seven Wonders of the World of Greek and Roman tradition.

Two brothers of Nebuchadnezzar, seven of his sons, and two daughters are known by name from reliable cuneiform sources.[28] One of his sons attempted to raise a rebellion against his father, and was imprisoned, an episode giving rise to a literary lament, and showing Nebuchadnezzar was not entirely secure in his rule. His wife may have been Amytis, the daughter of a king of Media.[29]

One year before he became king, Nebuchadnezzar as crown prince had inflicted a major defeat on the Egyptians under their pharaoh Necho at Carchemish on the Upper Euphrates. He captured Hamath on the river Orontes, thereby gaining at least nominal control over much of Assyria's

---

[26] The two words are clearly distinguished when they are written as logograms: GÁN for *ikû* ('field'), E for *īku* ('dyke').

[27] Xenophon, *Anabasis* II.5.   [28] See Streck 1998–2001: 197.   [29] See Brosius 1996: 21–39.

western empire. In 604, his first year as king, Nebuchadnezzar marched down almost to the frontier with Egypt, to push the Egyptians back to the Nile and protect the border. Ashkelon lay on the Mediterranean coast by the road leading into Egypt; like Hamath, it had the potential to block access to the Nile. His assault on Ashkelon showed how severely a ruler and his city would be punished for breaking off loyalty to Babylon and siding with Egypt: its king was seized, his city plundered, walls and buildings reduced to ruins. But since he is listed in a prism inscription as a king who contributed to the expenses of building the Southern Palace,[30] he must have been allowed to stay as a vassal king, so he was still there and able to make a donation. In his fourth year, Nebuchadnezzar marched towards Egypt and the two armies fought to a standstill with severe losses, such that each withdrew. The Babylonian king spent the next year in Babylon repairing the damage and re-equipping his army. That experience may have deterred an ambition to invade and conquer Egypt. In the following year he plundered 'numerous Arabs', perhaps to weaken Arabian alliances with Egypt and Palestine. From this time if not earlier, many groups of foreign soldiers were brought into Babylon to serve the king, and when they were retired from active service, they were given estates in the countryside to manage.[31] Antimenidas, the brother of Alcaeus, the Greek poet from the island of Lesbos, was serving the Babylonians as a foreign soldier, and Carians were included in the list of foreigners recorded on the prism inscription found in Nebuchadnezzar's Southern Palace.[32]

Three rock sculptures show the only images we know of the famous king.[33] Nebuchadnezzar II engraved two great panels of sculpture on the rock face at Brisa in a pass through the mountains of Lebanon, to 'the luxuriant forest of Marduk, sweetly fragrant', to proclaim that he controlled access to the cedar trees, so valuable for building palaces and temples:

> Strong cedars, massive and tall, of splendid beauty, supreme their stately appearance, huge yield of the Lebanon, I bundled together like river reeds, I perfumed the Euphrates and set them up in Babylon like Euphrates poplars.[34]

---

[30] Da Riva 2013a; 217.   [31] Hackl and Jursa 2015.

[32] Potts 2018 notes that some Carians may have come from Egypt to Babylonia in late Assyrian times. At this time the Greek philosopher and mathematician Pythagoras is thought by some to have studied among Chaldeans; see Robson 2006–8.

[33] The Schøyen stela of Nebuchadnezzar II is almost certainly a fake. See Dalley 2016: 754.

[34] Da Riva 2012b.

Diviners held cedar chippings in their mouths to purify their breath during rituals – a less well-known use. The king quoted from Hammurabi's Code to link his deeds to those of his famous predecessor. Very likely the spectacular rock carving also celebrated his success in driving the Egyptian army out of the region. Like Gilgamesh in the great *Epic of Gilgamesh*, and like Assyrian kings as depicted on their royal seal, he showed himself fighting a lion. Half a millennium later, the Roman emperor Hadrian carved at least 250 inscriptions in the same area, as if to show that he could compete with the legendary Babylonian ruler. An epic was almost certainly written to glorify Nebuchadnezzar's heroism, comparable to the *Epic of Nabopolassar*. Berossus gave a hint of it, narrating how, on hearing of his father's death, Nebuchadnezzar rushed back to Babylon from leading a campaign to Egypt: 'He set out with a few companions and reached Babylon by crossing the desert'. A comparable episode is found in the text of the Assyrian Esarhaddon who, on hearing of the death of the king his father, defied terrible conditions to rush back to the capital from abroad without waiting for his troops.[35]

Nebuchadnezzar is famous for sacking the first temple in Jerusalem, and deporting some of its people to Babylonia, as had been the custom in dealing with conquered rebels for many centuries. During the Assyrian empire, an Assyrian governor had been installed in Samaria and some Israelites from there had been deported to Assyrian territories. Around forty years later, small numbers of Judeans from Jerusalem had been taken to Nineveh by Sennacherib when Hezekiah yielded to pressure. Now, in 609, king Josiah had been killed trying to defend his country against Egyptian forces.[36] By the time his first son, Jehoiakim, ruled Judah (608–598), initially as the pharaoh Necho's vassal, Jerusalem was a very wealthy city. Although his predecessors had paid tribute and tax, collected from the whole land, to Assyria and later to Egypt, the city had never been occupied by foreign forces. Nebuchadnezzar, having defeated Egyptians in Syria and Palestine,[37] took control of the king in Jerusalem as a vassal of Babylon; but after Jehoiakim's death, his son Jehoiakin (597), then aged eight, succeeded him and rebelled, probably under renewed pressure from Egypt. He was taken prisoner to Babylon.[38] According to Ezekiel, Jehoiakin's captivity was Yahweh's punishment for breaking oaths:

---

[35] Leichty 2011: 13. Dillery 2015: 274 and 282–3, compares with a text relating to Antiochus I.
[36] 2 Kings 23:29.   [37] Grayson 1975b: chronicles 4 and 5.   [38] See Lipschits 1998.

> Will a man who has done this go unpunished?
> Can he break a treaty and go unpunished?
> As I live, I swear – it is the Lord Yahweh who speaks:
> In Babylon, in the country of the king who put him on the throne, whose
>   oath he has ignored, whose treaty he has broken – there will he die.

The *Babylonian Chronicle* gives a brief account of the first Babylonian action that resulted in the installation of another son, Zedekiah (596–586), as a client king:

> The seventh year, in the month of Kislev, the king of Akkad mustered his
> army and marched to Hattu. He encamped against the city of Judah and
> on the second day of the month of Addar he captured the city and seized
> the king (Jehoiakin). A king of his own choice (Zedekiah) he appointed to
> the city; taking a vast tribute, he brought it into Babylon.

The emphasis is on the wealth of Jerusalem, where the temple that Solomon had built centuries earlier and many of its accumulated treasures were presumably still intact. In his fourth year as ruler, Zedekiah or his representatives travelled to Babylon, probably to renew his oaths of loyalty before the overlord and confirm his status as a vassal king. Subsequent pressures proved too strong to resist: he approached the Egyptians for military aid against the Babylonians, as well as receiving ambassadors from Tyre, Sidon, Ammon, Moab, and Edom to put together an alliance. An opportunity for conspiracy against Babylon arose when Nebuchadnezzar had to deal with a rebellion within Babylonia and did not campaign in 595, his tenth year. In 595 Nebuchadnezzar had faced a rebellion in Babylon, recorded in the *Babylonian Chronicle*. In the following year, a named traitor was executed by having his throat cut for leading a conspiracy in which oaths of loyalty had been broken. The traitor's lands were confiscated. Despite the smooth prose of royal inscriptions with its veneer of success supported by the great gods, the Babylonian king was threatened within his homeland. Zedekiah's rebellion was one of many. So after nine years of an arrangement which seemed to be working well, with tribute delivered regularly, Nebuchadnezzar was obliged to take strong action in Jerusalem for a second time, and besieged it between c. 589 and 587:

> In the ninth year of Zedekiah king of Judah, in the tenth month,
> Nebuchadnezzar king of Babylon came against Jerusalem with his whole
> army and they besieged it. And on the ninth day of the fourth month of
> Zedekiah's eleventh year, the city wall was broken through. And all the
> princes of the king of Babylon came and took seats in the Middle Gate:

Nergal-šarezer of Simmagir, Nebo-sarsechim chief of the magnates, Nergal-šazban the military governor.[39]

The temple itself was thoroughly sacked under the command of Nebusaradan, one of Nebuchadnezzar's top officers.[40] Bronze fittings and furnishings in particular were taken to Babylon. The Babylonians did not damage the vessels they removed from the temple, but took them to serve Babylonian gods in Babylon's shrines, to symbolize subjugation.[41] The holy building was burned, and the city walls torn down, in a thorough destruction. Already the Babylonians had begun to set up a new centre for rule in Mizpeh to the north of Jerusalem. This was part of a strategic policy to purge the Judean capital of national and religious fervour that made Jerusalem so hard to control. To break the link with the royal House of David, Gedaliah, a moderate man and experienced administrator, was appointed and surrounded with Babylonian advisers. Top religious and military men were taken away and executed. Zedekiah was blinded. But a member of the royal family, helped by the king of Ammon, assassinated Gedaliah and escaped to Egypt. The Babylonian king's actions against Jerusalem should be set within the general context of his repeated campaigns to the west, to the states of Syria and Palestine, looking towards Egypt.[42]

Detailed information comes from biblical texts, which alone refer to the destruction of the first temple. The episode is not preserved in the fragmentary and laconic *Babylonian Chronicle*, nor did Nebuchadnezzar leave his own account of events. No epic is extant to give a literary version.

These events mark the beginning of Jewish exile: from Jerusalem, from Neirab in Syria, from Gaza and Ashkelon, to Babylonia. The number of people deported from Jerusalem when Jehoiakin was taken is given in 2 Kings 24:14 as 10,000 but by Jeremiah as 3,023; one can only guess at reasons for the difference. The city was largely deprived of its top citizens. Ration lists found in Nebuchadnezzar's palace in Babylon show that the displaced Judean king Jehoiakin and his family, among others, were allocated oil, barley, and dates.

Deportees settled in Babylonian villages which were sometimes named after the original home of their people: the 'village of Judeans', villages of

---

[39] Jeremiah 39:1–3. Jeremiah 39:3–14 gives an account in which the names and offices of Babylonian officers are recognizable, see Jursa 2010.

[40] The Akkadian Nabu-zer-iddina. His title in Hebrew is 'chief of butchers', referring to the appropriate slaughter of animals for sacrifice and royal meals; in Akkadian texts he is identified as 'chief of cooks/bakers', a high office at Nebuchadnezzar's court.

[41] 2 Chron 36:10 and Ezra 1–6.   [42] Lipschits 1998.

people from Neirab, from Gaza, from Ashkelon, and from Tyre, are all known from contemporary cuneiform texts. Each village was allocated fields in central Babylonia, which the exiles rented and farmed, paying taxes from the produce. The king 'arranged to assign to the prisoners (Jews, Syrians, and Tyrians) on their arrival settlements in the most suitable lands of Babylonia'.[43]

Contractual matters were recorded by Babylonian scribes in the service of the state; they still wrote on clay in cuneiform with an occasional name in Aramaic script on one of the edges of a clay tablet. Parts of their archives have been recognized, from Neirab-village and from the village of Judeans.[44] The Judeans, settled with their families, were reluctant to return to Jerusalem when the opportunity arose one or two generations later, despite being urged on by zealots who hoped they would come back to support the rebuilding of the temple but were often disappointed by the response. They flourished in Babylonia, and were still there nearly a century later, acting on the advice of the prophet Jeremiah (29:5–7):

> Build houses, settle down, plant gardens and eat what they produce, take wives and have sons and daughters, . . . Work for the good of the country to which I have exiled you, pray to Yahweh on its behalf, since on its welfare yours depends.

Babylonia had a higher standard of living than Palestine at that time, so a reluctance on the part of settled families to move back from Mesopotamia when opportunities arose is not surprising.[45] In some instances, archaeological excavation has supported the assumption of devastated cities in and around Jerusalem; but there is also a literary motif of a deserted waste land which implies mainly that there was no king in charge.[46] The Deuteronomic commandment that Hebrews should not make images of Yahweh can be considered alongside the recent discovery that official Babylonian seals by this time do not show deities in human form.[47] This similarity may have made integration easier for the Judeans who lived as exiles in Babylonia. They did not have to change their names, and from this time onwards Jews used Babylonian month-names, no matter where they lived.

Although the destruction of Ashkelon and then of Jerusalem should have opened up access for an invasion of Egypt, Nebuchadnezzar's

---

[43] Berossus according to Joseph., *Ap.* I, 138, trans. van der Spek.

[44] Pearce and Wunsch 2014. The interpretation given here follows that of Waerzeggers 2015b. None of the tablets comes from a known site, so a mixture of tablets from individual archives is likely.

[45] Barstad 1996: 66–7.   [46] Wiesehöfer 2003.

[47] Ornan 2005. Examples in Altavilla and Walker 2016.

subsequent siege of Tyre shows that other coastal cities had not yet been cowed into submission. Tyre consisted of a rocky island and a mainland settlement. Without ships, it was an unusually difficult task to capture both parts of the city. Details are lacking because there are no royal inscriptions for the later years of Nebuchadnezzar's long reign. The siege of Tyre lasted for thirteen years and must have drained some of Babylon's military resources as well as showing that its army was not invincible. When at last victory was achieved, Tyre's king Baal III became a vassal and is listed among all the other Levantine contributors to the building of the Southern Palace; Tyrians were deported to Babylonia, where a village, named 'Tyre', has been identified in texts.[48] Despite the difficulties of a long siege, the fabulous wealth of Tyre, transported to Babylon, would have added enormously to Nebuchadnezzar's coffers. Tyrian colonies presumably had their taxes diverted to the king of Babylon.[49] The victory had ramifications not least in the western Mediterranean, giving rise to later claims that Nebuchadnezzar had 'conquered' Iberia. His hard-won conquests gave him the reputation of a victor as far as the Pillars of Hercules (the Straits of Gibraltar), as related centuries later by Greek writers Josephus and Strabo.[50]

Ezekiel, living in Babylonia, attributed the overthrow of Tyre to the anger of Yahweh, stating that Babylon was acting under instruction from the displaced god of Judah:

> For the Lord Yahweh says this:
>
> From the North I am sending Nebuchadnezzar, king of Babylon, king of
>   kings, against Tyre
> With horses and chariots and horsemen, a horde of many races . . .
> By your wisdom and your intelligence you have amassed great wealth;
> You have piles of gold and silver inside your treasure houses.
> Such is your skill in trading, your wealth has continued to increase
> And with this your heart has grown more arrogant.
> And so, the Lord Yahweh says this:
> Since you consider yourself the equal of God,
> Very well, I am going to bring foreigners against you.[51]

Ezekiel's tomb is in southern Iraq, just north of the Shiʿa holy city of Nejef. Many scholars think his spectacular visions, in particular the chariot of Yahweh and the composite creatures – including winged bulls with human

---

[48] In avoiding the misleading term 'Phoenician', I follow Quinn 2018: ch. 2.
[49] Schaudig 2008.   [50] Röllig 2014–16.   [51] Ezekiel 26:7–8.

faces – which attended it, were inspired by witnessing the great festivals of Babylonian cities.

Campaigns and conquests during the latter part of Nebuchadnezzar's forty-three-year reign are recorded neither in chronicles nor in royal inscriptions, but he probably made at least one campaign eastwards and took control of Susa for a short time; the various strands of evidence are ambiguous.[52] On the island of Agarum (modern Failaka) at the head of the Arabian Gulf, Nebuchadnezzar exercised control to the extent of leaving an inscription there, nicely cut into a block of ashlar masonry: 'Palace of Nebuchadnezzar, king of Babylon', as well as an inscribed bronze bowl dedicated to the Sun-god; a Babylonian governor served there under Nabonidus not long afterwards.[53] He did not attempt to invade Egypt, as far as is known. One aspect of Nebuchadnezzar's policy was that he purposefully did not build any new royal palaces outside of Babylon, in contrast to the policy of Assyrian kings, whose governors had lived in identifiable palaces in the cities that they administered. His approach to Jerusalem, where he broke up a centre of zealous resistance and nationalist worship, and broke the continuity of the House of David, led to an arrangement that was satisfactory from the Babylonian point of view. He met reverses and difficulties, including an uprising led by nearby Borsippa, with immense determination. Although he did not invade Egypt,[54] Nebuchadnezzar took vigorous action to restrict its ambitions by surrounding the borders of Egypt with provinces which had reason to fear ferocious reprisals if they attempted rebellion.

His policy of keeping local rulers surrounded by Babylonian advisers, rather than putting a Babylonian governor in charge, was largely successful for a while, but eventually direct rule had to be imposed. Public loyalty was demonstrated by advertising foreign donations to his fabulous Southern Palace. Many local rulers, or their representatives, came to Babylon and renewed their oaths of loyalty at the New Year Festival. Trends towards the conflation of great gods and the use of symbols in preference to anthropomorphic images may help to explain how Jeremiah could call Nebuchadnezzar the servant of Yahweh, and how Nabonidus could call Cyrus II the servant of Marduk.[55]

The events of Jerusalem's downfall, and the biblical texts that refer to them, were well known to the Judeans of the diaspora, and so had a marked

---

[52] Potts 2016: 285–9.   [53] Potts 2009.

[54] Contra Berossus and the prediction of Ezekiel 29:17–21. See Streck 1998–2001: 199, 'Nebukadnezar II.A'.

[55] Jeremiah 25:9, 27:6; see also Isaiah 44:28.

effect on later understanding of Nebuchadnezzar's legacy. His reputation among Hebrews as a 'bad' king emanated mainly from Jerusalem, where the supposed misery and plight of deportees in Mesopotamia was exaggerated in biblical texts to encourage the deportees to return.[56] Therefore, in biblical tradition including the Book of Daniel, atrocity stories soon transformed the events leading up to the fall of Babylon, stereotyping Nebuchadnezzar as a mad and cruel king who was justly punished for Babylon's fate. The king was confused with Nabonidus, a man of very different character who was in fact the last king of the dynasty, whose son was Belshazzar, and whose dreams were described in unusual detail in his public royal inscriptions, giving a general link with the dreams in Daniel. Cuneiform sources do not record the dreams of Nebuchadnezzar. The tiresome length and complexity of Mesopotamian royal names easily led to confusion. Other traditions regarded Nebuchadnezzar II as a very great ruler, so that later would-be occupants of the throne in Babylon took his name: Nidinti-Bēl called himself Nebuchadnezzar III in 522 BC and an Armenian took the name Nebuchadnezzar IV in 521, both during the reign of Darius I.

The pursuit of business interests continued during Nebuchadnezzar's reign; they are represented by records from the Archive of Iddin-Marduk, who was associated with the business house of Egibi, involved in trade and in the taxation of agricultural produce.[57] Archives of clay tablets show that business activities continued through to Achaemenid occupation. Among them the Archive of Egibi, found in Babylon, bears witness to five generations of sales, loans, financial matters, legal decisions, marriages, adoptions, and inheritance spanning the period 602–482.[58] Members of the family held top positions in temple administration at Uruk, showing that the close links between Uruk and Babylon forged by Nabopolassar had continued under his successors. At least 1,700 texts have been identified there.

Nebuchadnezzar's most visible legacy was perpetuated by his monumental building works, carried out in at least eight of the greatest cities in Babylonia as well as in Babylon. Bricks inscribed by him have been found in astonishing abundance. His longer inscriptions record that he recognized inscriptions written by kings two thousand years earlier, for they could still be read by his well-trained scribes. Although no images of the king on stone monuments have been found, the rock-cut reliefs in the Lebanon show that there was no objection to showing his image there.[59]

---

[56] Waerzeggers 2015b.   [57] Wunsch 1993.   [58] Wunsch 2000.

[59] It should be noted, however, that some building work previously attributed to Nebuchadnezzar may be redated to the Seleucid period. There were many phases of repair and rebuilding.

Although he did not leave royal inscriptions describing his campaigns, Nebuchadnezzar II left detailed texts in cuneiform to show the organization behind his other achievements. His high officials were obliged to provide labour, drawn from the provinces or regions where they held responsibility.[60] In the palace he employed 800 Elamite guards and fourteen Elamite builders.[61] Treasures gained from his conquests and annual taxes from his empire financed building work on a grand scale. He continued and completed the work done by his father on the ziggurat E-temen-anki, and embellished the great temple Esagila. He made a wonderful new boat for Marduk to ride on festival journeys; he worked on the great walls of Babylon; and he continued construction on the new palace begun by his father, on the site where previous kings had also built, now known as the Southern Palace.[62] It consisted of three units, of which one contained a huge throne room. Later in his reign, he built another palace on a high mound at the northernmost part of the citadel. It is now known as the Summer Palace and is described below.

At the beginning of each year, coinciding with the spring equinox, a New Year Festival took place in Babylon. Its purpose was to renew the kingship for the following year, taking the king outside the city to the temple of the New Year Festival, which lay to the north beyond the citadel, to check whether renewal should be granted. During the first eleven days of the month of Nisan, which was associated with Babylon's constellation 'the field' (*ikû*, the Square of Pegasus), once kingship had been renewed, the king re-entered the citadel and the people celebrated his rule with processions through seven or more stations in the city. He was reinvested with royal robes, crown, and sceptre.[63] The architecture of the city centre was closely linked to these parades along the great Processional Way, through the imposing Ishtar Gate, and visits to temples: the temple gates, streets, and citadel walls served as stations promoting the king's authority associated with past glory. At each station, prayers and recitals performed in the presence of well-known statues with their inscriptions reinforced the accepted view of Babylon's fame in the cultural memory of its people and its visitors.[64] Two of these statues had been looted, perhaps a thousand years earlier, from Mari, where the men they depicted had served as famous

---

[60] Several of them had titles of office inherited from Assyrian government. See Da Riva 2013a.

[61] Pedersén 2005b.   [62] Margueron 2013.

[63] Evidence comes from a Seleucid text, and from an inscription of Nebuchadnezzar published by Meyer 1962: 231–4; on parts of the topographical list *Tintir*, see George 1992; for discussion, see Pongratz-Leisten 1994: 87–90, Beaulieu 2005, and Pongratz-Leisten 2006–8.

[64] See Jonker 1995; Young 1996; Oshima 2011: 65–8.

governors in the third millennium BC. Later the statues were modified to transform them into demi-gods who could intercede with the great gods.[65] The stations were linked to some of the divine names proclaimed for Marduk in the *Epic of Creation*, acknowledging particular powers assimilated to him from other gods. In his temple, Marduk as Bēl was seated on Tiamat, the Sea representing anarchy, and seats of various conquered composite creatures such as the lion monster *ugallu*, the dragon *ušumgallu*, and the serpent *bašmu* were there, too. A separate temple, or a room in the great temple (the word translated as 'house' can also mean 'room') was the House of the Pure Mound (E-dukuga), where Marduk's splendid ceremonial chariot was housed.

A cluster of shrines within the temple complex Esagila was central to the festival. Nabopolassar and Nebuchadnezzar II, who boast of their work in royal inscriptions, restored it to its earlier glory. But most of it has not been excavated because the remains lie far beneath later houses and tombs. Koldewey's sounding went dangerously deep (see the photograph in Figure 2.4, Chapter 2). For that reason only small parts of wall were identified, and the published plan is almost entirely a reconstruction. No clay tablets were found there, although many were retrieved from a space to the south.[66]

The following account combines details taken from this period and from Seleucid texts produced centuries later, which may include alterations in the ritual according to changing needs.[67] A few details are scattered among various texts of different dates, some complete, some fragmentary, allowing many uncertainties. As the sequence of events set out here has been gathered from more than one source, it may not accurately give the schedule for any particular period. Nebuchadnezzar and his successor Neriglissar both made improvements to ensure that the ceremonies were spectacular.[68] Very likely changes had been made to the ceremony ever since the First Dynasty of Babylon, when the western Storm-god Addu was the main participant. The day on which the battle between Marduk and Tiamat took place varies between at least three different days of the festival according to different records. Many features of the *Epic of Creation* can be recognized in various divine names and episodes. Prayers and incantations were recited at various stages; planets and stars were invoked. Purification of a temple was achieved by an exorcist in three ways: water from a well along the Tigris and from another well along the Euphrates was sprinkled;

---

[65] Sallaberger 2006–8.   [66] Many were of later date; see Clancier 2009: 142–4.
[67] As so often, there are gaps in the texts.   [68] Linssen 2003: 215–37 for an edition of sources.

cedar oil was smeared on doors; and a sheep was beheaded in the temple, which its carcass 'purifies' before being taken and thrown into the river.

Day 1: Marduk the Lord (Bēl), with priests and cult singers in attendance, set off from the shrine of Asarre, 'god of all heaven', which was uncovered in Koldewey's excavations at the bottom of the famous deep trench (see Figure 2.4). Marduk's statue was perhaps related to his name as Anshar, as proclaimed in the *Epic of Creation*. The cedar roofing beams of the shrine were plated with gold.

Day 2: Marduk was stationed in the forecourt of the shrine, in between curtains, where his name was proclaimed as Mes (Sumerian for 'hero').

Day 3: Marduk was on the pure holy hill, E-dukuga, where two fierce gods with Underworld connections stood each on a dais, symbolized as divine weapons.[69]

Day 4: Marduk entered the Shrine of Fates, where he also stayed later on days eight and eleven. The god's name there was proclaimed as 'King of the gods of heaven and earth'.[70] Also on that day, a *šešgallu*-priest blessed the temple (Esagila?), addressed *ikû*-Pegasus, and recited the *Epic of Creation*. Meanwhile in the adjacent temple of Nabu-of-Vats, which lay between the Southern Palace and the ziggurat, the king received the sceptre of kingship.

Day 5: Esagila was purified, using water from the two rivers, in preparation for the arrival of Nabu from Borsippa. A procession made its way along the street, coming along the Processional Way, perhaps beginning from the Ishtar Gate. It stopped again at the temple of Nabu-of-Vats, where Marduk was proclaimed as Asalluhi, and a Sumerian prayer to the god was part of the liturgy. The king entered, encountering the god for the first time. He laid down his royal insignia; his ears were pulled twice; he was slapped on the cheek. If his tears flowed, Bēl was well disposed. If his tears did not flow, Bēl was angry. He knelt before Marduk and declared himself to be free from sins committed against the cult and shrines, not to have damaged the privileges of the city – the *kidinnūtu*-status that freed the citizens from taxes and corvée work and forbade the bearing of weapons within the city walls – and not to have neglected the city walls. The statue of the god Nabu arrived by boat from Borsippa and processed to the temple of Ninurta, located nearest to the city gate, and the canal connecting Babylon to Borsippa.[71]

---

[69] They were named Enmesharra and Enbilulu.   [70] In Sumerian, *Lugal-dimmer-an-ki-a*.

[71] A text describing the sacred boat made for him by Šamaš-šum-ukin has been identified, though it is fragmentary. See Frame 1995: 256–7.

Day 6: Marduk's boat Sirsir, his dragon-boat, took part in the events of this day, mooring at the dais at the end of the river. The dragon represented Tiamat, controlled by Marduk as its steersman. The connections of the name may imply that a ritual performance demonstrated the combat in which the god was victorious over the forces of Chaos, but there is no certain evidence for a dramatic presentation by actors. Perhaps at this stage Marduk's title 'Enlil of the gods' was proclaimed, the title with which he is acknowledged on the glazed bricks at the Ishtar Gate.

Day 7: Marduk rode by boat – one of Nebuchadnezzar's Wonders – to the *akītu*-temple of the New Year Festival,[72] the temple of sacrifices. It was located outside the citadel wall, and probably surrounded by a garden; the gods assembled and were dressed in new robes. Nabu, as Sirsir, was proclaimed in a hymn of Nebuchadnezzar, when he proceeded from the temple of Ninurta to Esagila. Nebuchadnezzar described the boat that he made for Marduk:

The Sirsir boat, for transporting Marduk the lord of gods – its hull front and back, its dimensions, its capacity, its sides, the hoe emblem, the *mušhuššu*-dragon – I decorated it with fourteen talents twelve minas of red gold, 750 *sagallatu*-ornaments[73] of *hulālu*-agate, and shining lapis lazuli.

Day 8: At some stage in the events, Marduk was transported in his chariot, a superb vehicle whose various personified parts, such as the axle and dust-guard, represented mythical creatures.[74] It was drawn by two white horses chosen by divination. The diviner held the mane and hair while reciting an incantation as a request to authorize its appointment:

You, O horse, creature of holy mountains,
You are magnificent among the Pleiades.
You are set in heaven like a rainbow.
You were born in holy mountains.
You eat pure juniper,
You drink spring water from sacred mountains.
You are given for the chariot of Marduk the great Lord.

---

[72] 'Day One Temple' may have been another name for this temple. See Linssen 2003: 85 n. 457. Kosmin 2018 associates it with the new era inaugurated by Seleucus in 305 BC.

[73] This reading of the signs SÁ GÁL GUR is provisional. If correct, it describes the shape of a tuber from the sedge species Cyperus esculentus, which bears nut-shaped, edible nodules on the end of its main roots. See CDA s.v. *sagillatu*. Possibly used to denote a fringe with beads attached to the ends?

[74] Lambert 1973: 277–80.

> Its ritual [the diviner then addresses the priest]: you whisper the incantation three times into the horse's left ear through a sweet [hollow] reed; you place offerings before it as to gods.[75]

A procession reached the New Year Festival temple, where Marduk was proclaimed god of the temple. There the ceremony of sacred marriage took place between the king and a priestess, demonstrating the king's fertility which symbolized the whole country's productivity. The menu of a sumptuous banquet can be taken from the food and drink listed as offerings authorized for various deities in Nebuchadnezzar's inscriptions:

> fattened bulls, *pasillu*-sheep, strings of fish, wild birds, ducks and geese, reed rodents, eggs, honey, ghee, milk, best oil, wines 'as if water', beer, orchard fruits including apples, figs, pomegranates, grapes, dates of Dilmun (the best!), dried figs, raisins, abundant vegetables, fruits of the allotments, best beer, honey, butter, top quality pressed oil, date-sweetened emmer beer, barley beer, wine from mountains and other lands, all the best of everything produced of land and sea.[76]

Day 9: Does lack of information imply that the king and his subjects were still eating and drinking?

Day 10: When Marduk left that temple, he (and presumably the king) received gifts and homage from ambassadors and high-level representatives from all over his empire who would have taken part in the banquet and sworn oaths of loyalty in the presence of god and king, presenting gifts and tribute in person. Marduk's victory over Chaos and Babylon's control of an ordered world for the benefit of mankind was assured.

Day 11: Marduk was back in the shrine of fates; the gods assembled for the second time, and fates for the coming year were fixed for the king. A prayer was intoned for his health, success, and long life, accompanied by sacrifices.

This summary gives the merest sketch of the greatest festival recorded in cuneiform. A hymn of Nebuchadnezzar II to Nabu expresses the very close relationship between Nabu and Marduk, in which Nabu has the titles elsewhere ascribed to Marduk: 'Enlil of the gods' and

---

[75] Lambert 2007: 83; my translation. The word for the mane, *zappu*, is also the name of the Pleiades. Likewise an incantation was whispered into the ear of a sacrificial bull whose hide and tendons were then incorporated into the *lilissu*-drum that played an important role in rituals; Lenzi 2018.

[76] This list is taken from Schaudig 2001: text P2, which is similar to broken lists in several inscriptions of Nebuchadnezzar II.

> King of the gods of heaven and earth
> The one who gives the sceptre and throne of kingship to the king
> Creator of mankind
> The one who entrusted kingship to Nebuchadnezzar.

But the same prayer also invokes Marduk as creator of Nebuchadnezzar and calls upon him to exercise kingship.[77] In another hymn, Nabu is invoked as Asari, as Sirsir, and as Shazu, and is in charge of the Tablet of Destinies, taking the same names and roles as Marduk in the *Epic of Creation*, implying that there was a version of that epic in which Nabu took the role of conquering hero. The relationship between the two gods was not antagonistic; their symbols, hoe and stylus, are shown side by side on seals.

Other festivals celebrated the cults of various gods, including a Palm Festival in which the goddess Ishtar was victor in the cosmic battle; processions along ceremonial roads and canals to Borsippa and Kish are known, but the texts do not have the length or detail to allow reconstruction as is possible for the New Year Festival of Babylon.[78] That festival was the template for other celebrations at different times of year in different cities.[79] In Uruk, Ishtar and Anu were celebrated in that city's version.[80] In Babylon each month had a particular ritual, to call upon a constellation, depending on which one was at its height in the 'place of protection',[81] specifically to protect Esagil from invasion and to defend against usurpation. The rituals involved substitution for destruction, such as a fire laid on a brick and thrown into the river, or a shrine built to be burned instead of Esagila. Education in cuneiform was still a serious business: the temple of Nabu-of-Vats contained a votive deposit of elementary school texts dedicated to the god by junior scribes. Each gave his own name with a brief prayer to the god requesting long life or successful progeny.

Ever since the late second millennium or earlier, the orderly layout of the city with its citadel walls set with eight city gates had remained substantially the same. Elements of the plan were listed in the five-tablet composition *Tintir*, which gives names and epithets of the city, names of shrines and their occupants, ceremonial names of walls, canals, streets, and city quarters.[82]

---

[77] Oshima 2014: 473–80.   [78] See Linssen 2003: 90–1; George 2003.

[79] There were four 'new years' based on equinoxes and solstices.

[80] See Linssen 2003: 184–244.

[81] This interpretation gives the meaning 'protection' rather than 'secret' to *niširtu*, as in many inscriptions of Nebuchadnezzar concerning the defence of the city. See CAD and CDA s.v.

[82] *Tintir* is a name of Babylon, and the name of a text. For the text, see George 1992. A commentary on the text has been identified.

Babylon's wide Processional Way (*mašdahu*) had a raised, paved surface and with its monumental Ishtar Gate, 'The Entrance of Kingship', had many phases of development. The famous glazed bricks decorated with dragons and bulls in relief along the Processional Way and on the Ishtar Gate are usually attributed to Nebuchadnezzar; but an unglazed version preceded them. A replica reminiscent of Babylon's Ishtar Gate at Persepolis, with fragments of a *mušhuššu*-dragon on a glazed surface, is believed to have been built by Cyrus the Great.[83] It indicates that Babylon's example was followed by an Achaemenid king.

The Ishtar Gate, famous from its glorious reconstruction in Berlin, stood adjacent to the great temple of the Great Goddess (Nin-mah), adorned with blue-glazed baked bricks and at least one inscription of Nebuchadnezzar in white glaze.[84] It celebrated 'Ishtar' (which is used as a general term for any goddess) as the great goddess Nanaya, for whom a dedicatory inscription was written on a wall of the Processional Way. Nanaya was a great goddess in Uruk whose fame increased throughout the Near East in later times, although her temple in Babylon has not been identified.[85] Modelled figures of rampant bulls, golden with blue curls of body hair, hooves, and horns, white lions with golden manes, and Marduk's special creature, the scaly *mušhuššu*-dragon, white with golden claws and horn, were cleverly incorporated into the brickwork, set beneath two bands of geometric design separated by a wide band of rosettes – all coloured blue, gold, and white. The bull and *mušhuššu* figures were copied or adapted from those erected at Nippur by the ruler of Agade, Naram-Sin (2254–2218 BC) more than 1,500 years earlier.[86] Those images at Babylon on the Ishtar Gate reflect Marduk rather than Ishtar.

The temple of Marduk, Esagila, was an enormous complex that included three large internal courtyards, the whole extent measuring about 165 x 115 m. Shrines dedicated to other gods were contained within it. Roofing may have included vaults and domes.[87] The centre of worship and of many festivals was a glorious statue of Marduk wearing garments colourfully embroidered, shining with appliqué ornaments of gold and silver, his neck adorned with a huge cylinder seal of best lapis lazuli inscribed: 'Property of Marduk. Seal of the Storm-god Addu of Esagila', as if to remind us that more than a millennium earlier, Samsu-iluna son of Hammurabi had

---

[83] See Chaverdi and Callieri 2017: 394–7. The find-spot is Tol-e Ajori, a gateway or temple on the edge of the city, about 3 km west of the Persepolis Terrace.

[84] See Marzahn 2008: 46–53.   [85] George 1993a: nos. 794 and 1117.   [86] Joannès 2011.

[87] According to Strabo, buildings were traditionally roofed with brick vaults. Evidence for them has sometimes been found on other sites, such as Ur and Tell al-Rimah.

celebrated the New Year Festival for the Storm-god whose name was given to Marduk as victor in the *Epic of Creation*. The seal had been donated by Esarhaddon a century earlier.[88]

Nebuchadnezzar II described the Southern Palace and its vicissitudes:

> In Babylon, my favourite city which I love, there is a palace, a building which is the Wonder of Peoples, the anchor rope of the land, a pure residence, my royal dwelling, in the district of Babili in the middle of Babylon, extending from the city wall Imgur-Ellil to the eastern canal named Libil-hegalli ('May it bring abundance'), from the bank of the Euphrates to the street of Babylon [down which Marduk processed in the great New Year Festival] named Ay-ibur-shabu ('May the arrogant not flourish'), which Nabopolassar king of Babylon, the father who begot me, built out of mud brick, and there he lived.
>
> But its base had been weakened by floodwater, and the outside of that building became too low when the streets of Babylon were consolidated.
>
> I cleared away its walls which consisted of mud brick, and I opened up its foundation platform until I reached groundwater. I laid down [new] foundations for it against the groundwater and built it up as high as a mountain with bitumen and baked brick. I laid strong cedar beams across it to roof it. Cedar door leaves set with bronze bands, thresholds and door jambs made of copper I fixed at each of its gateways. Inside it I heaped up silver, gold, precious stones, all very valuable, in abundance – property and possessions worthy of admiration. Within it I stored treasure chests, a royal treasury. Since I did not wish the support of my kingship to be based in any other city, I did not build royal residences in every town, nor did I place possessions worthy of kingship in other parts of the country. Was not my royal building in Babylon a sufficient ornament for my kingship? In reverence for Marduk my divine lord, my heart was in Babylon, the city of my treasury, which I love. So I sought to improve my royal seat, but not to change its streets, not to weaken its base, not to block its watercourses by broadening the residence, 490 cubits of land alongside Nemetti-Enlil the city wall on the outside; I built two strong harbour walls out of bitumen and baked brick, and between them I made a baked-brick structure. On top of it I built a great residence very tall, out of bitumen and baked brick, for the seat of my kingship, and thus I improved upon my father's palace and made a more splendid royal seat. I laid strong cedars which come from high mountains, mighty firs, and choice cypresses from distant lands, to roof it. Door leaves of rosewood, cedar, cypress, ebony and ivory, set with silver and gold bands, encased in bronze, thresholds of silver and door jambs of copper I fixed at each of

---

[88] Leichty 2011: 248–9.

its gateways, and I encircled its top with a battlement-crown of lapis lazuli. I surrounded it with a strong inner wall of bitumen and baked brick, mountain-high.

Beside that wall of baked brick I built [another] great wall of strong stones split from great mountains and I made the top of it mountain-high. I made that house a Wonder, and filled it with riches for the admiration of all peoples. Its sides were surrounded with beauty, awe-inspiring the dread radiance of kingship, so that the wicked and unjust cannot come into it.[89]

From this inscription it appears that the palace had two parts, the one a treasury, and the other a royal residence. In the massive throne room, impressively roofed with towering vaults, the walls were built of glazed brick designed with friezes of stylized date palms and palmettes, coloured in two shades of blue, as well as white and gold, separated by narrow bands of rectangular design, and striding lions.

The palace took about ten years to build. In his dedicatory prism inscription, Nebuchadnezzar II invoked Marduk:

O Marduk, lord of lands, hear my utterances! May I enjoy the palace I made!

May I reach old age in it, in Babylon! May I have the satisfaction of growing very old! May I reach inside it the rich tribute of the kings of the regions of the whole inhabited world! May my offspring rule forever inside it!

Nebuchadnezzar would have hoped that the massive foundations would compensate for the inevitable subsidence. Having built the entire foundation platform for the Southern Palace, he probably set upon it only the first two of the four buildings excavated there, each with a separate entrance and separate drainage. Closest to the Ishtar Gate, where the great processions would pass through, was the Vaulted Building within the easternmost palace, and accommodation. Next to it was the building with the biggest of the internal courtyards, and the huge throne room. Then perhaps a later king (Cyrus?) built a third palace beside it, on the part of the foundation platform that was still bare, followed by a fourth (built by Darius I?), each with a large central courtyard in Babylonian style. Finally, beside the whole complex, beyond the western entrance, Artaxerxes built a delightful pillared pavilion where the shattered fragments of an inscription on stone in cuneiform script conveying Old Persian language name the king (see Figure 10.3).

[89] Clay cylinder inscription BM 85, 4–30, ii.1–56.

Many of Babylon's kings displayed to the public statues and relief sculptures of famous rulers from the past, to link themselves with a long-lived and illustrious culture. Some of them were collected from conquered lands. They were installed on the main streets, especially at gateways.[90] Among the best known are those of very early kings of the Middle Euphrates – the life-size diorite statue of Puzur-Eshtar, a governor of Mari dated to around 2000 BC, which may have been taken to Babylon by Hammurabi, found set alongside the north-east wall of the Processional Way; a neo-Hittite relief sculpture of the Storm-god; the inscribed lime-stone stela of Šamaš-rēš-uṣur, the 'honey-king' of Suhu, from the eighth century; and the gigantic, unfinished 'Lion of Babylon', perhaps represent-ing the late Assyrian conquest of Egypt when its kings ruled the city (see Figure 7.9).

Late in his reign, Nebuchadnezzar II built another palace, the Summer Palace, beyond the inner walls of the citadel, on a different mound now known as Babil, at the northern corner of the outer city wall.

> My heart impelled me to build a palace close to the baked-brick city wall where the north wind blows, for the treasures of Babylon, a match for the (other) palace of Babylon.

It is known as the Summer Palace because of its air ducts, which improved airflow within the rooms, affording some welcome relief from the stifling heat of summer. Clay records show that great temples in the old cities such as Uruk and Sippar supplied quantities of bricks in exchange for silver. This palace was entirely Nebuchadnezzar's own work, so he did not have to face the problems of an older building sinking into the water table. He founded it 'upon the breast of the Underworld', upon a mighty platform of brick-work that reached down sixty cubits. The location must have been a boon to the builders; by contrast, for example, the temple of Ninurta on the citadel mound had to be raised several times during Nebuchadnezzar's reign because of flooding and subsidence.

Since the river Euphrates flowed through the middle of the city, massive revetment was needed along the banks to prevent damage to central areas, since the height of the water could vary by many metres depending on the season. The bridge that connected the two banks in the city centre was very sturdily built upon shaped piers of stone, one of which was discovered by excavation, since the course of the Euphrates has shifted, leaving the old

---

[90] Klengel-Brandt 1990; Garrison 2012. The idea that these objects were collected in a 'museum' has been overturned by archaeological evidence.

Figure 8.3 Basalt (?) stela showing the Storm-god of Halab (Aleppo), with a Luwian text written in Hittite hieroglyphs on the back; found at Babylon. Height 1.28 m. Istanbul, Ancient Orient Museum. Credit: Koldewey 1900: pl. 1.

riverbed dry. In his inscriptions Nebuchadnezzar wrote that his father had begun the work on the bridge. Herodotus wrote that the stones of the bridge were bound together with iron and lead.

To Nebuchadnezzar II or to 'an Assyrian king reigning in Babylon', or to the legendary Semiramis, Greek writers variously gave the credit for creating the Hanging Garden 'of Babylon', one of the original Seven Wonders of the Ancient World.[91] Nebuchadnezzar's own inscriptions do not mention it. When Koldewey excavated at Babylon he expected to discover the garden located beside the Southern Palace of Nebuchadnezzar.

[91] See Dalley 2013.

Figure 8.4 Whitish limestone sculpture of the 'honey king', a local ruler of Suhu in the eighth century BC, on the Middle Euphrates, brought to Babylon as loot and installed along the Processional Way. He introduced beekeeping and claimed descent from Hammurabi. Note that the symbols of Marduk and Nabu are side by side. The porous stone is greasy from anointing. Height 1.18 m. Istanbul, Ancient Orient Museum. Credit: Koldewey 1932.

Disappointing many visitors and patrons, he was unable to find proof, for 'myth had invaded archaeology'. In desperation he suggested that it had been a roof garden within the north-eastern corner of the Southern Palace, perhaps overlooking the Ishtar Gate and the Processional Way. That corner, which formed a substantial wing of the huge building, was unusual for being built of baked brick with bitumen mortar, presumably designed to cope with unusual quantities of water. Its rooms on the ground level were topped by vaults roofed with large paving stones for the floor of an upper area. At ground level was a well with shafts on either side, comprising an installation for raising water vertically, perhaps as an elaborate bucket chain or paternoster. Koldewey was well aware that none of these features matched the layout of the garden or its water-raising equipment as described in detail by Greek writers, nor was the area shaped like a theatre, nor did it have an aqueduct bringing water in from higher ground, as those later writers specified. The building materials and the special water-raising

Fig 8.5 Life-size diorite statue of Puzur-Eshtar, ruler of Mari c. 2100–2000 BC. Probably looted from Mari by Hammurabi, then found installed with his father's statue by the north-east wall of the Processional Way, and partly recarved in the eighth/ seventh century to represent a protective, magical demi-god. Height 1.7 m. Credit: Commons.wikimedia, G. Dall'Orto, Istanbul Archaeological Museum.

installation suit the idea of a roof garden from which, one may speculate, the royal family could appear in public and witness processions, rather like an Egyptian 'window of appearances'. A royal garden of this time, the Juniper Garden, has been identified in texts, but it lay on the south side of the citadel, to the south of Esagila, a long way from Nebuchadnezzar's great palace, and has none of the features expected of the Hanging Garden.[92] Nevertheless, Nebuchadnezzar's fame as its creator continues to resonate in modern times, confused with Sennacherib because both kings attacked Jerusalem, and confused with Nabonidus in the Book of Daniel.

The rule of the Chaldean dynasty of Babylonian kings lasted for less than a century; but the fame of its first two kings in later generations was extraordinary, partly due to military achievements, including the sacking of the First Temple in Jerusalem and the siege of Tyre, but also their stupendous building works in the city of Babylon, funded by plunder taken from the great Assyrian cities.

---

[92] Clancier 2009: 117.

Let me see Babylon! Let me go up to Esagila! Let me go to Babylon!

Prayer to Marduk (Oshima 2011: 67)

Babylon

Amel-Marduk (Evil-Merodach, 561–560)
Neriglissar (Nergal-šarra-uṣur, 559–556)
La-abaši-Marduk (556)
Nabonidus (Nabu-naʾid, 555–539)   // Croesus of Lydia (580–546)
    (Belshazzar crown prince)   // Astyages the Mede of Ecbatana
                                       // Cyrus II of Anshan (559–530)
Cyrus II The Great (539–530)
    Cambyses crown prince, king in Babylon (538–537)
Cambyses (530–522)
Bardiya, Nebuchadnezzar III (522, for 3 months)

By the time of Nebuchadnezzar II's death, the kingdom of Babylon had expanded to include the Levant with its Phoenician cities, but had not conquered Egypt.[1] It continued to incorporate Assyria, Nabopolassar's conquest. The last king of the dynasty, Nabonidus, added north-west Arabia to the empire. To the north-west at that time the powerful kingdom of Lydia, now Western Turkey, had been a focus for campaigns by Neriglissar and perhaps also Nabonidus, but neither reached the capital Sardis.[2] Nabonidus' campaign against Lydia is implied by the record of prisoners of war donated to serve as slaves in the temples of Nabu and Nergal, but it was Cyrus who went on to capture Sardis. Meanwhile, Persian-speaking tribes had moved into the area of south-western Iran now called Fars, putting pressure on Elamite cities, not least the old Elamite royal city Anshan, near to which Cyrus built his garden city at Pasargadae and may have begun to create the famous ceremonial centre at Persepolis.

---

[1] The main text editions of royal inscriptions from this period are by Da Riva 2012a and 2012b, 2013a, 2013b; Schaudig 2001 for Nabonidus and Cyrus; Dandamaev 1998–2001. Chronicles: Grayson 1975b; astronomical diaries: livius.org.

[2] This information comes from a fragmentary part of the *Nabonidus Chronicle*. See p. 252.

Some tribes associated with the Elamites and Medes to support Cyrus in taking control of the city of Babylon, so Nabonidus was the last native Babylonian king. Cyrus was his usurper and conqueror from around the region of Ecbatana (modern Hamadan); his son and successor Cambyses made a lasting conquest of Egypt, which had briefly been added to the Assyrian empire by Ashurbanipal in the mid-sixth century. The language spoken by the new conquerors may have been foreign, but they still used cuneiform Babylonian for some records, and did not attempt to disturb the cultural continuity of Babylonia.

The stable reigns of Nabopolassar and Nebuchadnezzar were followed by three short reigns that attempted to perpetuate the royal lineage, to fulfil the prayer that Nebuchadnezzar had expressed to Marduk when he dedicated the Southern Palace.[3] His son **Amel-Marduk** (the biblical Evil-Merodach) was regarded with favour in biblical tradition because he released Jehoiakin after thirty-seven years of captivity, but later had the reputation as a 'bad' king. Amel-Marduk's accession was contested, perhaps because he had supposedly tried to seize his father's throne when Nebuchadnezzar was away from Babylon. He had been imprisoned, and wrote a prayer under his pre-throne name to Marduk in captivity:[4]

> Only Marduk among the gods unties the knot of deceit of the wicked . . .
> Marduk looks at squinting eyes with disfavour.
> He makes Girra the fire-god burn the defaming lips . . .
> Win victory over the doer of abominations, the tightener of my knot of
>   evil.
>
> ───
>
> The prayer of a weary and shackled man, whom a man of evil shackled, who reported to Marduk. By his prayer to Marduk may he be released so that people and the land will see his greatness.

A fragment of an epic-style text, probably written by Nabonidus to denigrate the sons of Nebuchadnezzar, describes Amel-Marduk as a man of poor judgement who failed in his duty to the gods. These are typical of the accusations made by a usurper against his predecessor.

Amel-Marduk was assassinated by his brother-in-law **Neriglissar**, who was probably son of the chief of the Puqudu tribe; he had strengthened his claim to belong to the dynasty by wedding a daughter of Nebuchadnezzar.

---

[3] See Da Riva 2008: 14–16.

[4] The attempt to usurp his father is known only from the much later *Wayiqrah Rabbah*. See discussion by Oshima 2011: 316–17. His pre-accession name may have been Nabu-šuma-ukin, but this is not certain.

He also arranged for his own daughter to marry into the family of Borsippa's priesthood. He has been identified as the *simmagir*-official named in the Old Testament who went to Jerusalem in the time of Nebuchadnezzar. During his four-year reign he carried out minor building works in Babylon and on canals around Babylon. He led a campaign to north Syria and beyond, to cross the border of the kingdom of Lydia, but did not reach its capital city Sardis, seat of the super-wealthy king Croesus who was linked by the marriage of his sister to the royal family of Medes based in Ecbatana, an alliance with the potential to diminish Babylon's access to several trade routes.[5] Neriglissar's son **La-abâši-Marduk** lasted less than a year on the throne. Attempts to continue connections with Nebuchadnezzar were frustrated when **Nabonidus**, a man with no known royal ancestry, took the throne and reigned for sixteen years.

Nabonidus had held an official position at the courts of Nebuchadnezzar and Neriglissar. He was already in his mid-fifties or older, and was ably supported by his adult son Belshazzar. Rather like Nabopolassar, Nabonidus described himself as 'an only son who has nobody [to promote him]', a claim which acknowledges that he was a usurper, and shows a certain pride as a self-made man; but the *Babylonian King-List* accepted him as a member of the dynasty following his predecessors. Predictably, he

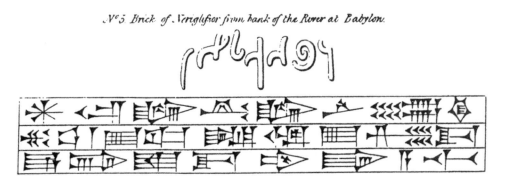

Figure 9.1 Inscriptions in cuneiform and alphabetic Aramaic written on a brick of Neriglissar. The cuneiform signs are archaic, typical of c. 1,200 years earlier.
Credit: Rawlinson 1861: pl. 8:5.

---

[5] Herodotus names one 'Labynetus' as the negotiator who had succeeded in making peace between Medes and Lydians in 585, but this date is probably too early to allow an identification with Nabonidus, whose name was quite common in Babylonia. See Dandamaev 1998–2001.

claimed to have been installed by his eager supporters with the full support of his divine lord Marduk.

His period of kingship was described as 'the dynasty of Harran' in a later text, *The Dynastic Prophecy*.[6] Harran, near modern Urfa, was one of the royal cities of Hanigalbat to which a branch of the late Assyrian royal family traced its origins.[7] Nabonidus' mother, Adda-guppi, a great lady with enormous influence over her son, is well known from three basalt slabs bearing long and informative inscriptions, hers and his, which were discovered in the great mosque at Harran. Two of them had been reset, face down, as threshold stones at the east and west entrances, as if to tread their names and pagan beliefs into the earth and down to the Underworld. In her youth, Adda-guppi had been a loyal subject of Ashurbanipal and his successors, who set up Harran as their royal city during the final years of Assyrian power. Her name is essentially Aramean, and strong Aramaic influence has been traced in her son's royal inscriptions, despite his scholarly use of Babylonian. She was a devotee of the Moon-god under the local name Ilteri. To the Moon-god alone she attributed her son's call to kingship, and that god, in answer to her prayer, appeared to her in a dream. He foretold that her son would restore his temple E-hulhul, the 'House of rejoicing', which had been damaged at the fall of Assyria; Nabonidus was destined to install replacement statues based on images surviving from the reign of Ashurbanipal.[8] Adda-guppi died while Nabonidus was in Arabia, and he wrote a nostalgic account of her life after her death. His maternal background helps to explain why Nabonidus took such an interest in explaining events of the late seventh century when, according to his interpretation, Marduk had chosen the Medes as his agents to conquer Nineveh and Harran in revenge for the earlier sack of Babylon by Sennacherib – the Moon-god controlled events on earth:

> I am Adda-guppi, mother of Nabonidus king of Babylon, worshipper of Sin, Nin-gal, Nusku, and Sadarnunna my gods. From my childhood I have sought after their divinity ... from the time of Ashurbanipal, king of Assyria, until the ninth year of Nabonidus king of Babylon, the son, offspring of my womb, 104 years of happiness, with the reverence which Sin, king of gods, inspired in me – he made me personally flourish: the vision of both my eyes is clear, I am excellent in understanding, my hands and feet are sound, my words are well-chosen, meat and drink agree with

---

[6] On *The Dynastic Prophecy*, see below, and van der Spek 2003: text no. 5.   [7] Fales 2014.
[8] They may have been made in Babylon. See Lee 1993: 131–6.

me, my flesh is good, my heart is glad, I have seen my descendants for four generations flourishing in themselves.

Nabonidus' son Belshazzar, whose name appropriately means 'O Lord, protect the king!', is best known from the biblical Book of Daniel, where he is confusingly presented as crown prince, son of Nebuchadnezzar. Belshazzar rather than the king is named in the dates on some 3,000 tablets that belong to the years when he took charge of Babylon during the middle of Nabonidus' reign. While his father was in Arabia, Belshazzar promulgated an edict concerning the management of temple lands and the obligation to pay taxes; it gave the general principles on which leases were granted, and set rates of pay for various categories of workmen.[9] Belshazzar took over duties that were normally expected to bear only the king's name; the edict gives the two royal names together.

Nabonidus' daughter was installed as priestess of the Moon-god at Ur. He wrote a detailed inscription telling how he had followed a very ancient precedent, as well as basing his action on his own interpretation of a lunar omen. An early king known to have installed a daughter in that role is Kudur-mabuk, the influential Elamite 'father' of two consecutive rulers of Larsa in Hammurabi's time. This act would have given Nabonidus a reliable informant watching over the loyalty of southern Mesopotamia, just as it had done for Kudur-mabuk.

Nabonidus' royal inscriptions are among the most extensive and varied of any Mesopotamian monarch. The chronicles that refer to his reign are known only from copies made more than two centuries later, during the Seleucid period.[10] Their information is normally considered to be reliable, but that is not true of the *Nabonidus Chronicle*, which is of questionable historical value. Another tricky text known as the *Counterfeit Literary Letter* contains judgements from the past, presumably aimed at an unknown current king. It was supposedly written by one early king to another (the beginning of the text is missing), and includes a tirade against priests of Ur, Uruk, and other cities, describing how early rulers had enjoyed success or failure as a direct consequence of their treatment of Esagila, linking Marduk's punishment to any ruler who had offended the gods of Babylon.[11]

---

[9] van Driel 2002: 166–71.   [10] Schaudig 2001: 47; but see Waerzeggers 2015a.

[11] Schaudig 2009: 15. Although a composition at the end of Nabonidus' reign would be appropriate, the extant copy dates from the time of Xerxes, who may have been using or adapting an earlier text.

Emphasizing his piety towards his most illustrious and successful predecessors, Nabonidus referred to Ashurbanipal and Nebuchadnezzar as his
role models. When he prepared the ground for work on the great temples in
the big cities, he relied on oracles to pick a favourable time in the traditional
way. Occasionally he unearthed inscriptions of earlier kings and was able to
read their names in the original texts: Sargon and Naram-Sin of Agade
from the mid-third millennium BC at Harran, Hammurabi at Larsa,
Samsu-iluna at Sippar, a stela of Nebuchadnezzar I at Ur, Ashurbanipal
at Agade, and many others. Modern scholars have sometimes called
Nabonidus an antiquarian or an archaeologist.[12] At each discovery he
treated the finds with reverence by anointing inscriptions, making sacrifices, and reinstalling them with statues of their gods. One particular
incident shows the long-term importance of his actions: finding a broken
statue of Sargon the Great of Agade from almost two thousand years earlier
when he was restoring a temple in Sippar, Nabonidus repaired and
reinstalled it. He then set up a cult for it which continued to be maintained
by Cyrus and Cambyses.[13] There was a special significance to the discovery
of Sargon because he, like Nabonidus, had not inherited his kingship but
had been selected, according to legend, by the goddess Ishtar.

Nabonidus' royal inscriptions give an impression of extreme piety, of
anxiety to link his building work restoring temples to previous work by
legendary kings, of overt reliance on dreams, visions, and omens for the
direction of his policies. An astonishing wealth and variety of royal inscriptions are known to us, written in a style that shows off a deep knowledge of
literature. He was well educated in the skills of the scribe in Sumerian and
Babylonian cuneiform. He described himself as 'offspring of Marduk the
sage of the gods' and 'the wise prince'. Some of his inscriptions, written in
the first person, contain quotations from the great works of literature such
as *Ludlul bēl nēmeqi* ('Let me praise the god of wisdom (Marduk)') and the
manual for divination by celestial omens, *Enūma Anu Enlil*. During this
general period, the great manuals of divination and astronomy were
reworked and expanded; concurrent versions allowed extra flexibility in
quotation, interpretation, and dispute by astrologers.[14] Nabonidus' preoccupation with dreams and their interpretation shows a great reliance on
that branch of divination. His keen and public involvement in the intrica-
cies of those sciences was later satirized in the verse account of his reign
written for Cyrus, and in the biblical Book of Daniel.

---

[12] Schaudig 2003.   [13] Sommerfeld 2009–11; Schaudig 2003.
[14] Hunger and Steele 2018; Koch-Westenholz 1999: 149.

One of Nabonidus' preoccupations was to allocate blame for the destruction of Nineveh and the fall of the Assyrian empire. On his Babylon Stela, which he installed in a prominent position at the Ishtar Gate, he related that Marduk had chosen the Median king to avenge an earlier sack of Babylon, taking responsibility for the fall of Nineveh. He blamed Babylonian allies for the damage done in looting the great Assyrian city, for he wrote that 'looting is anathema to Marduk'.[15] In the same text, as if to restore the reputation of Sennacherib, he claimed that Marduk had abandoned Babylon in anger,[16] allowing the great city to be sacked; later, he identified Marduk as responsible for the fall of the Assyrian empire because of the damage done to Babylon, even though he was a god who hated looting. His instrument of punishment was the barbaric Umman-manda – a term that may include the Medes – who once again got out of control. Nabonidus describes how Sennacherib (referred to only as 'king of Subartu') led Marduk by the hand to the city of Ashur, as if accompanying him to a new location for the New Year Festival. Thus Sennacherib was portrayed as the agent of Marduk. None of his inscriptions mention Esarhaddon, who claimed to have restored Babylon after its sack by Sennacherib. Nor is there mention of Ashurbanipal's sack of Babylon when he deposed his elder brother Šamaš-šum-ukin, for that sack of Babylon had been a just punishment for the treachery of the Assyrian king's brother and his Elamite allies.

Three phases of Nabonidus' reign can be distinguished: the first three years spent in Babylon arranging building works in many of the great cities; the next ten years spent in north-western Arabia, making his base at the great oasis city of Tayma and extending south down the coast; and the last four years following his return to Babylon, during which he arranged the restoration of the temple in Harran.

Near the beginning of Nabonidus' reign there was famine and hardship in Babylonia, which the king attributed to the sinful behaviour of citizens in all the great cities, including Babylon itself. A text in which the king's title, 'king of justice', harks back to Hammurabi the great lawgiver enumerates the corrupt and unjust practices that were common when Nabonidus came to the throne and describes the measures he took to control disorder by restoring good observance of law.[17] Like Nebuchadnezzar, Nabonidus

---

[15] Schaudig 2001: 516, also known as the Istanbul stela and the Basalt stela.

[16] The cause appears not to be specified, but the text is incomplete.

[17] See Schaudig 2001: 579–88, who argues that the 'king of justice' inscription should probably be ascribed to Nabonidus rather than Nebuchadnezzar, contra Lambert and Beaulieu.

Figure 9.2 and 9.3 'Babylon' stela of Nabonidus, basalt, reworked from a giant statue, with the symbol of Tanit, goddess of Sidon, on the base peg. Height c. 95+ cm. Found near the Ishtar Gate. Credit: Scheil 1896. Istanbul, Ancient Orient Museum.

recorded his restoration and maintenance of the wall of Babylon named Imgur-Enlil, and likewise described it as a Wonder, but most of his building work was carried out in other cities. His building inscriptions show the traditional piety to the relevant gods of Babylonia. Some of his royal inscriptions give details of his own personal life.

Early in his reign, Nabonidus was able to return to Susa the statues of Elamite gods that had been looted by the Assyrians. He campaigned against Lydia and took prisoners but failed to capture Sardis. In the south-east, a governor served him on the island of Dilmun (Bahrain), continuing to oversee trade.[18] Nabonidus referred to unsettled conditions around the area of Harran due to the Medes, but recorded how danger was averted later: his ally Cyrus had captured and looted Ecbatana, an act for which Nabonidus expressed his approval.

---

[18] Known from a rock inscription found near Tayma. See Potts 2009: 37.

Like Nebuchadnezzar, Nabonidus made expeditions to the mountains of Lebanon to obtain cedar wood for his new buildings, having won victories in forests west of the river Orontes; at Sippar he used 5,000 cedars for the roofing, doors, and gates of the temple of the Sun-god. A temple library has been found there with clay tablets stacked on shelves.

During the middle phase of his reign, Nabonidus left Babylon and with his army marched down to Tayma. This oasis site in north-west Arabia was not thought to have Bronze Age or early Iron Age remains, and Nabonidus' visit there was not paid much attention. But, contrary to expectation, recent excavations have discovered a walled town from the time of Hammurabi. The finds have been astonishing. Nabonidus himself left many traces of his activities along the roads and in the vicinity of Tayma: a rock inscription at a pass through the mountains in southern Transjordan on the way to the Hejaz; the names of his entourage of officials, known from clay tablets in Babylonia, found inscribed on rocks and boulders near the oasis of Tayma; several fragments of stone with dedications in cuneiform on the site;[19] a royal palace; a full-size statue of the king in sandstone; symbols of Marduk and Nabu on nearby rocks. The local economy was capable of supporting a royal presence: wine was produced there at that time, convenient for feasts at court.[20] Nabonidus conquered several Arabian tribes, including Dedan, whose ruler he killed; and he marched down towards Medina, leaving a rock inscription at Padakku (modern Fadak) beside the main road. By carving so many outdoor inscriptions written in cuneiform and other scripts, he proclaimed that he controlled the Hejaz, and could divert trade from Egypt.

Nabonidus remained in Arabia for ten years, leaving Belshazzar in charge in Babylon. More than one suggestion has been made to account for such an extraordinary decision. The first relates to strategy.[21] The conquests of Nebuchadnezzar at Carchemish, in the Levant, and in Palestine, which had driven the Egyptians back into the Nile Valley, meant that the king of Babylon could now control a substantial part of the Red Sea coast as well as routes eastwards towards Babylon, interfering with Egyptian access to spices, aromatics, and gems traded from Arabia. But was the king's personal presence needed so far from home, for ten years, to establish Babylonian control?

---

[19] Hausleiter and Schaudig 2016.
[20] See, e.g., Hausleiter 2010; Maraqten 1990: 17–31; Schaudig 2011–13.
[21] Magee 2014: 272–4.

The second suggestion concerns the king's ill health and the influence of the Moon-god. Among the Dead Sea Scrolls discovered at Qumran in the Judean desert was the *Prayer of Nabonidus*. It tells that the king in Teman (Tayma, Tayman) was cured of a leprous illness by a Judean doctor. The fragments are written in Aramaic on parchment:

> The words of the prayer that Nabonay king of Babylon the great king prayed [when he was smitten] with a bad skin disease by the decree of God in Tayman:
>
> 'I, Nabonay, was stricken with an evil disease for seven years, and when God set [his face on me, he healed me] and my sin was forgiven by him. A diviner who was a Judean fr[om the exiles came to me and said:] "Recount and record these things, to give honour to the name of the God Most High".
>
> 'And thus I wrote: "I was stricken with an evil disease in Teman [by the decree of the Most High God, and as for me], seven years I spent praying to the gods of silver and gold, bronze, iron, wood, stone, and clay, because I thought that they were gods . . ."'.[22]

When Nabonidus returned from Arabia, he elevated the Moon-god to the highest rank among the gods, but he did not ban rival deities. According to curses commonly listed at the end of treaties and other texts, the Moon-god caused skin diseases. For example:

> May the Moon-god clothe his whole body in a leprosy that will never lift; may [the deity] infect him with a skin disease and so put an end to his entry into palace and temple.[23]

Since the Moon, with its pale yellow, pitted surface, was associated with skin disease, it is possible that Nabonidus left Babylon because he was no longer able to enter any temple or participate in the New Year Festival. Once he was cured, he could return, face the people of Babylon without embarrassment, and take part in the festival without pollution. He would then have had a particular reason to attend to the temple of the Moon-god at Harran, which he admitted had long been neglected, and to cultivate a special relationship with the Moon-god. His personal reasons for special piety to the Moon-god do not necessarily imply a religious reform; cylinder and stamp seals from his reign show no increased frequency of lunar symbols.[24]

---

[22] Holm 2013: 336.   [23] See examples in CAD s.v. *saharšubbû*, and Herbordt et al. 2019: no. 5.
[24] Altavilla and Walker 2016: II, 118.

This interpretation supposes that Nabonidus' attempt to raise the Moon-god above all others in the Babylonian pantheon, which is apparent in his later inscriptions, did not develop until he was cured of his disease, and only then did he emphasize his mother's religious fervour when he paid special attention to the cult of the Moon-god in Harran and elsewhere. His last four years included building work at Ur and Harran, both centres for the worship of the Moon-god. He restored the great ziggurat at Ur, built by Ur-Namma and Shulgi in the late third millennium, and extolled the Moon-god by giving him the top titles: 'For Sin, lord of the gods of heaven and earth, king of the gods, god of gods'. He claimed that the Moon-god had selected him from birth to be king of Babylon, in the inscription found at Harran that he wrote in the name of his deceased mother. He made changes to the cult of Marduk. The inscriptions that date from this late phase also indicate the king's attempt to placate the priests of Esagila and pay lip service to the cult of Marduk. They show clearly that he tried to promote the Moon-god to a position above Marduk without actually supplanting him.

At this time, Cyrus had set out from the old Elamite capital at Anshan in Fars and was leading an army whose campaigns were to Babylon's advantage. Nabonidus' admiration for Cyrus is expressed with startling clarity in one of his inscriptions. Blaming the barbarous Umman-manda for creating dangerous conditions around Harran, he used vaguely unsettled times as an excuse for delaying the restoration of the temple E-hulhul (the 'house of rejoicing') dedicated to the Moon-god there. Marduk reassured him with a prophecy delivered in a dream.[25] 'Marduk, the Enlil of the gods, and Sin the light of heaven and earth' appeared to him, and spoke the following words:

> 'O Nabonidus, king of Babylon, carry bricks with the horses of your chariot, build E-hulhul and install Sin the great lord within it for his dwelling'. Reverently I spoke to Marduk, the Enlil of the gods: 'The temple that you order me to build: the Umman-manda are encircling it, and their strength is too massive'. Marduk spoke with me: 'The Umman-manda of whom you spoke, he, his land, and the kings who go at his side will no longer exist!'
>
> When three years had passed, against Ištumegu he raised Cyrus king of Anzan, his young servant, and with his small army he scattered the wide-ranging Umman-manda. He captured Ištumegu (Astyages), king of the Umman-manda, and took him to his country. I revered the word of

---

[25] Schaudig 2001: 416–17.

> Marduk the great lord and Sin the light of heaven and earth, whose
> command is not changed. I was anxious, I became worried, my face was
> troubled. I was not negligent, I was not careless, I did not avoid work. I
> summoned my far-flung troops from Gaza on the border of Egypt on the
> upper sea beyond the Euphrates to the lower sea, kings, princes, gover-
> nors, and wide-ranging troops which Sin, Shamash, and Ishtar had
> entrusted to me to rebuild E-hulhul . . .

Nabonidus, true to his learned character, gave the precise dates of the
ruin and rebuilding at Harran. This was a deliberate calculation: the gap
consists of three *saros* cycles (eighteen years each)[26] and indicates a symbolic use of chronology and astronomy related to the Moon. He paraded his
scholarship when he alluded to omens, divination, and traditional literature in his royal inscriptions.

Belshazzar had full authority in Babylon for the decade while his father
was abroad, and was content to keep the title of crown prince. By the time
Cyrus captured Babylon, Nabonidus was settled back in Babylon city, an
old man apparently at ease with Belshazzar's efficient control. In Babylon
city, the archive of the Egibi family firm was in its third generation during
Nabonidus' reign and continued without a break when Cyrus took the
kingship, when it assumed the new role of tax farming for its Persian
masters. The head of the firm began travelling to Iran to establish good
relationships with the cities there.[27] Record-keeping among Babylonians
continued when the Chaldean dynasty came to an end.

The biblical Book of Daniel, composed or copied around four centuries
after the fall of Babylon, has features that are recognizable in the *Prayer of
Nabonidus* that was found at Qumran among the Dead Sea Scrolls.
Although Daniel has substituted the name of Nebuchadnezzar for that of
Nabonidus, and perhaps madness for a skin disease,[28] the narrative makes
the substitution of the king's name clear by including Belshazzar, son of
Nabonidus. The naming of Teman in the Qumran text connects directly to
Arabian Tayma and Nabonidus' residence there. As in other instances
when names are substituted, one aim was to appeal to a Jewish readership
interested in the fate of Jerusalem's First Temple and the king responsible
for the Exile. In the Qumran text the list of materials from which the statues
of gods were made, and the implication that they were not gods, coincides
with chapter 4 of the Book of Daniel in which much more detail is given
within the context of the king's dream.[29] As for the famous 'writing on the

---

[26] For the details of this lunar cycle, see e.g. Walker 1996: 52–3.   [27] Baker 2004.
[28] See Newsom 2014.
[29] Holm 2013: 336–43. Only the main breaks are indicated in the translation given here.

wall' in Daniel chapter 5, dramatically painted by Rembrandt, the role of the Jewish diviner in the *Prayer of Nabonidus* allows it to be interpreted according to techniques of wordplay, well-known from Babylonian cuneiform manuals.[30] The words *mene mene tekel upharsin* can be understood in two ways: both literally – 'a mina, a mina, a shekel, and a half-mina' – and as a prophetic metaphor – 'counted, counted, weighed, and divided', referring to the end of Babylon's kingship. The story has been classified as apocalyptic, in the sense that a prophetic dream has a symbolic meaning referring to a final judgement at the end of time, or to a near-final disaster:

> There is going to be a time of great distress, unparalleled since nations first came into existence . . . of those who lie sleeping in the dust of the earth, many will awake, some to everlasting life, some to shame and everlasting disgrace.[31]

The prophet Ezekiel, who spent much of his life in exile in Babylonia during the sixth century and was buried there, wrote:

> Outside, the sword; inside, plague and famine. Anyone who is found in the countryside will die by the sword; anyone who is found in the city will be devoured by famine and plague. Their fugitives will run away and make for the mountains; I shall slaughter them all like doves of the valleys, each for his sin.[32]

An earlier prophecy provides an antecedent, arising from a dream experienced by the writer of the Babylonian epic *Erra and Ishum*, in which the furious god Erra threatens:

> I shall finish off the land and count it a ruin.
> I shall devastate cities and make of them a wilderness.
> I shall destroy mountains and fell their cattle.
> I shall stir up oceans and destroy their produce.
> I shall dig out reed thickets and graves, and I shall burn them like Girra.
> I shall fell people and I shall leave no life.

These quotations illustrate the rise of an apocalyptic vision, foreseeing the end of human life on Earth. **Cyrus'** capture of Babylon marks the end of Nabonidus' reign. The events surrounding it are known only from texts written some time after the event, and so most of them show Nabonidus in a bad light, contrasting with the image of Cyrus as a peace-loving, benevolent man who was justified in taking the city, supposedly without opposition.[33] This is the ideal image taken up by Greek writers such as

---

[30] Gzella 2016.   [31] Daniel 12:1, 3.   [32] Ezekiel 7:15–17.   [33] See Wiesehöfer 2001: 42–4.

Herodotus and Xenophon,[34] following Cyrus' self-representation and perhaps inspired by Greek philosophic interest in ideal kingship and the limitations of tyranny.[35] Before the cuneiform sources were found and published, those Greek accounts were the only evidence for Cyrus' reign as an Achaemenid Persian, so the heroic image gained from them was easily contrasted with the biblical image, equally polemical, of the Assyrians and Babylonians as aggressive and cruel people, with values supposedly different from those of the ancient Hebrews and Greeks. This has been described as a theory 'locating within Europe's Aryan inheritance all the virtues that set Europe apart from the rest of the world, and viewing the triumph of Aryan Europe as the providentially guided culmination of human history'.[36] It created racial stereotypes that still linger in modern nationalist movements and have spread into Asian countries where groups of Indo-Aryan/Indo-Iranian languages have been recognized.[37] Little did they know at the time the theory developed that Cyrus would mainly have spoken Elamite, a non-Aryan language.

When Cyrus marched against Babylon, Nabonidus took into safe custody at Babylon the statues of gods from the cities on the eastern flank of Mesopotamia that were in particular danger; but they did not save the city from invasion.[38] The *Babylonian Chronicle* tells of a fierce battle won by Cyrus at Upe (Greek Opis) east of the Tigris, which resulted in looting and the massacre of its citizens. That report gives a different picture of Cyrus from the ideal one that he promoted after becoming king in Babylon. He waited in Sippar on the Euphrates above Babylon, perhaps diverting branches of the river in order to weaken the defences of Babylon, until his general Gubaru 'of Gutium'[39] had done the dangerous work of penetrating the city and capturing Nabonidus. Troops under Gubaru's leadership captured Nabonidus, who had fled

---

[34] Cyrus the Pretender, whom Xenophon supported in his unsuccessful attempt to wrest the kingship from Artaxerxes II in 401 BC, is thought to be conflated deliberately with Cyrus II in the *Cyropaedia*. See Chapter 10 below.

[35] Wiesehöfer 2001: 43–51.

[36] For Aryan against a Mesopotamian background, see Cooper 1993: 178, with this quotation; and Cooper 1991. For an argument against the supposed exceptional brutality of Assyrians, see Frahm 2017: 8–9.

[37] See, e.g., Hoenigswald, Woodard, and Clackson 2006: 535; Jamison 2006: 673.

[38] See van der Spek 2014.

[39] Gubaru is Ugbaru in Babylonian (both forms are used in the *Nabonidus Chronicle*), Gobryas in Greek, Gaubarva in Persian. The name is Persian.

back to Babylon after the fall of Sippar, two days before Gubaru entered Babylon.[40]

The new king's triumphal entry into the city was staged about eighteen days later in October 539: 'His vast troops whose number, like the water in a river, could not be counted, were marching fully armed at his side'. Thus Cyrus could claim to have entered the city without a fight, to joyful acclaim, without interrupting the ceremonies and rituals of the great temples there: 'My vast troops were marching peaceably in Babylon, and the whole of Sumer and Akkad had nothing to fear'. Cyrus' account of his peaceful entry into Babylon was modelled on that of Sargon II and cannot be taken at face value.[41] He broke the exemption from military duty and the ban on bearing arms within the sacred city. In earlier times, as we have seen, the Babylonians had relied heavily on foreign allies to do their fighting for them but did not allow them inside Babylon. Now Cyrus, having lured away Elamite archers and the Median horsemen who had given support to Babylon in the past, let them into the holy city.[42] Some of the treasures from his earlier capture of Ecbatana and Sardis would have been put to use paying them for their support during his capture of Babylon. Guards were placed at the gates of Esagila and rituals in the city were not interrupted. Gubaru installed district officers in the huge province that included both Babylonia and Syria 'Across the River' (Eber-Nari). As a high official in Babylon, 'officer in charge of the land' (*šakin māti*), he kept his post for the next few years.

There are various different stories of Nabonidus' fate at the hands of the victor. He may have been exiled to Carmania (modern Kerman) close to the royal cities of Pasargadae and Persepolis[43] after a spell of imprisonment in Babylon. The region of Carmania had been a well-settled part of the Neo-Elamite cultural area, and was an integral part of the Achaemenid empire, so exile was not an extreme punishment. If this version is correct, Cyrus showed more mercy than when he had killed Croesus of Lydia, or when he plundered Opis and slaughtered its people before moving on to Sippar.

The royal inscriptions of Nabonidus have to be separated as far as possible from tendentious accounts which were written for Cyrus after

---

[40] Berossus reported that the king surrendered in nearby Borsippa when that city was besieged; the *Nabonidus Chronicle* says that Nabonidus was taken prisoner in Babylon.

[41] Kuhrt 1990.

[42] For the account of Cyrus' capture of Babylon given by Xenophon in the *Cyropaedia* VII.5.30, 150 years later, see Chapter 10 below.

[43] This account is given in *The Dynastic Prophecy*. Edition in van der Spek 2003: text 5, 311–34.

his accession to justify his conquest of Babylon by showing that his usurpation was approved by the Babylonian gods because Nabonidus no longer had their support. So he denigrated Nabonidus in the traditional way. Those accounts were composed for Cyrus by Babylonian scribes under his instruction for a Babylonian public. Every one of Nabonidus' supposed misdeeds is a stereotype found in earlier Babylonian and Assyrian royal inscriptions that justify a usurper, such as angering the gods by changing rites without proper authorization, neglect of temples, failing to maintain law and order, scattering the population, and being generally unfit to rule. Such themes, although they were standard justifications written by usurpers, have sometimes been misunderstood as exceptional because the usurper was not Babylonian but a foreigner from Elamite and Persian lands.[44]

Such was the reverence accorded to the city of Babylon and its indigenous kings that Nabonidus' monuments were not removed from the streets, nor were they defaced or displaced when the new dynasty came to power. No attempt, it seems, was made to remove the hundreds of clay cylinders, inscribed with foundation inscriptions giving an account of his deeds, that Nabonidus had written and installed. The rebel kings of Babylon who rose up at the beginning of Darius' reign would both take the name Nebuchadnezzar but also claim descent from Nabonidus: the reputation of the latter was not destroyed by Persian propaganda.

Under Cyrus' rule, the statues of gods that had been taken into protective custody were returned to their proper cities; and the library of literature in the temple of the Sun-god at Sippar survived the capture of the city. Carian mercenaries who had been brought into Babylon and Borsippa by Nebuchadnezzar continued to work for the new regime. Cyrus' building work in Babylon did not mention that Nabonidus had done work on the wall Imgur-Enlil, but he did acknowledge the work done previously by Ashurbanipal, and one can recognize Assyrian influence on his sculpture in his new royal city at Pasargadae. Elsewhere in Babylonia, too, Cyrus acted as an indigenous ruler, leaving inscribed bricks in Ur and Uruk. But having commissioned and publicized his right to rule in the Cyrus Cylinder and the *Verse Account of Nabonidus*, as described below, he wrote no more royal inscriptions in Babylonian cuneiform, as if to confirm that the campaigns of his reign were no longer relevant to a Babylonian public. His heart was in his new palaces and gardens at Pasargadae, but Babylon remained the seat of kingship.

---

[44] Kuhrt 1983.

Clay tablets with Elamite cuneiform rather than Old Persian were found in great quantities at Persepolis, representing imperial administration under subsequent Achaemenid kings. In Cyrus' palaces at Pasargadae, cuneiform inscriptions on stone were altered, probably changing the genealogy of Cyrus to match that of Darius I. However, it is disputed whether Cyrus ordered the change or whether it was Darius as a usurper who claimed that his genealogy had a precedent in the line of Cyrus the Great.[45]

Xenophon wrote *The Education of Cyrus* (*Cyropaedia*) early in the fourth century BC. He used the illustrious name of Cyrus to give a largely fictional narrative in which were blended the character and deeds of Cyrus the Great and of the much later Cyrus the Pretender who had tried in vain to usurp the throne of his brother Artaxerxes II. This mixture allowed Xenophon to invent a detailed account of the successful capture of Babylon by Cyrus the Great, which had taken place about 150 years earlier, and to imply that it was achieved by Cyrus the Pretender, whose cause failed despite Xenophon's support. He describes how the unnamed king of Babylon was killed in the fighting, reflecting the actual death of Cyrus the Pretender, but not that of Nabonidus. His details of the capture of Babylon may therefore be entirely fictitious.

To witness the downfall of two great empires – Assyrian and Babylonian – within one lifetime would have aroused curiosity. What caused those empires to fall? Were their failures due to the actions of the final ruler, whether good or bad? Due to the moral turpitude of increasingly over-indulged elites? Or to the wrath of city gods owing to neglect, such as the king failing to take part in the New Year Festival, or to acts of sacrilege? Were such terrible disasters due to the nature of kingship and 'tyranny'? Such questions would have been appropriate for Ionians and Macedonian Greeks to ask, because their early philosophers had tried to analyse the properties of a good ruler, a good life, a good society, and good government. Could the convulsions at Nineveh and then at Babylon – and in Lydia, as examined by Herodotus – be explained by comparing the deeds of the loser and the winner?

The Dynastic Prophecy was written during the Seleucid period. It gives a summary of certain reigns, treated as prophecies as if they had not yet happened but were 'destined' to be good or bad according to actual events.

---

[45] See Dandamaev and Lukonin 1989: 272–82; Stronach 2013; Henkelman 2011.

As with other prophecies, no names are specified. The reigns of Nabonidus and Cyrus are described as follows:

> A rebel prince will arise [*gap due to damage*]
> He will establish a dynasty of Harran.
> He will exercise kingship for seventeen years.
> He will be stronger than the land, and interrupt the festival of Esagila.
> He will build the wall in Babylon.
> He will plot evil against Akkad.
> A king of Elam will arise. He will take the royal sceptre from him.
> He will remove him from his throne, that king whom he dethroned –
> The king of Elam will change his place.
> He will settle him in another country.
> That king will be stronger than the land
> And all the lands will bring tribute to him.
> During his reign Akkad will live in safety.[46]

It is sometimes said that the Babylonians were collectors of facts, list makers rather than analysts, whereas users of the Greek language wanted to know reasons why. But this is a simplification. The clearest example of searching for an answer is the *Sin of Sargon* text, which explored possible reasons for Sargon II's death in battle when divination had presumably given an assurance of safety.[47] There is growing evidence from this time onwards that earlier cuneiform texts such as chronicles were revised to contribute to a more or less fictional account which engaged with causes. Many of those texts have been found in the library of Esagila, which mainly dates to the Seleucid and early Arsacid (Parthian) period. For instance, a copy of a tablet, now fragmentary, gave a fictional response of Šamaš-šum-ukin to Nabopolassar, the military leader who had taken the throne, though from a later king.[48] As we have seen, much earlier fictional correspondence of historical kings was composed before the reign of Hammurabi, seeking to assign blame to a particular king for catastrophic events. The *Nabonidus Chronicle*, like the *Verse Account*, mocks Nabonidus for excessive piety in dedicating his daughter to the Moon-god at Ur and his scholarly pretensions in engaging with the science of divination.[49]

As a man of mixed descent, Elamite and Persian, and so not a Semite, Cyrus was certainly not the first to claim the throne of Babylon as a foreigner; the long and successful dynasty of the

---

[46] van der Spek 2003: text 5 col. ii.   [47] See Chapter 7 above.
[48] Spar and Lambert 1988: no. 44, dated to the time of Alexander the Great.
[49] Schaudig 2001: 47; but see Waerzeggers 2015a.

Kassites and the short-lived Elamite dynasty suggest that a foreigner who took the trouble to assimilate with the local culture would soon count as a Babylonian and find a place among earlier dynasties. Before he captured Babylon, Cyrus had already been hailed by Nabonidus as the young servant of Marduk.

The story of Cyrus' birth and childhood, as related in Greek by Herodotus (I.107–30), is similar to a Mesopotamian one. In short, the baby Cyrus of noble birth was given to a herdsman to expose on a mountainside, because a dream had predicted that the child would usurp the throne. He was rescued and raised incognito until his identity became known, and eventually he did indeed seize the throne. A similar story is known from the Babylonian *Legend of Sargon of Agade's Birth*, set in a supposedly historical background of the third millennium BC, and sharing motifs with the biblical tale of the birth of Moses.[50] The tale was adapted from the birth and childhood of the legendary hero Gilgamesh, an episode which never became part of the standard Babylonian *Epic of Gilgamesh*, but may have served as a template for heroes including Moses, Sargon of Agade, and Seleucus I, each set in his own particular landscape and historical background.[51] The legend was surely spread by Cyrus to link himself with Babylonia's great past. Already in the late Assyrian period the fictitious *Letter of Gilgamesh* had made a connection between Marduk and Gilgamesh, calling the legendary hero 'beloved of Marduk' in order to bring the hero within the orbit of Babylon while continuing to refer to the royal cities in southern Babylonia, Uruk and Ur, with which he was originally associated.[52]

The royal cities of Susa, Pasargadae, Anshan, and Persepolis all lay east of Babylonia, and this marks a major change. Unlike the Kassites in Babylon, who had no royal city beyond Babylonia, the Elamite, Persian, and Achaemenid kings marked the core of their territory by their choices of royal cities. Babylon inevitably lost some of the focus of the new ruler, whose main attention would have been directed towards his home bases in Persia in addition to maintaining control of the empire bequeathed by Nabonidus. Cyrus may also have used the ceremonial centre at Persepolis before it was enlarged by Darius I,[53] and may have been responsible for a building recently uncovered at the western city gate of Persepolis; it was

---

[50] See Sommerfeld 2009–11: § 5.3. A literary legend of Sargon found at Kanesh shows that one such story was known in the early second millennium and so was not a much later invention.

[51] See Frayne 2010: 168–72 with references.

[52] It was found in the 'library' at Sultantepe near Harran. See George 2003: I, 117–19.

[53] Godard 1965: 108–9 thought that some building work at Persepolis was done before the reign of Darius.

created by Babylonian craftsmen using glazed brick with low-relief imagery relating to Marduk (the *mušhuššu*), showing extraordinary respect for Babylon.[54] Was this part of a plan to take the great ceremonies of kingship away from Babylon and transport them to Persepolis, the new Achaemenid city, or simply to replicate them?

The name Cyrus is almost certainly Elamite. His family was related to Astyages king of the Medes in Ecbatana, and he rose to power when the army of Astyages defected to him. With Median support Cyrus defeated Croesus, and adopted from Lydia the use of gold and silver coinage for currency, but the coins were measured by weight, according to Babylonian weights, in recognition of the widespread authority of Babylonian commerce. This was, however, a major change of practice – replacing metals in any form by weight under temple control with coinage from a royal mint. The Babylonians were slow to accept the change. Cyrus used the title 'king of Anshan' on some of his inscriptions, and 'king of Parsu' on others, acknowledging two linguistically distinct branches in his background. He traced his real or legendary ancestors to 'Teispes' when calling himself king of Anshan, but to 'Achaemenes' when calling himself king of Parsu.[55] In his texts intended for a Babylonian audience he acknowledged Marduk as patron god.

Cyrus came from a background in which literature was not written, and no written Persian literature has been found throughout the Achaemenid period. Later Persian literature was not integrated in any way with Babylonian literature. The Elamite language, which has no relationship to Persian, had been written in cuneiform for many centuries in the past, but was used by now only for brief royal inscriptions and for administrative purposes at Persepolis, where tens of thousands of clay tablets have been found. The Old Persian language did not begin to be written in a new adaptation of cuneiform script until a little later than Cyrus' lifetime. The language or languages of the Medes seem never to have been written. The three ethnic and linguistic groups, Elamite, Persian, and Median, had mixed and intermarried by this time, which may account for the use of both Elamite and Persian royal titles. Greek writers seem not to have known about the Elamites, despite a long-standing, literate administration and royal inscriptions in that language. They may have considered them to be Medes, about whom they knew.

The Babylonian text known as the *Verse Account of Nabonidus* was written for Cyrus in support of his claim to be a righteous ruler chosen

---

[54] Chaverdi and Callieri 2017: 394–7. [55] See Rollinger 2011–13; Stronach 2013.

by the great gods, and to give a popular description of the ousted king. It ridicules Nabonidus for his intellectual pretensions, especially his interpretation of omens connected with the moon and specifies offences against the gods. Among the latter is the accusation that Nabonidus had installed a moon-disc above the temple of Marduk in Babylon. To show that local officials had come over to Cyrus' side and continued to work for the new regime, the text names two top men, Zeriya, the head of temple administration (*šatammu*), and Rimut, the royal secretary (*zazakku*), who transferred their loyalty; their words endorsing the new ruler are given verbatim as they swore their new oath: 'Now we understand what the king has told us!'Administrative texts confirm that the two men, like many of their compatriots from elite families, continued to work for the new regime.[56] Much earlier examples – at Mari under Samsu-Addu, and at Larsa in the time of Hammurabi – show that regime change did not necessarily lead to the replacement of important officials, so what Cyrus did was in line with earlier Mesopotamian custom. But his treasurer Mitridata had a Persian name.

The Cyrus Cylinder[57] is a barrel-shaped record made of baked clay and conforms to a standard type of foundation inscription known from many earlier Assyrian and Babylonian examples. Its text was composed in the literary Babylonian language and in Babylonian script on a normal barrel cylinder which would not have been exhibited in public, but concealed within brickwork as a record for later builders. Two fragments of clay tablet (not parts of cylinders) have only recently been identified. From such a tablet the text would have been copied not only onto duplicate cylinders of the same shape, which were then baked and set into the city walls, but also onto other media for public display. It is not, therefore, a unique document, as was often claimed before these fragments were discovered. As a literary, almost epic-style document composed by a Babylonian scribe (whose name is preserved on one of the fragments), the text contains near-quotations from the *Epic of Creation*. The only god named in the text is Marduk, to whom the inscription is dedicated. Although Cyrus ruled over Susa and called himself 'king of Anshan city', the text mentions no Elamite or Persian deities. This confirms the current understanding that Persian kings writing for a Babylonian public invoked the main Babylonian god. In Egypt, Cambyses and Darius would later respect Egyptian gods in their Egyptian inscriptions, and Darius would acknowledge the Persian god

---

[56] Jursa 2007a.   [57] Finkel 2013.

Figure 9.4 Clay foundation cylinder recording building work done by Nabonidus (right); clay foundation cylinder recording conquest of Babylon by Cyrus II (left). Both inscribed in Babylonian cuneiform. Credit: Commons.wikimedia/Mike Peel (BM 1880.0617 1941); and by kind permission of the Ashmolean Museum (AN 262-857); photo Ian Cartwright.

Ahura-Mazda in Persia. The language and script show that the Cyrus Cylinder's intended audience was restricted to the people of Babylon and of Babylonia; it was not translated into other languages.

The text presents Cyrus as the new and righteous king, giving reasons why Nabonidus was not fit to continue. It would have been written around the time Cyrus celebrated his first New Year Festival to legitimize the usurpation. Nabonidus' misdeeds are described in purely traditional terms – failure to perform rituals properly, neglecting temples, giving the gods cause for anger and rejection – as found in earlier Assyrian and Babylonian texts whenever a usurper was required to justify his takeover:

> The gods of the land of Sumer and Akkad which Nabonidus, to the fury of the lord of gods, had brought into Babylon: at Marduk's command, I

returned them unharmed to their shrines in the sanctuaries that make them happy.

Thus Nabonidus' far-sighted security measures were made to look like an offence to Marduk.

Cyrus did not entirely succeed in ruining Nabonidus' reputation. Two successive claimants to the throne at the death of Cambyses called themselves Nabonidus' son, an unlikely claim had Nabonidus been considered mad or a failure. On the contrary, he was a successful king who had persevered through the trials of military actions, held on to the empire gained by his predecessors, extended it at least in the Hejaz, and in northern Syria secured control over Harran. His title 'king of the world' was well earned.

The text of the Cyrus Cylinder mentions that divine images and the people of the cities endangered by Cyrus' invasion were allowed and encouraged to return to their original homes, using virtually the same words as Hammurabi in his Code: 'I collected together all of their people and returned them to their settlements'. The cities are named, and they are all in eastern Babylonia, the area nearest to Cyrus' own lands; there is no mention of any western or southern cities. It was therefore particularly urgent to please and pacify those in eastern places. Nevertheless, Old Testament prophets interpreted his statement as extending to a much wider area in the hope of attracting talent and manpower for rebuilding the temple in Jerusalem that Nebuchadnezzar had sacked.

Plentiful records of Judean settlers recently discovered in towns of eastern and south-eastern Babylonia give no sign that Judeans moved back to Palestine in the reign of Cyrus or subsequently. Nor did they avoid names that were compounded with that of Yahweh, which implies that they did not have to give up or hide their religion. Their families continued to work on agricultural land, many paying taxes to official tax collectors of the Egibi firm. Like the Babylonians and Assyrians before him, Cyrus was aware that a settled, peaceful city with agricultural hinterland was productive and could therefore pay regular taxes. There is no hint that Cyrus was more tolerant of foreign gods than any other kings of the time, and it was normal to recognize foreign deities in polytheistic societies.[58] On previous occasions Assyrian kings had returned a statue of Marduk to Babylon, and had allowed deported people to return to Babylonia, so Cyrus and his successors were simply following a long-standing tradition in those respects.[59]

---

[58] Henkelman 2008: 55–7.   [59] Kuhrt 1983; van der Spek 2014: 246–7.

The Cyrus Cylinder contains one of history's most misused texts. 'Some documents are less important for what they say than for what people wrongly think that they say', as Jonathan Sumption has put it, and are misappropriated to serve a modern political agenda.[60] A misinterpretation of the text accounts for how a replica of the Cyrus Cylinder came to be displayed in the United Nations building in New York, wrongly proclaimed as a unique document with the first statement of human rights and 'freedom'. In fact it has nothing to do with special treatment for Judean deportees. Its false prestige inspired a very faulty attempt to copy the cuneiform onto fossilized leg bones of oxen in China,[61] a forgery that attracted international attention because the find supposedly linked China with the great empire of Persia and a new attitude to granting freedom, until the two fragments of clay tablets giving parts of the inscription were found to disprove its supposedly unique character.[62]

Cyrus left no Babylonian inscriptions recording the deeds of the later part of his reign. Chronicles, on which one hopes to rely, had apparently been discontinued in the reign of Neriglissar; none are known from Babylon until the end of the Achaemenid period, when their composition was perhaps resumed.[63] Individual deeds of Achaemenid kings were apparently recorded in Babylonia neither in chronicle form nor in royal narrative inscriptions. Such a long gap accounts for the over-reliance on Greek texts by scholars in modern times. Some less formal records continued to be written on organic materials.[64]

Cyrus' campaigning as 'king of lands' made it impossible for him to perform regular ceremonial duties in Babylon. For a year he made his son **Cambyses** 'king of Babylon': the *Babylonian Chronicle* records that Cambyses was invested in the temple of Nabu-of-Vats in Babylon, where he would have received the sceptre of kingship as co-regent with his father. Cambyses was also known as 'governor'; some documents have Cyrus and Cambyses side by side in their dating. There is an echo of the arrangement

---

[60] Said of Magna Carta during a lecture to the Friends of the British Library, March 2015.

[61] Schaudig 2001: 551. For possible motive and opportunity, see Yang 2002.

[62] See the British Museum webpage on the Cyrus Cylinder, www.britishmuseum.org/collection/object/W_1880-0617-1941. The two fragments come from a tablet (not a cylinder), found at Dailem near Babylon, and represent the 'original' text to be copied on to numerous cylinders.

[63] Waerzeggers 2012: 297. Note that the Weidner 'Chronicle' is now recognized as a literary work in the school curriculum, the *Dynastic Chronicle* as a work linked to the *Sumerian King-List*, and Chronicle P as a historical epic. See Waerzeggers 2012: 289 and 288 n. 15; and Waerzeggers 2015a.

[64] Henkelman and Folmer 2016.

made by Ashurbanipal for his brother Šamaš-šum-ukin, in which the latter was invested with the insignia of kingship but was treated as the governor of the city only. What happened to the annual festivals in the city for the rest of Cyrus' reign is unknown. From this time onwards Babylon was not the main residence of its ruler, so royal participation in major festivals must have been intermittent. But the city's status remained very high as a centre for various kinds of literature, including the great manuals of astronomy and divination, and for texts required for religious ceremonies.

Cambyses, whose name is Persian, is best known for his conquest of Egypt. He brought back to Babylonia Carian prisoners of war who joined those whom Nebuchadnezzar had brought to Babylon. Some took Babylonian names but are still recognized as Carians in Babylonian texts from the reign of Darius I.[65] Cambyses is also known for the atrocity story told by Greek authors of the killing of the Apis bull in Egypt. This is one of several tales of sacrilege told by Greek historians more than a century after the supposed event; some of them have been proved grossly exaggerated by non-Greek, contemporary inscriptions and by archaeological evidence.

Elamite culture was still recognized. It was not subsumed under Persian domination, and the administration of the Persian empire was mainly recorded in Persepolis in the Elamite language, written in cuneiform script on clay tablets. Centuries later a red-purple 'Elamite' robe of Nebuchadnezzar II was put on display for Antiochus III, for a ceremony of kingship in Borsippa.[66] Gubaru remained the governor of Babylon and the province Across the River, acting as a viceroy until the accession of Darius, when he was replaced by one Ushtanu. Throughout that time it was possible for administrators and scribes to consult old records; as with public monuments, the new regime did not destroy old texts, although there may have been some 'weeding' of the collections.[67]

The city of Babylon at this time was still dominated by the huge buildings erected by Nabopolassar and Nebuchadnezzar. No new buildings in the city can be attributed to Nabonidus. As for Cyrus and Cambyses, since royal inscriptions and chronicles were no longer being written in cuneiform (if at all), only much later Greek sources mention Babylon's architecture, and they are unreliable for several reasons, not least that Babylon and Nineveh were confused.[68] Many fine gates were set into the city's great walls, but they had more than one name, ceremonial and vernacular, so not even their number is certain for any particular period. The many canals running through the city and the branches of the Euphrates in the vicinity would have confused

[65] Zadok 2005.   [66] See below Chapter 10.   [67] Clancier 2009: 222.   [68] Dalley 2013: 107–26.

western visitors. Aerial photographs of the site where Babylon stood show that the Euphrates changed its course through the city. The change, which must have done terrible damage to the layout of the city, was once too confidently placed in the mid-fifth century BC; the dating is now less certain.[69] Marshland to the west of the city may have affected the change, but no clear evidence has yet been found.

What is certain is that ceremonial streets and canals were still the imposing setting for great processions. Many stelas and statues from earlier times were still on public display to remind citizens and visitors of a glorious past continuing into the present;[70] many great temples are known from Babylonian texts and from excavation, while others no doubt wait to be found.[71] Imperfections due to persistent problems of a high water table and the subsidence of large buildings must have required endless repairs and rebuilding.

When Cambyses died, a rebellion broke out centred on Babylon. Early in his reign Cambyses had grown suspicious of his own brother Bardiya, who was also known as Smerdis (Herodotus' name for him), and is said to have killed him and hushed up the murder. The aftermath was later referred to by Darius in his own long inscription at Bisotun, and Herodotus gave a lurid account a century later. The secrecy allowed a look-alike named Gaumata (Darius' name for him), also known as Smerdis, to claim that he was Bardiya; and when Cambyses died, Gaumata-Bardiya-Smerdis claimed the throne of Babylon and ruled for three months before Darius caught up with him and killed him. Different versions make it impossible to disentangle the core events. But this brief summary serves to introduce Darius I, with whose reign the next chapter begins.

Cyrus and Cambyses did not attempt to close down the worship of Mesopotamian deities, nor did they install cults of their own deities in Babylon. Evidence for the selection of priests shows judicial concern for the ethnicity of an initiate, so Persians presumably could not take over religious duties in Mesopotamian temples.[72] Persians and Elamites had royal cities in the east, so Babylon was no longer the main royal city, and no longer exempt from taxation. Relics of the past were not removed, and temple scribes stood firm in continuing to copy texts in Babylonian cuneiform and to create or adapt new texts that gave a new slant on old history. Mixed marriages between Babylonians and Persians were accepted. The theme in

---

[69] See Boiy 2004: 55–72, 78–98.
[70] Klengel-Brandt 1990: 41–6 showed that many of the statue fragments were found in various places on the citadel, and were on public display around the ceremonial area.
[71] George 1992.   [72] Lohnert 2010.

literature, that the king must be supported despite his failings because he was chosen and supported by the great gods, goes back to the *Epic of Gilgamesh* in Hammurabi's time, and to *The Righteous Sufferer* (*Ludlul*) in the Kassite period; both works were still in circulation. The new foreign rulers may have aimed for the ideal of direct succession, but often had to settle for less during the later phases of Babylon's history. Whatever their circumstances, they all prized Babylon's formal recognition of their kingship.

10 | Darius I to Alexander, and Seleucid to Parthian Rule[1]

When that great Kings return to clay
    Or Emperors in their pride,
Grief of a day shall fill a day,
    Because its creature died.
But we – we reckon not with those
    Whom the mere Fates ordain,
This Power that wrought on us and goes
    Back to the Power again.

                  (Rudyard Kipling, *The Burial*, 1902)

The Achaemenid Persians who occupied Babylon from the time of Darius I built Persepolis as their main ceremonial centre, and kept Susa as a royal city. Their administrative records were written in Elamite cuneiform. The attention they paid to Babylon was calculated to prevent uprisings and to avoid disturbing the flow of tax revenue, festivals, and scholarship. After 200 years, having accumulated an even bigger empire than before, they were defeated by Alexander the Macedonian, who appreciated Babylonian culture and passed on his interest to his Seleucid Greek successors. They in turn maintained an empire for about 164 years. In Babylon, the library long established at Esagila with its astronomers, diviners, and rituals for confirming kingship, gave the city an authority that was not displaced by Persepolis or Antioch. The Parthians who took over from the Seleucids continued to appreciate Babylon's scholarship, while cuneiform script and literature, resilient for more than two millennia, gradually gave way to alphabetic scripts and organic writing materials.

After Nabonidus's reign ended, kingship and Babylon were no longer as closely linked under Persian rule. Although the Kassites a thousand years earlier had also been foreigners rather than Semitic rulers from within

---

[1] This chapter relies on recent entries on Livius.org, not least for the chronicles currently identified, ongoing work on the astronomical diaries, and various recent publications of van der Spek, including entries in Goldberg and Whitmarsh 2016; also van der Spek 2009–11; Waerzeggers (various), Boiy 2004, Clancier 2009, Pedersén 2005a, and others.

Mesopotamia, they had maintained Babylon as a holy city, and had no urban centres elsewhere to divide their loyalties. But Achaemenid rule was different: the Persians had taken over Elamite royal cities and built others of their own to the east of Mesopotamia. So in Babylon certain forms of literature and scholarship were no longer directly related to a king surrounded by scholars: henceforth no royal decree would prompt the insertion of an intercalary month into the calendar, which came under temple authority; henceforth the main purpose of divination would no longer focus on the safety of the king alone; henceforth astronomy could broaden its scope, no longer tied to a king's requirements. Anyone could now consult an astronomer for a horoscope, but diviners relying on astronomical events were as respected as before: great kings still took advice for their actions from the seers of Babylon. Surprisingly, from the capture of Babylon by Cyrus onwards, the city adapted to each foreign regime. It continued to celebrate its festivals, to recite the *Epic of Creation*, to study ancient texts, to make radical discoveries in astronomy, and to accumulate uninterrupted archives of businessmen and lawyers. Very few Persian words are to be found in Babylon's cuneiform texts.

Babylon's Chaldean astrologers had enormous international prestige. During the early part of the First Dynasty of Babylon around 1800 BC, a very large number of men had practised the profession of the extispicy diviner (*bārû*); clay models of livers bear witness to their expertise. Then a written manual of such omens came into being. Gradually extispicy lost some of its prestige to the later sciences of celestial and terrestrial omens, and the number of *bārû*-diviners decreased relative to the number of astronomer-astrologers. The earliest astronomical diaries (known as 'regular observations') began to record daily events in the city of Babylon at this time.[2] Mathematical astronomy developed as an abstract subject.

Under Persian rule the duty of announcing the beginning of the month and intercalation as required was relegated to the temple.[3] Calculations were done by mathematical prediction, not dependent on observation and weather conditions. The prediction of lunar and solar eclipses remained crucial, using the data set out in the manuals *Plough Star* (*Mul.Apin*) and *When Anu and Enlil* (*Enūma Anu Enlil*). Babylonian month-names continued to be used in Mesopotamia. Intermittent political and military events are briefly noted, and they are dated when the condition of the clay tablets allows.

---

[2] A much earlier date for the first astronomical diary has now been discounted.   [3] Steele 2011.

The astronomer Nabu-rimannu put his name on mathematical computed tables of celestial observations, and was famous among Greek writers more than three centuries later.[4] The posts of astronomers in Babylon were mainly hereditary, so the scholarship developed there and in few other cities; no Persian loanwords are found in the new types of text. Texts of mathematical astronomy found at Babylon and Uruk span a long period of time, from around 400 to 50 BC, but it is often impossible to tell whether a text dates to the Achaemenid or to the Seleucid period, despite the very considerable differences between the two regimes. The advantage of purely numerical texts is that, unlike cuneiform words, they transfer easily to the writing systems of all other languages.

Astrology was very closely connected to astronomy. The basic concept underlying the 'science' of astrology is expressed in a cuneiform text:

> The signs of Earth together with those of Sky produce a signal. Sky and Earth both bring us portents, each separately but not differently, since Sky and Earth are linked. A sign that is evil in Sky is evil on Earth, a sign that is evil on Earth is evil in Sky.

This basic concept is expressed in the *Epic of Creation*, when Marduk splits the body of Tiamat and forms earth and sky from the mirror-image halves: 'He sliced her in half like a fish for drying'. The zodiac, a circle consisting of twelve equal segments of thirty degrees each, represents the months of the year, each segment is connected to a constellation, and each hour is represented by fifteen degrees. The scheme thus links time with constellations. It is first found around the fifth/fourth century BC, about the same time as new types of horoscope are found: birth omens, also known as nativities.[5] All of them were 'touched' by the moon. A few of the real and imaginary creatures that gave their names to segments of the zodiac were sculpted much earlier, on *kudurru*-stones from the late second millennium onwards, and a few are known as pictures described in words in a small group of texts.[6] An artificial but systematic correlation between body parts and the names of the zodiac creatures allowed an application to medicine, and other links widened the range of forecasts. Such associations became more numerous when the micro-zodiac was formulated in which each

---

[4] See Röllig 1998–2001. Nabu-rīmannu was known in Greek as Naburiannos. His work was especially valued by Posidonius, who came from Apamea-on-the-Orontes where a cult of Bēl persisted.

[5] Fincke 2016: 133. The signs of the zodiac probably reached Egypt directly from Babylonia rather than through Greek intermediaries; see Ossendrijver and Winkler 2018: 410–11. For Babylonian influence on 4QZodiac Calendar, found at Qumran, see Jacobus 2014: 81–2.

[6] Beaulieu et al. 2018.

segment was divided into twelve further sections.[7] Combinations of data were used to predict a wide range of topics including enemy attacks, the price of barley, and the weather. This astrological concept, no longer considered valid in modern western scholarship, was elaborated alongside serious mathematics.[8]

1 Achaemenid Persian Period

(3 short-lived non-Persian usurpers, 7 of 9 Achaemenid rulers)

Nebuchadnezzar IV (521)
Darius I (521–486)
Xerxes (485–465)
Bel-šimanni, Šamaš-eriba (482)
Artaxerxes I (464–424)
Darius II (423–405)
Artaxerxes II Arsaces (404–359)
  (Cyrus the Pretender)
Artaxerxes III Ochus (358–338)
Darius III (335–331)

Although the Achaemenids themselves did not absorb Mesopotamian literature as the Kassites had done in earlier times, knowledge of traditional myths, epics, chronicles, and astronomical and divinatory compendia continued within Babylonia. Temple scholars made copies and adaptations of the many older religious, historical, and narrative texts in their libraries.[9] The great business archives found in Babylon and Nippur continued to record the administration of agricultural estates in north-western and south-eastern Babylonia as before. Families were free to use Persian, Babylonian, or Greek personal names according to personal taste; ethnic pride was not necessarily involved. The public monuments of earlier times were not removed from the streets of Babylon. Although a columned building was added to the Southern Palace, the major development took place in the Merkes district, east of the Processional Way, the great temple, and the ziggurat – probably far enough from the river to avoid sinking and

---

[7] Monroe 2016: 119–38.

[8] Recently a calculus type text has been identified by Ossendrijver on a clay tablet in which a numerical graph plots velocity against time.

[9] Waerzeggers 2015a: ch. 5 suggests that some late tablets were not reworkings of earlier ones. This is disputed.

subsidence. This area, previously developed in Kassite times, was filled with the houses of merchants and their domestic tombs. It flourished well into the early period of Parthian rule.[10]

Royal roads and horse relays had developed in the Near East from at least the late second millennium; they were not a Persian invention, but were improved and extended at this time.[11] Law and order were still enforced along traditional lines: the prologue to Hammurabi's Code was still copied and studied in cuneiform, and a new law code with different formulations but similar content is known from a small cuneiform fragment, even though the official language of communication was the standardized Imperial Aramaic written in ink on parchment. Babylonian cuneiform written on clay was used in fewer and fewer spheres of activity. Gold and silver coins showing the king's portrait were based on a Babylonian standard shekel weight (sixty to a mina, rather than the 'Greek' rate of fifty to a mina), an affirmation of Babylonia's central role in trade.[12] Darius minted his own gold and silver coinage likewise, and named them darics after himself. His coins were used mainly for paying troops, and they portrayed the king in military pose, as an archer.[13] Within Babylonia the change to coinage was very slow because the traditional use of metals by weight, with verifiable purity, was satisfactory.

Under Achaemenid rule the city was still important, not least because it housed treasures extracted from the conquest of Assyria, to which loot and tribute from the conquests of Nebuchadnezzar, Nabonidus, and Cyrus had been added. The ground plan of walls and moats around the Southern Palace on Babylon's citadel show how well the core was protected, and a garrison of mercenaries was stationed in the city. A stela of Darius I with a copy of (a version of) his Bisotun Inscription in Babylonian cuneiform stood close to a stela of Nabonidus near the Ishtar Gate. At the western end of the great palace, a pillared first floor addition was perhaps built in Persian style; very damaged remains of a pillar base and an animal-headed capital resembling those at Persepolis were found by Koldewey. But there are no Achaemenid building inscriptions, nor temples to their deities, nor any apparent interest in Babylonian literature.

When Cambyses died and rebellions broke out in Babylon, at least four men were recognized as kings in Babylonian texts.[14] The first of them was

---

[10] See Invernizzi 2008a: 239–48, and 2008b: 251–75; and the sketch suggesting fluctuations in the river's course and their dating at 2008b: 530.
[11] Radner 2002: 3–4.   [12] van der Spek 2017.
[13] Cool Root 1979: 116–18, but such coins have not been found in Babylon.
[14] Pearce and Wunsch 2014: xxxix, note with bibliography.

Figure 10.1 Stone fragments of a scene from the top of a stela of Darius I, set up by the Ishtar Gate in Babylon. Restored by comparison with the great rock sculpture at Bisotun. Credit: after Seidl 1999; illustration by C. Wolff.

Gaumata, who claimed to be a son of Cyrus, brother of Cambyses. He was soon killed when Darius, a usurper from the family of a Persian administrator, dashed to Babylon from Media and took him by surprise. Then Nidinti-Bēl 'son of Nabonidus' rose up, taking the name Nebuchadnezzar (III) and the title 'king of Babylon'. His claim to be a son of Nabonidus implies that Nabonidus had a good reputation in Babylon, contrary to Cyrus' propaganda. He took cult statues from southern cities to Babylon for safety, presumably in response to Darius mobilizing his army, but ruled for only a few months before Darius caught him and his nobles, and impaled them in Babylon. Araha, who came from the area of Armenia (Urartu) in 521,[15] called himself Nebuchadnezzar (IV), 'king of Babylon'

---

[15] Beaulieu 2014: 17–26.

inscriptions

inscriptions

Figure 10.2 Part of the scene carved on the rock at Bisotun, showing Darius I victorious over recumbent rebel leader. Credit: King and Thompson 1907: pl. XIII.

and 'king of lands', claiming also that he was a son of Nabonidus. In reprisal, Darius 'destroyed' the walls and gates of Babylon, and impaled about 3,000 men from the top echelon of society.[16] The usurpers were called 'liar kings' by Darius, and their gods were false, not because of religious fervour, or an attempt to impose Persian gods on the conquered people, but because they were incapable of winning success for the rebels. Darius' actions against the three consecutive rebels are recorded in the great multilingual inscription carved on the rockface at Bisotun near Ecbatana, at a narrow pass where every traveller could see it. The Babylonian version of the long text contains no allusions to Babylonian or other literary works, and there is no evidence that Achaemenid Persians or Elamites had a written literature of their own.

Darius I ('holding the good'), followed the example set by Cyrus in taking the Babylonian title 'king of Babylon' in Babylonian texts, and taking Egyptian royal titles in Egypt, showing a pragmatic and flexible approach in order to express his control and ingratiate himself with each particular nation. To remind the citizens of their failed rebellion, he had a copy of the

[16] Hdt III.159.1.

central scene from his great rock sculpture at Bisotun set up in Babylon, on the Processional Way to the north of the Ishtar Gate.

Darius is portrayed with his foot on the supine figure of the rebel Gaumata, whose arms are raised in submission, just as he is shown on the rock. But there is a significant difference: the name of Ahura-mazda is replaced by the name Bēl, which by this time was commonly used for Marduk, a replacement clearly designed for a Babylonian public.[17] The king strengthened his connections with Babylon by marrying the daughter of its Persian governor, Gubaru. Unlike Cyrus, who had married an Egyptian, Darius and his descendants married Persian women as their first wives, but were more flexible in taking secondary wives.

Some of his royal name seals and inscriptions, notably on the rock at Bisotun, were inscribed in three or four languages and scripts: Elamite as the primary one, Babylonian, Old Persian (which he took particular pride in writing),[18] and (at Elephantine in Egypt) Aramaic; Darius thereby disseminated his authority and achievements to different language groups throughout his empire.

The Iranian god Ahura-mazda, promoted in later written tradition in the religion of Zoroaster, is prominent as the only god named in the Bisotun rock inscriptions. Ahura-mazda is first found in an Assyrian list of gods of the seventh century, as Assara-mazaš,[19] so presumably he was worshipped in Assyria at that time, but there is no evidence for a cult dedicated to him in Babylon. According to other monuments in Iran, tolerant polytheism continued under the Achaemenids. No attempt was made to impose any kind of monotheism; Persian gods, with the exception of Anahita (in the reign of Artaxerxes II), were not introduced into Babylonian cults, nor were temples in Babylon closed down.[20] During Darius' reign a statue of Bēl was installed, with prebends allocated for offerings, in a shrine to the god Ninurta.[21] Some artistic elements in Achaemenid art, such as the winged disc, show Mesopotamian influence.[22]

When Babylonian craftsmen created a replica of Babylon's Ishtar Gate in glazed brickwork at Persepolis,[23] it was perhaps because Persepolis was intended to supplant or to imitate Babylon as the main centre for the

---

[17] Seidl 1999: 101–4.
[18] The word used by Darius can be translated either as 'Aryan' or as 'Iranian'.
[19] See Dandamaev and Lukonin 1989: 321.
[20] Dandamaev and Lukonin 1989: 320–66; Henkelman 2008: 342.
[21] Baker 2011b. For a definition of prebends, see Chapter 6, p. 154.
[22] There is no evidence for Zoroaster at this time. See Messerschmidt 2006; Henkelman 2008.
[23] See Chapter 9, p. 267.

celebration of kingship. The immense amount of building done at Persepolis under Darius and his successors placed a heavy burden on subject peoples including Babylonians; the protected status of Babylon's own citizens may not have continued under Achaemenid rule. The fact that cuneiform records on clay belonging to Judean settlers have been found in central Babylonia shows that not all of them returned to Jerusalem at this time.[24]

Xerxes, whose name means 'ruling over heroes', kept the title 'king of Babylon' for local consumption, as did his son Artaxerxes.[25] In his second year, 484, he introduced a regular system of seven intercalated months in cycles of nineteen years, presumably on the advice of Babylonian astronomers, a move that showed he was in control of calendrical order.[26] It was a reform that must have facilitated administration throughout his empire. Under Darius, Babylon had been part of a single huge province; its governor Ushtanu may only have kept his post for a few years until Xerxes divided it into two, putting the western part, Across the River (Eber-Nari), under a man named Tattanu.

Rebellions led by two Babylonians were suppressed. This led to many top officials being replaced, often by Persians, in a purge that extended to some of the other northern cities.[27] Babylon and its sympathizers would have suffered, but the New Year Festival in Babylon continued to be celebrated. Around this time at Uruk the ancient temple Eanna was abandoned, the gods of Babylon Bēl and Bēltiya were expelled along with priests who had come from Babylon, and two enormous new temples were built, dedicated to the Sky-god Anu. They contained at least one scholarly library. This indicates that Xerxes intended to weaken the centralizing control that Babylon had exerted.[28] Uruk became a major rival, both in the magnificence of its temples, and in cherishing and developing its libraries and scholarship; but it paid homage to Babylon's leadership by naming its ceremonial gates after those of Babylon, and modelled its New Year Festival on that of Bēl-Marduk.[29] The *Uruk King-List* of kings and sages may have been written or copied at this time, as part of Uruk's efforts to rival Babylon.[30]

At least three business archives, those of Egibi, Iddin-Marduk, and Nappahu, had been maintained throughout the changes from indigenous rule to the reigns of Cyrus and then Darius. But they came to an end at this

---

[24] See Chapter 8.   [25] See various studies in Waerzeggers and Seire 2019.
[26] This is known misleadingly as the Metonic Cycle. See, e.g., Jones 2017: 77–81.
[27] Borsippa, Kish, and Sippar. See Waerzeggers 2003: 4, and Hackl 2018.   [28] Beaulieu 2018a.
[29] George 1995: 194.   [30] See Neujahr 2012.

time as part of Xerxes' purge, which must have led to the impoverishment of many businessmen who failed to adapt.

Xerxes' undeserved reputation as the destroyer of Babylonian cults has been refuted by firm new evidence derived from legal and administrative texts showing that he allowed new loyal local administrative groups to arise, rather than replacing them with Persian ones. A supposed atrocity story perpetuated by Greek texts tells of a statue of an unidentified man removed from Esagila (not Marduk or any other divine image, as previously supposed), and the killing of a priest who tried to prevent the removal. Also contrary to older opinions, Xerxes did not put a stop to the celebration of the New Year Festival in Babylon,[31] but introduced a new and reliable calendar for planning its celebration. Although a temple library of cuneiform tablets at Sippar came to an end at this time, Xerxes did not destroy the library of Esagila in Babylon.

The tale that Xerxes destroyed the ziggurat and deliberately damaged temples at Babylon belongs to the atrocity genre; Herodotus described the ziggurat in all its glory a few decades later, but may have relied on an earlier written account if he did not go there himself, as some have claimed. As discussed in previous chapters,[32] the ziggurat would have deteriorated without human agency, but the period when it became too ruined to function is uncertain.

Artaxerxes I's links with Babylon are implied by the account written by his Greek doctor Ctesias: that he had sons by at least two Babylonian women, one of them probably the mother of Darius II. Ctesias' writings, preserved only in later extracts, are of dubious historical value, for he presented atrocity tales to make his work more enticing. These were the early days of development for a new genre of literature, the novel.[33] Ctesias' salacious description of the Achaemenid court gave the impression that it was a hotbed of the scandalous behaviour to be expected of immoral easterners. Some events described strikingly in Ctesias' writings and in Xenophon's *Anabasis* and *Cyropaedia* are found neither in the fragments of Berossus' history nor in the *Babylonian Chronicle* nor in the astronomical diaries.[34] Both Greek writers show a great interest in the characters involved in the fall of Nineveh and the conquest of Babylon.

During this reign signet rings, a Greek fashion, became popular among high officials in Babylon.[35] This significant introduction follows the peace

---

[31] Boiy 2004: 278.   [32] Chapter 7 p. 205 and Chapter 8 p. 222.
[33] See, e.g., Morgan 2007: II, 552–64.   [34] Da Riva 2017a.
[35] Signet rings are known from impressions on dated clay tablets; see Altavilla and Walker 2016: 21.

concluded between Greece and Persia in 448 BC. Long before Alexander's conquest, therefore, Greeks were making their mark in Babylon.

Some Judeans are thought to have returned to Jerusalem from exile in Babylonia at this time.[36] The best-known version of the Hebrew Book of Esther was a court novel with love interest emanating from a brilliant heroine, set in the court of a great king 'Ahasuerus' in Babylon. Whether the name is intended to indicate Xerxes, Artaxerxes I, or a later Artaxerxes, or is deliberately ambiguous, is unknown.[37] Although the main action takes place in Babylon and the story was evidently popular under Achaemenid rule, it uses earlier material taken from the Assyrian campaigns of Ashurbanipal against Susa and from the ritual calendar of Ishtar-of-Nineveh.[38]

A major archive, now known as the Kasr Archive, found on the citadel mound, records the activities of the sub-governor of Babylon, a native Babylonian called Belshunu, who was subordinate to the Persian satrap Gubaru.[39] From those texts it is clear that he was already a property owner and manager, one of few Babylonians to succeed in rising to high office. The properties involved were in north-western Babylonia; similar business activities recording the management of properties in south-eastern Babylonia have been found at Nippur in the Murashu Archive of the same period. That area, too, was under the control of the satrap Gubaru.

The period from this reign to the end of Achaemenid rule, about 120 years, was a productive time for the astronomers attached to Esagila. In exchange for holding prebends (see Chapter 6, p. 154) and then fixed allowances when prebends were replaced, astronomers had duties in observation and recording, thereby extending their understanding of celestial movements;[40] but priests from families of Babylon were replaced in all the major temples of northern Babylonian cities.[41]

Herodotus, writing in the reign of Artaxerxes I, claimed that the ziggurat in Babylon had eight stages. Other elements in his description, including the spiral stairway, cannot be confirmed from contemporary cuneiform texts.[42] At least ten different reconstructions of the ziggurat's remains have been proposed.[43] The Greek historian may have relied on second-hand information, since it is unlikely that the tower was in good repair when he

[36] See Chapter 8, p. 230; Edelman 2005: 195.
[37] An intriguing mention in the *Babylonian Talmud, Tractate Megillah*, tells that a version of the story was known in the Elamite language; see Epstein 1959.
[38] See also Chapter 7, p. 211; Dalley 2007, using the work of Gunkel 1917.
[39] Stolper 1990. In Greek, their names were Belesys and Gobryas, respectively.
[40] Beaulieu 2006a: 5–22. For a definition of 'prebend', see Chapter 6, p. 154.   [41] Hackl 2018.
[42] Hdt I.180.   [43] Vicari 2000.

wrote, and may no longer have been safe for recording celestial observations – if indeed that was ever its function. Even when the tower became a ruin, cuneiform texts prolonged detailed knowledge of its existence, especially an invaluable listing of Babylon's temples, gates, and streets known as *Tintir*, and the Esagila Tablet, which includes measurements of the structure.

Under **Darius II**, Belshunu continued his career and was promoted to full governorship of the province of Syria known as 'Across the River', where he built himself a palace with an extensive park in the region of Aleppo (Halab).[44] Nearby villages belonged to the half-Babylonian mother of Cyrus the Pretender. In the king's accession year, the governor of Babylon (*šakin ṭēmi*) was following Greek fashion in using a signet ring, but it was engraved with the motif of a man in contest with a lion reminiscent of the motif of the late Assyrian royal stamp seal rather than a Greek-style design.[45]

The library of Esagila was not found in the temple of Marduk itself (of which only a tiny part was reached by excavation in the deep trench, see Figure 2.4), but was excavated on adjacent land to the south; there may have been more than one collection.[46] It may have been 'weeded' at this time to make space for new texts and for copies of old, damaged texts, but essentially it flourished as before, providing the staff and facilities for scholarly research.[47] Individual temple scholars were active until around 69 BC. This means that a wide variety of texts were kept, copied, and revised for many centuries: chronicles, epics, astronomical diaries, and some royal correspondence. The temple libraries and scholars in Uruk were Babylon's main rivals. The great libraries of Babylon and Uruk preceded those founded later at Alexandria in Egypt and at Pergamum in north-western Anatolia.

Soon after the death of Darius II, his son Cyrus the Pretender marched on Babylon from distant Sardis, hoping to supplant his elder brother. His allies included the Greek writer Xenophon, who led an army of Greek mercenaries. Xenophon's *Anabasis* or *March of the Ten Thousand* mentions that Cyrus destroyed the palace and park of the Babylonian satrap Belshunu. Students of ancient Greek often read the text at an early stage of their studies, and understand it literally as a real adventure story with a great hero. However, the account is questionable

---

[44] Stolper 1987.   [45] Altavilla and Walker 2016: 17, 85, and 173, no. 532.
[46] See Clancier 2009: 143
[47] Clancier 2009: 222; 231 n. 994; 233–9 suggested an alternative explanation in an increased preference for writing-boards and parchment.

in many respects, for Xenophon described events that had taken place more than thirty years earlier; the passage of time gave him the opportunity to adjust the details and burnish his own reputation.[48] The site where the battle took place in 401 at which Cyrus the Pretender was defeated and killed was named Cunaxa by Xenophon but has not been identified.[49] Following the death of the Pretender, his mother killed the king's official consort as well as a probable son-in-law of the king, and then retired or was exiled to Babylon or Babylonia. Belshunu managed to keep his position after the battle, and **Artaxerxes II Arsaces** kept the throne, celebrating by building a pillared pavilion alongside the vast Southern Palace in Babylon. Column bases similar to those familiar from Persepolis are among very few relics of Persian architecture found in Babylon. Artaxerxes II introduced the cult of the Persian goddess Anaitis into Babylon for the benefit of Persians in the city, certainly not to force Persian religion upon the Babylonians, whose cults continued as before.[50]

A famous Babylonian astronomer named Kidinnu lived in Babylon around this time. He may have invented 'System B' which describes the synodic arc for each planet by means of a linear zigzag function.[51] His reputation was high in later times among Greek astronomers.[52] As before, clay tablets were collected and copied in a location to the immediate south of Esagila for access, safekeeping, and revision.

The mother of **Artaxerxes III** was a Babylonian, perhaps a union made, as before, to strengthen the ties between the ruling family and Babylon as the most prestigious city in the world. Artaxerxes III is known chiefly for his capture of Sidon, from where he deported prisoners of war to Babylon. His satrap for Across the River, bore the same name as the earlier satrap, Belshunu (Xenophon calls him Belesys), causing some unfortunate confusion; but it is notable that a man with a Babylonian name was appointed on both occasions. Most other high officials by this time were Persians, and Persian words were used for their professions, such as *databara* ('judges'). Artaxerxes' son Arses reinstated or extended a tax exemption for Babylonians during his brief reign, an act which would have earned him some popularity.

---

[48] See, e.g., Azoulay 2004.

[49] The vicinity of Hiritum has been suggested, near one end of the northern cross-country wall, where at least two previous battles had been fought against would-be usurpers. See Boiy and Verhoeven 1998: 21, 147–58, and map 5.

[50] Dillery 2015: 46.   [51] For an explanation of this see, e.g., Walker 1996: 60.

[52] Hunger 1976–80.

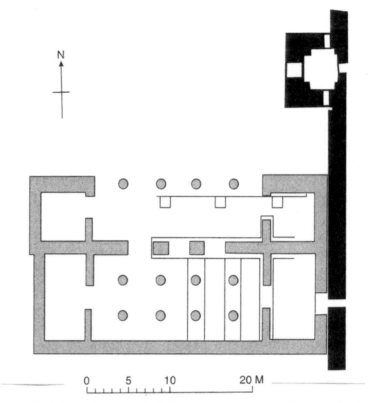

N

0   5   10   20 M

Figure 10.3 Plan of a pavilion built for Artaxerxes II outside the west side of the Southern Palace. Credit: after Koldewey 1931: pl. 28.

The Achaemenid period of Persian rule came to an end when Alexander defeated **Darius III** at the battle of Gaugamela to the east of Nineveh.[53] At that time a Persian satrap named Mazaeus was responsible for Across the River and Cilicia, apparently contemporary with the second Belshunu, who by then had been promoted to governor of Babylon.[54]

2   Alexander and Civil War, 331–305

Alexander III (The Great) of Macedon (331–323)
(Civil War)
Alexander IV with Antigonus (323?–305?)

---

[53] The name of the battleground includes the name of the nearby ancient town at Tell Gomel and the adjacent river Gomel.
[54] Badian 2015.

Alexander had invaded Asia from his kingdom Macedonia. His capital, Pella, lay 40 km west of modern Thessaloniki, in the north of the Greek peninsula, distant from Babylon by about 2,760 km on foot. At this time, the kingdom had language, deities, and the study of arts and sciences in common with the Greek city states. One can distinguish them in art: Macedonians were clean-shaven, but southern Greeks sported beards. From Alexander's conquests onwards, the two groups were barely distinguished, and the term 'Hellenistic' applies to both.

As Alexander marched towards Babylon in 331 BC after winning the battle at Gaugamela,[55] he was warned by Chaldean diviners not to approach the city from the east. That route would have been the obvious one because the western approach was so marshy, dangerous for an army trained to travel on foot. Alexander ignored the advice, but it is significant that he received the warning: his subsequent illness and death in Babylon would have been interpreted as an example of how dangerous it was to ignore the advice of Babylonian experts. Greek authors by this time used the term 'Chaldean' to signify scholars including diviners, and perhaps also citizens of Babylon more widely. It was also used to denote the Aramaic language.

Alexander entered Babylon three weeks after the battle. He supposedly took the city without a fight because the Persian satrap Mazaeus opened the gates to him and was duly rewarded with the right to retain his post as Babylon's top Achaemenid official under Macedonian authority. In public written messages to the Babylonians the new king promised not to allow the entering of houses, reprisals, or looting, which, if true, indicates iron discipline. Mazaeus was one of many Persians who retained high office under Alexander; one of his sons had a Babylonian name, Ardu-Bel. Alexander kept him in charge in Babylon, presumably keen to win favour by not interrupting the smooth flow of festivals, sacrifices, and economic life. Mazaeus instituted a mint at Babylon; examples of his coin, the 'double daric', have been found there. He died in 328 while Alexander still ruled.

Alexander only spent thirty-four days in Babylon before setting off to Susa and Persepolis on new conquests. Popular accounts perpetuate the shocking exaggeration that Alexander the Great burnt Persepolis to the ground, but archaeological evidence has shown this 'atrocity story' to be a gross exaggeration.[56]

Alexander moved the great treasuries of Persepolis and of Susa, first to Ecbatana, and then to the Southern Palace in Babylon, thus increasing the

---

[55] van der Spek 2003. [56] Sancisi-Weerdenberg 1993.

Figure 10.4 Coin of Mazaeus, bearded Iranian satrap of Babylon in the time of Artaxerxes III, Darius III, and Alexander. Credit: Commons.wikimedia/Classical Numismatic Group Inc.

wealth of Babylon enormously and giving hope that the temples, especially the huge ziggurat E-temen-anki, could be restored to their former glory. Strabo wrote that 'Alexander preferred Babylon, since he saw that it far surpassed [other cities], not only in its size, but also in all other respects'.[57] But plans to rebuild Babylon with the labour of ten thousand men did not materialize, and the ruined ziggurat was never rebuilt. It lay abandoned amid huge heaps of collapsed brickwork. Alexander's treasurer Harpalus, ignoring the tradition of using wealth for pious works, funded an extravagant lifestyle for himself with Babylon's enormous treasury. Its depletion was exacerbated by the death first of Alexander's bosom companion Hephaistion, whose funeral in Babylon was extravagant and spectacular, and then of Alexander himself, which was followed by another spectacular funeral. Antimenes from Rhodes, who replaced Harpalus, revived an old import tax of 10 per cent, thus milking wealthy visitors, who were dazzled by the ceremonies, festivals, and markets in the great city. Alexander may have had a Greek theatre built in Babylon using bricks of Nebuchadnezzar; alternatively, the theatre may be a later construction. A substantial amount of revenue must have been diverted from Babylon to the building of a new port of Alexandria, perhaps the largest in his empire, at the junction of the river Karun and the Tigris. The site was not far from the head of the Gulf at that time. It harboured a fleet of a thousand warships which would have

[57] Strabo, *Geography* XV.3.10.

been able to explore the east coast of Arabia and facilitate trade between Susa and the Gulf.[58]

When Alexander returned to Babylon in 323, he fell ill and died, having been unable to spend much time in the city or take part in the New Year Festival there. Perhaps as a result of his illness, Bēl-Marduk was identified with Sarapis (a Hellenized Egyptian god) in his aspect as a healing god. The syncretism picked up a much earlier assimilation of Marduk with Asalluhi, the Sumerian god of healing and incantations, and the match was continued by Seleucus I.[59] In accordance with Babylonian beliefs, the sick king adopted the traditional custom of appointing a substitute king in the hope of diverting divine anger, for the substitute, accepted as king by the gods, was put to death.[60] Alexander and his companions certainly engaged with some Babylonian beliefs and traditions, but whether he personally took celestial divination seriously before he fell ill is not known. However, in Babylonia and Assyria the idea was ingrained that a ruler who ignored the results of divination would die; it went back to the death of king Naram-Sin in the third millennium.

Alexander's rule in Babylon was marked by engagement with the city's scholarship not only in astrology. The great philosopher Aristotle asked his nephew Callisthenes to forward to him Babylonian astronomical observations.[61] As for Babylonian literature, considerable interest is known to have existed among Alexander's followers because Eudemus of Rhodes, having studied in Athens under Aristotle and served under Alexander in India, made a Greek translation of the *Epic of Creation*. His Greek version was used by Damascius, the last head of the School of Athens in the early sixth century AD, an astonishing eight centuries later.[62] Thus the Babylonian *Epic of Creation* was known to Greek scholars in some form for more than 800 years. Several aspects of Babylonian mathematics have been detected in Greek mathematical works from Eudemus' time.[63] The library of Esagila with its scholars was certainly not a closed institution, and Greek scholars took an active interest in their work. There is no evidence for the reverse: Babylonians did not start writing plays, nor did they translate Plato's works. They already had their own 'wisdom' dialogues from a long tradition of wisdom literature that probed issues of loyalty, integrity, and the good life.

---

[58] A silver tetradrachm of Alexander type, minted in Babylon around 315 BC, was found in a hoard at al-Ayun in central Arabia, suggesting that Babylon's trade directly across the great deserts was active soon after Alexander's death. Potts 2010: 96.

[59] van der Spek 2014.   [60] Ambos 2005.   [61] Beaulieu 2006b.   [62] Dillery 2015: 235–40.
[63] Friberg 2007.

By the time Alexander the Great's successors (the *diadochi*) were fighting for the throne of Babylon, the ziggurat was completely derelict. Debris
from it was eventually carried off by elephants supplied from India and
Bactria and dumped to form the mounds of the Homera district and
elsewhere. Nothing now remains, in contrast to the imposing remains of
the ziggurat at Borsippa. Xerxes was blamed for its ruination by foreigners
who enjoyed 'atrocity stories' and did not understand the long-term problem of subsidence on Babylon's citadel and the weaknesses of tall brick
structures.[64] Some Greek writers supposed that the edifice covered the
tomb of a hero, and referred to it as the 'Tomb of Bēl'. This deduction
presumably arose from a comparison of the solid brick ziggurat with
Egyptian stone pyramids containing chambers that held the bodies of
deceased pharaohs. We can only imagine the tales told by guides to gullible
tourists in Babylon. *Plus ça change.*

Alexander's coinage, based in part on that of Tarsus (where Sennacherib
had built a temple with statues to commemorate his father's death), shows
that he paid at least lip service to the divinity of great rulers by allowing his
head to be shown with a pair of horns, comparable to those of Naram-Sin,
king of Akkad in the third millennium BC. On his travels, Alexander would
have seen Naram-Sin's rock sculptures and other stone monuments,
already 2,000 years old. Coinage was widely used from this time, usually
counted rather than weighed as earlier forms of currency, notably 'hack-
silver', had been.

Babylonian citizens held on to their own rituals and administrative
practices: an attempt to introduce Macedonian month-names did not
displace the traditional Babylonian ones. Greek roof tiles eventually
replaced earlier roofing on the Summer Palace, one of few changes that
would have altered the skyline, and the first version of the Greek theatre
may have been built during or just after Alexander's rule (see below,
Chapter 11). Plans were afoot to collect tithes in order to clear debris as a
first stage in restoring Esagila, but were presumably postponed when
Alexander died and the fights for succession began.[65]

How might the Babylonians have regarded Alexander and his legacy?
The *Babylonian King-List*, laconic as ever, is a poor guide to the chaotic
succession of Macedonian rulers in Babylon. Alexander had never managed to celebrate the New Year Festival in order officially to receive
kingship. The attempt to establish a dynasty was desperate. Alexander

[64] The fact that sun-dried brickwork tolerates the stress of heavy loading far better than baked
brickwork may not have been appreciated by foreign rulers when repairs were attempted.
[65] Boiy 2010: 211–13.

produced no children during his lifetime. The baby on the throne, **Alexander IV**, was Alexander's posthumous (and only) son by a Bactrian princess, and the baby's co-regent was Alexander's mentally deficient half-brother. Neither of them had support within Babylon; both were murdered by feuding relatives. The Babylonian *Epic of Gilgamesh* makes it clear that a proper king should have several sons to commemorate their father after his death. Alexander had no plausible heirs. A consequence of that failing was a series of wars between 323 and 306 that impoverished the region, its coffers already depleted by inappropriate extravagances. Alexander had rejected the advice of astrologers on approaching the city. Towards the end of his life, having marched to India, he returned without first obtaining adequate knowledge of the barren mountainous terrain along the Iranian coast, and he lost a large part of his army. He arrived back in Babylon exhausted, fell sick, and died. Clearly the gods had not supported the king.

When Seleucus I at last took the throne, he set up no cult of Alexander, nor is there any known memorial to the hero's achievements. No boys are named after the great conqueror; not until 150 BC did a king in Babylon, Alexander Balas, bear his name. This suggests that Trajan's pilgrimage to the place where Alexander died (see Chapter 11, p. 318), was part of a much later phenomenon, encouraged when the legends of his fame had taken root elsewhere despite the realities of Babylon's experience.

A buried treasure including 14 kg of silver bullion was unearthed by Hormuzd Rassam in 1882. It had been hidden during the uncertain times that followed Alexander's death.[66] Prices rose very high during the civil wars, but returned to normal again and stayed steady from about 300 to 140 BC.[67] During the civil war one of the hopefuls, **Antigonus**, the one-eyed commander of the armed forces, authorized documents to be dated by his name and title as general (*stratēgos*), usurping the baby king's prerogative without actually giving himself the title of king. Seleucus, having served as commander of the royal shield-bearers under Alexander, was promoted to commander of companion cavalry during the struggles. He introduced a new era, now called the Seleucid, by which documents began to be dated using his name from 312/11 onwards in rivalry with Antigonus; his era overlaps the end of the short-lived Macedonian dynasty.[68] It was Antigonus and Seleucus, both top military men, who fought out their claim to the kingship of Babylon. At times there was fighting in Babylon for control of the palace, and for the Temple of Nabu-of-Vats where the gods bestowed

---

[66] Almost all of it was melted down by the Ottoman authorities soon after the discovery.
[67] van der Spek 2006.   [68] Boiy 2012.

kingship. On several occasions 'dust' had to be removed from Esagil, as reported in the *Babylonian Chronicle of Successors*. But chronicles and astronomical diaries continued to be written during those troubled times.

3   Seleucid Kings, 305–141 BC

(7 Seleucid kings of 12)

Seleucus I 'Conqueror' (305–281)
Antiochus I 'Saviour' (281–261)
Antiochus II 'God' (261–246)
Seleucus II 'Gloriously Victorious' (246–226/5 or 225/4)
Seleucus III 'Thunderbolt' (225–222)
Antiochus III 'The Great' (222–187)
Antiochus IV 'Manifest God' (175–164)
First Parthian conquest (141)

Crowned king in Antioch-on-the-Orontes in 305, **Seleucus I** 'Conqueror', whose name means 'shining white' in Greek, nevertheless took Babylon as a royal city. It was still surrounded by rich agricultural estates. Towns and farms filled with foreign soldiers and foreign deportees helped to do the work that added to tax revenues. The *Babylonian King-List* continued its record throughout the Seleucid period. Until recently the history of the Seleucid dynasty has concentrated on Anatolia, where information from Greek texts is plentiful. That has now changed, with study concentrated on fragments of chronicles and astronomical diaries, rich new sources which are yielding surprising results.[69]

Like the Macedonian kings, their Seleucid successors looked very different from Persian kings: even in Babylon they were clean-shaven, so they were easily distinguished from the bearded Babylonians and Persians. They were sympathetic to the local people: Persian titles of high officials were dropped; local Babylonian families filled top positions and had posts with Babylonian names. Archives and libraries continued as before. The city's reputation in gaining divine support for kings and the institution of kingship was undiminished, the authority of its astronomers and diviners unquestioned since Alexander's death had been foretold. As a financial and ceremonial centre, the city did not lose its importance at this time, although the blocking of some roads, which led to shortages of grain, caused at least one local famine and concomitant fighting. The astronomical diary for 274 records

[69] The site Livius.org is frequently updated with ongoing results.

that 'purchases in Babylon and the cities were made with copper coins of Ionia', which suggests Anatolian-Greek rivalry to dominate trade.[70]

The Seleucids of western Asia and the Ptolemies of Egypt were all of Macedonian ancestry, and were rivals for the possession of western Asia and Arabia. Where Seleucus and his immediate successors founded or refounded cities to the west of Babylon, a cult of Babylonian Bēl can be found.[71] Among them are Dura Europus, Palmyra, Apamea-on-the-Orontes, Edessa, and Antioch-on-the-Orontes. The ambiguity of the title Bēl allowed a wide interpretation – as the Sun-god or the Storm-god, for instance, but the title itself was Babylonian as distinct from the western Ba'al. Seleucus' promotion of the cult reinforced the claim that Syria belonged to Babylonia and was not open to easy invasion by the Ptolemies, whose incursions into Asia were repulsed with difficulty in the Six Syrian Wars.

On taking possession of Babylon, **Seleucus** took the title '*stratēgos* of Asia'. The new era for dating documents with his name, already promoted in 311, was inscribed on a wide range of objects to disseminate acceptance and familiarity.[72] His genuine interest in preserving the city of Babylon is indicated by the installation of a *na*-gauge used for measuring the height of the Euphrates so that the danger of severe flooding could be anticipated.

Two misconceptions have coloured the perception of the Hellenistic kings in Babylon. One is the assumption that the New Year Festival was no longer celebrated by the king. Newly researched chronicles and astronomical diaries mention the celebration, which continued into early Parthian times.[73] The festival was presumably modified when the king himself was absent. Another assumption is that the practice of offering prayers to the gods for the well-being of the king was a new introduction; in fact, it had been common among the Assyrian and Babylonian kings of much earlier times, and did not imply a high level of divinity.[74] Throughout the Seleucid period, rituals for Babylonian gods were performed not only in Babylon but also in Uruk, Borsippa, Kutha, and Nippur, and at least on some occasions in other cities.[75]

[70] Pirngruber 2017: 107–20.
[71] A cuneiform tablet was found at Dura Europus, probably mid-second millennium; another at Antioch-on-the-Orontes, probably Neo-Assyrian, now in Princeton. See Di Giorgi 2016: 38.
[72] Kosmin 2018 maintains that this new era was commemorated in the Day One temple, which is generally thought to be a name for (a part of?) the temple of the New Year Festival.
[73] The temple of the New Year Festival is mentioned in the astronomical diary for 80 BC.
[74] Mitsuma 2015.
[75] van der Spek 2009–11: 381. A temple library in Sippar was excavated in 1987; see Gasche and Tanret 2009–11.

A variety of cuneiform texts continued to be written and copied: tablets belonging to at least twenty chronicles have been identified, as well as astronomical diaries, astronomical tables, almanacs, hemerologies, and other kinds of text relating to divination and medicine. Since these are easier to recognize than literary texts among the thousands of surviving fragments, current emphasis on their predominance may be misleading. The events that had led up to the fall of Assyria and to the conquest of Babylon continued to be of enormous interest which can be traced on cuneiform tablets written in the Seleucid period.

The colour-glazed bricks, moulded with bulls and *mušhuššu*-dragons on the walls of the Ishtar Gate and with lions on the Processional Way, may have been made in this period, perhaps replacing an unglazed version that was unearthed beneath them. Since the whole Kasr mound suffered from subsidence, the heavy structures needed frequent renewal, but there is little or no evidence for dating the different layers.

With the construction of a new harbour (named Alexandria, then Antiochia, then Charax Spasinou) on the Lower Tigris, and a new administrative centre at Seleucia (previously Upe) on the Middle Tigris, a shift in activity from the Lower Euphrates was inevitable. Trade up the Euphrates to the west is not well attested on clay tablets, with Aramaic written on parchment now preferred, but Babylon continued to collect agricultural taxes and maintained its fame through ritual festivities and architecture.

Seleucus and his son **Antiochus I** (who is famous for using elephants in his army) took possession of land on both sides of the Euphrates around Babylon and Borsippa. The deed must have been deeply unpopular; but the kings did their best to integrate themselves into indigenous tradition. A clay cylinder found at Borsippa, the only royal Babylonian cuneiform inscription known from the whole Seleucid dynasty, conforms in almost every way to the long tradition of foundation cylinders. It records the intention of Antiochus I, co-regent with his father, to do building work on Esagila in Babylon and Nabu in Borsippa, with the emphasis on Nabu as son of Marduk.[76] The Greek god Apollo, regarded as the Greek equivalent of Nabu, was hailed as founder of the dynasty, so the temple in Borsippa had a particular significance. Western bricks were explicitly used to symbolize the link between the Greek-Macedonian west and Babylonia. The inscription ends with a prayer for his stepmother Stratonice, who was his father's second wife and became Antiochus' wife while his father Seleucus I

---

[76] A corrected reading describes Nabu as writing 'on your exalted writing-board, which fixes the boundary of heaven and earth'; see Stevens 2012.

still ruled. In order to establish and guard hereditary succession, sons were mainly named after the two great founders for nearly two centuries a policy that led to some inbreeding. A notable exception is the name of Stratonice's father, Demetrius 'besieger of cities', who had won renown under Alexander.

Seleucus had founded a sanctuary for the Greek god Apollo, close to Antioch-on-the-Orontes. A legend known only from a Latin text concerning the birth of Seleucus narrates his mother's liaison with Apollo, who thus became the divine founder of the dynasty.[77] The legend of divine parentage would have associated Seleucus with ancient Mesopotamian heroes who claimed a divine parent: Gilgamesh, Sargon of Agade, and Ashurbanipal.[78] The epithet 'God' taken by Antiochus II and shown on his coinage may be understood in the light of this surprising story and from traces in later legends, as well as from the cult that was established for Seleucus and his sons.[79] One public sign that Antiochus I was aware of the need to integrate into a Babylonian tradition of artistic conventions was that, after the death of his father, he introduced coins and seals on which Seleucus' head had small horns protruding from the forehead, as if to claim some measure of divine status. In this he imitated Alexander and the much earlier kings of Agade.[80]

Antiochus I, by marrying his father's wife, would have been the butt of lewd laughter among the scribes who composed the cylinder inscription – which he could not read in cuneiform for himself. Stratonice's name was punningly rendered in Babylonian as 'Astarte-nīqu' (the former part being the goddess of love and the latter the Babylonian for 'copulation'), and two writings used for the word 'heir, son' in referring to the god Nabu, gave a phonetic reading similar to the name Apollo (*aplu, ibila*).[81] Stratonice was recognized as queen until her death, which was recorded by the astronomical diary for 256 BC, along with the sacrifices in Esagila that Antiochus II made to Bēl and Bēltiya.

Nothing has been found to identify the existence of the royal family in Babylon. They presumably lived in some part of the great Southern Palace when they were not abroad, but no trace has been found of their presence. The cylinder inscription from Borsippa can be compared with the Cyrus Cylinder as an attempt to integrate the new dynasty into Babylonian tradition.

---

[77] Justin, *Epitome of Philippic Histories of Pompeius Trogus* 15.4.
[78] Several Greek authors wrote dramas loosely based on the life of Stratonice. See *Oxford Classical Dictionary* 4th ed., 'Stratonice'.
[79] van der Spek 2016a.   [80] Dirven 2015.   [81] Kosmin 2014.

Various tales indicate a fascination with the great upheavals in Babylon and Assyria three and four centuries earlier. Mesopotamian history and literature permeated the Mesopotamian lands ruled by Seleucus and his successors. The new rulers speculated, as their subjects had done under earlier rulers, on the causes of the downfall of great empires, no doubt continuing to wonder why the gods had allowed such convulsions, and why diviners had not been able to prevent disaster. For instance, a story about the late Assyrian court inscribed in Aramaic in the Amherst Papyrus dates from around this time, perhaps as a copy of an earlier text. It includes the desperate and unsuccessful attempt of an Assyrian princess to arbitrate between her warring brothers, ending in Ashurbanipal's sack of Babylon. The biblical Book of Daniel, set in Babylon under Nebuchadnezzar II, refers to successive empires, 'predicting' with hindsight that Babylon will fall to a foreign power. It relates to the fall of Babylon during the reign of Nabonidus and his son Belshazzar, as we have seen.[82]

The Tigris with its deeper channel benefitted from the decision to house the fleet at the new Alexandria – the harbour city that gave direct access to the Gulf.[83] Seleucia-on-the-Tigris was founded by Seleucus I as a new city c. 307 BC, transforming the older town of Upe to serve as a centre for Macedonian administration. It became the chief residence of the satrap, where the Seleucid administration kept records on parchment in Greek and Aramaic (only clay *bullae* survive to prove this); clay tablets were not used there. Since Babylon, on the Euphrates, remained a pivotal point for trade up into Syria and further west as well as the major centre for traditional cuneiform scholarship and worship, the networks of the two cities were complementary. The great festivals in honour of Babylon's gods continued to draw merchants and crowds from far and wide: Babylon retained its special status and was never demoted to a mere provincial capital, as was once thought.[84] During those times cuneiform sources record that rivalry within the king's family living in Babylon led to occasional street fighting there.

Contrary to an earlier opinion, few Babylonians shifted from Babylon to Seleucia-on-the-Tigris. Greek writers are now thought to have misrepresented a delegation of Babylon's leading citizens who went to Seleucia around 275 BC, presumably to negotiate tax exemptions and the terms of the relationship between the two cities. To Macedonian eyes the old areas of Babylon, especially the debris around the ruined ziggurat, would have looked quite shabby compared with the new buildings of Seleucia, but

---

[82] See Chapter 9, pp. 233 and 260.
[83] The shoreline of the alluvium was certainly much further north than at present.
[84] Nielsen 2015.

Figure 10.5 Statue of the goddess of Fortune holding a palm of victory, crowned,
celebrating the defeat of Chaos, represented as a beardless man with lower body
submerged in water (River Orontes?) on whom she places her foot, a local adaptation of
the *Epic of Creation*'s main theme. Roman copy in marble of a bronze public sculpture
made for Seleucus I at Antioch c. 305 BC by the sculptor Eutychides. Height 88 cm.
Credit: Commons.wikimedia, Carole Raddato, Flickr. Vatican Museum Inventory 2672.

Babylonians preferred evidence of antiquity. A wealth of new information from clay tablets found in Babylon shows that the city had lost little if any of its importance at that time. If the treasury was depleted to defend the city against Ptolemaic invasions during the Six Syrian Wars, tax revenues from the great empire may have compensated and certainly prices remained steady. Seleucus and his successors refounded various towns or cities that had flourished in previous centuries – a less expensive policy than building a whole new city.[85]

Seleucus I had founded the city of Antioch-on-the-Orontes (modern Antakya) on the site of a town that had existed at least since Assyrian times. To mark his coronation there he commissioned a statue from the Greek sculptor Eutychides of Sicyon, whose innovative design suggests that a local version of the *Epic of Creation* was recited at royal ceremonies, as it was in Babylon. The statue depicted Chaos defeated, upon whom the crowned Tyche (Greek for 'Fortune') sat elegantly with her foot holding him down. The conquered prisoner was half submerged in water, holding his arms outstretched, no doubt locally representing the unpredictable waters of the Orontes.[86] In Babylonian terms, chaos was Tiamat, the sea, mother of the gods, who was defeated by Marduk. At Antioch, the genders are reversed in accordance with local conditions: Orontes as a male, the city's Fortune as a female. Following this lead, under the Roman empire later rulers in other cities who continued to worship Bēl of Babylon and celebrate the victory of Bēl-Marduk over Chaos put the same design on the reverse of their coins, adjusting gender to local interpretations.[87]

In the time of Seleucus I and Antiochus I, a Babylonian scholar named Berossus was top temple administrator and high priest (*šatammu*) of Esagila. His post was hereditary, and he held it concurrently with his father. His control extended beyond Marduk's temple Esagila to the city's other temples and to urban administration, and he exerted influence over other great cities. The impression of his large seal of office has been recognized on many dated clay tablets; it was engraved with the *mušhuššu*-dragon of Marduk and inscribed 'Property of the god Bēl'.[88] Berossus was certainly literate in cuneiform writing and was bilingual in Greek and Babylonian. He wrote a hugely significant account in Greek for his royal Seleucid

---

[85] They include Susa (Seleucia-by-Eulaios), Damara (Dura-Europos), and Antioch-on-the-Orontes. Seleucia-on-the-Tigris had previously been known as the substantial town Upe, and Dur-Kurigalzu likewise as Parsa.

[86] He is not 'a swimmer', as he is sometimes described. Swimmers in antiquity are shown with the whole body horizontal in water.

[87] See Dalley 2014: 70–1.   [88] Wallenfels 2017: no. 21

patrons, to transmit to them the essentials of Babylonian history, myth, and cosmography. His *Babyloniaca* has not survived, but it was paraphrased, perhaps altered, misread, misunderstood, then relayed in short extracts by much later writers who were not familiar with his background. Whereas versions of the *Sumerian King-List* gave Eridu or Kish as the first city, created by the gods, Berossus gave that status to Babylon – which was partly true because the name of Eridu had been given to a quarter within Babylon at least as early as the reign of Nebuchadnezzar I.[89] The reinterpretation of the *Sumerian King-List*, already implied in the *Epic of Creation*, allowed Babylon to have a mythic past that went back before the Flood.[90]

The surviving extracts of the *Babyloniaca* can no longer be attributed strong Hellenistic influence. Berossus clearly made direct use of Babylonian chronicles as well as Nabonidus' Babylon Stela (still publicly visible in Babylon)[91] and the Harran Cylinder text for historical sections; he used a version of the *Epic of Creation* for his account of creation, as well as the traditional *Myth of the Seven Sages*;[92] and his ethnographic information is of a kind exemplified in late eighth/seventh-century Assyrian texts.[93] The astronomical section of Berossus' work dealing with cosmology rather than astronomy was based on concepts found, for instance, in the star catalogue *Plough Star*, of which the latest known copy dates from after 312 BC,[94] and in the manual of celestial observations *When Anu and Enlil*. In his day there were at least fourteen astronomers, 'scribes of *Enūma Anu Enlil*' employed by the temple of Marduk.[95] Berossus deliberately selected traditional knowledge from times of native rule, excluding the developments in mathematical astronomy that occurred under Persian and Seleucid kingship.[96] Babylonian words transcribed in Greek letters, used by Berossus and presumably excerpted from his original text, are listed in the Oxyrhynchus Glossary, and are specifically attributed to him.[97] His work was available in the library in Alexandria, which had been founded by Ptolemy I or II in the first half of the third century BC around the time Berossus was active, and perhaps also in the library in Pergamum. Scholarship under the aegis of Esagila and its library had continued despite

[89] The Arab historian al-Ṭabarī (AD 838–923) wrote that Babylon shared with Susa the honour of being the first cities. See Rosenthal's translation, al-Ṭabarī 1989: I, 341.
[90] Dillery 2015: xxx and 235.
[91] van der Spek 2008; Waerzeggers 2015a. See Figures 9.2–3, above.
[92] The myth is known only from partial and indirect references. See, e.g., Dillery 2015: 69.
[93] E.g. the letter to the gods written by Sargon II, and some of Esarhaddon's campaign accounts.
[94] Steele in press; Dillery 2015: 240.   [95] van der Spek 2006: 277.   [96] See Steele 2013.
[97] Schironi 2009. The text fragments are dated to around the first century BC, but include much earlier material; and Schironi 2013.

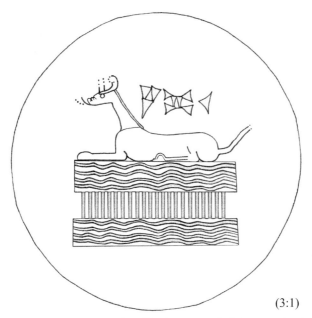

(3:1)

Figure 10.6 Design on the official stamp seal of the top priest/administrator of the temple Esagila; probably used by Berossus, and by his successors. Credit: by kind permission of Wallenfels 2017.

political and military troubles. The Goal Year texts, which predicted the relations of the periods of the Moon and five planets for the coming year, a work invaluable for astrologers, were available for compiling the astronomical diaries and almanacs. A copy of the Esagil Tablet, a metrological text giving dimensions for the ziggurat, as described in Chapter 8, and for some parts of the temple Esagila, was made on clay around this time.

Sudines, a renowned Babylonian astronomer also known for his knowledge of the 'science' of stones, served as an expert scholar to Attalus I, king of Pergamum in north-western Anatolia (269–197 BC) and father of Eumenes II, who built the famous library there and very likely took as a gift a copy of Berossus' *Babyloniaca* to encourage and then celebrate the inauguration of the new library.[98] Pergamum was in competition with Alexandria to make its library the most famous in the world.[99] When it was destroyed in AD 262, many of its contents, mainly written on parchment, were transferred to Alexandria, perhaps including the *Babyloniaca*. Copies of Berossus' sources which have now been recognized indicate that

---

[98] See Schmidt 2011–13. His name has not yet been recognized in cuneiform texts. Attalus' son Eumenes II was the official founder of Pergamum's library.

[99] Marck 2016: 243–4.

scribes in Babylon were still interested in them; old though they were, they had not been supplanted by newer types of texts and were readily available in the library of Esagila or on royal stelas that still stood on display in the streets. The preserved fragments of Berossus' text emphasize the fall of the great empires, as in much literature of the early Seleucid period, which suggests that the emphasis was not simply due to selection by those who quoted his text in much later times.[100] In later times Berossus was connected with the sibyls of Rome; a faint echo of his writing may be discerned in the First Sibylline Oracle,[101] and Pliny records that a statue of Berossus as a supremely famous astronomer was erected in Athens.[102] He retired to the Aegean island of Kos, where an altar dedicated to Bēl of Tadmor (Palmyra) has been found.[103]

Antiochus I followed the example set by his father by making his own son **Antiochus II**, co-regent with him, a move that must have eased the burdens of ceremonial and military duties across such a huge empire. Continuing his father's work, he took charge of removing debris from Esagila and the ziggurat E-temen-anki with the help of elephants sent as a gift from Bactria, perhaps inspired by his mother, who was Bactrian. Unused to the untidy debris of an ancient mud-brick city, he stumbled in public, which was inevitably interpreted as a bad omen. In 275/4 BC a huge number of bricks were moulded for reconstructing or repairing Esagila, but it is not certain that they were put to use there.

Laodice, wife of Antiochus II and mother of Seleucus II, was not repudiated when her husband's second marriage with Ptolemy II's sister Berenice offered superior advantages, a marriage that marked the end of the Second Syrian War but did not preclude the Third Syrian War against Egypt. Laodice was granted estates east of the Tigris in Babylonia, following the Assyrian tradition of royal women owning land there.[104] Antiochus II also gave much land to his sons. In an act of great munificence they and their mother donated it, free of some taxes, to the temples of Babylon, Borsippa, and Kutha, to be administered locally. Borsippa and Kutha were both close to Babylon so the deed strengthened loyalty in that region in the face of the rise of Uruk, city of Gilgamesh, in the south. Some stages of the transactions were authorized by the administrator (*šatammu*) of Esagila and were recorded on a *kudurru*-stone set up in a courtyard within the temple of Bēl-Marduk. A text written on clay in 173 BC, about a century

---

[100] Da Riva 2014.   [101] Lightfoot 2007: 216–19.   [102] Pliny *Natural History* VII.37.123.

[103] Drawing in Dalley et al. 1998: 115, fig. 55.

[104] Notably Naqia, mother of Esarhaddon, and Libbali-šarrat, wife of Ashurbanipal; centred on the town Lahiru.

after the initial transaction, takes the form of a long letter that the administrator of Esagila wrote to the temple's assembly (*kiništu*) in 236 BC. Decades later it was copied onto clay tablets in the form of a speech delivered by him to the assembly of Esagila.[105] An assembly of that kind would have taken place in the 'house of counsel' (*bīt milki*) in the Juniper Garden.[106] As relations with Egypt deteriorated, the fortunes of the southern city of Uruk began to rise, while street fighting in Babylon in two separate years was recorded in astronomical diaries. Antiochus' mother Stratonice died during his reign in 254, and the sacrifices made on her behalf show that the king used the occasion for a very public memorial in Babylon.

Seleucus II inherited the kingship from his father. He had been brought up among powerful royal women who were each determined to secure the kingship for their respective sons. His kingship had to be confirmed in Uruk rather than Babylon owing to the civil war that had broken out between Seleucus and his brother. This marks a low point in Babylon's prestige. Uruk was the main rival to Babylon among the old cities of Mesopotamia, where Seleucus inaugurated a huge new temple dedicated to the Sky-gods Anu and Antu, and two top Babylonian officials took alternative Greek names. Uprisings, and an invasion at the beginning of his reign by Ptolemy III 'the Benefactor', to whom Seleucus was related by marriage, mark the beginning of the Third Syrian War. Ptolemy managed to reach Babylon and besieged it, but was pushed back and did not take the throne. While the Seleucid dynasty teetered on the edge of disaster, in the distant satrapy of Partha, the Parthians took the opportunity to establish their own dynasty with kings who took the name of their founder, Arsaces in 247/6. As a result, the Parthian dynasty is also known as the Arsacid dynasty. A new era for dating their own Parthian documents began at the same time, sometimes used alongside Seleucid-era dates on clay tablets.

The early Parthians were heavily bearded horsemen and archers, clad in baggy trousers, skilled riders with stirrups which enabled them to turn in the saddle at a gallop to deliver the Parthian (parting) shot behind them without losing control of their horse. They had fought with Darius III against Alexander, and some of their leaders later claimed descent from Artaxerxes II, which shows that their loyalties did not necessarily lie with the Seleucids. Their interest in Babylon was due to their passion for trade as they opened up routes between China and western Asia, across the wilds of central Asia, and hoped to benefit from access to Babylon and cities to the

---

[105] Jursa and Spar 2014: no. 148.   [106] Boiy 2004: 204; Clancier 2009: 182–5.

west. Jugglers, acrobats, and ostrich eggs were among their contributions to diplomatic relationships, but benefit from trade in silk was the main prize. Babylon was disrupted when the Parthians invaded Mesopotamia while Seleucid troops were fighting in the west, and uncertain times led to street fighting in Babylon. The finances of the city would have been depleted, but new wealth soon flowed in.

In 224 BC, soon after the accession of **Seleucus III**, the *šatammu* of Esagil offered eleven bulls, 1,000 ewes, and eleven ducks to Bēl and Bēltiya in honour of the new king and his sons, taking money from the royal treasury for the great gods as well as for Seleucus and his sons.[107] In those turbulent times exceptional measures were needed to re-establish loyalty and stability. The king celebrated the New Year Festival in Babylon at least once during his reign, and he subsidized it, showing how important that great ceremony was for reaffirming kingship and for keeping the *Epic of Creation* at the forefront of Babylonian myths.

His successor **Antiochus III** is known to have occupied the palace built by Nebuchadnezzar, and was living in Babylon when he was summoned to Antioch-on-the-Orontes for his coronation. A clay tablet records that a large wooden writing-board was used during his reign for writing down a sequence of astronomical observations for the astronomical diaries, which shows that clay tablets were not the only medium for that enormously important compilation.[108] In 205 BC he took part in the New Year Festival at Babylon, and at the end of his long reign he took part in rituals there. At the ceremony he was shown, or wore, the purple robes of Nebuchadnezzar II, and was presented with gold items and a crown weighing 1,000 gold shekels. He visited the Day One temple (perhaps a name for the temple of the New Year Festival), and travelled in ceremony to Borsippa and back to Babylon. These acts showed a commitment to piety and tradition. They linked the king to the great Nebuchadnezzar II and showed that Seleucid kings still accepted the city as a vital centre for divine worship connected to successful rule. From this reign onwards, offerings of an ox and some sheep for the great gods were made during the New Year Festival in Babylon for the well-being of the royal family.[109]

This was all the more necessary because Antiochus faced a serious rebellion led by a Persian satrap who managed to seize Seleucia-on-the-Tigris, a move that led to the Fourth Syrian War. Seleucid rule certainly extended beyond the shores of Babylonia into the Gulf and north-eastern Arabia, but it was impossible to defend the homeland in every direction at

---

[107] van der Spek 2016a: 27. [108] Mitsuma 2013: 54. [109] Mitsuma 2015.

once.[110] From the success of a naval expedition which demonstrated his control of the harbour on the Tigris, Antiochus enriched Babylon by receiving a tribute from Gerrha, a walled desert oasis, a remarkable city where families lived underground in dwellings carved out of salt rock to protect them from extremes of temperature. Its client king delivered to Antiochus 500 talents of silver, 1,000 talents of frankincense, and 200 talents of a superior type of myrrh – just one instance of how far-ranging was Antiochus' reputation, and how enormous the wealth from which Babylon profited, even while danger appeared close to home and elsewhere.

The harbour city of Alexandria in the eastern Sealand had been planned by Alexander the Great at the mouth of the Karun and the Tigris. Now renamed Antiochia, it was key to expanding Seleucid trade and political control throughout the Arabian Gulf, reflected in the icon of an anchor on Seleucid coins. It stood within the province of Elymais/Maysan, which could control the harbour. Antiochus was killed in Elymais after pillaging a temple of Bēl, far from his army's successes in the Fifth Syrian War against Egypt. During this period, a leader campaigning abroad whose funds were depleted would identify a wealthy temple to raid and refill his war chest.

Antiochus IV refounded the city of Babylon, probably giving it the new status of a *polis*, which would have given Greeks and Macedonians official citizenship.[111] He introduced a new colony of Greeks there, apparently with a separate administration. The Greek theatre with its adjoining gymnasium (*palaistra*) had been built using recycled bricks bearing an inscription of Nebuchadnezzar II. First built perhaps by Alexander, but certainly rebuilt on a larger scale after the refoundation of the city, it continued to be used, with several phases of rebuilding and enlargement, into the Parthian period.[112] Its decorative style was distinctly Greek and fragments of friezes found in plasterwork include a key pattern.[113]

Antiochus appointed a jeweller as the new bishop/administrator (*šatammu*), combining the role with the post of finance minister (*zazakku*). The very brief victory he won over Egypt in the Sixth Syrian War may have given a much-needed boost to Babylon's finances. Like his father, he died in the Sealand territory of Elymais. Babylon's new semi-Greek status did not allow the next three short-lived kings, one of them named after the

---

[110] Not only the island of Ikaros (Failaka), but also Gerrha (Thaj) on the mainland, a site within modern Kuwait. See, e.g., Kosmin 2013.

[111] Or possibly Antiochus III. Clancier 2009: 276.

[112] van der Spek 2001; Potts 2011. Neither of the two texts found there is closely datable.

[113] André-Salvini 2008: 263, pls. 211–13.

Macedonian hero Alexander, to neglect their duty to the temples. So they continued the dynasty, assailed by enemies in a much-reduced empire, including incursions from Parthians, leading to the successful invasion of 141 BC. Lower Babylonia – the Sealand – split into semi-independent groups. Meanwhile, businesses in Babylon continued to keep some records on clay, and astronomers recorded their work in cuneiform on clay, regularly producing astronomical diaries and chronicles strictly focused on Babylon. They, and some literary texts, survive in fragments. The fine wooden writing boards and parchment scrolls on which most records and much literature were now written, and the palm sticks, have long decayed and turned to dust, beyond recovery.[114]

---

[114] The *Uruk King-List* of kings and sages may have been written or copied at this time, as part of the effort made by Uruk to rival Babylon. Neujahr 2012: 50–7, prefers a date late in the reign of Nebuchadnezzar II for the original composition.

11 | First Parthian Conquest, 141 BC, to the Visit of Trajan in AD 116[1]

> Babylon, which is the capital of the Chaldean tribes, long held the highest renown among the cities in the whole world.
>
> Pliny, *Natural History* VI.xxx.121 (first century AD)

Late Seleucid Kings

Demetrius II 'Conqueror' (first reign 145–141, Babylon briefly occupied by Mithradates I)

Antiochus VII 'From the town Side' (138–129, Babylon briefly occupied by Phraates II)

Demetrius II (second reign 129–125, Babylon briefly occupied by Artabanus I)

Early Parthian and Other Kings, Some as Rulers in Babylon

(a selection of early kings from a Persian dynasty that lasted for c. 474 years)

Arsaces I (c. 247/8–217 founder of dynasty in Persia)

Mithradates I (171–139/8, interrupted rule in Babylon of Demetrius II)

Phraates II (139/8–128, interrupted rule in Babylon of Antiochus VII)

Artabanus I (128–124/3, Babylon briefly occupied by Hyspaosines)

    Hyspaosines of Elymais/Maysan (127–122)

    Hyspaosines as king in Babylon (124/3)

Mithradates II (124/3–88/7)

Gotarzes I 'Ox-crusher' (91/90–81/80)

Osroes (AD 108–27/8) interrupted in Babylon by Trajan

    Trajan Roman emperor in Babylon AD 116.

---

[1] The dates by years for the Parthian kings are taken from Wiesehöfer 2001: 317; but some uncertainties persist.

Seleucid rule began to break up when periodic invasions by Parthians and Elamites interrupted the dynastic line. It took the Parthians a long time to confirm their control over Babylon, so desirable for its wealth and trading connections. Information is sparse and confusing; occasionally Seleucids and Parthians appear to have reigned in Babylon during the same period.

When Parthia had broken free from Seleucid rule, it began its own system for dating years. The first year of the Arsacid Era corresponded to 247 BC, at the end of Antiochus II's rule in Babylon, long before Babylon received any Parthian king. The era's introduction by Arsaces I serves as a mark of intent, a challenge to the Seleucids and their era, and encouraged subsequent rulers to name themselves Arsaces, to the confusion of modern historians. The first Parthian victory over Babylon was short-lived, beaten back by the Seleucid king. Not until 141 BC was a more or less continuous dynasty established in the city, marked by Mithradates I, who celebrated a New Year Festival in Babylon, dutifully respecting the city's ancient traditions. The tradition of composing chronicles and astronomical diaries continued, independent of changes of power. Frequent skirmishes between Seleucids and Parthians are recorded in the astronomical diaries, which can be put into a chronological sequence whenever the state of preservation of the clay tablets allows. Parthian rule in Babylon survived the death of Mithradates and continued for ten years under Phraates II until Antiochus VII regained the city; cuneiform documents from Babylon and other cities were often dated by both eras.

Hyspaosines' independence as ruler of Maysan in the deep south of Babylonia combined a local revival of south-eastern Sealand and of Elamite power, reflected in Elymais, one of the names of his kingdom.[2] In 133, not long before he claimed independence, serious trouble had arisen in Babylon when a man proposed a new cult of Bēl-Marduk which was opposed by the temple hierarchy. Turmoil followed, encouraging rebellion elsewhere. In that year Hyspaosines 'plundered the harbour of ships together with their possessions'. Taking control of Alexander's great harbour on the Tigris, he renamed it Charax Spasinou after himself, in a ceremony attended by a Babylonian astrologer, and 'restored' it, as had Antiochus V twenty-five years earlier.[3] As an independent and successful leader of a trading kingdom, he minted his own coins in a style similar to that of the Seleucid kings; his face on the obverse is unmistakably clean-shaven, as if based on Greek custom. A Greek inscription discovered on

---

[2] His kingdom was variously known as Characene, Elymais, and Maysan.
[3] Its previous names had been first Alexandria and second Antiochia.

Bahrain indicates that he ruled the island (ancient Dilmun) and Failaka (ancient Agarum, Greek Ikaros), as the Seleucids had done before him.[4] In appreciation of his long heritage, he took ancient statues of the Sumerian governor Gudea and installed them in his own palace at Telloh, a city whose history went back to Sumerian times. Gudea had been one of the greatest writers of literary Sumerian and had ruled the area in the late third millennium BC. There were still scholars in Babylon and Uruk who could read his inscriptions, though Hyspaosines wrote his own brick and coin inscriptions in Aramaic.[5] Hyspaosines briefly took the title 'king of Babylon' in 124/3 before he was pushed out by a short-lived Parthian claimant, whose successor Mithradates II had a powerful rival to Babylon's throne in the 'satrap of satraps' Gotarzes. The latter changed his name to Arsaces when Mithradates died, claiming a link with the founder of the Parthian dynasty. Thus Babylon was still a magnet for usurpers early in the last century BC.

The Greek theatre in Babylon was completely rebuilt in brick as before under Mithradates II, who had taken the throne shortly after Hyspaosines in c. 121 BC.[6] The **expenditure** implies interest and prosperity. Whether the theatre was used for staged entertainments is not known, but astronomical diaries locate the public announcement of royal decrees and results of battles there. In accordance with the popularity of athletic competitions in Greek society, a list of winners of such competitions, written in Greek on clay, is dated c. 109 BC. It implies that athletic competitions were publicly valued under Parthian rule. But they had also been held in Assyria (the race of Nabu, known from seventh-century Nineveh) and in Egypt, so one should not put too much emphasis on the Greek nature of the activity.

Babylon's name was not changed. Greek authors attest that it was still used as a royal residence for Parthian kings, and that is confirmed by cuneiform texts found there. No change in the architectural style of temples is known, so presumably repairs and rebuilding followed traditional practice. The layout of processional streets and gateways, the temple of Ishtar-of-Babylon – rebuilt by Apil-Sin in the nineteenth century BC – all survived into the Parthian period.[7] The temple of the New Year Festival is mentioned in the astronomical diary for 80 BC, and in 78 BC the temple of Nabu-of-Vats, where the royal sceptre was given to the king during the

---

[4] Kosmin 2013.   [5] Clancier 2011: 761.

[6] Or Mithradates III. The discovery of a gymnasium at Jebel Khalid, a late Seleucid garrison town on the Middle Euphrates, supports the view that gymnasia were more common than used to be supposed. See Clarke and Connor 2016: V, ch. 3.

[7] Boiy 2004: 81–92.

New Year Festival. The street layout in the Merkes area, which had been unchanged since at least the time of Nabopolassar, still had its well-built, spacious houses, having continued to enjoy prosperity throughout the Achaemenid and Seleucid periods. Many rich tombs have been found there. Offerings to the great gods for the well-being of the king or a top official were continued by at least one Parthian king, still recorded on clay in cuneiform.[8] Long after Nebuchadnezzar II had built the first version of the Summer Palace high up on the edge of the citadel, Greek roof tiles with decorative antefixes giving the building a Mediterranean appearance replaced a local style of roofing, creating a small but significant change in the skyline.[9] The place where Alexander died would have attracted pilgrims at least from the late Seleucid period, providing a source of revenue; a revival of interest in Alexander's heroic achievements in the mid-second century is suggested by the choice of royal names Demetrius and Alexander rather than Seleucus and Antiochus at that time.

In the 1860s the French consul in Baghdad, Louis Delaporte, had made the discovery of a Parthian hypogeum containing five tombs which included a brick of Nebuchadnezzar II (highly prized), cylinder seals of various earlier periods, vases, a tripod, lamps, terracotta figurines and masks. Rubies were found as inserts in the eyes and navel of an alabaster statuette representing a naked goddess crowned with a bronze lunar crescent; rubies were also found on the site of Gerrha in north-east Arabia, upstaging the carnelian popular as a red gemstone in earlier times.[10] The contents of the tomb were reassembled in Paris for a striking display within the exhibition on Babylon at the Louvre.[11]

New kinds of texts were produced on clay by Babylon's scholars: the ephemerides and procedure texts which predict, by mathematical formulae, dates of lunar and planetary phenomena, and describe the methods for making the calculations; summaries of predicted events for a single year; almanacs that tried to predict celestial phenomena from observations taken in the preceding relevant period. Wide-ranging discussion and rivalry between scholars in Babylonian and Greek traditions show that the early Parthian period was a dynamic time for the development of astronomy.[12]

At least three archives written in cuneiform on clay tablets have been identified in museum collections as texts from Babylon dated to this period. One is the Archive of Rahimesu, from the early first century BC, relating to

[8] Mitsuma 2015.   [9] See Andre-Salvini 2008: 262 photo no. 209.   [10] Al-Zahrani 2011: 172.
[11] André-Salvini 2013: 196, fig. 10.
[12] Clancier 2009: 233–7. They contradict the old view that rigid, conservative scholars were dying out in a temple no longer relevant internationally.

transactions carried out in silver for the temple of the goddess Gula – which in itself is a sign of continuing worship in a temple or shrine in Babylon. Those records also refer to the temple Eturkalama of 'the Lady of Babylon'. Some of the tablets are thought from their contents to come from the Esagila temple. Another is the Archive of Mušēzib, a family of astrologers; it includes both literary and archival texts. Especially unexpected is a scholarly exercise, copying from an inscription on alabaster, a letter-order of the Assyrian king Ashurbanipal requesting that tablets be sent from Babylon and Borsippa for his library at Nineveh. The response to that letter has also been found. This shows that scribes were still interested in and taught about the deeds of Ashurbanipal, and they knew that he had taken cuneiform texts from Babylonian cities to his library at Nineveh.[13] A third archive or group of tablets consists of astronomical diaries and related texts.[14] Some of the late tablets give evidence that documents written in Aramaic and in Greek were used in parallel.[15]

Many famous works from much earlier times were still studied, such as the Sumerian *Lament Over Sumer and Ur*, written around 1,700 years earlier, now recopied in 287/6 BC. This shows that it is not necessarily mistaken to look for echoes of very early literature in later compositions. The last-known astronomical diary was written on clay in 61 BC, but other astronomical texts continued until at least AD 41–2. As was mentioned in the previous chapter, purely mathematical texts on Babylonian astronomy could be transferred easily into other languages, since numbers do not represent the same complications as words written in cuneiform.

At Uruk the copying of texts was thought to have come to an end around 168 BC, much earlier than in Babylon, until an almanac text from Uruk was found dated to AD 79/80, about four years later than one from Babylon dated AD 74/5.[16] The discovery illustrates the peril of drawing grand conclusions from scanty information.

The following list of texts shows how broad a range was still available on clay in Babylon under early Parthian rule:

A copy of *Plough Star* (*Mul.Apin*) was made on clay in Babylon at the beginning of the second century BC.[17]

When Anu and Enlil (*Enūma Anu Enlil*) was copied continuously until at least the first century BC.[18]

The latest known fragment from the *Epic of Gilgamesh* is dated c. 127 BC.[19]

---

[13] Frame and George 2005.   [14] Boiy 2004: 187.   [15] Hackl 2016.
[16] Hunger and de Jong 2014.   [17] Hunger and Steele 2018: 130.   [18] Fincke 2016: 119.
[19] George 2003: 740 with n. 11.

A copy of the wisdom text *A Poor Forlorn Wren* dates to 69 BC.[20]

A copy of *Tintir*, which lists the temples, streets, and gates of Babylon, was made in 61/60 BC.

A prayer to Marduk was copied from a text in Babylon in 34 BC.[21]

For sure they could no longer be read centuries later when the Neoplatonist philosopher Damascius, who became head of a school of philosophy at Athens around AD 515, knew the substance and perhaps the whole text of the *Epic of Creation*, presumably from the Greek translation made by Eudemus in the time of Alexander the Great. Damascius would have inherited the interests of Eudemus, who had been a highly rated pupil of Aristotle at the Lyceum School in Athens. That link was made in the time of Berossus, when Babylonian and Greek texts could both be read with relative ease in Babylon.

Among undated texts are the intriguing bilingual Graeco-Babylonian Tablets. They represent the extreme difficulties of transferring Babylonian cuneiform texts into a Greek alphabet. A very approximate date in the first or second century AD has been suggested.[22] The bilingual tablets may have been written by Babylonians to try out the Greek alphabet as a phonetic representation of some established cuneiform texts such as *Tintir*. Such a rendering might have had a magical or liturgical value, allowing a Greek-speaking participant to learn and recite a text required for the sufferer who followed an itinerary of sacred stations in *The Poem of the Righteous Sufferer*:[23]

> I, who had descended to the grave, entered the Gate of the Rising Sun again.
> In the Gate of Abundance, …
> In the Gate of the … Divine Guardian, my tutelary god (*lamassu*) approached me.
> In the Gate of Health, I encountered Health.
> In the Gate of Life, I was granted Life.
> In the Gate of the Rising Sun, I was counted among the living.
> In the Gate of Bright Amazement, my signs became clear.
> In the Gate of Release from Guilt, my binding was undone.
> In the Gate of Praise, my word became thoughtful.
> In the Gate of Release from Sighing, my sighing was removed.
> In the Gate of Pure Water, I was sprinkled with water of purification.

---

[20] Jiménez 2017: 330.   [21] Oshima 2011: 83.

[22] Boiy 2004: 292; Maul 1991; George 1997a: Appendix, 137–43. Clancier 2009: 247 rejects Geller's very late dating, as others have done.

[23] Oshima 2011: 65–8.

In the Gate of Health, I met Marduk.

In the Gate of Sprinkling Abundance, I kissed the feet of Zarpanitu.[24]

Diogenes 'of Babylon' (c. 240–152 BC), who was head of the Stoa in Athens, made a visit to Rome in 156/5, as recorded by Cicero. The name Diogenes is Greek, but there are a few well-known examples of elite Babylonians using both a Greek and a Babylonian name.[25] Some recent scholars, assuming that cuneiform traditions had died out by the time of that visit, have supposed that 'Babylon' stands for Seleucia-on-the-Tigris, but the hyper-correction is unnecessary in view of the evidence for scholarship in Babylon continuing for at least a century after Diogenes' lifetime. New evidence for one of his writings has come to light in papyri found at Herculaneum, where a long summary of his work on music has been identified.[26] In Athens, as Pliny asserts, Berossus was hugely admired as an astronomer 'to whom, due to his marvellous predictions, the Athenians publicly erected in the gymnasium a statue with a "gilded tongue"',[27] which stood in the company of statues of other famous men, all with Greek names: Berossus was the only foreigner.

The fact that cuneiform scholarship continued into the last century BC may also support the possibility that genuine Babylonian material underlies one of the Sibylline oracles, and Berossus' supposed connection with that tradition.[28]

The difference between Babylonian and Greek philosophy is tradition-ally judged to be so wide that Seleucid Greek rule brought the reason and logic of Hellenism to Mesopotamia, where the old superstitions of divin-ation and astrology were supposedly replaced or overlaid by new and better ways of thinking. The idea that reason and logic, from Greek culture onwards, constituted a 'cognitive superpower' is questioned by scholars of several disciplines, epitomized by Charles F. Kettering (1876–1958):

'Logic is an organized way of going wrong with confidence'.

The need to gain the confidence to make decisions and arrive at the truth is crucial for both Babylonian divination and Socratic dialogues: confi-dence wins battles and inhibits indecision with the assurance that the gods in heaven are giving support.[29] The Seleucid period in Babylon shows no evidence for Greek influence on literature, ritual, astronomy, or architec-ture (until the theatre was built and the Summer Palace reroofed with tiles). Meanwhile, there is much evidence for Greek interest in Babylonian

---

[24] Tablet IV, 38–51.   [25] See, e.g., Beaulieu 1998–2001; Boiy 2005.   [26] See Janko 2002: 32.
[27] Pliny, *Natural History* VII.37.123.   [28] See Chapter 10, p. 303.
[29] Maul 2018: 253–7; Mercier and Sperber 2017: 4, 197–9.

divination at the highest level, as is clear from the deeds of Xenophon and Alexander.[30] The great cuneiform compendia, which served as databases for Babylonian astronomers and diviners, and the rituals for averting a predicted calamity continued into the Parthian period with no evidence of Greek intrusions. On the contrary, some knowledge of Babylonian astronomy was perpetuated through Ptolemy and other scholars who wrote in Greek.[31] Early Greek reasoning and logic are characterized by the Socratic dialogues, a format for probing questions of ethics and the good life in a discussion. The dialogue format in general is found, for example, in Sumerian (*The Instructions of Shuruppak*) and Babylonian (*Counsels of Wisdom* and *Theodicy*), while Plato's dialogue *Cratylus* shows a technique of philological argument which has been found in much earlier Babylonian compositions.[32]

The cult of Bēl spread widely beyond Babylon to prosperous cities. On the Orontes at Antioch, the defeat of the sea representing Chaos, displayed in public in the famous statue by Eutychides, refers to a local adaptation of the *Epic of Creation* (see Chapter 10), and the motif was adapted to other cities in other media. At Dura Europus a temple to Bēl was founded in 33 BC; there a precious dupondius (a coin made of the yellow metal orichalcum) for Severus Alexander, Roman emperor from AD 222 to 235, was found showing the same motif.[33] Within the temple an internal wall was decorated with a painting showing a priest officiating in the tall white hat characteristic of 'Chaldean' priests, recognizable also on a stone altar found at Killiz north of Aleppo. At Apamea-on-the-Orontes, a stone altar was dedicated to Bēl;[34] the city was famous for its Chaldean Oracles that were quoted and commented on by Neoplatonist philosophers during the Roman empire.

Babylon was still important enough in AD 24/5 to attract merchants from Palmyra 'who are in Babylon'; these men dedicated a statue from which an inscribed fragment has been found in Palmyra, where the huge temple had been dedicated to Bēl in AD 32.[35] Within the building a stone relief sculpture on an internal wall showed a scene from the *Epic of Creation* in Roman dress where Tiamat, sea goddess of Chaos, was recognizable by her snaky lower body.[36] Because Palmyra was so splendidly built in stone in the Roman period, visitors and scholars alike have assumed that it had no earlier history; the discovery of a clay tablet from the second millennium

[30] Maul 2018: 219.   [31] See Pingree 1998: ch. 6, 125–37 for detailed information.
[32] Erler 2011; Jiménez 2018: 87–105.   [33] Kosmin 2011: pl. 28.
[34] Dalley and Reyes 1998: 122 gives illustrations.   [35] Boiy 2004: 54
[36] For different ways of representing Tiamat in art, see Heffron and Worthington 2012.

Figure 11.1 Plaque of Palmyra limestone from Dura Europus, temple of Fortune (Gadde) AD 159, showing the goddess of Fortune on a lion throne being crowned victor over Chaos, who is shown as a woman offering her right breast, with lower body submerged in water. The motif is derived from a version of the *Epic of Creation*. Credit: by kind permission of Yale University Museum, accession 1938.5313.

BC, and references to the city as Tadmor in other cuneiform texts tell a different story, showing that a mud-brick oasis town existed long before the imposing stone structures covered it. In Elymais a temple of Bēl was looted by Antiochus III in 187 BC. On the Aegean island of Kos, where Berossus had settled late in life, Palmyrenes dedicated an altar to Bēl of Tadmor.[37] In Hatra, the wonderful city in the desert west of the Tigris which Trajan failed to conquer, the temple of the Sun-god was called Esagila, probably early in the second century AD. At Edessa (modern Urfa) the defeated figure of Chaos, represented in one case as a female offering a breast, is found on coins where Syriac texts affirm that a New Year Festival was still celebrated among a largely Christian population.[38] Nabu (Nebo in Syriac) was the

---

[37] See Dalley 1998: 115, fig. 55, inscribed in Aramaic and Greek.
[38] Segal 1970: 52–3. For more examples on coins, see Dalley 2014: 70–1.

Figure 11.2 Part of a stone frieze from inside the temple of Bēl at Palmyra, showing a heroic scene in Roman dress. Victory as an archer in a chariot defeats Chaos as a female (?) with snaky lower parts. The motif is derived from a version of the *Epic of Creation*. Credit: Marion Cox† after Seyrig 1934 pl. 20.

hero-god who participated in a version of that great myth, which shows how the Babylonian epithet Bēl ('Lord'), was transferable to fit local tradition, hinting at the assimilation of two great Babylonian gods.[39]

Long after the Assyrian empire came to an end, the people of Ashur, Nineveh, and Erbil had their own versions, in different languages, of a New Year Festival with appropriate calendars and public architecture. In the many cities where a cult dedicated to Bēl persisted, a variety of versions of the *Epic of Creation* in liturgical use would have been known; iconography supplements alphabetic texts as evidence.

In the mid-first century AD the Roman emperor Nero spent four million sesterces on Babylonian coverlets for sumptuous dining, testifying to the reputation of Babylonian textiles and the existence of a thriving industry, especially for pattern weaving.[40] Babylon's theatre was repaired in the second century AD. As late as the third century, five temples remained in Babylon, when Jewish communities lived in the city.[41] The Greek traveller Pausanias, writing in the second century AD, described Babylon as inhabited only by priests, but the dating of repairs on the theatre implies that he, like other Greek and Roman visitors, misinterpreted the rubble-strewn streets and brick walls with crumbling plaster, the hole in the ground where the great ziggurat had stood, for ruin and abandonment.

---

[39] Pomponio 1998–2001.   [40] Pliny, *Natural History* VIII.lxxiv.196.   [41] Boiy 2004: 189.

The Summer Palace was still a place to visit where the ghost of Alexander lingered. In AD 116 the Roman emperor **Trajan** briefly took control of Babylonia and paid a visit to Babylon in order to pay homage to the place where his great hero Alexander had died. The hero's body, embalmed by Egyptians in Babylon, had eventually been taken to Alexandria in Egypt, but knowledge of his deathbed in Babylon still lived on, 439 years later. Trajan 'had gone there both because of its fame – though he saw nothing but mounds and stones and ruins to justify this – and because of Alexander, to whose spirit he offered sacrifice in the room where he had died'.[42] Babylon had become a place of pilgrimage dedicated to the Macedonian king of Babylon; the design of the antefixes predates Trajan's visit by at least two centuries, which suggests that pilgrims were already coming long before he came to make his offering. The foreign visitor could still enter the palace of Nebuchadnezzar II and make a sacrifice there.

By AD 116, very few if any clay tablets were still in use, and Romans who came to Mesopotamia would have had no knowledge of Babylon's literature, apart from its astronomical observations and divinatory practices. Its libraries and archives now lay far beneath the ground, awaiting discovery by travellers 1,500 years later. For the Romans, ancient literature was Greek, written with an alphabetic script from which their own was derived, and they modelled their own literature on that of ancient Greeks. The rich culture of Babylon, so closely linked to its cuneiform writing system, had vanished.

[42] Cass. Dio LXVIII.30; Wetzel, Schmidt, and Mallwitz 1957: 24 and pl. 23c.

Appendix: Genesis 14:1–16 and Possible Links with Foreign Rulers Early in the Reign of Hammurabi

The background to this appendix is given in Chapter 3. Over half a century ago many scholars thought that there were references to Babylonian history in the Hebrew Book of Genesis 14:1–16, including the garbled names of kings known from cuneiform texts in the time of Hammurabi.[1] A reaction then arose, dominating the subject and solving the problems by simply rejecting them. However, as many more texts became available, particularly those excavated at Mari, a return to the earlier view was suggested by Jean-Marie Durand based on the possible identification of the name Arioch with Arriuk.[2] In support of this, one can now suggest identifying Tidal not as the historical Hittite king Tudhaliya, but as a very high-ranking man in pre-Hittite times, as described below. The first element *chedor-* in the English translation of the Hebrew as Chedor-laomer has been linked to the Elamite *kudur-*, but the second element, *laomer*, has still not been identified among several names of Elamite leaders in the eighteenth-century texts, found mainly at Mari, Tell al-Rimah, Shemshara, Tell Leilan, and Kanesh. This is not surprising, since there were several concurrent Elamite leaders in that period. They are often referred to by their title, such as 'grand vizier', rather than by name.

The first part of the episode in Genesis 14:1–9 is given here in the translation of the Jerusalem Bible:

> It was in the time of **Amraphel** king of **Shinar**, **Arioch** king of **Ellasar**, **Chedor-laomer** king of **Elam**, and **Tidal** king of the **Goiim**.
>
> These made war on Bera king of Sodom, Birsha king of Gomorrah, Shinab king of Admah, Shemeber king of Zeboiim, and king of Bela (that is, Zoar).
>
> These latter all banded together in the Valley of Siddim (that is, the Salt Sea).

---

[1] For a translation of the supposed texts, see Foster 2005: 369–75.　　[2] See Durand 2005.

For twelve years they had been under the yoke of Chedor-laomer, but in the thirteenth year they revolted.

In the fourteenth year Chedor-laomer arrived and the kings who were on his side. They defeated the Rephaim at Asteroth-karnaim, the Zuzim at Ham, the Emim in the plain of Kiriathaim, the **Horites** in the mountainous district of Seir as far as El-paran, which is on the edge of the wilderness.

Wheeling round, they came to the Spring of Judgement (that is, Kadesh); they conquered all the territory of the Amalekites and also the **Amorites** who lived in Hazazon-tamar.

Then the kings of Sodom, Gomorrah, Admah, Zeboiim and Bela (that is, Zoar) marched out and took up battle positions against them in the Valley of Siddim, against Chedor-laomer king of Elam, Tidal king of the Goiim, Amraphel king of Shinar and Arioch king of Ellasar: four kings against five!

Amraphel	Either Hammurabi with an unexplained suffix -*el*, or Amud-pi-El, king of Qaṭna, with the common misreading of the letter *r* for *d*; possibly a confusion of the two names.
Shinar	The place name Shinar, as the name of the western Kassite tribe Šamharu, later used for Babylonia in general, is already attested by the sixteenth century.[3]
Arioch	Arriuk, who served the Elamites in Upper Mesopotamia, and ruled from Kawalhum (later Kalhu, Nimrud) on the Upper Tigris.[4]
Ellasar	Possibly Ilansura, which may have been located at modern Hasankeyf on the Upper Tigris.[5]
Chedor-laomer	Long recognized as a rendering of an Elamite name, perhaps Kudur-Lagamar, but not currently found as a name for one of the many Elamite rulers of any period. The Elamites appear to have had several concurrent 'rulers' in the time of Hammurabi.
Elam	The Babylonian name for the kingdoms of south-western Iran, based largely on Susa.
Tidal	New evidence for identifying Tidal, long recognized as an abbreviation for the Hittite royal name Tudhaliya, is

[3] See Wilhelm 2009–11.   [4] See Charpin and Ziegler 2003: 226.
[5] See Eidem and Ristvet 2011: 25–6 and Astour 1992.

found on a clay tablet from the pre-Hittite Assyrian merchant colony at Kanesh. He was a 'chief cupbearer', which is a title for a military leader.[6] At that time Kanesh was conquered by Pithana, king of the unidentified city Kuššara, home to the ancestors of the earliest Hittite kings. Pithana was a contemporary of Hammurabi and Samsu-iluna; his inscribed seal has been recognized on a tablet found at Tell al-Rimah.[7]

Goiim
: The Goiim 'peoples' in biblical Hebrew may refer to pre-Hittites, Hurrians, and others groups in central Anatolian city states.[8]

Horites
: Hurrians, known from the late third millennium in northern Mesopotamia.

Amorites
: These originally West Semitic people connect the biblical text with the period of Babylon's first dynasty. Subsequently, the term fell out of use.

Other Mesopotamian themes, not necessarily from the time of Hammurabi's dynasty, found in Genesis and recognized as Babylonian, are the stories of the Flood and the Tower of Babel.

In Syria and Palestine, evidence for the importance of Qaṭna has been uncovered in excavations. Finds of cuneiform texts at Haṣor, Megiddo, and Hebron indicate knowledge of Babylonian there.

The apparent identification of names found in cuneiform texts of Hammurabi's time, and the episode in Genesis, as already suggested by Durand in 2005, has been strengthened by subsequent research. It would support an element in the 'documentary hypothesis' which claims that some biblical text incorporates reworked records written originally beyond Palestine.

[6] See Wilhelm 2014–16 and Barjamovic et al. 2012: 39, text Kt 89/K 379.
[7] See Lacambre and Nahm 2015 and Langlois 2017: 35–6.   [8] See Schachner 2011: 56–68.

Bibliography

Abbreviations

AOAT	Alter Orient und Altes Testament
ARM	Archives Royales de Mari
CAD	Chicago Assyrian Dictionary for *The Assyrian Dictionary of the Oriental Institute of the University of Chicago*, ed. A. Oppenheim, E. Reiner et al., Chicago: Oriental Institute, 1956–2010
CDA	*A Concise Dictionary of Akkadian*, ed. J. Black, A. George, and N. Postgate. 2nd (corrected) printing. Wiesbaden: Harrassowitz, 2000
CDLI	Cuneiform Digital Library Initiative
CLeO	Classica et Orientalia
CUSAS	Cornell University Studies in Akkadian and Sumerian
ERC	Éditions Recherches sur les Civilisations
ETCSL	Electronic Text Corpus of Sumerian Literature
KUB	Keilschrifturkunden aus Boghazköi
NABU	*Nouvelles Assyriologiques Brèves et Utilitaires*
NINO	Nederlands Instituut voor het Nabije Oosten
OBO	Orbis Biblicus et Orientalis
OLA	Orientalia Lovaniensia Analecta
PNAE	*Prosopography of the Neo-Assyrian Empire*
RAI	Rencontre Assyriologique Internationale
RIMAP	Royal Inscriptions of Mesopotamia Assyrian Periods
RIMBP	Royal Inscriptions of Mesopotamia Babylonian Periods
RIMEP	Royal Inscriptions of Mesopotamia Early Periods
RlA	*Reallexikon der Assyriologie*
SAA	State Archives of Assyria
SBL	Society of Biblical Literature
SEPOA	Société pour l'étude du Proche-Orient Ancien
TIM	Texts in the Iraq Museum
VS	*Vorderasiatische Schriftdenkmäler der Staatlichen Museen zu Berlin*, 22 vols. Leipzig: J. C. Hinrich, 1907–17
WVDOG	Wissenschaftliche Veröffentlichung der Deutschen Orient-Gesellschaft

Abraham, K. and Gabbay, U. (2013) 'Kaštiliašu and the Sumundar Canal: A New Middle Babylonian Royal Inscription', *Zeitschrift für Assyriologie* 103: 183–95.

Abraham, K. and van Lerberghe, K. (2017) *A Late Old Babylonian Temple Archive from Dūr-Abiešuh. The Sequel*. CUSAS 29. Bethesda, MD: CDL Press.

Abu Assaf, A. (1992) 'Eine Alabastervase des Königs Salmanassar III im Nationalmuseum zu Damaskus', in *Von Uruk nach Tuttul. Eine Festschrift für Eva Strommenger*, ed. B. Hrouda, S. Kroll, and P. Spanos. Munich: Profil Verlag, 29–32.

Abusch, T. (2014) 'Notes on the History of Composition of Two Incantations', in *From Source to History: Studies on Ancient Near Eastern Worlds and Beyond, Dedicated to Giovanni Battista Lanfranchi*, ed. S. Gaspa, A. Greco, D. Morandi Bonacossi, S. Ponchia, and R. Rollinger. AOAT 412. Münster: Ugarit-Verlag, 1–10.

  (2019) 'Some Observations on the Babylon Section of *Enūma Eliš*', *Revue d'Assyriologie et d'archéologie orientale* 113: 171–3.

Adams, R. (1965) *Land Behind Baghdad*. Chicago: Oriental Institute Publications.

al-Qaddūmī, Ghāda al-Hijjāwī (1996) *Book of Gifts and Rarities: Selections Compiled in the Fifteenth Century from an Eleventh-century Manuscript on Gifts and Treasures*. Cambridge, MA: Harvard Centre for Middle Eastern Studies.

Al-Rawi, F. (1992) 'A New Hymn to Marduk from Sippir', *Revue d'Assyriologie* 86: 79–83.

Al-Rawi, F. and Dalley, S. (2000) *Old Babylonian Texts from Private Houses at Abu Habbah, Ancient Sippir*. London: NABU Publications.

al-Ṭabarī (1989) *History*, Vol. 1: *General Introduction and From the Creation*, trans. F. Rosenthal. Albany: State University of New York Press.

Altavilla, S. and Walker, C. (2016) *Late Babylonian Seal Impressions on Dated Tablets in the British Museum, Part 2 Babylon and Its Vicinity*. NISABA 28. Messina: Di.Sc.A.M.

Al-Ubaid, I. (1983) Unpublished Cuneiform Texts from Old Babylonian Period Diyala Region, Tell Muhammad. MA diss., Baghdad University.

Alvarez-Mon, J., Basello, G., and Wicks, Y. (eds.) (2018) *The Elamite World*. London: Routledge.

al-Zahrani, A. A. (2011) 'Thaj and the Kingdom of Gerrha', in *Roads of Arabia: The Archaeological Treasures of Saudi Arabia*, ed. U. Franke, A. Al-Ghabban, J. Gierlichs, and S. Weber. Exhibition catalogue, Museum für islamische Kunst. Berlin: Wasmuth, 168–75.

Ambos, C. (2005) 'Missverständnisse bei Ersatzkönigsritualen für Ashurbanipal und Alexander den Grossen', in *Die Welt der Rituale: von der Antike bis heute*, ed. C. Ambos, S. Hotz, G. Schwedler, and S. Weinfurter. Darmstadt: Wissenschaftliche Buchgesellschaft, 96–101.

(2009) 'Eunuchen als Thronprätendenten und Herrscher im alten Orient', in *Of Gods, Trees, Kings and Scholars: Neo-Assyrian and Related Studies in Honour of Simo Parpola*, ed. M. Luukko, S. Svärd, and R. Mattila. Helsinki University Press, 1–7.

(2013) *Der König im Gefängnis und das Neujahrsfest im Herbst. Mechanismen der Legitimation des babylonischen Herrschers im 1. Jahrtausend v. Chr. und ihre Geschichte*. Dresden: Islet.

André-Salvini, B. (2008) *Babylone. À Babylone, d'hier et d'aujourd'hui*. Exhibition catalogue. Paris: Hazan; Musée du Louvre.

(ed.) (2013) *La Tour de Babylone*. Rome: CNR-Louvre.

Annus, A. (2001) *The Standard Babylonian Epic of Anzu*. SAA Cuneiform Texts III. Helsinki University Press.

Archi, A. (2010) 'Hadda of Halab and His Temple in the Ebla Period', *Iraq* 72: 3–17.

Armstrong, J. and Brandt, M. (1994) 'Ancient Dunes at Nippur', in *Cinquante-deux Réflexions sur le Proche-Orient Ancien, offertes en hommage à Leon de Meyer*, ed. H. Gasche. Mesopotamian History and Environment Occasional Paper 2. Leuven: Peeters, 255–63.

Arnaud, D. (2007) 'Documents à contenu historique', *Aula Orientalis* 25/1: 5–84.

Aro, J. (1970) *Mittelbabylonische Kleidertexte der Hilprecht-Sammlung Jena*. Berlin: Akademie-Verlag.

Aruz, J., Benzel, K., and Evans, J. M. (eds.) (2008) *Beyond Babylon: Art, Trade, and Diplomacy in the Second Millennium B.C.* Exhibition catalogue, Metropolitan Museum of Art. New Haven, CT: Yale University Press.

Asher, A. (ed. and trans.) (1907) *The Itinerary of Rabbi Benjamin of Tudela*. New York: Hakesheth Publishing.

Astour, M. (1992) 'The North Mesopotamian Kingdom of Ilanṣura', in *Mari in Retrospect*, ed. G. Young. Winona Lake, IN: Eisenbrauns, 1–35.

Azoulay, V. (2004) 'Exchange and Entrapment: Mercenary Xenophon?', in *The Long March: Xenophon and the Ten Thousand*, ed. R. Lane Fox. New Haven, CT: Yale University Press, 289–304.

Badian, E. (2015) 'Mazaeus', *Encyclopaedia Iranica*, https://iranicaonline.org/articles/mazaeus.

Bahrani, Z. (2003) *The Graven Image*. Philadelphia University Press.

(2017) *Mesopotamia Ancient Art and Architecture*. London: Thames and Hudson.

Baker, H. (2004) *The Archive of the Nappāḫu Family*. Archiv für Orientforschung Beiheft 30. Vienna: Institut für Orientalistik der Universität Wien.

(2011a) 'Šamaš-šumu-ukin', in *PNAE*, Vol. 3, Part II: *Š–Z*, ed. H. D. Baker. Helsinki University Press.

(2011b) 'The Statue of Bēl in the Ninurta Temple at Babylon', *Archiv für Orientforschung* 52: 117–20.

Baker, H. and Pearce, L. (2001) 'Nabu-zuqup-kenu' in *PNAE*, Vol. 2, Part II: *L–N*, ed. H. D. Baker. Helsinki University Press.

Barberon, L. (2012) *Les religieuses et le culte de Marduk dans le royaume de Babylone*. Mémoires de NABU 14. Paris: SEPOA.

Bardet, G., Joannès, F., Lafont, B., Soubeyran, D., and Villard, P. (eds) (1984) *Archives administratives de Mari I*. ARM XXIII/1. Paris: ERC.

Barjamovic, G. and Larsen, M. (2008) 'An Old Assyrian Incantation against the Evil Eye', *Altorientalische Forschungen* 45: 144–55.

Barjamovic, G., Hertel, T., and Larsen, M. (2012) *Ups and Downs at Kanesh*. Leiden: NINO.

Barrelet, M.-T. (1977) 'Un inventaire de Kar-Tukulti-Ninurta', *Revue d'Assyriologie* 71: 51–92.

Barstad, H. (1996) *The Myth of the Empty Land: A Study in the History of Judah during the 'Exilic' Period*. Oslo: Scandinavian University Press.

Bartelmus, A. (2007) '*Talimu*: The Relationship between Aššurbanipal and Šamaš-šum-ukin', *SAA Bulletin* 16: 287–302.

   (2010) 'Restoring the Past: A Historical Analysis of the Royal Temple Building Inscriptions from the Kassite Period', *Kaskal* 7: 143–72.

Barth, R. (1969) *Ethnic Groups and Boundaries: The Social Organization of Culture Differences*. Oslo: Universitetsforlaget.

Beaulieu, P.-A. (1998) 'Ba'u-asītu and Kaššaya, daughters of Nebuchadnezzar II', *Orientalia* 67: 173–201.

   (1998–2001) 'Nikarchos', in *RlA*, Vol. 9, 315–16.

   (2005) 'Eanna's Contribution to the Construction of the North Palace at Babylon', in *Approaching the Babylonian Economy*, ed. H. Baker and M. Jursa. AOAT 330. Münster: Ugarit-Verlag, 45–73.

   (2006a) 'The Astronomers of the Esagil Temple in the 4th Century BC', in *If a Man Builds a Joyful House: Assyriological studies in honor of Erle V. Leichty*, ed. A. Guinan, M. de J. Ellis, A. Ferrara, S. Freedman, M. Lutz, L. Sassmannshausen, S. Tinney, and M. Waters. Cuneiform Monographs 31. Leiden: Brill, 5–22.

   (2006b) 'De l'Esagil au Mouseion: l'organisation de la recherche scientifique au IVe siècle av. J.-C.', in *La Transition entre l'empire achéménide et les royaumes hellénistiques*, ed. P. Briant and F. Joannès. Persika 9. Paris: De Boccard, 17–36.

   (2014) 'An Episode in the Reign of the Babylonian Pretender Nebuchadnezzar IV', in *Extraction and Control: Studies in Honor of Matthew W. Stolper*, ed. M. Kozuh, W. Henkelman, C. Jones, and C. Woods. Chicago: Oriental Institute, 17–26.

   (2018a) 'Uruk before and after Xerxes: The Onomastic and Institutional Rise of the God Anu', in *Xerxes and Babylonia: The Cuneiform Evidence*, ed. C. Waerzeggers and M. Seire. OLA 277. Leuven: Peeters, 189–206.

   (2018b) *A History of Babylon 2200 BC–AD 75*. Chichester: Wiley-Blackwell.

Beaulieu, P.-A., Frahm, E., Horowitz, W., and Steele, J. (2018) *The Cuneiform Uranology Texts: Drawing the Constellations*. Philadelphia: American Philosophical Society Transaction.

Beckman, G. (1999) *Hittite Diplomatic Texts.* 2nd ed. Atlanta, GA: Society of Biblical Literature.

(2014) *The Babilili Ritual from Hattusa (CTH 718).* Winona Lake, IN: Eisenbrauns.

Bergamini, G. (1977) 'Levels of Babylon Reconsidered', *Mesopotamia XII*: 111–52.

(2013) 'Fondations dans l'eau', in *La Tour de Babylone*, ed. B. André-Salvini. Rome: CNR-Louvre, 43–64.

Biga, M. (2014) 'Inherited Space – Third Millennium Political and Cultural Landscapes', in *Constituent, Confederate and Conquered Space*, ed. E. Cancik-Kirschbaum and E. Christiane. Topoi 17. Berlin: de Gruyter, 93–110.

Biggs, R. (2000) 'Conception, Contraception, and Abortion in Ancient Mesopotamia', in *Wisdom, Gods and Literature: Studies in Assyriology in Honour of W. G. Lambert*, ed. A. George and I. Finkel. Winona Lake, IN: Eisenbrauns, 1–13.

Birot, M. (1974a) *Lettres de Yaqqim-Addu, gouverneur de Sagaratum.* ARM XIV. Paris: Geuthner.

(1974b) Review of J. J. Finkelstein, 1972, *Late Old Babylonian Documents and Letters*, Yale Oriental Series XIII, *Bibliotheca Orientalis* 31: 271–2.

(1993) *Correspondance des Gouverneurs de Qaṭṭunân.* ARM XXVII. Paris: ERC.

Birot, M., Kupper, J.-R., and Rouault, O. (1979) *Répertoire analytique I: Noms propres.* ARM XVI/1. Paris: Geuthner.

Black, J., Cunningham, G., Robson, E., and Zólyomi, G. (2004) *The Literature of Ancient Sumer.* Oxford University Press.

Blocher, F. (1988) 'Einige altbabylonische Siegelabrollungen aus Kiš im Louvre', *Revue d'Assyriologie* 82: 33–46.

(2012) 'Zum Zweck der Bastion Warad-Sins in Ur', in *Stories of Long Ago: Festschrift für Michael D. Roaf*, ed. H. Baker, K. Kaniuth, and A. Otto. Münster: Ugarit-Verlag, 45–56.

Böck, B. (2013) 'Medicinal Plants and Medicaments Used for Conception, Abortion, Fertility Control in Ancient Babylonia', *Journal Asiatique* 301/1: 27–52.

Boiy, T. (2004) *Late Achaemenid and Hellenistic Babylon.* Leuven: Peeters.

(2005) 'Akkadian-Greek Double Names in Hellenistic Babylonia', in *Ethnicity in Ancient Mesopotamia*, Papers read at the 48th RAI 2002, ed. R. Kalvelagen and D. Katz. Leiden: NINO, 47–60.

(2010) 'Temple Building in Hellenistic Babylonia', in *From the Foundations to the Crenellations: Essays on Temple Building in the Ancient Near East and Hebrew Bible*, ed. M. Boda and J. Novotny. AOAT 366. Münster: Ugarit-Verlag, 211–19.

(2012) 'The Birth of an Era', in *The Ancient Near East, A Life! Festschrift Karel van Lerberghe*, ed. T. Boiy, J. Bretschneider, A. Goddeeris, H. Hameeuw, G. Jans, and J. Tavernier. OLA 220. Leuven: Katholieke Universiteit, 43–58.

Boiy, T. and Verhoeven, K. (1998) 'Arrian, *Anabasis* VII.21.1–4 and the Pallukkatu Canal', in *Changing Watercourses in Babylonia: Towards a Reconstruction of the Ancient Environment in Lower Mesopotamia*, ed. H. Gasche and M. Tanret. Mesopotamia History and Environment Series II Memoirs IV. Ghent: University of Ghent, 147–58.

Bonechi, M. (1991) 'Relations amicales syro-palestinennes: Mari et Haṣor au XVIIIe siècle', in *Florilegium marianum. Recueil d'études en l'honneur de Michel Fleury*, ed. J.-M. Durand. Mémoires de NABU 1. Paris: ERC, 9–22.

Bongenaar, A. (1999) 'Silver and Credit in Old Assyrian Trade', in *Trade and Finance in Ancient Mesopotamia*, ed. J. Dercksen. Leiden: NINO, 55–83.

Borger, R. (1979) *Babylonisch-Assyrische Lesestücke*, Vol. 1. 2nd ed. Rome: Pontifical Biblical Institute.

(2000) 'Šurpu II, III, IV and VIII in Partitur', in *Wisdom, Gods and Literature: Studies in Assyriology in Honour of W. G. Lambert*, ed. A. George and I. Finkel. Winona Lake, IN: Eisenbrauns, 15–90.

Börker-Klähn, J. (1982) *Altvorderasiatische Bildstelen und vergleichbare Felsreliefs.* Mainz: P. von Zabern.

Breniquet, C. and Michel, C. (2014) *Wool Economy in the Ancient Near East and the Aegean.* Oxford: Oxbow.

Breton, J.-F. (1999) *Arabia Felix from the Time of the Queen of Sheba: Eighth Century BC to First Century AD*, trans. Albert Lafarge. Notre Dame, IND: Notre Dame University Press.

Brinkman, J. (1969) 'Ur: The Kassite Period and the Period of the Assyrian Kings', *Orientalia* 38: 310–48.

Brinkman, J. A. (1976–80) 'Kassiten', in *RlA*, Vol. 5, 464–73.

(1980–3a) 'Pešgaldaramaš', in *RlA*, Vol. 10, 436.

(1980–3b) 'Marduk-zakir-šumi II', in *RlA*, Vol. 7, 379.

(1981–2) 'The Western Asiatic Seals Found at Thebes in Greece: A Preliminary Edition of the Inscriptions', *Archiv für Orientforschung*, 28: 73–7.

(1984) *Prelude to Empire: Babylonian Society and Politics, 747–626 B.C.* Philadelphia: Occasional Publications of the Babylonian Fund.

(1998–2001a) 'Nebuchadnezzar I', in *RlA*, Vol. 9, 192–4.

(1998–2001b) 'Nabu-naṣir', in *RlA*, Vol. 9, 5–6.

(2001) 'Assyrian Merchants at Dūr-Kurigalzu', *NABU* no. 73.

(2017) 'Babylonia under the Kassites: Some Aspects for Consideration', in *Karduniaš: Babylonia under the Kassites*, ed. A. Bartelmus and K. Sternitzke. Berlin: de Gruyter, 1–44.

Brisch, N. (2007) *Tradition and the Poetics of Innovation: Sumerian Court Literature of the Larsa Dynasty (c. 2003–1763 BCE).* AOAT 339. Münster: Ugarit-Verlag.

Brosius, M. (1996) *Women in Ancient Persia, 359–331 BC.* Oxford University Press.

Bryce, T. (2002) *Life and Society in the Hittite World.* Oxford University Press.

(2005) *The Kingdom of the Hittites.* 2nd ed. Oxford University Press.

Buchanan, B. (1966) *Catalogue of Ancient Near Eastern Seals in the Ashmolean Museum*, Vol. 1: *Cylinder Seals*. Oxford: Clarendon Press.

Çagirgan, G. and Lambert, W. (1991–3) 'The Late Babylonian Kislimu Ritual for Esagil', *Journal of Cuneiform Studies* 43–5: 89–106.

Calderbank, D., Robson, E., Shepperson, M., and Slater, F. (2017) 'Tell Khaiber: An Administrative Centre of the Sealand Period', *Iraq* 79: 21–46.

Campbell, S., Hauser, S., Killik, R., Moon, J., Shepperson, M., and Dolesalkova, V. (2018) 'Charax Spasinou: New investigations at the Capital of Mesene', *Zeitschrift für Orient Archäologie* 11: 212–39.

Cancik-Kirschbaum, E., van Ess, M., and Marzahn, J. (eds.) (2011) *Babylon: Wissenskultur in Orient und Okzident*. Topoi. Berlin Studies of the Ancient World 1. Berlin: de Gruyter.

Cathcart, K. (1994) 'Edward Hincks (1792–1866): A Biographical Essay', in *The Edward Hincks Bicentenary Lectures*, ed. K. Cathcart. University College Dublin, 1–29.

Cavigneaux, A. (2013) 'Les fouilles irakiennes de Babylone et le temple de Nabû-ša-hare', in *La Tour de Babylone*, ed. B. André-Salvini. Rome: CNR-Louvre, 65–76.

Charles, M. (1913) *The Books of Adam and Eve in the Apocrypha and Pseudepigrapha of the Old Testament in English*. Oxford: Clarendon.

Charpin, D. (1985) 'La chronologie des souverains d'Ešnunna', in *Miscellanea Babylonica. Mélanges offerts à Maurice Birot*, ed. J.-M. Durand and J.-R. Kupper. Paris: Editions Recherche sur les civilisations, 51–66.

(1986) *Le clergé d'Ur au siècle d'Hammourabi (XIXe–XVIIIe siècles av. J.-C.)*. Paris: Librairie Droz.

(1988) 'Lettres de Yarim-Addu à Zimri-Lim', in *Archives Epistolaires de Mari* 1/2, ed. D. Charpin, F. Joannès, S. Lackenbacher, and B. Lafont. ARMT XXVI/2. Paris: ERC, 159–86.

(1990) 'Une alliance contre l'Elam et le ritual du *lipit napištim*', in *Mélanges Jean Perrot*, ed. F. Vallat. Paris: ERC, 109–18.

(1995) 'La fin des archives dans le palais de Mari', *Revue d'Assyriologie* 89: 29–40.

(2000) 'Les prêteurs et le palais: les édits mîšarum des rois de Babylone et leurs traces dans les archives privées', in *Interdependency of Institutions and Private Entrepreneurs: Proceedings of the Second MOS Symposium*, ed. A. C. V. M. Bongenaar. Leiden: NINO, 185–211.

(2004) 'Histoire politique du Proche-Orient Amorrite (2002–1595)', in *Mesopotamien. Die altbabylonische Zeit, Annäherungen 4*. OBO 160/4. Fribourg: Academic Press, 25–480.

(2010) 'Un édit du roi Ammi-ditana de Babylone', in *on Göttern und Menschen. Beiträge zu Literatur und Geschichte des Alten Orients. Festschrift für Brigitte Groneberg*, ed. D. Shehata, F. Weiershäuser, and K. Zand. Cuneiform Monographs 41. Leiden: Brill, 17–46.

Charpin, D. and Durand, J.-M. (2013) 'La "suprématie élamite" sur les amorrites. Réexamen, vingt ans apres la XXXVIe RAI (1989)', in *Susa and Elam*, ed. K. de Graef and J. Tavernier. Leiden: Brill, 329–39.

Charpin, D. and Ziegler, N. (2003) *Mari et le Proche-Orient à l'époque amorrite: essai d'histoire politique*. Florilegium marianum V, Mémoires de NABU 6. Paris: SEPOA.

Chaverdi, A. and Callieri, P. (2017) 'Appendix: The Monumental Building of Tol-e Ajori', in *Persian Religion in the Achaemenid Period*, ed. W. Henkelman and C. Rédard. Wiesbaden: Harrassowitz, 394–7.

Civil, M. (2011) 'The Law Collection of Ur-Namma', in *Cuneiform Royal Inscriptions and Related Texts in the Schøyen Collection*, ed. A. George. CUSAS 17. Bethesda, MD: CDL Press, 221–86.

Clancier, P. (2009) *Les bibliothèques en Babylonie dans la deuxième moitié du 1er millénaire av. J.-C.* AOAT 363. Münster: Ugarit-Verlag.

  (2011) 'Cuneiform Cuture's Last Guardians: The Old Urban Notability of Hellenistic Uruk', in *Oxford Handbook of Cuneiform Culture*. ed. K. Radner and E. Robson. Oxford University Press, 752–73.

Clarke, G. and Connor, P. (2016) *Jebel Khalid on the Euphrates*, Vol. 5. Sydney University Press.

Clayden, T. (2011) 'Glass Axes of the Kassite Period from Nippur', *Zeitschrift für Orient-Archäologie* 4: 92–135.

Cline, E. (2014) *1177 B.C., The Year Civilization Collapsed*. Princeton University Press.

Cogan, M. and Tadmor, H. (1988) *II Kings: Anchor Bible Commentary*. New York: Doubleday.

Cohen, Y. (2012) 'Where Is Bazi, Where Is Zizi? The List of Early Rulers in the *Ballad* from Emar and Ugarit, and the Mari Rulers in the Sumerian King List and Other Sources', *Iraq* 74: 137–52.

  (2013) *Wisdom from the Late Bronze Age*. Atlanta, GA: Society of Biblical Literature.

  (2015) 'The Problem of Theodicy – The Mesopotamian Perspective', in *Colères et repentirs divins: actes du colloque organisé par le Collège de France, Paris, les 24 et 25 avril 2013*, ed. J.-M. Durand, L. Marti, and T. Römer. OBO 278. Fribourg: Academic Press, 243–70.

  (2018) 'Why "Wisdom"? Copying, Studying and Collecting Wisdom Literature in the Cuneiform World', in *Teaching Morality in Antiquity: Wisdom Texts, Oral Traditions, and Images*, ed. T. Oshima. Tübingen: Mohr Siebeck, 41–59.

  (2019) 'Cuneiform Writing in "Bronze Age" Canaan', in *The Social Archaeology of the Levant: From Prehistory to Present*, ed. A. Yasur-Landau, E. Cline, and M. Yorke. Cambridge University Press, 245–64.

Colbow, G. (1994) 'Abrollungen aus der Zeit Kaštiliašus', in *Beiträge zur altorientalishen Archäologie und Altertumskunde, Festschrift für Barthel Hrouda*, ed.

P. Calmeyer, K. Hecker, L. Jakob-Rost, and C. Walker. Wiesbaden: Harrassowitz, 61–6.

Cole, S. (1994) 'Marsh Formation in the Borsippa Region and the Course of the Lower Euphrates', *Journal of Near Eastern Studies* 53: 81–109.

(1996) *Nippur IV: The Early Neo-Babylonian Governor's Archive from Nippur.* Chicago: Oriental Institute.

Cole, S. and Machinist, P. (1998) *Letters from Priests to the Kings Esarhaddon and Assurbanipal.* SAA XIII. Helsinki University Press.

Colonna d'Istria, L. (2012) 'Epigraphes alphabétiques du pays de la Mer', *NABU* no. 3/48: 61–2.

Cook, S. (1903) *The Laws of Moses and the Code of Hammurabi.* London: A. and C. Black.

Cool Root, M. (1979) *King and Kingship in Achaemenid Art: Essays on the Creation of an Iconography of Empire.* Leiden: Brill.

Cooley, J. (2013) *Poetic Astronomy in the Ancient Near East.* Winona Lake, IN: Eisenbraun.

Cooper, J. (1991) 'Posing the Sumerian Question, Race and Scholarship in the Early History of Assyriology', *Aula Orientalis* 9: 47–66.

(1993) 'Sumerian and Aryan: Racial theory, Academic Politics and Parisian Assyriology', *Revue de l'histoire des Religions*, CCX/2: 169–205.

Dalley, S. (1995) 'Bel at Palmyra and Elsewhere in the Parthian Period', *ARAM* 7: 137–51.

(2001) Review of R. Mattila, *The King's Magnates*, *Bibliotheca Orientalis* 58: 197–206.

(2003) 'Why Did Herodotus Not Mention the Hanging Garden?', in *Herodotus and His World*, ed. P. Derow and R. Parker. Oxford University Press, 171–89.

(2005a) *Old Babylonian Texts in the Ashmolean Museum.* OECT XV. Oxford: Clarendon Press.

(2005b) 'The Language of Destruction and Its Interpretation', *Baghdader Mitteilungen* 36: 275–85.

(2007) *Esther's Revenge at Susa.* Oxford University Press.

(2009) *Babylonian Tablets from the First Sealand Dynasty in the Schøyen Collection.* CUSAS 9. Bethesda, MD: CDL Press.

(2010) 'Old Babylonian Prophecies at Uruk and Kish', in *Opening the Tablet Box: Near Eastern Studies in Honor of Benjamin R. Foster*, ed. S. Melville and A. Slotsky. Leiden: Brill, 85–97.

(2013a) *The Mystery of the Hanging Garden of Babylon.* Oxford University Press.

(2013b) 'Gods from North-Eastern and North-Western Arabia in Cuneiform Texts from the First Sealand Dynasty, and a Cuneiform Inscription from Tell en-Nasbeh, c. 1500 BC', *Arabian Archaeology and Epigraphy* 24/2: 177–85.

(2014) 'From Mesopotamian Temples as Sacred Groves to the Date-Palm Motif in Greek Art and Architecture', in *Le Jardin dans l'Antiquité: introduction et huit exposés suivis de discussions*, ed. K. Coleman with P. Derron. Fondation Hardt, Entretiens sur l'antiquité classique 60. Vandœuvres: Fondation Hardt, 53–80.

(2016) review of Andre-Salvini, *La Tour de Babylone*, *Bibliotheca Orientalis* 72: 751–5.

(2020) 'The First Sealand Dynasty: Literacy, Economy, and the Likely Location of Dur-Enlil(e) in Southern Mesopotamia at the End of the Old Babylonian Period', in *Studies on the First Sealand and Kassite Dynasties*, ed. S. Paulus and T. Clayden. Proceedings of the 2016 RAI, Philadelphia. Boston, MA: de Gruyter.

Dalley, S., Hawkins, J., and Walker, C. (1976) *Old Babylonian Tablets from Tell al-Rimah*. London: British School of Archaeology in Iraq.

Dalley, S. and Reyes, A. (1998) 'Mesopotamian Contact and Influence in the Greek World (2)', in *The Legacy of Mesopotamia*, ed. S. Dalley. Oxford University Press, 107–24.

Dalley, S., Reyes, A., Pingree, D., Salvesen. A. and McCall, H. (1998) *The Legacy of Mesopotamia*. Oxford University Press.

Dalley, S. and Yoffee, N. (1991) *Old Babylonian Texts in the Ashmolean Museum: Texts from Kish and Elsewhere*. Oxford Editions of Cuneiform Texts XIII. Oxford: Clarendon Press.

Dandamaev, M. (1998–2001) 'Nabonid A', in *RlA*, Vol. 9, 6–11.

Dandamaev, M. and Lukonin, V. (1989) *The Culture and Social Institutions of Ancient Iran*. Cambridge University Press.

Daniels, P. (1994) 'Edward Hincks's Decipherment of Mesopotamian Cuneiform', in *The Edward Hincks Bicentenary Lectures*, ed. K. Cathcart. University College Dublin, 30–57.

(1995) 'The Decipherment of Ancient Near Eastern Scripts', in *Civilizations of the Ancient Near East*, Vol. 1, ed. J. Sasson, J. Baines, G. Beckham, and K. S. Rubinson. New York: Scribners, 81–93.

Da Riva, R. (2008) *The Neo-Babylonian Royal Inscriptions: An Introduction*. Guides to the Mesopotamian Textual Record 4. Münster: Ugarit-Verlag.

(2012a) 'BM 67405 and the Cross Country Walls of Nebuchadnezzar II', in *The Perfumes of Seven Tamarisks: Studies in Honour of W. G. E. Watson*, ed. G. Del Olmo Lete, J. Vidal, and N. Wyatt. AOAT 394. Münster: Ugarit Verlag, 15–18.

(2012b) *The Twin Inscriptions of Nebuchadnezzar at Brisa (Wadi esh-Sharbin): A Historical and Philological Study*. Archiv für Orientforschung Beiheft 32. Vienna: Institut für Orientalistik der Universität Wien.

(2013a) 'Nebuchadnezzar II's Prism (ES 7834): A New Edition', *Zeitschrift fur Assyriologie* 103: 196–229.

(2013b) *The Inscriptions of Nabopolassar, Amel-Marduk, and Neriglissar*. Studies in Ancient Near Eastern Records 3. Berlin: de Gruyter.

(2014) 'Assyrians and Assyrian Influence in Babylonia (626–539 BCE)', in *From Source to History: Studies on Ancient Near Eastern Worlds and Beyond,*

Dedicated to Giovanni Battista Lanfranchi, ed. S. Gaspa A. Greco, D. Morandi Bonacossi, S. Ponchia, and R. Rollinger. AOAT 412. Münster: Ugarit-Verlag, 55–71.

(2017a) 'The Figure of Nabopolassar in Late Achaemenid and Hellenistic Historiographic Tradition: BM 34793 and CUA 90', *Journal of Near Eastern Studies* 76: 75–97.

(2017b) 'A New Attestation of Habigalbat in Late Babylonian Sources', *Welt des Orients* 472: 250–64.

Da Riva, R. and Frahm, E. (1999–2000) 'Šamaš-šum-ukin, die Herrin von Ninive und das babylonische Königssiegel', *Archiv für Orientforschung* 46–7: 156–82.

Darshan, G. (2016) 'The Calendrical Framework of the Priestly Flood Story in Light of a New Akkadian Text from Ugarit (RS 94.2953)', *Journal of the American Oriental Society* 136: 507–14.

de Boer, R. (2013) 'An Early Old Babylonian Archive from the Kingdom of Malgium?', *Journal Asiatique* 301/1: 19–25.

De Graef, K. (2013) 'The Use of Akkadian in Iran', in *Oxford Handbook of Ancient Iran*, ed. D. Potts. Oxford University Press.

de Jong, M. (2007) *Isaiah among the Ancient Near Eastern Prophets*. Leiden: Brill.

de Roos, J. (2006) 'Materials for a Biography: The Correspondence of Puduhepa' in *The Life and Times of Hattusili III and Tuthaliya IV*, ed. T. van den Hout. Leiden: NINO, 17–26.

Dercksen, J. and Pigott, V. (2017) 'Zinn', in *RlA*, Vol. 15, 301–4.

Devecchi, E. (2017) 'Of Kings, Princesses, and Messengers: Babylon's International Relations during the 13th Century', in *Karduniaš. Babylonia under the Kassites*, ed. A. Bartelmus and K. Sternitzke. Boston, MA: de Gruyter, 112–22.

Dietrich, M. (2003) *The Babylonian Correspondence of Sargon II and Sennacherib*. SAA XVII. Helsinki University Press.

Di Giorgi, A. (2016) *Ancient Antioch from the Seleucid Era to the Islamic Conquest*. Cambridge University Press.

Dillery, J. (2015) *Clio's Other Sons: Berossus and Manetho*. Ann Arbor: University of Michigan Press.

Dio Cassius (2014) *Roman History*, Vol. 7: *Books 61–70*, trans. E. Cary. Loeb Classical Library 176. Cambridge, MA: Harvard University Press.

Diodorus Siculus (1933) *Library of History*, Vol. 1, trans. C. H. Oldfather. Loeb Classical Library 279. Cambridge, MA: Harvard University Press.

Dirven, L. (2015) 'Horned Deities of Hatra: Meaning and Origin of a Hybrid Phenomenon', *Mesopotamia* 50: 243–60.

Dossin, G. (1978) *Correspondance féminine*. ARM X. Paris: Librairie orientaliste Paul Geuthner.

Drewes, A. and Ryckmans, J. (2016) *Les inscriptions sudarabes sur bois dans la collection de l'Oosters Instituut conservée dans la bibliothèque universitaire de Leiden*. Wiesbaden: Harrassowitz.

Durand, E. (1880) 'Extracts from Report on the Islands and Antiquities of Bahrein', *Journal of the Royal Asiatic Society* 12: 189–201.

Durand, J.-M. (1986) 'Fragments rejoints pour une histoire Elamite', in *Fragmenta Historiae Elamicae: Mélanges offerts à M.-J. Steve*, ed. L. de Meyer, H. Gasche, and F. Vallat. Paris: ERC, 111–28.

(1988) *Archives épistolaires de Mari* 1/1. ARM XXVI/1. Paris: ERC.

(1990a) 'Cité-état d'Imar', in *Mari Annales de Recherches Interdisciplinaires 6*. Paris: ERC, 39–92.

(1990b) 'Fourmis blanches et fourmis noires', in *Mélanges offerts à Jean Perrot*, ed. F. Vallat. Paris: ERC, 101–8.

(1992) 'Rapports entre l'Elam et Ourouk', *NABU* no. 62: 47–8.

(1993) 'Le mythologème du combat entre le dieu de l'orage et la mer en Mésopotamie', in *Mari Annales de Recherches Interdisciplinaires 7*. Paris: ERC, 41–61.

(1997–2000) *Les documents épistolaires du palais de Mari*. Paris: Cerf.

(2005) 'De l'époque amorrite à la Bible: le cas d'Arriyuk', Memoriae Igor M. Diakonoff. *Babel und Bibel* 2: 59–69.

(2013) 'La suprématie Elamite sur les Amorrites: Réexamen, vingt ans après la XXXVI RAI (1989)', in *Susa and Elam*, ed. K. De Graef and J. Tavernier. Leiden: Brill, 329–40.

Edelman, D. (2005) *The Origins of the 'Second' Temple: Persian Imperial Policy and the Rebuilding of Jerusalem*. London: Equinox.

Edzard, D.-O. and Farber, G. (1974) *Répertoire Géographique des Textes Cunéiformes, 2: Die Orts- und Gewässernamen der Zeit der 3. Dynastie von Ur*. Wiesbaden: Dr. Ludwig Reichert Verlag.

Eidem, J. and Laessøe, J. (2001) *The Shemshara Archives*, Vol. 1: *The Letters*. Copenhagen: Kongelige Danske Videnskabernes Selskab.

Eidem, J. and Ristvet, L. (2011) *The Royal Archives from Tell Leilan: Old Babylonian Letters and Treaties from the Lower Town Palace East*. Leiden: NINO.

Ensor, G. (1904) *Moses and Hammurabi*. London: Religious Tract Society.

Epstein, I. (ed.) (1959) *Babylonian Talmud, Tractate Megillah*. London: Soncino Press.

Erler, M. (2011) 'Chaldäer im Platonismus', in *Babylon. Wissenskultur in Orient und Okzident*, ed. E. Cancik-Kirschbaum, M. van Ess, and J. Marzahn. Topoi 1. Berlin: de Gruyter, 225–37.

Evers, S. (1993) 'George Smith and the Egibi Tablets', *Iraq* 55: 107–17.

Fales, M. (2014) 'The Two Dynasties of Babylon', in *From Source to History: Studies on Ancient Near Eastern Worlds and Beyond, Dedicated to Giovanni Battista Lanfranchi*, ed. S. Gaspa, A. Greco, D. Morandi Bonacossi, S. Ponchia, and R. Rollinger. AOAT 412. Münster: Ugarit-Verlag, 201–37.

Falkenstein, A. (1963) 'Inschriftenfunde Uruk-Warka 1960–61', *Baghdader Mitteilungen* 2: 56–71.

Farber, W. (2014) *Lamaštu: An Edition of the Canonical Series*. Winona Lake, IN: Eisenbrauns.

Feeney, D. (2016) *Beyond Greece: The Beginnings of Latin Literature*. Cambridge, MA: Harvard University Press.

Fincke, J. (2016) 'The Oldest Mesopotamian Astronomical Treatise: *Enūma Anu Enlil*', in *Divination as a Science*. Winona Lake, IN: Eisenbrauns, 107–46.

Finkel, I. (1988) 'Adad-apla-iddina, Esagil-kin-apli, and the Series SA.GIG', in *A Scientific Humanist: Studies in Memory of Abraham Sachs*, ed. E. Leichty, M. de J. Ellis, and P. Gerardi. Philadelphia: University Museum, 143–59.

(2006) 'Report on the Sidon Cuneiform Tablet', *Archaeology and History in Lebanon* 24: 114–20.

(2013) *The Cyrus Cylinder: The King of Persia's Proclamation from Ancient Babylon*. New York: I. B. Tauris.

Finkel, I. and Seymour, M. (2008) *Babylon: Myth and Reality*. London: British Museum.

Finlayson, B. (2014) 'Introduction to the Levant during the Neolithic Period', in *Oxford Handbook of the Archaeology of the Levant*, ed. M. Steiner and A. Killebrew. Oxford University Press, 123–33.

Fischer-Elfert, H.-W. and Krebernik, M. (2016) 'Zu den Buchstabennamen auf dem Halaham Ostrakon aus TT.99 (Grab des Sennefri)', *Zeitschrift für ägyptische Sprache und Altertumskinde* 143: 169–76.

Foster, B. (2005) *Before the Muses*. 3rd ed. Bethesda, MD: CDL Press.

(2014) 'Diorite and Limestone: A Sumerian Perspective', in *He Has Opened Nisaba's House of Learning: Studies in Honor of Ake Sjøberg*, ed. L. Sassmannshausen. Leiden: Brill, 51–6.

Frahm, E. (1997) *Einleitung in die Sanherib Inschriften*. Archiv für Orientforschung Beiheft 26. Vienna: Institut für Orientalistik der Universität Wien.

(2010) 'Counter-Texts, Commentaries, and Adaptations: Politically Motivated Responses to the Babylonian Epic of Creation in Mesopotamia, the Biblical World, and Elsewhere', in *Conflict, Peace and Religion in the Ancient Near East*, ed. A. Tsukimoto. Orient XLV. Tokyo: Society for Near Eastern Studies in Japan, 3–33.

(2011) *Babylonian and Assyrian Commentaries: Origins of Interpretation*. Münster: Ugarit-Verlag.

(2013) 'Creation and the Divine Spirit in Babel and Bible: Reflections on *Mummu* in *Enūma Eliš* I. 4 and *rûaḥ* in Genesis 1.2', in *Literature as Politics, Politics as Literature: Essays on the Ancient Near East in Honor of Peter Machinist*, ed. D. Vanderhooft and A. Winitzer. Winona Lake, IN: Eisenbrauns, 97–116.

(2016) 'Of Doves, Fish, and Goddesses: Reflections on the Literary, Religious, and Historical Background of the Book of Jonah', in *Sibyls, Scriptures, and*

Scrolls: John Collins at Seventy, ed. J. Baden, H. Najman, and E. Tigchelaaret. Leiden: Brill, 432–58.

(2017) 'Assyria and the South: Babylonia', in *A Companion to Assyria*, ed. E. Frahm. Hoboken, NJ: Wiley Blackwell, 286–98.

(2018) 'The Exorcist's Manual: Structure, Language, *Sitz im Leben*', in *Sources of Evil. Studies in Mesopotamian Exorcistic Lore*, ed. G. van Buylaere, M. Luukko, D. Schwemer, and A. Mertens-Wagschal. Leiden: Brill, 9–47.

Frame, G. (1987) *Assyrian Rulers of the Early First Millennium BC*, Vol. 1: *1114–859*. RIMAP 2. Toronto University Press.

(1992) *Babylonia 689–627 B.C.: A Political History*. Leiden: NINO.

(1995) *Rulers of Babylonia from the Second Dynasty of Isin to the End of Assyrian Domination (1157–612 BC)*. RIMBP 2. Toronto University Press.

(1999) 'My Neighbour's God: Aššur in Babylonia and Marduk in Assyria', *Bulletin of the Canadian Society for Mesopotamian Studies*, 34: 5–22.

Frame, G. and George, A. (2005) 'The Royal Libraries of Nineveh: New Evidence for King Ashurbanipal's Tablet Collecting', *Iraq* 67: 265–84.

Frankena, R. (1966) *Briefe aus dem British Museum*. Altbabylonische Briefe in Umschrift und Übersetzung 2. Leiden: Brill.

Franklin, N. (2019) 'Megiddo and Jezreel Reflected in the Dying Embers of the Kingdom of Israel', in *The Last Days of the Kingdom of Israel*, ed. S. Hasegawa, C. Levin, and K. Radner. Beihefte zur Zeitschrift für der alttestamentliche Wissenschaft, Band 511. Berlin: de Gruyter, 189–208.

Frayne, D. (1990) *The Old Babylonian Period (2003–1595)*. RIMEP 4 Early Periods. Toronto University Press.

(1992) *The Early Dynastic List of Geographical Names*. New Haven, CT: American Oriental Society.

(2010) *Gilgamesch, Ikonographie eines Helden*, ed. H.-U. Steymans. OBO 245. Fribourg: Academic Press, 168–72.

Friberg, J. (ca. 2007) *Amazing Traces of a Babylonian Origin in Greek Mathematics*. Hackensack, NJ: World Scientific.

Fuchs, A. (1994) *Die Inschriften Sargons II. aus Khorsabad*. Göttingen: Cuvillier Verlag.

(2011) 'Sargon', in *PNAE*, Vol. 3, Part II: *Š–Z*, ed. H. D. Baker. Helsinki University Press, 1239–47.

(2017) 'Die Kassiten, das mittelbabylonische Reich und der Zagros', in *Karduniaš. Babylonia under the Kassites*, ed. A. Bartelmus and K. Sternitzke. Boston, MA: de Gruyter, 123–65.

Fuchs, A. and Parpola, S. (2001) *The Correspondence of Sargon II, Part III: Letters from Babylonian and the Eastern Provinces*. SAA XV. Helsinki University Press.

Gadd, C. (1973) *The Cambridge Ancient History*, Vol. I, Part 2: *Early History of the Middle East*, ed. I. Edwards, C. Gadd, and N. Hammond. 3rd ed. Cambridge University Press, 220–7.

Garrison, M. (2012) 'Antiquarianism, Copying, Collecting', in *Companion to the Archaeology of the Ancient Near East*, ed. D. T. Potts. Hoboken, NJ: Wiley Blackwell, 27–47.

Gasche, H. (2013) 'Le Südburg de Babylone: une autre visite', in *La Tour de Babylone. Études et recherches sur les monuments de Babylon*, ed. B. André-Salvini. Rome: Istituto di studi sulle civiltà dell'Egeo e del vicino Oriente, 115–26.

Gasche, H., Armstrong, J., Cole, S., and Gurzadyan, V. (1998) *Dating the Fall of Babylon: A Reappraisal of Second-Millennium Chronology*. Mesopotamia History and Environment Series II, Memoirs IV. Ghent: University of Ghent/Chicago: Oriental Institute of the University of Chicago.

Gasche, H. and Tanret, M. (1998) *Changing Watercourses in Babylonia: Towards a Reconstruction of the Ancient Environment in Lower Mesopotamia*. Mesopotamia History and Environment. Memoirs 5/1. Chicago: Oriental Institute of the University of Chicago.

(2009–11) 'Sippar', in *RlA*, Vol. 12, 528–47.

George, A. (1992) *Babylonian Topographical Texts*. OLA 40. Leuven: Peeters.

(1993a) *House Most High*. Winona Lake, IN: Eisenbrauns.

(1993b) 'Babylon Revisited: Archaeology and Philology in Harness', *Antiquity* 67: 734–46.

(1995) 'The Bricks of Esagil', *Iraq* 57: 173–98.

(1997a) 'Bond of the Lands: Babylon, the Cosmic Capital', in *Die Orientalische Stadt. Kontinuität, Wandel, Bruch*, ed. G. Wilhelm. Saarbrücken: Druckerei und Verlag, 126–45.

(1997b) 'Marduk and the Cult of the Gods of Nippur at Babylon', *Orientalia* 66: 65–70.

(2000) 'Four Temple Rituals', in *Wisdom, Gods and Literature: Studies in Assyriology in Honour of W. G. Lambert*, ed. A. George and I. Finkel. Winona Lake, IN: Eisenbraun, 259–99.

(2003) *The Babylonian Gilgamesh Epic: Introduction, Critical Edition and Cuneiform Texts*. Oxford University Press.

(2005–6) 'The Tower of Babel: Archaeology, History and Cuneiform Texts', *Archiv für Orientforschung* 51: 75–95.

(2009) *Babylonian Literary Texts in the Schøyen Collection*. CUSAS 10. Bethesda, MD: CDL Press.

(2011) *Cuneiform Royal Inscriptions and Related Texts in the Schøyen Collection*. CUSAS 17. Bethesda, MD: CDL Press.

(2015) 'On Babylonian Lavatories and Sewers', *Iraq* 77: 75–106.

Giovino, M. (2007) *The Assyrian Sacred Tree*. OBO 230. Fribourg: Academic Press.

Glassner, J.-G. (2004) *Mesopotamian Chronicles*. Writings from the Ancient World 19. Atlanta, GA: Society of Biblical Literature.

Godard, A. (1965) *The Art of Iran*. London: Allen and Unwin.

Goddeeris, A. (2002) *Economy and Society in Northern Babylonia in the Early Old Babylonian Period (c. 2000–1800 BC)*. OLA 109. Leuven: Peeters.

Goldberg, S. and Whitmarsh, T. (eds.) (2016) *Oxford Classical Dictionary*. Oxford University Press.

Goring-Morris, A. and Belfer-Cohen, A. (2014) 'The Southern Levant (Cisjordan) during the Neolithic Period', in *Oxford Handbook of the Archaeology of the Levant*, ed. M. Steiner and A. Killebrew. Oxford University Press, 147–69.

Grayson, A. (1972) *Assyrian Royal Inscriptions*, Vol. 1: *Records of the Ancient Near East*. Wiesbaden: Harrassowitz.

  (1975a) *Babylonian Historical-Literary Texts*. Toronto University Press.

  (1975b) *Assyrian and Babylonian Chronicles*. Texts from Cuneiform Sources 5. New York: J. J. Augustin.

  (1983) 'Königslisten und Chroniken', in *RlA*, Vol. 6, 77–135.

  (1987) *Assyrian Rulers of the Third and Second Millennia BC (to 115 BC)*. RIMAP 1. Toronto University Press.

  (1996) *Assyrian Rulers of the Early First Millennium BC (858–745 BC)*. RIMAP 3/2. Toronto University Press.

Grayson, A. and Novotny, J. (2012) *The Royal Inscriptions of Sennacherib Part 1*. RIMAP 3/1. Winona Lake, IN: Eisenbrauns.

  (2014) *The Royal Inscriptions of Sennacherib Part 2*. RIMAP 3/2. Winona Lake, IN: Eisenbrauns.

Grigson, C. (2007) 'Culture, Ecology and Pigs from the Fifth to the Third Millennium BC around the Fertile Crescent', in *Pigs and Humans. 10,000 Years of Interaction*, ed. U. Albarella, K. Dobney, A. Ervynck, and P. Rowley-Conwy. New York: Oxford University Press, 83–108.

Grimme, H. and Pilter, W. (1907) *The Law of Hammurabi and Moses: A Sketch*. London: Society for Promoting Christian Knowledge.

Groß, M. and Pirngruber, R. (2014) 'On Courtiers in the Neo-Assyrian Empire: *ša rēši* and *manzaz pāni*', *Altorientalische Forschungen* 14/2: 161–75.

Guichard, M. (2014a) *L'épopée de Zimri-Lim*. Florilegium marianum XIV, mémoires de NABU 16. Paris: SEPOA.

  (2014b) 'Political Space – Local Political Structures in Northern Syria: The Case of the Country of Ida-maraṣ in the 18th Century BC', in *Constituent, Confederate and Conquered Space: The Emergence of the Mittani State*, ed. E. Cancik-Kirschbaum and E. Christiane. Topoi. Berlin Studies of the Ancient World 17. Berlin: de Gruyter, 147–60.

Gunkel, H. (1916) *Esther*. Tübingen: J. C. B. Mohr.

Gurney, O. (1977) *Some Aspects of Hittite Religion*. Oxford: Oxford University Press.

Gzella, H. (2016) 'The Scribal Background of the "Mene tekel" in Daniel 5', www.bibleinterp.com/articles/2016/04/gze408029.shtml.

Haas, V. (1994) *Geschichte der hethitischen Religion*. Leiden: Brill.

Hackl, J. (2016) 'New Additions to the Rahimesu Archive: Parthian Texts from the British Museum and the World Museum, Liverpool', in *Silver, Money and*

Credit: Festschrift for R. van der Spek, ed. K. Kleber and R. Pirngruber. Leiden: NINO, 87–106.

(2018) 'The Esangila Temple during the Late Achaemenid Period', in *Xerxes and Babylonia: The Cuneiform Evidence*, ed. C. Waerzeggers and M. Seire. OLA 277. Leuven: Peeters, 165–87.

Hackl, J. and Jursa, M. (2015) 'Egyptians in Babylonia in the Neo-Babylonian and Achaemenid Periods', in *Exile and Return*, ed. J. Stökl and C. Waerzeggers. Berlin: de Gruyter, 157–80.

Hamidović, D. (2014) 'Alphabetical Inscriptions from the Sealand', *Studia Mesopotamica* 1: 137–55.

Hammond, N. (2017) 'Pot Fragments Seal the Deal on Naming Lost Kings of Commerce', *The Times*, Saturday 22 April 2017.

Harper, P., Aruz, J., and Tallon, F. (eds.) (1992) *The Royal City of Susa: Ancient Near Eastern Treasures in the Louvre*. New York: Metropolitan Museum of Art.

Hauser, S. (1999) 'Babylon in arsakidischer Zeit', in *Babylon, Focus mesopotamischer Geschichte, Wiege früher Gelehrsamkeit, Mythos in der Moderne*, ed. J. Renger. Saarbrücken: Druckerei und Verlag, 207–39.

Hausleiter, A. (2010) 'Ancient Tayma', in *Roads of Arabia: The Archaeological Treasures of Saudi Arabia*, ed. U. Franke, A. Al-Ghabban, J. Gierlichs, and S. Weber. Exhibition catalogue, Museum für islamische Kunst. Berlin: Wasmuth, 102–24.

Hausleiter, A. and Schaudig, H.-P. (2016) 'Rock Relief and Cuneiform Inscription of King Nabonidus at al-Ḥāʾiṭ (Province of Ḥāʾil, Saudi Arabia), Ancient Padakku', *Zeitschrift für Orient-Archäologie* 9: 224–40.

Hawkins, J. David (2000) *Inscriptions of the Iron Age: Corpus of Hieroglyphic Luwian Inscriptions*, 3 vols. Berlin: de Gruyter.

Heeßel, N. (2017) 'Zur Standardisierung und Serialisierung von Texten während der Kassitenzeit am Beispiel der Opferschau-Omina', in *Karduniaš: Babylonia under the Kassites*, ed. A. Bartelmus and K. Sternitzke. Boston, MA: de Gruyter, 219–28.

Heffron, Y. and Worthington, M. (2012) 'Tiamat', in *RlA*, Vol. 13. 643–5.

Heimpel, W. (2003) *Letters to the King of Mari*. Winona Lake, IN: Eisenbrauns.

Heltzer, M. (1981) *The Suteans*. Naples: Istituto universitario orientale.

Henkelman, W. (2008) *The Other Gods Who Are: Studies in Elamite-Iranian Acculturation Based on the Persepolis Fortification Texts*. Achaemenid History IV. Leiden: NINO.

(2011) 'Cyrus the Persian and Darius the Elamite: A Case of Mistaken Identity', in *Herodotus and the Persian Empire*, ed. R. Rollinger, B. Truschnegg, and R. Bichler. CLeO 3. Wiesbaden: Harrassowitz, 577–634.

Henkelman. W. and Folmer, M. (2016) 'Your Tally Is Full! On Wooden Credit Records in and after the Achaemenid Empire', in *Silver, Money, Credit: A Tribute to Robartus J. van der Spek on the Occasion of His 65th Birthday*, ed. K. Kleber and R. Pirngruber. Leiden: NINO, 133–239.

Herbordt, S., Mattila, R., Parker, B., Postgate, J., and Wiseman, D. (2019) *Documents from the Nabu Temple and from Private Houses on the Citadel*. Cuneiform Texts from Nimrud VI. London: British Institute for the Study of Iraq.

Herodotus (2003) *The Histories*, trans. A. de Sélincourt. Harmondsworth: Penguin.

Herrmann, G. and Laidlaw, S. with H. Coffey (2009) *Ivories from the North West Palace (1845–1992)*. Ivories from Nimrud VI. London: British Institute for the Study of Iraq.

Hertel, T. (2013) *Old Assyrian Legal Practices*. Leiden: NINO.

Hinke, W. J. (1907) *A New Boundary Stone of Nebuchadrezzar I from Nippur*, ed. H. Hilprecht. The Babylonian Expedition of the University of Pennsylvania, Series D: Researches and Treatises 4. Philadelphia: University of Pennsylvania.

Hoenigswald, H., Woodard, R., and Clackson, J. (2006) 'Indo-European', in *The Cambridge Encyclopaedia of the World's Ancient Languages*, ed. R. Woodard. Cambridge University Press, 534–50.

Hoffmann, F. and Quack, J. (2007) *Anthologie der demotischen Literatur*. Berlin: LIT Verlag.

Hoffner, H. and Beckman, G. (1999) *Hittite Diplomatic Texts*, 2nd ed. Atlanta, GA: Society of Biblical Literature.

Holm, T. (2007) 'The Sheikh Fadl Inscription in Its Literary and Historical Context', *Aramaic Studies* 5: 193–224.

(2013) *Of Courtiers and Kings: The Biblical Daniel Narratives and Ancient Story Collections*. Winona Lake, IN: Eisenbrauns.

Horowitz, W. (1998) *Mesopotamian Cosmic Geography*. Winona Lake, IN: Eisenbrauns.

(2000) 'Astral Tablets in the Hermitage, St. Petersburg', *Zeitschrift für Assyriologie* 90: 194–206.

Horowitz, W., Oshima, T., and Sanders, S. (2018) *Cuneiform in Canaan: The Next Generation*. Philadelphia: Eisenbrauns.

Horsnell, M. (1999) *The Year-Names of the First Dynasty of Babylon*, 2 vols. Hamilton: McMaster University Press.

Høyrup, J. (1990) 'Algebra and Naïve Geometry: An Investigation of Some Basic Aspects of Old Babylonian Mathematical Thought', *Altorientalische Forschungen* 17: 27–69, 262–354.

Hunger, H. (1976–80) 'Kidinnu', in *RlA*, Vol. 5, 589.

(1992) *Astrological Reports to Assyrian Kings*. SAA VIII. Helsinki University Press.

(2011–13) 'Sternkunde', in *RlA*, Vol. 13, 150–61.

Hunger, H. and de Jong, T. (2014) 'Almanac W22340a from Uruk', *Zeitschrift für Assyriologie* 104: 182–94.

Hunger, H. and Steele, J. (2018) *The Babylonian Astronomical Compendium MUL. APIN*. London: Routledge.

Hurowitz, V. (1997) 'Reading a Votive Inscription: Simbar-šipak and the Ellilification of Marduk', *Revue d'Assyriologie* 91: 39–45.

(2013) 'What Was Codex Hammurabi, and What Did it Become?', *Maarav* 18: 89–100.

Invernizzi, A. (2008a) 'Babylone sous domination Perse', in *Babylone*. Exhibition catalogue. Paris: Hazan–Musée du Louvre, 239–48.

(2008b) 'Les dominations Grecque et Parthe', in *Babylone*. Exhibition catalogue. Paris: Hazan–Musée du Louvre, 251–75.

Ionides, M. (1937) *The Regime of the Rivers Euphrates and Tigris*. London: E. and F. N. Spon.

Ismail, M. (2011) *Wallis Budge*. Kilkerran: Hardinge Simpole.

Izre'el, S. (1997) *The Amarna Scholarly Tablets*. Cuneiform Monographs 9. Groningen: Styx.

Jacobus, H. (2014) *Zodiac Calendars in the Dead Sea Scrolls*. Leiden: Brill.

Jacquet, A. (2012) 'Funerary Rights and the Cult of Ancestors during the Amorite Period', in *(Re-)constructing Funerary Rituals in the Ancient Near East*, ed. P. Pfälzner. Wiesbaden: Harassowitz, 123–36.

Jamison, S. (2004) 'Sanskrit', in *The Cambridge Encyclopaedia of the World's Ancient Languages*, ed. R. Woodard. Cambridge University Press, 673–99.

Janko, R. (2002) 'The Herculaneum Library: Some Recent Developments', *Estudios Clássicos* 121: 25–41.

Janssen, C. (1991) 'Samsu-iluna and the Hungry *Naditums*', *Northern Akkad Project Reports* 5: 3–39.

Jean, C.-F. (1950) *Lettres Diverses*. ARM II. Paris: Imprimerie Nationale.

Jeremias, J. (1903) *Moses und Hammurabi*. Leipzig: J. C. Hinrichs.

Jeyes, U. (1989) *Old Babylonian Extispicy: Omen Texts in the British Museum*. Leiden: NINO.

Jiménez, E. (2017) *The Babylonian Disputation Poems: With Editions of the Series of the Poplar, Palm and Vine, the Series of the Spider, and the Story of the Poor, Forlorn Wren*. Cultures and History of the Ancient Near East 87. Leiden: Brill.

(2018) '"As your name indicates": Philological Arguments in Akkadian Disputations', *Journal of Ancient Near Eastern History* 5: 87–105.

Joannès, F. (1982) *Textes Economiques de la Babylonie récente*. Paris: ERC.

(2011) 'L'écriture publique du pouvoir à Babylone sous Nabuchodonosor II', in *Wissenskultur in Orient und Okzident*, ed. E. Cancik-Kirschbaum, M. van Ess, and J. Marzahn, Topoi 1. Berlin: de Gruyter, 113–20.

Jones, A. (2017) *The Portable Cosmos*. Oxford University Press.

Jones, A. and Steele, J. (2018) 'Diodorus on the Chaldeans', in *The Scaffolding of Our Thoughts. Essays on Assyriology and the History of Science in Honor of Francesca Rochberg*, ed. J. Crisostomo, N. Heessel, and T. Abusch. Leiden: Brill, 333–52.

Jonker, G. (1995) *The Topography of Remembrance: The Dead, Tradition, and Collective Memory in Mesopotamia*. Leiden: Brill.

Josephus (1926) *Contra Apionem*, in *The Life; Against Apion*, trans. H. Thackeray. Loeb Classical Library 186. Cambridge, MA: Harvard University Press.

Jursa, M. (2007a) 'The Transition of Babylonia from the Neo-Babylonian Empire to Achaemenid Rule', in *Regime Change in the Ancient Near East and Egypt: From Sargon of Agade to Saddam Hussein*, ed. H. Crawford. London: British Academy, 74–92.

(2007b) 'Die Söhne Kudurrus und die Herkunft der neubabylonische Dynastie', *Revue d'Assyriologie* 101: 125–36.

(2010) 'Der neubabylonische Hof', in *The Achaemenid Court*, ed. B. Jacobs and R. Rollinger. Wiesbaden: Harrassowitz, 67–106.

Jursa, M. and Spar, I. (2014) *Late Babylonian Archival and Administrative Tablets in the Metropolitan Museum of Art*. Metropolitan Museum of Art Cuneiform Texts IV. Winona Lake, IN: Eisenbrauns.

Justin (2011) Epitome *of the* Philippic History *of Pompeius Trogus*, Vol. II: *Books 13–15. The Successors to Alexander the Great*, trans. J. Yardley. Oxford University Press.

Kammenhuber, A. (1987–90) 'Marduk', in *RlA*, Vol. 7, 370–2.

Kämmerer, T. and Metzler, K. (2012) *Das babylonische Weltschöpfungsepos Enūma eliš*, AOAT 375. Münster: Ugarit-Verlag.

Kaniuth, K. (2017) 'Isin in the Kassite Period', in *Karduniaš: Babylonia under the Kassites*, ed. A. Bartelmus and K. Sternitzke. Berlin: de Gruyter, 492–507.

Kataja, L. and Whiting, R. (1995) *Grants, Decrees and Gifts of the Neo-Assyrian Period*. SAA XII. Helsinki University Press.

Katz, D. (2003) *The Image of the Underworld in the Sumerian Sources*. Winona Lake, IN: Eisenbrauns.

Keetman, J. (2009) 'Form, Zweck, und Herkunft der verschiedenen Teile der Esangil-Tafel', *Revue d'Assyriologie* 103: 111–30.

Kepinski, C. (2012) 'Organization of Harrâdum, Suhum, 18th–17th Centuries B.C.', in *Organization, Representation and Symbols of Power in the Ancient Near East*, ed. G. Wilhelm. 54th RAI Würzburg. Winona Lake, IN: Eisenbrauns.

King, L. (1912) *Babylonian Boundary Stones and Memorial Tablets in the British Museum*. London: British Museum.

King, L. and Thompson, R. (1907) *The Inscription of Darius the Great at Behistun*. London: British Museum.

Klengel, H. (1983) 'Bemerkungen zu den altbabylonische Rechtsurkunden und Wirtschaftstexten aus Babylon (VS 22: 1–82)', *Altorientalische Forschungen* 10: 5–48.

(1990) 'Halab – Mari – Babylon. Aspekte syrisch-mesopotamischer Beziehungen im altbabylonischer Zeit', in *De la Babylonie à la Syrie, en passant par Mari. Mélanges offerts à M. Kupper*, ed. Ö. Tunca. Liège: Université de Liège, 163–75.

Klengel-Brandt, E. (1990) 'Gab es ein Museum in der Hauptburg Nebukadnezars II. in Babylon?', *Forschungen und Berichte* 28: 41–6.

Knapp, A. (2015) *Royal Apologetic in the Ancient Near East*. Atlanta, GA: Society of Biblical Literature.

Koch-Westenholz, U. (1995) *Mesopotamian Astrology*. Copenhagen: Museum Tusculanum Press.

(1999) 'The Astrological Commentary Šumma Sin ina tāmartišu, Tablet 1', in *La Science des Cieux. Sages, mages, astrologues*, ed. R. Gyselen. Res Orientales XII. Bures-sur-Yvette: Groupe pour l'étude de la civilisation du Moyen-Orient, 149–65.

Koldewey, R. (1900) *Die hethitische Inschrift gefundenen in der Königsburg von Babylon*. Leipzig: Hinrichs.

(1911) *Die Tempel von Babylon und Borsippa nach den Ausgrabungen durch die Deutsch-Orient Gesellschaft*. WDVOG 15. Leipzig: Hinrichs.

(1931) *Die Königsburgen von Babylon 1: die Südburg*. WVDOG 54. Leipzig: Hinrichs.

(1932) *Die Königsburgen von Babylon 2: die Hauptburg und der Sommerpalast Nebukadnezars im Hügel Babil*. WVDOG 55. Leipzig: Hinrichs.

Kosmin, P. (2011) 'The Foundation and Early Life of Dura-Europos', in *Dura-Europos. Crossroads of Antiquity*, ed. L. Brody and G. Hoffman. Chestnut Hill, MA: McMullen Museum of Art, Boston College, 150–76.

(2013) 'Rethinking the Hellenistic Gulf: The New Greek Inscription from Bahrain', *Journal of Hellenic Studies* 133: 61–79.

(2014) 'Seeing Double in Seleucid Babylonia: Re-Reading the Borsippa Cylinder of Antiochus I', in *Patterns of the Past: Epitedeumata in the Greek Tradition: Festschrift for Oswyn Murray*, ed. A. Moreno and R. Thomas. Oxford University Press, 173–98.

(2018) *Time and Its Adversaries in the Seleucid Empire*. Cambridge, MA: Harvard University Press.

Kraus, F. (1964) *Briefe aus dem British Museum*. Altbabylonische Briefe 1. Leiden: Brill.

(1968) *Briefe aus dem Archive des Shamash-hazir*. Altbabylonische Briefe IV. Leiden: Brill.

(1977) *Briefe aus dem British Museum*. Altbabylonische Briefe VII. Leiden: Brill.

(1983) 'Spät-altbabylonische Briefe aus Babylon (VS 22: 83–92)', *Altorientalische Forschungen* 10: 49–63.

(1984) *Königliche Verfügungen in altbabylonischer Zeit*. Leiden: Brill.

(1985) *Briefe aus kleineren westeuropäischen Sammlungen*. Altbabylonische Briefe X. Leiden: Brill.

Krecher, J. and Müller, H.-P. (1975) 'Vergangenheitsinteresse in Mesopotamien und Israel', *Saeculum* 26: 13–44.

Kuehne, H. (2002) 'Thoughts about Assyria after 612 BC', in *Of Pots and Plans: Papers on the Archaeology and History of Mesopotamia and Syria Presented to David Oates in Honour of His 75th Birthday*, ed. L. Al-Gailani-Werr, J. Curtis, and A. McMahon. London: NABU Publications, 171–5.

(2017) 'Early Iron in Assyria', in *Overturning Certainties in Near Eastern Archaeology: Festschrift in Honor of K. Aslihan Yener*, ed. Ç. Maner, M. Horowitz, and A. Gilbert. Leiden: Brill, 318–40.

Kuhrt, A. (1983) 'The Cyrus Cylinder and Achaemenid Imperial Policy', *Journal for the Society for Old Testament Studies* 25: 83–97.

(1990) 'Alexander and Babylon', in *Achaemenid History Workshop V*, ed. H. Sancisi-Weerdenburg. Groningen University Press, 121–30.

Kupper, J.-R. (1954) *Correspondance de Bahdi-Lim*. ARM VI. Paris: Imprimerie nationale.

(1959) 'Lettres de Kiš', *Revue d'Assyriologie* 53: 19–38, 177–82.

(1987–90) 'Mari post-mariotes', in *RlA*, Vol. 7, 389–90.

Labat, R. (1994) *Manuel d'épigraphie akkadienne*. 6th ed., rev. F. Malbran-Labat. Paris: Paul Geuthner.

Labat, R. and Malbran-Labat, F. (1995) *Manuel d'épigraphie akkadienne*. Paris: Paul Geuthner.

Lacambre, D. and Nahm, W. (2015) 'Pithana, an Anatolian Ruler in the Time of Samsu-iluna of Babylon: New Data from Tell Rimah (Iraq)', *Revue d'Assyriologie* 109: 17–28.

Lackenbacher, S. (1982) 'Un text vieux-babylonien sur la finition des textiles', *Syria* 59: 129–49.

(1998) 'Les lettres de Yanṣib-Addu', in *Archives épistolaires de Mari 1/2 Part III*, ed. D. Charpin, F. Joannès, S. Lackenbacher, and B. Lafont. ARM XXVI. Paris: ERC, 359–70.

Lambert, W. (1973) 'Antediluvian Kings and Marduk's Chariot', in *Symbolae biblicae et Mesopotamicae Francisco Mario Theodoro de Leagre Böhl*, ed. M. Beek. Leiden: Brill, 271–80.

(2007) *Babylonian Oracle Questions*. Winona Lake, IN: Eisenbrauns.

(2011) 'Babylon: origins', in *Wissenskultur in Orient und Okzident*, ed. E. Cancik-Kirschbaum, M. van Ess, and J. Marzahn. Topoi 1. Berlin: de Gruyter, 71–6.

(2013) *Babylonian Creation Myths*. Winona Lake, IN: Eisenbrauns.

Landsberger, B. (1965) *Brief des Bischofs von Esagila an König Asarhaddon*. Amsterdam: Noord-Hollandsche Uitg. Mij.

Langlois, A.-I. (2017) *Les archives de la princesse Iltani découvertes à Tell al-Rimah (XVIIIe siècle av. J.-C.) et l'histoire du royaume de Karana/Qaṭṭara*. Mémoires de NABU 18, Archibab 2. Paris: SEPOA.

Larsen, M. (1995) 'The "Babel/Bibel" Controversy', in *Civilizations of the Ancient Near East I*, ed. J. Sasson and J. Baines. New York: Scribner, 95–106.

(1996) *The Conquest of Assyria*. London: Routledge.

(2015) *Ancient Kanesh*. Cambridge University Press.

Layard, H. (1853) *Discoveries in the Ruins of Nineveh and Babylon*. London: John Murray.

Leclant, J. and Clerc, G. (1995) 'Fouilles et travaux, Metzamor', *Orientalia* 64/3: 225–355.

Lee, T. (1993) 'The Jasper Cylinder Seal of Aššurbanipal and Nabonidus' Making of Sin's Statue', *Revue d'Assyriologie* 87: 131–6.

Leichty, E. (1986) *Catalogue of the Babylonian Tablets in the British Museum VI*. London: Trustees of the British Museum.

(2011) *The Royal Inscriptions of Esarhaddon, King of Assyria (680–669 BC)*. RINAP 4. Winona Lake, IN: Eisenbrauns.

Lenzi, A. (2008) 'The Uruk List of Kings and Sages and Late Mesopotamian Scholarship', *Journal of Ancient Near Eastern Religions* 8: 137–69.

(2018) 'Material, Constellation, Image, God: The Fate of the Chosen Bull According to KAR 50 and Duplicates', in *The Scaffolding of Our Thoughts: Essays on Assyriology and the History of Science in Honor of Francesca Rochberg*, ed. J. Crisostomo, N. Heessel, and T. Abusch. Leiden: Brill, 58–96.

Lewis, B. (1980) *The Sargon Legend: A Study of the Akkadian Text and the Tale of the Hero Who Was Exposed at Birth*. Boston, MA: American Schools of Oriental Research.

Lewis, T. (1996) 'CT13.33–34 and Ezekiel 32: Lion-Dragon Myths', *Journal of the American Oriental Society* 116: 28–47.

Lightfoot, J. (2007) *The Sibylline Oracles*. Cambridge University Press.

Lim, T., (2017) 'An Indicative Definition of the Canon', in *When Texts Are Canonized*, ed. T. Lim. Brown Judaic Studies. Atlanta, GA: Society of Biblical Literature, 1–24.

Linssen, M. (2003) *The Cults of Uruk and Babylon: The Temple Ritual Texts as Evidence for Hellenistic Cult Practices*. Leiden: Brill-Styx.

Lipschits, O. (1998) 'Nebuchadrezzar's Policy in "Hattu-Land"', *Ugarit Forschungen* 30: 468–87.

Livingstone, A. (1986) *Mystical and Mythological Explanatory Works of Assyrian and Babylonian Scholars*. Oxford: Clarendon Press.

(2013) *Hemerologies of Assyrian and Babylonian Scholars*. CUSAS 25. Bethesda, MD: CDL Press.

Llop, J. and George, A. (2001–2) 'Die babylonische-assyrische Beziehungen und die innere Lage Assyriens in der Zeit der Auseinanderetzung zwischen Ninurta-tukulti-Aššur und Mutakkil-Nusku nach neuen keilschriftlichen Quellen', *Archiv für Orientforschung* 48–9: 1–23.

Lloyd, S. (1947) *Foundations in the Dust: A Story of Mesopotamian Exploration*. Oxford University Press.

Lohnert, A. (2010) 'Reconsidering the Consecration of Priests', in *Your Praise Is Sweet: A Memorial Volume for Jeremy Black*, ed. H. Baker, E. Robson, and G. Zólyomi. London: British Institute for the Study of Iraq, 183–91.

Longrigg, S. (1960) 'Badra', *Encyclopaedia of Islam*, Vol. 1: *A–D*, ed. H. A. R. Gibb and editorial committee, 3rd ed. Leiden: Brill, 870–87.

Luukko, M. (2012) *The Correspondence of Tiglath-pileser III and Sargon II from Calah/Nimrud*. SAA XIX. Helsinki University Press.

Luukko, M. and van Buylaere, G. (2002) *The Political Correspondence of Esarhaddon*. SAA XVI. Helsinki University Press.

Machinist, P. (2014) 'Tukulti-Ninurta-Epos', in *RlA*, Vol. 14, 180–1.

Magee, P. (2014) *The Archaeology of Prehistoric Arabia*. Cambridge University Press.

Malbran-Labat F. (2004) 'Inscription no. 4001', in *Kition dans les Textes*, ed. M. Yon. Paris: ERC, 345–54.

Mallowan, M. (1966) *Nimrud and Its Remains*. London: Collins.

Maraqten, M. (1990) 'The Aramaic Pantheon at Tayma', *Arabian Archaeology and Epigraphy* 7: 17–31.

Marchesi, G. (2010) 'The Sumerian King List and the Early History of Mesopotamia', in *Ana turri gimilli. Studi dedicati al Padre Werner R. Mayer, S.J.*, ed. M. Biga and M. Liverani. Vicino Oriente, Quaderno V. Rome University Press, 231–48.

  (2017) 'Appendix 5: Inscriptions from the Royal Mounds of A'ali (Bahrain) and Related Texts', in *The Royal Mounds of A'ali in Bahrain: The Emergence of Kingship in Early Dilmun*, ed. S. Terp Laursen. Denmark: Jutland Archaeological Society – Moesgaard Museum, 425–32.

Marchetti, N. (2014–16) 'Tilmen Höyük', in *RlA*, Vol. 14, 48–50.

Marck, C. (2016) *In the Land of a Thousand Gods: A History of Asia Minor in the Ancient World*. Princeton University Press.

Marcus, M. (1991) 'The Mosaic Glass Vessels from Hasanlu, Iran: A Study in Large-Scale Stylistic Trait Distribution', *The Art Bulletin* 73: 536–60.

Margueron, J.-C. (2013) 'Le Palais de Nabuchodonosor à Babylone', in *La Tour de Babylone*, ed. B. André-Salvini. Rome: CNR-Louvre, 77–114.

Marzahn, J. (1994) *The Ishtar Gate: The Processional Way: The New Year Festival of Babylon*. Berlin: Staatliche Museen zu Berlin, Vorderasiatisches Museum.

  (2008) 'Koldewey's Babylon', in *Babylon*, ed. M. Seymour. London: British Museum Exhibition Catalogue, 46–53.

Marzahn, J., Schauerte, G., Müller-Neuhof, B., Sternitzke, K., Wullen, M., and Strzoda, H. (2008) *Babylon: Mythos und Wahrheit*. Exhibition catalogue. Munich: Hirmer.

Matthews, D. (1990) *Principles of Composition in Near Eastern Glyptic of the Later Second Millennium B.C.* Göttingen: Vandenhoek and Ruprecht.

Maul, S. (1991) 'Neues zu den 'Graeco-Babyloniaca', *Zeitschrift zur Assyriologie* 81: 87–107.

  (1992) *Die Inschriften von Tall Bderi*. Die Ausgrabungen von Tall Bderi 1. Berliner Beiträge zum Vorderen Orient Texte 2. Berlin: Reimer.

  (2018) *The Art of Divination in the Ancient Near East: Reading the Signs of Heaven and Earth*, trans. B. McNeil and A. Edmonds. Waco, TX: Baylor University Press.

May, N. (2012) 'Ali-talīmu – What Can Be Learned from the Destruction of Figurative Complexes', in *Iconoclasm and Text Destruction in the Ancient Near East and Beyond*, ed. N. May. Chicago Oriental Institute Seminars 8. Chicago: Oriental Institute, 187–230.

McMeekin, S. (2010) *The Berlin-Baghdad Express: The Ottoman Empire and Germany's Bid for World Power 1898–1911*. London: Allen Lane.

Melville, S. (1999) *The Role of Naqia/Zakutu in Sargonid Politics*. SAA Studies IX. Helsinki University Press.

(2016) *The Campaigns of Sargon II King of Assyria, 721–705 BC*. Oklahoma University Press.

Mercier, H. and Sperber, D. (2017) *The Enigma of Reason: A New Theory of Human Understanding*. London: Allen Lane.

Messerschmidt, W. (2006) Review of Curtis and Tallis, *Forgotten Empire*, *Bryn Mawr Classical Review*.

Meyer, G. (1962) 'Zur Inschrift des Nebukadnezar am Ischtar-Tor', in *Durch vier Jahrtausende altvorderasiatischer Kultur*, 2nd ed. Berlin: Vorderasiatisches Museum, 231–4.

Michalowski, P. (2011) *Correspondence of the Kings of Ur: An Epistolary History of an Ancient Mesopotamian Kingdom*. Winona Lake, IN: Eisenbrauns.

Michalowski, P. and Rutz, M. (2016) 'The Flooding of Ešnunna, the Fall of Mari: Hammurabi's Deeds in Babylonian Literature and History', *Journal of Cuneiform Studies* 68: 15–43.

Michaux, A. (1800) 'Cabinet des Antiques de la Bibliothèque nationale', *Magasin Encyclopédique ou Journal des Sciences, des Lettres et des Arts* 6/3: 86–7.

Michel, C. and Veenhof K. (2010) 'The Textiles Traded by the Assyrians in Anatolia (19th–18th Centuries BC)', in *Textile Terminologies in the Ancient Near East and Mediterranean from the Third to the First Millennia BC*, ed. C. Michel and M.-L. Nosch. Oxford: Oxbow, 210–71.

Miglus, P. (2000) 'Das Thronpodest des Salmanassar III aus Kalhu und die damalige babylonische Politik der Assyrer', in *Variatio delectat: Iran und der Westen: Gedenkschrift für Peter Calmeyer*, ed. R. Dittmann, B. Hrouda, U. Low, P. Matthiae, R. Mayer-Opificius, and S. Thurwachter. AOAT 272. Münster: Ugarit-Verlag: 447–67.

Mitchell, P. (2018) *The Donkey in Human History*. Oxford University Press.

Mitsuma, Y. (2013) 'Large Wooden Writing Board Mentioned in the Astronomical Diary -213', *NABU* no. 54.

(2015) 'The Offering for Well-Being in Seleucid and Arsacid Babylon', *Archiv für Orientforschung* 53: 117–27.

Mofidi-Nasrabadi, B. (2018) 'Elamite Architecture', in *The Elamite World*, ed. J. Alvarez-Mon, G. Basello, and Y. Wicks. London: Routledge, 507–30.

Monroe, M. Willis (2016) 'Micro-Zodiac in Babylon and Uruk: Seleucid Zodiacal Astrology', in *The Circulation of Astronomical Knowledge in the Ancient World*, ed. J. Steele. Leiden: Brill, 119–38.

Moorey, P. Roger (1978) *Kish Excavations 1923–1933*. Oxford: Clarendon Press.

(1999) *Ancient Mesopotamian Materials and Industries: The Archaeological Evidence*. Oxford: Oxford University Press.

Moortgat, A. (1988) *Vorderasiatische Rollsiegel*. Berlin: Gebr. Mann Verlag.

Mora, C. (2010) 'Seals and Sealings of Karkamiš Part III', in *Luwian and Hittite Studies Presented to J. David Hawkins*, ed. I. Singer. Tel Aviv University Press, 170–81.

Moran, W. (1991) 'Assurbanipal's Message to the Babylonians (ABL 301)', in *Ah, Assyria ... Studies in Assyrian History and Ancient Near Eastern Historiography Presented to Hayim Tadmor*, ed. M. Cogan and I. Eph'al. Scripta Hierosolymitana 33. Jerusalem: Magnes Press, 320–31.

(1992) *The Amarna Letters*. Baltimore, MD: Johns Hopkins University Press.

Morgan, J. (2007) 'Fiction and History: Historiography and the Novel', in *A Companion to Greek and Roman Historiography*, Vol. 2, ed. J. Marincola. Chichester: Wiley Blackwell, 552–64.

Mumford, L. (1961) *The City in History: Its Origins, Its Transformations, and Its Prospects*. New York: Harcourt, Brace and World.

Munro, A. (2014) *The Paper Trail: An Unexpected History of the World's Greatest Invention*. London: Allen Lane.

Neu, E. (1996) *Das hurritische Epos der Freilassung 1: Untersuchungen zu einem hurritisch-hethitischen Textensemble aus Hattusha*. Studien zu den Bogazköy-Texten XXXII 14. Wiesbaden: Harrassowitz.

Neujahr, M. (2012) *Predicting the Past in the Ancient Near East: Mantic Historiography in Ancient Mesopotamia, Judah, and the Mediterranean World*. Brown Judaic Studies 354. Providence, RI: Brown Judaic Studies.

Newsom, C. A. (2013) 'Now You See Him, Now You Don't: Nabonidus in Jewish Memory', in *Remembering Biblical Figures in the Late Persian and Early Hellenistic Periods: Social Memory and Imagination*, ed. D. Edelman and E. Ben Zvi. Oxford University Press, 270–82.

(2014) *Daniel: A Commentary*. Louisville, KY: Westminster John Knox Press.

Nielsen J. (2015) 'I Overwhelmed the King of Elam: Remembering Nebuchadnezzar in Persian Babylonia', in *Political Memory in and after the Persian Empire*, ed. J. Silverman and C. Waerzeggers. Atlanta, GA: Society for Biblical Literature, 53–73.

Novotny J. (2015a) 'On the *Šēdus*, *Lamassus*, and *Rābiṣus* Mentioned in Esarhaddon's Babylon Inscriptions', *NABU* 3: 127–8.

(2015b) 'New Proposed Chronological Sequence and Dates for Composition of Esarhaddon's Babylon Inscriptions', *Journal of Cuneiform Studies* 67: 145–68.

Novotny, J. and Watanabe, C. (2008) 'After the Fall of Babylon: A New Look at the Presentation Scene on Assurbanipal's Relief BM ME 124945-6', *Iraq* 70: 105–25.

Oates, D. (1968) *Studies in the Ancient History of Northern Iraq*. Oxford University Press.

Oates, D. and Oates J. (1976) 'Early Irrigation Agriculture in Mesopotamia', in *Problems in Economic and Social Archaeology*, ed. G. de Sieveking, I. Longworth, K. Wilson, and G. Clark. London: Duckworth: 109–35.

Oppenheim, A. (1966) 'Mesopotamia in the Early History of Alchemy', *Revue d'Assyriologie* 60: 29–45.

Oppenheim, A., Saldern, A., and Barag, D. (1988) *Glass and Glassmaking in Ancient Mesopotamia*. New York: Corning Museum of Glass.

Ornan, T. (2005) *The Triumph of the Symbol: Pictorial Representation of Deities in Mesopotamia and the Biblical Image Ban*. Fribourg: Academic Press.

(2012) 'The Life of a Dead King', *Bulletin of the American Schools of Oriental Research*, 366: 1–23.

(2019) 'The Relief on the Hammurabi Louvre Stele Revisited', *Journal of Cuneiform Studies* 71: 85–109.

Oshima, T. (2006) 'Marduk the Canal-Digger', *Journal of the Ancient Near Eastern Society* 30: 77–88.

(2011) *Babylonian Prayers to Marduk*. Tübingen: Mohr Siebeck.

(2013) *The Babylonian Theodicy*. SAA Cuneiform Texts IX. Helsinki University Press.

(2014) *Babylonian Poems of Pious Sufferers: Ludlul bēl nēmeqi and the Babylonian Theodicy*. Tübingen: Mohr Siebeck.

Ossendrijver, M. (2016) 'Ancient Babylonian Astronomers Calculated Jupiter's Position from the Area under a Time-Velocity Graph', *Science* 351/6272: 482–4.

Ossendrijver, M. and Winkler, A. (2018) 'Chaldeans on the Nile: Two Egyptian Astronomical Procedure Texts with Babylonian Systems A1 and A2 for Mercury', in *The Scaffolding of Our Thoughts: Essays on Assyriology and the History of Science in Honor of Francesca Rochberg*, ed. C. Cristostomo, A. Escobar, T. Tanaka, and N. Veldhuis. Leiden: Brill, 382–419.

Otto, E. (1994) 'Aspects of Legal Reforms and Reformulations in Ancient Cuneiform and Israelite Law', in *Theory and Method in Biblical and Cuneiform Law: Revision, Interpolation and Development*, ed. B. Levinson. Journal for the Study of the Old Testament Supplement Series 181. Sheffield Academic Press, 160–96.

Owen, D. (1993) 'Some New Evidence on Yahmadiu = Ahlamu', in *The Tablet and the Scroll. Near Eastern Studies in Honor of William W. Hallo*, ed. M. Cohen, D. Snell, and D. Weisberg. Bethesda, MD: CDL Press, 181–4.

Parpola, S. (1997) *Assyrian Prophecies*. SAA IX. Helsinki University Press.

Parpola, S. and Watanabe, K. (1988) *Neo-Assyrian Treaties and Loyalty Oaths*. SAA II. Helsinki University Press.

Paulus, S. (2014) *Die babylonische Kudurru-Inschriften von der kassitischen bis zur frühneubabylonische Zeit: untersucht unter besonderer Berücksichtigung Gesellschafts- und rechtshistorischer Fragestellungen*. AOAT 51. Münster: Ugarit Verlag.

(2017) 'The Babylonian *Kudurru*-Inscriptions and Their Legal and Socio-Historical Implications', ed. A. Bartelmus and K. Sternitzke, *Karduniaš: Babylonia under the Kassites*. Boston, MA: de Gruyter, 229–44.

(2018) 'Fraud, Forgery, and Fiction: Is There Still Hope for Agum-kakrime?', *Journal of Cuneiform Studies* 70: 115–66.

Pearce L. and Wunsch, C. (2014) *Documents of Judean Exiles and West Semites in Babylonia in the Collection of David Sofer*. CUSAS 28. Bethesda, MD: CDL Press.

Pedersén, O. (1998) *Archives and Libraries in the Ancient Near East 1500–300 B.C.* Bethesda, MD: CDL Press.

(2005a) *Archive und Bibliotheken in Babylon. Die Tontafeln der Grabung Robert Koldeweys 1899–1917.* Saarbrücken: Druckerei und Verlag.

(2005b) 'Foreign Professionals in Babylon: Evidence from the Archive in the Palace of Nebuchadnezzar II', in *Ethnicity in Ancient Mesopotamia*, ed. W. van Soldt, R. Kalvelagen, and D. Katz. Leiden: NINO, 267–72.

(2009) 'Assyrians in Babylon', in *Of Gods, Trees, Kings and Scholars: Neo-Assyrian and Related Studies in Honour of Simo Parpola*, ed. M. Luukko, S. Svärd, and R. Mattila. Helsinki University Press: 1–7.

Pientka, R. (1998) *Die spätaltbabylonische Zeit. Abi-ešuh bis Samsu-ditana. Quellen, Jahresdaten, Geschichte.* IMGULA 2. Münster: Rhema.

Pientka-Hinz, R. (2006–8) 'Samsu-iluna', in *RlA*, Vol. 11, 642–7.

Pingree, D. (1998) 'Legacies in Astronomy and Celestial Omens', in *The Legacy of Mesopotamia*, ed. S. Dalley. Oxford University Press, 124–37.

Pirngruber, R. (2017) *The Economy of Late Achaemenid and Seleucid Babylonia.* Cambridge University Press.

Pliny the Elder (1951) *Natural History*, Vol. VI: *Books 20–23*, trans. W. H. S. Jones, Loeb Classical Library 392. Cambridge, MA: Harvard University Press.

(1956) *Natural History*, Vol. VII: *Books 24–27*, trans. W. H. S. Jones, Loeb Classical Library 393. Cambridge, MA: Harvard University Press.

(1963) *Natural History*, Vol. VIII: *Books 28–32*, trans. W. H. S. Jones, Loeb Classical Library 418. Cambridge, MA: Harvard University Press.

Podany, A. (2002) *The Land of Hana: Kings, Chronology and Scribal Tradition.* Bethesda, MD: CDL Press.

(2016) 'The Conservatism of Hana Scribal Tradition', in *Cultures and Societies in the Middle Euphrates and Habur Areas in the Second Millennium BC 1. Scribal Education and Scribal Traditions*, ed. S. Yamada and D. Shibata. Studia Chaburensis 5. Wiesbaden: Harrassowitz, 69–98.

Pomponio, F. (1998–2001) 'Nabû', in *RlA*, Vol. 9, 16–24.

Pongratz-Leisten, B. (1994) *Ina Šulmi Īrub*. Baghdader Forschungen 16. Mainz: von Zabern.

(2006–8) 'Prozession(sstrasse) A', in *RlA*, Vol. 11, 98–103.

Porada, E. with Buchanan, B. (1948) *Corpus of Ancient Near Eastern Seals in North American Collections*, Vol. 1: *The Collection of the Pierpont Morgan Library*. New York: Pantheon Books.

Porada, E. and Collon, D. (2016) *Catalogue of the Western Asiatic Seals in the British Museum: Cylinder Seals IV*. London: British Museum Press.

Porter, B. (1993) *Images, Power, and Politics: Figurative Aspects of Esarhaddon's Babylonian Policy*. Philadelphia: American Philosophical Society.

Porter, B. and Radner, K. (1998) 'Aššur-ahu-iddina', in *PNAE*, Vol. I, Part I: *A*, ed. K. Radner. Helsinki University Press.

Potts, D. (1997) *Mesopotamian Civilization: The Material Foundations*. London: The Athlone Press, 30–9.

(2009) 'The Archaeology and Early History of the Persian Gulf in Antiquity', in *The Persian Gulf in History*, ed. L. Potter. New York: Palgrave Macmillan, 27–56.

(2010) 'Old Arabia in Historic Sources', in *Roads of Arabia: The Archaeological Treasures of Saudi Arabia*, ed. U. Franke, A. Al-Ghabban, J. Gierlichs, and S. Weber. Exhibition catalogue, Museum für islamische Kunst. Berlin: Wasmuth, 86–101.

(2011) '*The Politai and the Bīt Tāmartu: The Seleucid and Parthian Theatres of the Greek Citizens of Babylon*', in *Babylon: Wissenkultur in Orient und Okzident*, ed. E. Cancik-Kirschbaum, M. van Ess, and J. Marzahn. Topoi 1. Berlin: de Gruyter, 239–52.

(2016) *Archaeology of Elam*, 2nd (rev.) ed. Cambridge University Press.

(2018) 'The Carian Villages', *Cuneiform Digital Library Bulletin*: 1–7.

Pritchard, J. (1969) *Ancient Near Eastern Texts Relating to the Old Testament*, 3rd ed. with Supplement. Princeton University Press.

Quinn, J. (2018) *In Search of the Phoenicians*. Princeton University Press.

Rabbi Benjamin of Tudela (1907) *The Itinerary of Rabbi Benjamin of Tudela*, trans. and ed. A. Asher. New York: Hakesheth Publishing Co.

Radner, K. (2002) *Die neuassyrischen Texte aus Tall Šeh Hamad*. Berlin: Dietrich Reimer Verlag.

(2005) *Die Macht des Namens: altorientalische Strategien zur Selbsterhaltung*. Wiesbaden: Harrassowitz.

(2010) 'The Stele of Sargon II of Assyria at Kition', in *Interkulturalität in der Alten Welt*, ed. R. Rollinger, B. Gußler, M. Lang, and I. Madreiter. Wiesbaden: Harrassowitz, 429–49.

Radner, K. and van Koppen, F. (2009) 'Ein Tontafelfragment aus der diplomatischen Korrespondenz der Hyksosherscher mit Babylonien', Beiträge in M. Bietak and I. Forstner-Müller, 'Der Hyksospalast bei Tell ed-Dabʿa. Zweite und dritte Grabungskampagne', *Aegypten und Levante* 19: 91–120.

Rassam, H. (1897) *Asshur and the Land of Nimrod, being an Account of the Discoveries Made in the Ancient Ruins of Nineveh, Asshur, Sepharvaim, Calah, Babylon, Borsippa, Cuthah, and Van, Including a Narrative of Different Journeys in Mesopotamia, Assyria, Asia Minor, and Koordistan*. New York: Eaton and Mains.

Rawlinson, H. (1861) *The Cuneiform Inscriptions of Western Asia*, Vol. 1. London: British Museum.

Reade, J. (1986) 'Rassam's Babylonian Collection: The Excavations and the Archives', in *Catalogue of the Babylonian Tablets in the British Museum*, Vol. VI: *Tablets from Sippar I*, ed. E. Leichty. London: British Museum, xii–xxxvi.

   (1993) 'Hormuzd Rassam and His Discoveries', *Iraq* 55: 39–62.

   (2008a) 'Early Travellers on the Wonders: Suggested Sites', in *Babylon: Myth and Reality*, ed. I. Finkel and M. Seymour. London: British Museum Press, 112–17.

   (2008b) 'The Search for the Ziggurat', in *Babylon: Myth and Reality*, ed. I. Finkel and M. Seymour. London: British Museum Press, 124–5.

Redford, D. (2003) *The Wars in Syria and Palestine of Thutmose III*. Leiden: Brill.

Reiner, E. (1995) *Astral Magic in Babylonia*. Philadelphia: American Philosophical Society.

Reiner, E. and Pingree, D. (1975) *Babylonian Planetary Omens*, Vol. 1: *The Venus Tablet of Ammi-ṣaduqa*. Bibliotheca Mesopotamica 2/1. Malibu: Undena Publications.

Renger, J. (ed.) (1999) *Babylon: Focus mesopotamische Geschichte, Wiege früher Gelehrsamkeit; Mythos in der Moderne*. Topoi 1. Saarbrücken: Druckerei und Verlag.

Reynolds, F. (2003) *The Babylonian Correspondence of Esarhaddon and Letters to Assurbanipal and Sin-šarra-iškun from Northern and Central Babylonia*. SAA XVIII. Helsinki University Press.

Rich, C. (1839) *Narrative of a Journey to the Site of Babylon in 1811*. London: Duncan and Malcolm.

Richardson, S. (2005) 'Trouble in the Countryside *ana tarṣi* Samsuditana: Militarism, Kassites and the Fall of Babylon', in *Ethnicity in Ancient Mesopotamia: Papers Read at the 48th RAI*, ed. W. van Soldt, K. Kalvelagen, and D. Katz. Leiden: NINO, 273–89.

Richter T. (2004) *Untersuchungen zu den lokalen Panthea Süd- und Mittel-babyloniens in altbabylonischer Zeit*. 2nd (rev.) ed. Münster: Ugarit-Verlag.

Roaf, M. (1996) *Art and Architecture of the Ancient Orient*, ed. H. Frankfort. 5th (rev.) ed. New Haven, CT: Yale University Press.

Robson, E. (2006–8) 'Pythagoras', in *RlA*, Vol. 11, 134–5.

   (2008) *Mathematics in Ancient Iraq: A Social History*. Princeton University Press.

Rogers, R. (1915) *A History of Babylonia and Assyria*. 6th ed. New York: Abingdon Press.

Röllig, W. (1980–3) 'Kumme', in *RlA*, Vol. 6, 336–7.

   (1998–2001) 'Nabu-rīmannu', in *RlA*, Vol. 9, 32.

   (2009–11) 'Sardanapal(l)os', in *RlA*, Vol. 12, 36–7.

   (2014–16) 'Tyros A', in *RlA*, Vol. 14, 250–3.

Rollinger, R. (2011–13) 'Teispes', in *RlA*, Vol. 13, 508–9.

Rositani, A. (2003) *Rīm-Anum Texts in the British Museum*. Nisaba 4. Messina: Dipartimento de Scienze dell'Antichità.

(2014) 'More Rīm-Anum's Texts from the *bīt asīrī*', in *Semitica*. Cahiers publiés par l'Institut d'Études Sémitiques du Collège de France 56. Paris: Editions Jean Maisonneuve – Librairie d'Amérique et d'Orient, 35–64.

Roth, M. (1995) *Law Collections from Mesopotamia and Asia Minor*. Atlanta, GA: Scholars Press.

Rutten, M. (1960) 'Un lot de tablettes de Manana III', *Revue d'Assyriologie* 54: 19–40.

Saggs, H. (1988) *The Greatness That Was Babylon: A Survey of the Ancient Civilization on the Tigris-Euphrates Valley*. 2nd rev. ed. London: Sidgwick and Jackson.

Sallaberger, W. (2006–8) 'Puzur-Eshtar', in *RlA*, Vol. 11.

(2013) 'The Management of Royal Treasure: Palace Archives and Palatial Economy in the Ancient Near East', in *Experiencing Power, Generating Authority: Cosmos, Politics, and the Ideology of Kingship in Ancient Egypt and Mesopotamia*, ed. J. Hill, P. Jones, and A. Morales. Philadelphia: Pennsylvania University Press, 219–55.

Sallaberger W. and Schrakamp, I. (eds) (2015) *History and Philology: Associated Regional Chronologies*. ARCANE III. Turnhout: Brepols.

Salvini, M. (1993–7) 'Menua', in *RlA*, Vol. 8, 63–4.

Samet, N. (2014) *The Lamentation over the Destruction of Ur*. Winona Lake, IN: Eisenbrauns.

Sancisi-Weerdenberg, H. (1993) 'Alexander and Persepolis', in *Alexander the Great: Reality and Myth*, ed. J. Carlsen. Rome: L'Erma di Bretschneider, 177–88.

Sasson, J. (2015) *From the Mari Archives*. Winona Lake, IN: Eisenbrauns.

Sayce, A. (1923) *Reminiscences*. London: Macmillan.

Schachner, A. (2011) *Hattuscha, Auf der Suche nach dem sagenhaften Grossreich der Hethiter*. Munich: C. H. Beck.

Schaudig, H.-P. (2001) *Die Inschriften Nabonids von Babylon und Kyros' des Grossen samt den in ihrem Umfeld entstandenen Tendenzschriften*. AOAT 256. Münster: Ugarit-Verlag.

(2003) 'Nabonid, der Archäologe auf dem Königsthron', in *Festschrift für Burkhart Kienast: zu seinem 70. Geburtstag dargebracht von Freunden, Schülern und Kollegen*, ed. G. Selz. AOAT 274. Münster: Ugarit-Verlag, 447–97.

(2008) 'A Tanit-Sign from Babylon and the Conquest of Tyre by Nebuchadrezzar II', *Ugarit Forschungen* 40: 533–45.

(2009) 'The Colophon of the Sippar Text of the Weidner Chronicle', *NABU* no. 15.

(2011–13) 'Tēmā', in *RlA*, Vol. 13, 513–15.

(2016/18) 'Cuneiform Texts from Tayma, Seasons 2004–2015', in *Tayma II: Inscriptions from the Saudi-German Excavations*, Part I, ed. M. Macdonald, H. Schaudig, R. Eichmann, A. Hausleiter, and M. Al-Najem. Riyadh: Saudi Commission for Tourism and National Heritage, 2–20.

Scheil, V. (1896) 'Inscription de Nabonide', *Recueil de Travaux rélatifs à la philology et à l'archéologie égyptiennes et assyriennes* 18: 15–29.

(1902) *Délégation en Perse. Mémoires Tome IV. Textes élamites – sémitiques.* 2nd series. Paris: Ernest Leroux.

Schironi, F. (2009) *From Alexandria to Babylon: Near Eastern Languages and Hellenistic Erudition in the Oxyrhynchus Glossary* (P. Oxy 1802 + 4812). Berlin: de Gruyter.

(2013) 'The Early Reception of Berossos', in *The World of Berossus*, ed. J. Haubold, G. Lanfranchi, R. Rollinger, and J. Steele. CLeO 5. Wiesbaden: Harrassowitz, 235–54.

Schmidt, K. (2010) 'Göbekli Tepe – the Stone Age Sanctuaries', *Documenta Praehistorica* 37: 239–54.

(2011–13) 'Sudines', in *RlA*, Vol. 13, 242–3.

Schürer, E. (1986) *The History of the Jewish People in the Age of Jesus Christ*, III/1, rev. G. Vermes, F. Millar, and M. Goodman. Edinburgh: T&T Clark.

Schwemer, D. (2001) *Die Wettergottgestalten Mesopotamiens und Nordsyriens im Zeitalter der Keilschriftkulturen.* Wiesbaden: Harrassowitz.

Sciandra, R. (2012) 'The Babylonian Correspondence of the Seleucid and Arsacid Dynasties: New Insights into the Relations between Court and City during the Late Babylonian Period', in *Organization, Representation and the Symbols of Power in the Ancient Near East*, ed. G. Wilhelm. Winona Lake, IN: Eisenbrauns, 225–56.

Segal, J. (1970) *Edessa 'the Blessed City'.* Oxford: Clarendon Press.

Seidl, U. (1989) *Die babylonischen Kudurru-reliefs: Symbole mesopotamischer Gottheiten.* OBO 87. Freiburg: Universitätsverlag.

(1998–2001) 'Nabû B', in *RlA*, Vol. 9, 24–9.

(1999) 'Ein Monument Darius' I aus Babylon', *Zeitschrift für Assyriologie* 89: 101–14.

(2001) 'Das Ringen um das richtige Bild des Šamaš von Sippar', *Zeitschrift für Assyriologie* 91: 120–32.

Seymour, M. (2014) *Legend, History and the Ancient City Babylon.* London: I.B. Tauris.

Shear, I. (1998) 'Bellerophon Tablets from the Mycenaean World? A Tale of Seven Bronze Hinges', *Journal of Hellenic Studies* 118: 187–9.

Slanski, K. (2007) 'Rod and Ring: Icon of Righteous Kingship and Balance of Power between Palace and Temple', in *Regime Change in the Ancient Near East and Egypt from Sargon of Agade to Saddam Hussein*, ed. H. Crawford. Proceeding of the British Academy 136. Oxford University Press, 37–69.

Sollberger, E. (1987) 'A Bead for Sennacherib', in *Language, Literature, History, Philological and Historical Studies Presented to Erica Reiner*, ed. F. Rochberg-Halton. American Oriental Society 67. New Haven, CT: American Oriental Society, 379–81.

Sollberger, E. and Walker, C. (1985) 'Hammurapi à Mari et à Sippar', in *Miscellanea Babylonica: Mélanges offerts à Maurice Birot*, ed. J.-M. Durand and J.-R. Kupper. Paris: ERC, 257–64.

Sommerfeld, W. (2009–11) 'Sargon von Akkade', in *RlA*, Vol. 12, 48–9.

Spar, I. (1988) *Tablets, Cones and Bricks of the Third and Second Millennia B.C.* Cuneiform Texts in the Metropolitan Museum of Art 1. New York: Metropolitan Museum of Art.

Spar, I. and Jursa, M. (2014) *The Ebabbar Temple Archive and Other Texts from the Fourth to the First Millennium B.C.* Cuneiform Texts in the Metropolitan Museum of Art 4. New York: Metropolitan Museum of Art.

Spar, I. and Lambert, W. (2005) *Literary and Scholastic Texts of the First Millennium BC.* Cuneiform Texts in the Metropolitan Museum of Art 2. New York: Metropolitan Museum of Art.

Spycket, A. (1968) *Les statues de culte dans les textes mésopotamiens, des origines à la 1er dynastie de Babylone.* Paris: J. Gabalda.

Starr, I. (1983) *Rituals of the Diviner.* Malibu: Undena Publications.

(1990) *Queries to the Sungod: Divination and Politics in Sargonid Assyria.* SAA IV. Helsinki University Press.

Steele, J. (2011) 'Making Sense of Time: Observational and Theoretical Calendars', in *Oxford Handbook of Cuneiform Culture.* ed. K. Radner and E. Robson. Oxford University Press, 470–85.

(2013) 'The "Astronomical Fragments" of Berossos in Context', in *The World of Berossus*, ed. J. Haubold, G. Lanfranchi, R. Rollinger, and J. Steele. CleO 5. Wiesbaden: Harrassowitz, 99–113.

(in press) 'Citation and Use of MUL.APIN in the Neo-Assyrian and Late Babylonian Periods', in *Proceeding of RAI 2016*, ed. G. Frame. Philadelphia: Eisenbrauns.

Steiner, R. (1997) 'The Aramaic Text in Demotic Script', in *The Context of Scripture*, ed. W. Hallo and K. Lawson Younger. Leiden: Brill, 309–27.

Steinkeller, P. (2001) 'New Light on the Hydrology and Topography of Southern Babylonia in the Third Millennium', *Zeitschrift für Assyriologie* 91: 22–84.

(2003) 'An Ur III Manuscript of the Sumerian King List', in *Literatur, Politik und Recht in Mesopotamien. Festschrift für Claus Wilcke*, ed. W. Sallaberger, K. Volk, and A. Zgoll. Orientalia Biblica et Christiana 14. Wiesbaden: Harrassowitz, 267–92.

(2004) 'A History of Mashkan-shapir and Its Role in the Kingdom of Larsa', in *Anatomy of a Mesopotamian City: Survey and Soundings at Mashkan-shapir*, ed. E. Stone and P. Zimansky. Winona Lake, IN: Eisenbrauns, 26–42.

Sternitzke, K. (2017) 'Bestattungen in der Kassiten- und Isin II-Zeit', in *Karduniaš: Babylonia under the Kassites*, ed. A. Bartelmus and K. Sternitzke. Untersuchungen zur Assyriologie und vorderasiatischen Archäologie 11. Boston, MA: de Gruyter, 351–420.

Stevens, K. (2012) 'Collations to the Antiochus Cylinder (BM 36277)', *NABU* no. 35.

Stol, M. (1976) *Studies in Old Babylonian History*. Leiden: NINO.

(1981) *Letters from Yale*. Altbabylonische Briefe IX. Leiden: Brill.

(2006–8) 'Sabum B', in *RlA*, Vol. 11, 479–80.

Stolper, M. (1987) 'Belšunu the Satrap', in *Language, Literature, and History: Philological and Historical Studies Presented to Erica Reiner*, ed. F. Rochberg-Halton. New Haven, CT: American Oriental Society, 389–402.

(1990) 'The Kasr Archive', in *Achaemenid History IV: Centre and Periphery*, ed. A. Kuhrt and H. Sancisi-Weerdenburg. Proceedings of the Groningen 1986 Workshop on Achaemenid History. Leiden: NINO, 195–205.

(2004) 'Elamite', in *The Cambridge Encylopaedia of the World's Ancient Languages*, ed. R. Woodard. Cambridge University Press: 60–94.

Stone, E. (1977) 'Economic Crisis and Social Upheaval in Old Babylonian Nippur', in *Mountains and Lowlands: Essays in the Archaeology of Greater Mesopotamia*, ed. L. Levine and T. C. Young. Bibliotheca Mesopotamica 7. Malibu: Undena Publications, 266–89.

Stone, E., Lindsley, D., Pigott, V., Harbottle, G., and Ford, M. (1998) 'From Shifting Silt to Solid Stone: The Manufacture of Synthetic Basalt in Ancient Mesopotamia', *Science* 280: 2091–3.

Strabo (1961) *Geography*, Vol. 7: *Books XV–XVI*, trans. H. L. Jones. Loeb Classical Library 241. Cambridge, MA: Harvard University Press.

Streck, M. (1998–2001a) 'Nebukadnezar II', in *RlA*, Vol. 9, 194–206.

(1998–2001b) 'Ninurta', in *RlA*, Vol. 9, 512–22.

(1998–2001c) 'Nitokris', in *RlA*, Vol. 9, 590–1.

Streck, M. and Wasserman, N. (2008) 'The Old Babylonian Hymns to Papulegarra', *Orientalia* 77: 335–58.

(2012) 'More Light on Nanaya', *Zeitschrift für Assyriologie* 102: 183–201.

Stronach, D. (2013) 'Cyrus and the Kingdom of Anšan: Further Perspectives', *Iran* 51: 55–69.

Sulaiman, M. and Dalley, S. (2012) 'Seven *Naptanum*-Texts from the Reign of Rim-Sin I of Larsa', *Iraq* 74: 153–65.

Tadmor, H. (1994) *The Inscriptions of Tiglath-Pileser III, King of Assyria*. Jerusalem: Israel Academy of Sciences and Humanities.

Tadmor, H., Landsberger, B., and Parpola, S. (1989) 'The Sin of Sargon and Sennacherib's Last Will', *SAA Bulletin* 3/1: 3–51.

Taylor, J. (2011) 'Tablets as Artefacts, Scribes as Artisans', in *Oxford Handbook of Cuneiform Cultures*, ed. K. Radner and E. Robson. Oxford University Press, 5–31.

Teissier, B. (1994) *Sealings and Seals on Texts from Kültepe Karum Level 2*. Leiden: NINO.

Tenney, J. (2016) 'The Elevation of Marduk Revisited: Festivals and Sacrifices at Nippur during the High Kassite Period', *Journal of Cuneiform Studies* 68: 153–80.

Thelle, R. (2018) *Discovering Babylon*. London: Routledge.

Vallat, F. (1993) 'Kuk-našur et Ammi-ṣaduqa', *NABU* no. 39.

van der Kooij, A. (1996) '"The Story of Genesis 11.1–9 and the Culture of Ancient Mesopotamia", Review of C. Uehlinger, *Weltreich und 'eine Rede', eine neue Bedeutung von sogenannten Türmbauerzählung*(1990)', *Bibliotheca Orientalis* 53/1–2: 27–38.

van der Spek, R. (2001) 'The Theatre of Babylon in Cuneiform', in *Veenhof Anniversary Volume: Studies Presented to Klaas R. Veenhof on the Occasion of His Sixty-Fifth Birthday*, ed. W. van Soldt, J. Dercksen, N. Kouwenberg, and T. Krispijn. Leiden: NINO, 445–56.

(2003) 'Darius III, Alexander the Great, and Babylonian Scholarship', in *A Persian Perspective: Essays in Memory of Heleen Sancisi-Weerdenburg*, ed. W. Henkelman and A. Kuhrt. Achaemenid History XIII. Leiden: NINO, 289–346.

(2006) 'The Size and Significance of the Babylonian Temples under the Successors', in *La Transition entre l'empire achémenide et les royaumes hellenistiques*, ed. P. Briant and F. Joannès. Persika 9. Paris: De Boccard, 261–307.

(2008) 'Berossus as a Babylonian Chronicler and Greek Historian', in *Studies in Ancient Near East View and Society: Presented to Marten Stol*, ed. R. van der Spek and G. Haayer. Bethesda, MD: CDL Press, 277–318.

(2009–11) 'Seleukiden', in *RlA*, Vol. 12, 369–83.

(2014) 'Cyrus the Great, Exiles, and Foreign Gods: A Comparison of Assyrian and Persian Policies on Subject Nations', in *Extraction and Control, Studies in Honor of Matthew W. Stolper*, ed. M. Kozuh, W. Henkelman, C. Jones, and C. Woods. Studies in Ancient Oriental Civilization 68. Chicago: Oriental Institute, 233–64.

(2016) 'The Cult for Seleucus II and His Sons in Babylon', *NABU* no. 27.

(2017) '*Manûtu ša Babili*: The Babylonian Sub-division of the Mina', *NABU* no. 20.

van Dijk, J. (1970) 'Remarques sur l'histoire d'Elam et d'Ešnunna', *Archiv für Orientforschung* 23: 63–71.

van Driel, G. (2002) *Elusive Silver*. Leiden: NINO.

van Koppen, F. (2006) 'Letters from Southern Mesopotamia', in *The Ancient Near East, Historical Sources in Translation*, ed. M. Chavalas. Maldon, MA: Blackwell, 127–30.

(2011) 'The Scribe of the Flood Story and His Circle', in *Oxford Handbook of Cuneiform Culture*, ed. K. Radner and E. Robson. Oxford University Press, 140–66.

van Koppen, F. and Lehmann, M. (2012–13) 'A Cuneiform Sealing from Tell ed-Dabʿa and Its Historical Context', *Aegyten und Levante* 22–3: 91–4.

van Lerberghe, K. (2008) 'The Clergy and the Religious Institutions of Nippur in the Later Old Babylonian Period', in *Studies in Ancient Near Eastern World View and Society: Presented to Marten Stol*, ed. R. van der Spek. Bethesda, MD: CDL Press, 127–30.

van Lerberghe, K. and Voet, G. (2009) *A Late Old Babylonian Temple Archive from Dūr-Abiešuh*. CUSAS 8. Bethesda, MD: CDL Press.

(2016) 'Dūr-Abiešuh and Venice: Settlements in-between Great Rivers', in *Libiamo ne' lieti calici: Ancient Near Eastern Studies Presented to Lucio Milano on the Occasion of His 65th Birthday*, ed. P. Carò, E. Devecchi, N. De Zorzi, M. Maiocchi, and S. Ermidoro. Münster: Ugarit-Verlag, 557–62.

van Soldt, W. (1990) *Letters in the British Museum*, vol 1. Altbabylonische Briefe XII. Leiden: Brill.

(1994) *Letters in the British Museum*, vol 2. Altbabylonische Briefe XIII. Leiden: Brill.

(2008) 'The Location of Idu', *NABU* no. 55.

(2011) 'The Role of Babylon in Western Peripheral Education', in *Babylon: Wissenskultur in Orient und Okzident*, ed. E. Cancik-Kirschbaum, M. van Ess, and J. Marzahn. Topoi 1. Berlin: de Gruyter, 197–211.

Veenhof, K. (1993) 'On the Identification and Implications of some Bullae from Acemhöyük and Kültepe', in *Aspects of Art and Iconography: Anatolia and Its Neighbors. Studies in Honor of Nimet Özgüç*, ed. M. Mellink, E. Porada, and T. Özgüç. Ankara: Türk Tarih Kurumu, 645–57.

(1997–2000) 'The Relation between Royal Decrees and Laws in the Old Babylonian Period', *Jaarbericht. Ex Oriente Lux* 35–6: 49–84.

(2005) *Letters in the Louvre*. Altbabylonische Briefe XIV. Leiden: Brill.

Veenhof, K. and Eidem, J. (2008) *Mesopotamia: The Old Assyrian Period*, ed. M. Wäfler. OBO 160/5. Fribourg: Academic Press.

Veldhuis, N. (2008) 'Kurigalzu's Statue Inscription', *Journal of Cuneiform Studies* 60: 25–51.

Vicari, J. (2000) *La Tour de Babel*. Paris: Presses Universitaires de France.

Villard, P. (2008) 'Les cérémonies triomphales', in *Les armées du Proche-Orient ancien: IIIe–Ier mill. av. J.-C.*, ed. P. Abrahami and L. Battini. Oxford: Hadrian Books, 257–70.

Volk, K. (1995) *Inanna und Šukaletuda: zur historisch-politischen Deutung eines sumerischen Literaturwerkes*. Wiesbaden: Harrassowitz.

(2014–16) 'Wachstafel', in *RlA*, Vol. 14, 609–13.

Waerzeggers, C. (2003–4) 'The Babylonian Revolts against Xerxes and the End of Archives', *Archiv für Orientforschung* 50: 150–73.

(2010) 'Babylonians in Susa: The Travels of Babylonian Businessmen to Susa Reconsidered', in *The Achaemenid Court*, ed. B. Jacobs and R. Rollinger. Wiesbaden: Harrassowitz: 777–813.

(2012) 'The Babylonian Chronicles: Classification and Provenance', *Journal of Near Eastern Studies* 71: 285–98.

(2015a) 'Facts, Propaganda, or History? Shaping Political Memory in the Nabonidus Chronicle', in *Political Memory in and after the Persian Empire*, ed. J. Silverman and C. Waerzeggers. Atlanta, GA: Society for Biblical Literature, 95–124.

(2015b) Review of L. Pearce and C. Wunsch, *Documents of Judean Exiles and West Semites in Babylonia in the Collection of David Sofer* (2014), *Strata* 33: 179–94.

(2018) 'Cuneiform Writing and Control at the Exilic Village of Yahudu in Babylonian, c. 570–480 BC'. Delivered at University College London on 19 February 2018.

Waerzeggers, C. and Seire, M. (eds.) (2019) *Xerxes and Babylonia: The Cuneiform Evidence*. OLA 277. Leuven: Peeters.

Walker, C. (1980) 'Some Assyrians at Sippar in the Old Babylonian Period', *Anatolian Studies* 30: 15–22.

(1982) 'Babylonian Chronicle 25: A Chronicle of the Kassite and Isin II Dynasties', in *Zikir Šumim: Assyriological Studies Presented to F. R. Kraus*, ed. G. van Driel, T. Krispijn, M. Stol, and K. Veenhof. Leiden: Brill, 398–417.

(1995), appendix in D. Collon, *Ancient Near Eastern Art*. London: British Museum, 230–8.

(1996) *Astronomy before the Telescope*. London: British Museum Press.

Wallenfels, R. (2017) 'The Office Seal of the Šatammu of E-Sangil during the Hellenistic Period: A Résumé', *NABU* no. 21.

Wasserman, N. (2015) 'On the Author of the Epic of Zimri-Lim and Its Literary Content', *Archiv für Orientforschung* 53: 52–6.

Watkins, C. (2004) 'Hittite', in *The Cambridge Encyclopaedia of the World's Ancient Languages*, ed. R. Woodard. Cambridge University Press, 551–75.

Weippert, M. (1976–80) 'Kedor-laomer', in *RlA*, Vol. 5, 543–4.

Wells, C. and Magdalene, R. (2009) *Law from the Tigris to the Tiber: The Writings of Raymond Westbrook*, Vol. 1. Winona Lake, IN: Eisenbrauns.

West, M. (1995) 'The Date of the *Iliad*', *Museum Helveticum* 52/4: 203–19.

(1997) *The East Face of Helicon*. Oxford University Press.

Westenholz, A. (1987) *The 'Akkadian' Texts, the Enlilemaba Texts, and the Onion Archive: Old Sumerian and Old Akkadian Texts in Philadelphia*, Part II. Copenhagen: Carsten Niebuhr Institute.

Weszeli, M. (2003–5) 'Pferd', in *RlA*, Vol. 10, 469–81.

Wetzel, F., Schmidt, E., and Mallwitz, A. (1957) *Das Babylon der Spätzeit*. WVDOG 62. Berlin: Gebr. Mann.

Wiesehöfer, J. (2001) *Ancient Persia*. 2nd ed. London: I. B. Tauris.

(2003) 'The Medes and the Idea of the Succession of Empires in Antiquity', in *Continuity of Empire: Assyria, Media, Persia*, ed. G. Lanfranchi, M. Roaf, and R. Rollinger. Padua: S.a.r.g.o.n. Editrice e Libreria: 391–6.

Wiggermann, F. (2008) 'A Babylonian Scholar in Assur', in *Studies in Ancient Near Eastern World View and Society Presented to Marten Stol*, ed. R. van der Spek and G. Haayer. Bethesda MD: CDL Press, 203–34.

Wilcke, C. (1989) 'Genealogical and Geographical Thought', in *DUMU-E₂-DUB-BA-A. Studies in Honor of A. W. Sjøberg*, ed. H. Behrens, D. Loding, and M. Roth. Philadelphia: University Museum, 557–71.

(1990) 'Kudur-mabuk in Terqa', in *De la Babylonie à la Syrie, en passant par Mari: Mélanges offerts à Monsieur J.-R. Kupper à l'occasion de son 70e anniversaire*, ed. Ö. Tunca. Université de Liège, 179–81.

(2007) *Early Ancient Near Eastern Law: A History of Its Beginning*. Rev. ed. Winona Lake: Eisenbrauns.

Wilhelm G. (2004) 'Hurrian', in *Cambridge Encyclopaedia of the World's Ancient Languages*, ed. R. Woodard. Cambridge University Press, 95–118.

(2009) 'Die Götter der Unterwelt als Ahnengeister und altanatolischen Quellen', in *JHWH und die Götter der Völker, Symposium zum 80-Geburtstag von Klaus Koch*, ed. F. Hartenstein and M. Rösel. Neukirchen-Vluyn: Neukirchener Verlag, 59–75.

(2009–11) 'Šanhara', in *RlA*, Vol. 12, 11–12.

(2014–16) 'Tuthalija', in *RlA*, Vol. 14, 66–75.

Wilson, R. (1977) *Genealogy and History in the Biblical World and the Ancient Near East*. Yale University Press.

Winter, I. (2008) 'Touched by the Gods: Visual Evidence for the Divine Status of Rulers in the Ancient Near East', in *Religion and Power: Divine Kingship in the Ancient World and Beyond*, ed. N. Brisch. Chicago: Oriental Institute, 75–101.

Woods, C. (2004) 'The Sun-God Tablet of Nabu-apla-iddina Revisited', *Journal of Cuneiform Studies* 56: 23–103.

Woolley, C. Leonard (1965) *The Kassite Period and the Period of the Assyrian Kings*. Philadelphia: Publications of the Joint Expedition of the British Museum and of the University of Pennsylvania to Mesopotamia.

Wu, Y. (1994) *A Political History of Eshnunna, Mari and Assyria during the Early Old Babylonian Period (from the End of Ur III to the Death of Šamši-Adad)*. Changchun: Institute for the Study of Ancient Civilizations.

Wunsch, C. (1993) *Die Urkunden des babylonischen Geschäftsmannes Iddin-Marduk zum Handel mit Naturalien im 6. Jahrhundert v.Chr.* Cuneiform Monographs 3. Groningen: Styx.

(2000) *Das Egibi-Archiv*. Cuneiform Monographs 20. Groningen: Styx.

Xenophon (1914) *Cyropaedia*, trans. W. Miller. Cambridge, MA: Harvard University Press.

(2001) *Anabasis*, trans. C. Brownson, rev. J. Dillery. Cambridge, MA: Harvard University Press.

Yang, X. (2002) *White Tiger*. Hong Kong: Chinese University.

Yener, K. (2000) *The Domestication of Metals: The Rise of Complex Metal Industries in Anatolia*. Leiden: Brill.

Young, J. (1996) 'Memory/Monument', in *Critical Terms for Art History*, ed. R. Nelson and R. Shiff. Chicago University Press, 234–47.

Zadok, R. (2005) 'On Anatolians, Greeks and Egyptians in "Chaldean" and Achaemenid Babylonia', *Tel Aviv* 32: 76–106.

(2014) 'Hit in Suhu', *Kaskal* 11: 1–22.

(2017) 'A Cylinder Inscription of Aššur-ketta-lēšir II', in *'Now It Happened in Those Days': Studies in Biblical, Assyrian, and Other Ancient Near Eastern Historiography Presented to Mordecai Cogan on His 75th Birthday*, Vol. 1, ed. A. Baruchi-Unna, T. Forti, S. Ahituv, I. Eph'al, and J. Tigay. Winona Lake, IN: Eisenbrauns: 309–40.

Ziegler, N. (2007) *Les musiciens et la musique d'après les archives de Mari.* Mémoires de NABU 10, Florilegium marianum 9. Paris: ERC.

Zohary, D. (1996) 'The Mode of Domestication of the Founder Crops of Southwest Asian Agriculture', in *The Origins and Spread of Agriculture and Pastoralism in Eurasia*, ed. D. Harris. University College London Press, 142–58.

Zomer, E. (2019) *Middle Babylonian Literary Texts from the Frau Professor Hilprecht Collection, Jena.* Wiesbaden: Harrassowitz.

Index